CONTINUING BONDS

CONTINUING BONDS
New Understandings
of Grief

Edited by

Dennis Klass, Phyllis R. Silverman,
and Steven L. Nickman

Taylor & Francis
Publishers since 1798

USA	Publishing Office:	Taylor & Francis
		1101 Vermont Ave., N.W., Suite 200
		Washington, DC 20005-3521
		Tel: (202) 289-2174
		Fax: (202) 289-3665
	Distribution Center:	Taylor & Francis
		1900 Frost Road, Suite 101
		Bristol, PA 19007-1598
		Tel: (215) 785-5800
		Fax: (215) 785-5515
UK		Taylor & Francis Ltd.
		1 Gunpowder Square
		London EC4A 3DE
		Tel: 071 405 2237
		Fax 071 831 2035

CONTINUING BONDS: New Understandings of Grief

1 2 3 4 5 6 7 8 9 0   B R B R   9 8 7 6 5

This book was set in Times Roman by Brushwood Graphics, Inc. The editors were Christine Williams and Randall Frey. Cover design by Michelle Fleitz. Printing and binding by Braun-Brumfield, Inc.

A CIP catalog record for this book is available from the British Library.
∞ The paper in this publication meets the requirements of the ANSI Standard Z39.48-1984 (Permanence of Paper)

Library of Congress Cataloging-in-Publication Data
Continuing bonds : new understandings of grief / edited by Dennis Klass, Phyllis R. Silverman, and Steven L. Nickman.
    p.   cm.—(Series in death education, aging, and health care)
    Includes bibliographical references.
    1. Grief.   2. Grief—Cross-cultural studies.   3. Bereavement—Psychological aspects.
4. Children—Death—Psychological aspects.   5. Parents—Death—Psychological
aspects.   I. Klass, Dennis.   II. Silverman, Phyllis R.   III. Nickman, Steven L.   IV.
Series.
BF575.G7C67   1996
155.9′37—dc20   95-35022
                                                                              CIP

ISBN   1-56032-336-1 (case)
ISBN   1-56032-339-6 (paper)
ISSN   0275-3510

Contents

PART FIVE   Parental Bereavement

Chapter 12   **The Deceased Child in the Psychic and Social Worlds of Bereaved Parents During the Resolution of Grief**   199

Dennis Klass

Chapter 13   **The Wounded Family: Bereaved Parents and the Impact of Adult Child Loss**   217

Simon Shimshon Rubin

PART SIX   Bereaved Siblings

Chapter 14   **Basic Constructs of a Theory of Adolescent Sibling Bereavement**   235

Nancy Hogan and Lydia DeSantis

Acknowledgments

As this book took form, we have often depended upon insights, encouragement, and help from others. Hannelore Wass immediately saw the possibilities in the project. Elaine Pirrone, our editor at Taylor & Francis, has given a steady stream of intelligent questions, practical advice, and perspective-saving humor. Cathy Heidemann, secretary in the Webster University Religion Department, kept track of communications with the authors, oversaw the movement of manuscripts among editors and authors, and assembled the parts into one product. Cathy figured out how to convert the many computer programs used by the authors into files that could be shared among the editors and then used for typesetting. Webster work-study students Melinda Frohlich, Lauren Syrek, and Patricia Talton did word processing, checked manuscripts, and chased down references. As we worked with the publisher, with the contributors, and with the Webster staff, we have always felt on this project that we were doing it with friends.

Contributors

DAVID E. BALK
Kansas State University
  HDFS Department
303 Justin Hall
Manhattan, KS 66506-1403
David E. Balk is associate professor
of Human Development and Family
Studies at Kansas State University.
Among the courses he teaches are
Middle Childhood and Adolescence,
Program Evaluation, Death and the
Family, The Helping Relationship, and
Coping with Life Crises. Balk is the
author of *Adolescent Development:
Early Through Late Adolescence* and
of several research studies into adolescent bereavement. His 1981 dissertation study of sibling death during
adolescence formed the pioneering
effort for contemporary investigations
of adolescent grief responses. He is
married to Mary Ann Balk, whose
counsel he frequently seeks and probably more often should, and is the
father of Janet Renee Balk, whose
spirit and enthusiasm for life he
greatly enjoys.

BETTY C. BUCHSBAUM
515 Greenhaven Road
Rye, NY 10580
Betty C. Buchsbaum is the director of
Psychology Training at the Center for
Preventive Psychiatry, White Plains,
New York; and adjunct assistant clini-
cal professor of Psychology, Depart-
ment of Psychiatry, New York
Hospital-Cornell Medical Center,
Westchester Division, White Plains,
New York.

ROBERTA DEW CONANT
44 Burroughs Street
Jamaica Plains, MA 02130
Roberta Dew Conant is a clinical psychologist on the staff of Outpatient
Mental Health at Boston Regional
Medical Center, Stoneham, Massachusetts. Dr. Conant graduated from
Oberlin College in 1967, obtained a
degree in special education from
Boston University and earned a Psy.D.
in 1992 from Massachusetts School of
Professional Psychology. She worked
with Dr. Phyllis Silverman in the
development of her dissertation topic.
Dr. Conant has advanced training in
family therapy, including the use of
narrative approaches, through Family
Institute of Cambridge. She special-
izes in child and family therapy.

LYDIA DESANTIS
University of Miami School of Nursing
P.O. Box 016960
D2-5 Royce Bldg.
Miami, FL 33101
Lydia DeSantis is a nurse and an
anthropologist specializing in culturally focused care, adolescent and
immigrant health issues, and qualitative research methodology. She has
also done research on the concept of
loss as experienced by women who
have had a mastectomy. She has been
collaborating with Nancy Hogan on
adolescent sibling bereavement
research, development of a theory of
adolescent sibling bereavement, and
exploring cultural variations in
bereavement. She has published
widely on the cultural dimension of
health care and adolescent sibling
bereavement.

KENNETH GERGEN
Department of Psychology
Swarthmore College

500 College Avenue
Swarthmore, PA 19081-1397
Kenneth J. Gergen is the Mustin Professor of Psychology at Swarthmore College. Among other works, he is the author of *The Saturated Self* and *Realities and Relationships*.

MARY GERGEN
Mary Gergen is an associate professor of Psychology and Women's Studies at Pennsylvania State University, Delaware County Campus, and is the editor of *Feminist Thought and the Structure of Knowledge*. She is currently writing a book on feminist postmodernism in psychology.

NANCY HOGAN
School of Nursing
University of Miami
P.O. Box 016960
D2-5 Royce Building
Miami, FL 33101
Nancy Hogan is associate professor of Nursing at the University of Miami School of Nursing in Coral Gables, Florida. She is a nurse and a psychologist who has worked extensively with grieving parents and children. Her research centers on developing valid and reliable instruments designed to measure childhood and adulthood bereavement, and the generation of a theory of adolescent sibling bereavement from which to construct effective and age-appropriate interventions. Her research also includes conducting studies to measure the effectiveness of grief interventions.

HELENA ZNANIECKA LOPATA
Center for the Study of Comparative
    Social Roles
Loyola University
6525 North Sheridan Road
Chicago, IL 60626
Helena Znaniecka Lopata was born in Poland and came to the United States during World War II. She obtained her B.A. and M.A. from the University of

Illinois, and her Ph.D. from the University of Chicago. She is a professor of sociology at Loyola University of Chicago. Among her book publications are: *Occupation: Housewife; Widowhood in an American City; Women as Widows: Support Systems; City Women: Chicago; City Women: America; Polish American; Circles and Settings: Role Changes of American Women*. Forthcoming is *Current Widowhood: Myths and Realities*. She is also editing a series of books on *Current Research on Occupations and Professions*.

SAMUEL J. MARWIT
Suite 106, 7750 Clayton Road
St. Louis, MO 63117
Samuel J. Marwit is former director of Counseling Services and current associate professor of psychology at the University of Missouri at St. Louis. He holds a Diplomate in clinical psychology with the American Board of Professional Psychology and is a Fellow in the American Academy of Professional Psychology (ABPP). Dr. Marwit received his B.A. from the University of Michigan and his Ph.D. from the State University of New York at Buffalo. He is a co-founder of Resources for Crisis and Change, which is a multidisciplinary organization dedicated to the study and treatment of grief and significant life change. Dr. Marwit has published in the areas of diagnosing grief, the relationship of personality to grief, and the nature of support following death and divorce. He has also published in the areas of psycholinguistics, psychological testing, self-perceived body image, and issues related to professional psychological training.

SUSAN MILLER-HAVENS
151 Brattle Street
Cambridge, MA 02138
Susan Miller-Havens is a developmental psychologist. Born in New Jersey

in 1944, she holds a doctorate in Human Development from Harvard University. A clinician and adoption researcher, she is the immediate past director of the Education Department of the American Adoption Congress, Washington, D.C.

MIRIAM S. MOSS
8120 Brookside Road
Elkins Parks, PA 19117
Miriam S. Moss is a senior research sociologist at the Philadelphia Geriatric Center, where she has been engaged in a range of gerontological research since 1970. Her work has focused on family and social relationships, caregiving for elderly persons, the characteristics of the last year of life, and death and dying. She and her husband, Sidney, have written together extensively, and they were joint recipients of the Richard Kalish Award of the Gerontological Society of America. She is currently co-principal investigator in a study of the death of an elderly parent.

SIDNEY Z. MOSS
8120 Brookside Road
Elkins Parks, PA 19117
Sidney Z. Moss is a clinical and research social worker. He is a Family Therapist and Certified Grief Counselor, in private practice, who has specialized in issues of separation and grief. He has published widely about family losses over the life cycle, including reunions of parents and children, remarriage after widowhood or divorce, and death of the very old. He is currently working at the Philadelphia Geriatric Center on a study of the meaning of the death of an elderly parent for a middle-aged child.

CLAUDE L. NORMAND
8933 rue Clark
Montréal, QC H2N 1R7, Canada
Claude L. Normand obtained her Ph.D. from the University of Waterloo, Waterloo, Ontario, Canada in 1995 using the Massachusetts General Hospital/Harvard Medical School Child Bereavement Study data. She has been studying in the field of suicide prevention and bereavement since 1983. She developed and taught a course on death, dying, and bereavement in families at the School of Child and Youth Care at the University of Victoria, Victoria, British Columbia, in 1993. She is presently conducting post-doctoral research with the Groupe de recherche sur l'inadaptation psychosociale chez l'enfant (G.R.I.P.) at the Université de Montréal, Montréal, Québec, Canada.

PAUL C. ROSENBLATT
University of Minnesota
2900 McNeal Hall
1985 Buford Avenue
St. Paul, MN 55108-6140
Paul Rosenblatt has a Ph.D. in Psychology and is a professor in the Department of Family Social Science at the University of Minnesota. His recent research on grief over death and other losses includes studies of couples with a child whose life is sustained by equipment that supports breathing, couples who have had a child die, and farm families who have lost a family member in a farm accident. He is working on a book on grief in family systems and maintains a continuing interest in grief cross-culturally, including the grief of victims of human rights abuses.

SIMON SHIMSHON RUBIN
Department of Psychology
University of Haifa
Mount Carmel, Haifa, Israel, 31999
Simon Shimshon Rubin, Ph.D., is currently an associate professor of Psychology at the University of Haifa in Israel and a visiting associate professor in the Department of Psychiatry at the Harvard Medical School in Boston. Dr. Rubin joined the University of Haifa

faculty in 1980 and served as chairman of the Clinical Psychology Program from 1988 to 1993. Active in clinical and professional affairs in the United States and Israel, Dr. Rubin directed the State of Israel's Haifa Child, Adolescent and Family Clinic from 1984 to 1990. Dr. Rubin received his Ph.D. from Boston University in 1977 and was employed as a clinical psychologist at the Michael Reese Medical Center in Chicago from 1974 to 1980. Dr. Rubin has lectured and published internationally in the areas of loss and bereavement; professional ethics; training and supervision in psychotherapy; and the emotional problems of children, adults and families. He has served on and chaired committees concerned with health service delivery, professional regulation, and ethics.

MARGARET STROEBE
Department of Clinical and Health
    Psychology
University of Utrecht
Heidelberglaan 1,
    P.O. Box 80.140.3508
TC Utrecht, The Netherlands
Margaret Stroebe is lecturer in Clinical and Health Psychology at the University of Utrecht. Her abiding research interest lies in the field of bereavement. She is one of the editors (along with R. Hansson and W. Stroebe) of the *Handbook of Bereavement: Theory, Research and Intervention* and author (with W. Strobe) of *Bereavement and Health: The Psychological and Physical Consequences of Partner Loss.*

WOLFGANG STROEBE
Department of Clinical and Health
    Psychology
University of Utrecht
Heidelberglaan 1,
    P.O. Box 80.140.3508
TC Utrecht, The Netherlands

Wolfgang Stroebe is professor of Social, Organizational, and Health Psychology at the University of Utrecht. He is the author of a wide range of books, chapters, and articles on topics of social and health psychology, including *Social Psychology and Health* (with M. Stroebe), and is the co-editor of the *European Review of Social Psychology* (with M. Hewstone).

KIRSTEN TYSON-RAWSON
East Carolina University
CDFR Dept/HESC
Greenville, NC 27858- 4353
Kirsten Tyson-Rawson, Ph.D., is assistant professor in the Marriage and Family Therapy Program, Department of Child Development and Family Relations, East Carolina University. She received her doctorate in Marriage and Family Therapy from Kansas State University. Her primary clinical and research interests lie in the areas of bereavement, gender, and marital interaction.

LORA HEIMS TESSMAN
82 Kirkstall Road
Newtonville, MA 02160
Lora Heims Tessman is a practicing psychoanalyst in Newtonville, Massachusetts. She is on the faculty of the Massachusetts Institute for Psychoanalysis and Harvard Medical School; affiliate scholar member of the Boston Psychoanalytic Society and Institute; member of the Institute for Psychoanalytic Training and Research, New York. She is the author of the book, *Children of Parting Parents* and more recently has written a series of papers about father/daughter relationships, female development, and other topics. She is currently at work on the topic of changes in how the psychoanalyst is experienced in the inner psychic life of the analysand in the years following termination.

Preface

This book examines the continuing bond with the deceased in the resolution of grief. The continuing bond has been overlooked or undervalued in most scholarly and clinical work. The idea for the book grew out of several discussions among the three of us. We were sharing what each of us was finding in our respective and somewhat different research with families who had experienced a significant death (that of a child, a spouse, or a parent) and with families into which a child had been adopted. Initially, we became aware that both bereaved children and bereaved adults were struggling to find a way of maintaining a connection to the deceased. We were surprised when we found parallels in the experience of adoptees who had a relationship with a "fantasy" birth parent, even when they were adopted at birth. We found that older adoptees who had known their birth families were also maintaining a continuing internal connection with them. Our respective findings are more fully reported in individual chapters in this book. The following are some examples that show the direction of those early conversations.

Research interviews with children whose parent had died revealed that in the first years after the death, they developed a set of memories, feelings, and actions that kept them connected to their deceased parent. Rather than letting go, they seemed to be continuing the relationship. We observed that they kept this relationship by dreaming, by talking to the parent, by believing that the parent was watching them, by keeping things that belonged to the parent, by visiting the grave, and by frequently thinking about the dead parent. It was also clear that these connections were not static, but developed over time so that the parent–child relationship was developmentally appropriate to the child and to the child's present circumstances. These findings supported Silverman's finding that college-age women whose parents died when they were young reported a desire to know more about their deceased parents from the perspective of a young adult, to connect to the deceased in a different manner.

In a study of a self-help group of bereaved parents, it was apparent that the processes by which they resolved their grief involved intense interaction with their dead children. The bereaved parents were sustaining these interactions using similar means to those of the bereaved children. The poetry these parents wrote to clarify their experience to themselves and to each other was about learning to go on without the living child while at the same time maintaining the child as a presence in their lives. They learned to live without social roles and interpersonal interactions centered around parenting while at the same time the child became part of their inner world, and to the extent possible, part of their social reality. In a poem one mother wrote:

Will you forgive me if I go on?
If you can't make this earthly journey through time with me,
Will you then come along in my heart and wish me well?

Indeed, the members regarded the very life of the group as an extension of their relationship with their children. The refrain of the song adopted by the national organization says, "Our children live on in the love that we share." Parents regularly reported sensing their child's presence, hearing their child's voice, or seeing the influence of their child on their thoughts or on events in their world. As they shared their experiences with others and defined their experiences as normal, they discovered that they were moving toward "resolution" of their grief. In the resolution, the experiences of their child became part of their everyday world.

In research and clinical interviews adoptees repeatedly expressed a sense of sadness or of an important absence from their lives. These feelings could not be attributed to psychopathology. It became increasingly clear that this experience could be attributed at least in part to two factors: the nonexistence of the birth parents in the adoptees' life and the lack of opportunity to remediate this absence by means of a culturally condoned and encouraged mechanism of "grieving." Once the adoptees learned of their adoptive status they began trying to construct a mental image of their absent birth parents. They reported that an internal dialogue sometimes took place with this inner representation. The relationship to the inner representation had many of the elements that we saw between the bereaved and their dead relatives. Even though the adoptees almost never knew their birth parents directly, they reported powerful emotions and detailed thoughts about their absent birth parents. This complex of thought and emotion operated on both a conscious and an unconscious level, influencing emotions, behaviors, and life choices. In essence and without giving it a name, the adoptees were grieving for birth parents who were a part of their lives even when they had never known them.

As each of us looked at the data from our respective research, we realized that we were observing phenomena that could not be accounted for within the models of grief that most of our colleagues were using. It appeared that what we were observing was not a stage of disengagement, which we were educated to expect, but rather, we were observing people altering and then continuing their relationship to the lost or dead person. Remaining connected seemed to facilitate both adults' and children's ability to cope with the loss and the accompanying changes in their lives. These "connections" provided solace, comfort and support, and eased the transition from the past to the future.

We also observed that there was little social validation for the relationship people reported with the deceased or absent person. In adoption practice, the adoptive family was counseled to believe that the child would not need to know anything about the birth parent and that he or she should be treated exactly as though born into the adoptive family. Bereaved parents and children were encouraged to put the past behind, to mourn the loss, and to make new connections in the present. Many parents whose children had died young were encouraged to have other children as if the death of one child could be compensated for by the birth of another.

As we brought together the various threads of our work, each of us felt an excitement about the new linkages we were making. Silverman recalled for us a frustrating exchange she had with a colleague, almost a decade earlier, at the First International Conference on Bereavement held in Israel in November 1985. In a small work group, Silverman was trying to open up a discussion about the need to recognize what she was hearing from the bereaved who talked about their continued bond with the dead. A colleague insisted that dealing with bereavement involved putting the past behind and this required letting go of the relationship with the deceased. The colleague had developed tie-breaking rituals to accomplish this with his clients. He was pleased with his ability to overcome his clients' resistance to his advice to let go of the past. When this colleague could not convince Silverman that he was correct in spite of her data to the contrary, he said it was like having a baby: the baby is pushed out by the mother, gets slapped on the behind, cries, and "That's it." At that moment Silverman understood the nature of their differences. Birth is not about letting go, but about change in the nature of the mother's connection to her infant. Silverman had recently witnessed her grandson's birth and watched as the midwife gently facilitated the birth and placed the newborn on his mother's abdomen, his umbilical cord still attached. The child was surrounded by loving parents, aunt and uncle, and grandparents. His father carefully cut the cord. This delivery did not break a relationship; rather it led to a new set of relationships, with new dimensions and possibilities. The child was no less attached to his mother, and now attachment within an extended network of bonds was possible. The bereaved, like the new mother, have to change their relationship to the deceased. It does not mean that the relationship ends, though it changes in a decisive way. These ongoing connections and changes are the focus of this book.

The implication of our new understanding of grief goes further than the fact that people maintain a relationship to the deceased or absent birth parent. It requires that we look at the way we see relationships in general in our society. We need to bring into our professional dialogue the reality of how people experience and live their lives, rather than finding ways of verifying preconceived theories of how people should live.

As we recognized this congruence in our thinking, Silverman proposed that we edit a book that would call attention to these issues and their impact on bereavement processes. As we decided to edit this book, we realized that we each knew other scholars and clinicians whose findings were similar to ours. It was natural that we turned to those writers whose work had so informed and influenced our own. The response we received was gratifying, though not everyone was able to fit the project into their schedule. Silverman was in Israel on a Fulbright Fellowship for the 1993–94 academic year, and Nickman was in Boston. Klass and the fax machine managed to keep it together despite the geographical distances.

One of the rewards of editorship has been extended conversations by phone, fax, and letter with the contributors. From conception to final product, this book has been about dialogue. Now, we hope the readers will join us as the conversation continues. A new model of grief is embedded within the contributors' critiques of the current model of grief and within their descriptions of their subjects. We hope further conversation will clarify the new model, and we hope the readers will be part of that conversation.

Organization of the Book

The book's organization is quite simple: This Preface and the Introduction (Chapter 1) provide the framework for the book. Chapter 1 constitutes Part One, Examining the Dominant Model (of grief). In it, the editors trace the development of the 20th century model, showing how at critical points the data demonstrated that mourners maintained, rather than severed, their bonds with the deceased; however, the data were not integrated into the theory. The chapter describes the positive value placed on autonomy in our culture and the negative value placed on dependence, and how these values work to maintain the prevailing model of grief. The editors also begin to spell out what an alternative paradigm might look like. The core of the book, in which the paradigm is explored and further expanded, is divided into Parts Two through Eight, followed by Part Nine, the Conclusion. Short introductory comments for each of the seven main parts provide continuity from one part to another.

In Part Two (Chapters 2, 3, and 4), Setting the Stage, problems with the dominant model are examined. In Chapter 2, Margaret Stroebe, Mary Gergen, Kenneth Gergen, and Wolfgang Stroebe point to the cultural/historical relativism of the idea of grief work. In Chapter 3, Paul Rosenblatt summarizes several of his studies to show that the idea that people "get over" grief is false, for surges of feelings and thoughts that are very much like those experienced right after a death continue over a lifetime. In Chapter 4, Dennis Klass shows how the rituals of ancestor worship in Japan function to maintain the bond with the dead.

In Part Three (Chapters 5, 6, 7, and 8), The Inner Representation of the Deceased, the chapters are arranged according to the population studied. First the focus is on bereaved children, one of whose parents died. Chapter 5, by Phyllis Silverman and Steven Nickman, and Chapter 6 by Claude Normand with Silverman and Nickman, use data from the longitudinal MGH/Harvard Medical School Child Bereavement Study. In Chapter 7, Betty Buchsbaum relates children's memories of the deceased to the children's developmental stage. Chapter 8 by Kirsten Tyson-Rawson reports on her study of college women whose fathers had died. She discusses both positive interactions and those that are frightening and intrusive.

Widows and widowers are then discussed in Part Four (Chapters 9, 10, and 11), Spousal Bereavement. Chapter 9 by Helena Znaniecka Lopata reviews her concept of the widow's sanctification of her dead husband. Lopata first published this idea over two decades ago and it has been virtually ignored by subsequent scholars. In Chapter 10, on remarriage among the elderly, Sidney and Miriam

Moss show how the inner representation of the deceased spouses are part of the subsequent marriage, not left outside the marriage. Chapter 11 by Roberta Conant looks at the comforting sense of presence.

Part Five (Chapters 12 and 13) is about Parental Bereavement. In Chapter 12, Dennis Klass traces the interchange between the inner representation of the dead child as an inner reality and as a social reality in The Compassionate Friends, a self-help group. Simon Shimson Rubin's Chapter 13, based on his studies in Israel, gives a detailed account of his two-track model of bereavement. He documents how it is insufficient to evaluate resolution of grief on the basis of present functioning without also including how the bereaved relate to the deceased.

Part Six, Bereaved Siblings, contains only Chapter 14, a fact that reflects the paucity of good studies on the subject. Nancy S. Hogan and Lydia DeSantis report their study of siblings in which they triangulate the constructs of grief, personal growth, and attachment.

Early on there was some discussion among the editors over whether the dynamics of loss for adoptees is similar to those bereaved by death. Nickman argued the case strongly in the face of Klass's skepticism. Nickman's ideas were convincing. Thus, Part Seven (Chapters 15 and 16), Adoptee Losses, presents data that have not been examined in the context of bereavement research. In Chapter 15, Nickman synthesizes his many years of clinical practice with adoptees and their families. Fantasies that adoptees have about their birth parents are examined by Susan Miller-Havens in Chapter 16.

Part Eight (Chapters 17, 18, and 19), Meanings and Implications, deals with various clinical and research findings. In Chapter 17, Samuel Marwit and Dennis Klass asked a general population to recall a significant person who had died and to describe the role that person plays in present life. David Balk in Chapter 18 studied the intensity of attachment to the dead and the degree of distress in college students. He finds that strong attachment is associated with higher distress. Balk's findings are in some ways a counterpoint to the majority of the contributions to the book and so call for careful thinking. In Chapter 19, Laura Tessman gives us a detailed report of psychotherapy with the adult child of a Nazi war criminal. We can see the complexity of retaining the bond with the father while rejecting so much of the father.

The book ends with Part Nine (Chapter 20, Concluding Thoughts). Like most conversations, the one in this book develops themes and points of agreement/disagreement in ways that made sense to us but were not not always systematic. The chapter begins to give systematic form to the conversation. If in sharing this conversation we help others to join in, the book's purpose will have been fulfilled.

Dennis Klass
Phyllis R. Silverman
Steven L. Nickman

Part One

Examining the
Dominant Model

Chapter 1

Introduction:
What's the Problem?

Phyllis R. Silverman and Dennis Klass

This book was conceived to give voice to an expanded view of the bereavement process. Specifically, this book reexamines the idea that the purpose of grief is to sever the bonds with the deceased in order to free the survivor to make new attachments. We offer an alternative model based on the mourner's continuing bonds with the deceased.

A model is an ideal set of interactions or processes that make sense of multifarious data. As such, a model is a conceptual archetype. "By archetype I mean a systematic repertoire of ideas by means of which a given thinker describes by analogical extension, some domain to which those ideas do not immediately and literally apply" (Black, 1962, p. 241). Models are intellectual schemata, but as we will note, they are part of the Zeitgeist, the spirit of a particular age. Very often the assumptions in the model we use are unexamined. Batson (1980) wrote,

> Now, an explanation is a mapping of the pieces of a description onto a tautology, and an explanation becomes acceptable to the degree that you are willing and able to accept the links of the tautology. If the links are "self-evident" (i.e., if they seem undoubtable to the self that is you), then the explanation built on that tautology is satisfactory to you. That is all. It is always a matter of natural history, a matter of faith, imagination, trust, rigidity, and so on of the organism, that is of you or me. (p. 93)

This means that people persistently hold on to models, even in the face of contrary evidence. Bowlby (1961) linked the difficulty of abandoning old intellectual models to the pain of grief.

> The painfulness of new ideas, and our habitual resistance to them, can also be seen in this context. The more far-reaching a new idea, the more disorganization of existing theoretical systems has to be tolerated before a new and better synthesis of old and new can be achieved. (p. 335)

The authors in this book present data from populations who differ in the origins of their grief. We think that the net effect of all these contributions is to show that the resolution of grief involves a continuing bond that the survivor maintains with the deceased. We hope that this book demonstrates the rich possibilities of what we see as healthy, enduring bonds with the dead.

This chapter will

  1   outline the model of grief in general use, and show how this model of grief was developed in the face of data that suggested its inadequacy;
  2   discuss the assumptions of this dominant model of grief, which are part of the passing world view of modernity;
  3   explore the way inadequate assumptions about the nature of the self as well as assumptions about what is good social scientific methodology contributed to the remarkable resiliency of this model in the face of contrary data;
  4   begin to sketch out another model of grief, leaving the other chapters in the book to provide a fuller, more complex understanding of this model.

We realized in reviewing the contributions to this volume that the majority of the authors did qualitative, not quantitative, research. This realization about method brought us full circle, for it seems to us that the quantitative method, with its roots so deep in the logical positivism of modernity, is based on the same inadequate assumptions underlying the model of grief that this book sets out to correct. At the end of the chapter, we comment on an alternate methodological paradigm.

DISENGAGING AS A GOAL OF GRIEF

The view of grief most accepted in this century holds that for successful mourning to take place the mourner must disengage from the deceased, and let go of the past (Abraham, 1927; Clayton, Desmarais, & Winokur, 1968; Edelstein, 1984; Furman, 1984; Hofer, 1984; Peppers & Knapp, 1980; Pollock, 1975; Rando, 1986; Raphael, 1983; Sanders, 1989; Volkan, 1981; Weizman & Kamm, 1985). To experience a continuing bond with the deceased in the present has been thought of as symptomatic of psychological problems (Dietrich & Shabad, 1989; Horowitz, Wilner, Marmor, & Krupnick, 1980; Jackson, 1957; Miller, 1971). A continued attachment to the deceased was called unresolved grief. Some practitioners likened unresolved grief to other forms of phobic avoidance, which have been treated successfully by exposure to the avoided situation, such as the treatment of obsessive-compulsive and phobic patients (Mawson, Marks, Ramm, & Stern, 1981). Temporarily "hypercathecting" to the dead person was normal because "in the normal process of mourning . . . the person reacts to a real object loss by effecting a temporary introjection of the loved person. The main purpose of this hypercathecting is to preserve the person's relationship to the lost object" (Volkan & Showalter, 1968, p. 359).

  In this model the bond with the deceased is not a part of the resolution of grief, but is an attempt to preserve the relationship by fighting against the reality that the person is dead. In this formulation such resistance to reality is doomed to failure, for eventually the person must accept the fact that death is real and permanent, and in the end the bond must be relinquished.

In this view, maintaining an ongoing attachment to the deceased was considered symptomatic of pathology. Indeed, pathology was defined in terms of sustaining a relationship to the dead. Jackson (1957), in a book that was popular with clinicians for many years, said that attempts to maintain ties with the deceased is "a form of regression and psychological incorporation that should be discounted and discouraged. Regression is not cured by accepting it. It must be actively opposed, for it becomes worse if it is encouraged" (p . 65).

This theory led to some rather brutal clinical techniques. Though he later abandoned it in favor of more traditional psychoanalytic reliance on the productions of the unconscious and on managing the transference, Volkan's (1985) "re-griefing" psychotherapy received wide attention. Part of his report on the case of a 16-year-old girl whose mother committed suicide is as follows:

> Instead of talking with her about her mother as a dead person, her mother was referred to as an inanimate object consisting of degenerating anatomic structures such as skin, muscle, and bone. Such an attempt, after the phase of abreaction, serves to hasten the actual return to normal reality testing while paradoxically giving impetus to repression of some conflictual ideas expressed. As can be readily seen, this somewhat harsh technique does not provide for full emotional insight but rather serves to repress some instinctual demands, especially the patient's "death wishes" toward the lost object. . . . The therapist must be authoritative but at the same time he must be understanding. In this way the "strong" therapist can take over most of the guilt that the patient had been experiencing. (Volkan & Showalter, 1968, p. 370)

HISTORICAL PERSPECTIVE

This model of grief is a 20th-century phenomenon. Only in the past 100 years have continuing bonds been denied as a normal part of bereavement behavior. In this section we will trace some of the development of the modern understanding of grief. We will show how, as the theory grew, observations of the continuing bond with the dead were made, but the data were not integrated into the conceptual framework that guided most practice.

The modern idea of bereavement began with Freud's (1917/1961a) definition of mourning as the sad process by which "Each single one of the memories and situations of expectancy which demonstrate the libido's attachment to the lost object is met by the verdict of reality that the object no longer exists" (p. 255).

Freud was not talking about grief after a death in this definition. The loss Freud described was the child giving up the direct attachment (Oedipal love) to the parent. He theorized that grief is different from depression in that he thought depression is caused by internalizing the parent, who then remains as a critical voice in the ego ideal. Grief, as Freud saw it, frees the ego from the attachment to the deceased: "When the work of mourning is completed the ego becomes free and uninhibited again" (1917/1961a, p. 245). Freud never applied this theory to cases of grief after a significant death.

Freud's life has particular significance to us, because he generated a world view for those who followed him. We will examine Freud's personal difficulties in mourning rather closely, because his life clearly shows the dilemmas created by a modern world view (Homans, 1989). We know that his personal experience with grief did not support his theoretic model of grief. After important deaths, Freud seemed unable to find new attachments and unable to find a sense of transcendent connection that he seemed to think necessary if his bond with the deceased were to be continued. As Freud framed it for himself, the problem was that he could not allow himself to acknowledge any experience of a transcendent connection. When a friend said religion was based in an "oceanic feeling," Freud said he could find no such experience in himself except in regressive infantile narcissism (1961b). The idea that transcendent feelings are regressive led him to some interesting ideas about the nature of civilization, but did not serve him well when he became a mourner. When his daughter Sophie died, he wrote:

> Since I am profoundly irreligious there is no one I can accuse, and I know there is nowhere to which any complaint could be addressed. "The unvarying circle of a soldier's duties" and the "sweet habit of existence" will see to it that things go on as before. Quite deep down I can trace the feeling of a deep narcissistic hurt that is not to be healed. My wife and Annerl are terribly shaken in a more human way. (Jones, 1957, p. 20)

We later see that Freud was equally shaken, but could not allow himself the luxury of expressing his distress directly. In another letter written immediately after Sophie's death, he discussed the kind of control he tried to exercise: "It is such a paralyzing event, which can stir no afterthoughts when one is not a believer and so is spared all the conflicts that go with that. Blunt necessity, mute submission" (Jones, 1957, p. 19).

Nine years later, on what would have been his daughter's 36th birthday (April 11, 1929), Freud wrote to his friend Ludwig Binswanger after he learned that Binswanger's son had died. Freud acknowledged that after such a death he could not go on as before:

> Although we know that after such a loss the acute state of mourning will subside, we also know we shall remain inconsolable and will never find a substitute. No matter what may fill the gap, even if it be filled completely, it nevertheless remains something else. And actually this is how it should be. It is the only way of perpetuating that love which we do not want to relinquish. (Freud, 1961a, p. 239)

When Sophie's son died at age 4:

> It was the only occasion in his life when Freud was known to shed tears. He told me afterward that this loss had affected him in a different way from any of the others he had suffered. They had brought about sheer pain, but this one had killed something in him for good. . . . A couple of years later he told Marie Bonaparte that he had never been able to get fond of anyone since that misfortune, merely retaining his old attach-

ments; he had found the blow quite unbearable, much more so than his own cancer. (Jones, 1957, p. 92)

The connection Freud had drawn between grief and depression played out in a more complex way in his own life than in his theory. After his grandson died, Freud said that the boy had represented for him all children and grandchildren. After that death, he was unable to enjoy life. "It is the secret to my indifference [toward his cancer]—people call it courage—toward the danger to my own life" (Jones, 1957, p. 92).

From his own experience Freud understood that grief work did not turn out to be a process that could ever be completed, nor did it turn out to be a process that resulted in cutting old attachments and forming new attachments, but he did not give theoretical form to these feelings. Instead he responded to these important deaths in his life with deep depression, against which his only defense was a determined stoicism.

We can hear echoes of Freud's experience in his later metapsychology that saw human suffering as an expression of the tension between Eros, the drive for union, and Thanatos, the tendency to separate and dissolve. He saw that a harmony between Eros and Thanatos could be a solution to the pain of existence, but the method he had chosen, the analysis of the psyche of autonomous individuals, only led to further isolation, not to the sense of bonding with others or to membership in a community. Thus, while he describes the misery of the human condition brilliantly, in the end we can only understand, but there is nothing we can do about it (see Wilber, 1995, p. 331). This late metapsychology was never translated into clinical practice and never applied to the theory on grief.

Freud's early theory, not his experience or his later metapsychology, dominated subsequent formulations of appropriate grieving behavior. The theory took on a life of its own, and Freud's writing about his own experience with grief was not integrated into psychoanalytic thought. The post-Freud paradigm for understanding grief has maintained the idea that the primary goal of grieving is to cut the bond with the deceased so that new attachments can be formed. As we examine the history, we find that phenomena indicating that survivors do maintain bonds with the deceased have been rediscovered many times, but each time the insight fails to be passed on and incorporated into the next generation of research and theory.

Psychoanalysis has continued to study internalized object relations, including the relationship between an individual and a person who has died. What is imperfectly explained by psychoanalytic theory is the nature and extent of changes that occur in the relationship between the living individual and a dead person, who is absent from the external world and represented only, or largely, by mental constructs (inner representations).

Because the Oedipal conflict ended with the loss of direct cathexis with the parents and with the internalization of the parent in the form of the ego ideal (superego as the theory developed later), the psychoanalytic group soon developed the concept of internalization as part of grief work. Internalization is precisely the kind of psychological transformation of the bond with the dead that seems to be useful with our own data, and with the data we will see in many of the chapters of this book. Unfortunately, this idea of internalization soon got caught up in questions of pathology. Rather than simply examining data, the psychoanalytic scholars developed the idea that internalizing the dead is merely a preliminary stage to letting them go. They also severely limited the kinds of internalization they considered healthy. Only recently has psychoanalytic theory become more flexible with regard to interactions with the dead.

Abraham (1927) is credited with the basic idea that built on Freud's earlier work. He said that the mourner introjected the lost object in order to retain it. Schafer (1968, 1976) would later elaborate this idea of internalization in a way that formed the basis for most current discussion in psychoanalytic theory. Schafer distinguished between two kinds of internalization: identification and introjection. Volkan (1981) applied Schafer's idea directly to grief. His definition of identification would support the idea of a continuing attachment to the deceased. In identification, he says,

> The mourner no longer has a compulsive need to cling to the representation of the dead person. Meanwhile, however, paradoxically, the mourner identifies with certain aspects of the dead and comes to resemble him in these particulars. Thus, when such mourning is concluded, the ego will often have been enriched. (p. 67)

Introjection, on the other hand, is regarded as an unhealthy result of mourning, for in introjection the ego is split in a harmful way as the "object representation is felt as existing within the patient himself, and is perceived by some patients as an ongoing and persistent phenomenon" (Volkan, 1981, p. 70). Volkan thought of the introject as a frozen entity remaining in the psyche, not available to change nor enabling the survivor to establish healthy interactions in the present. These internalized representations are described as *unchanging*. Dietrich and Shabad (1989) emphasize the paradoxical character of the inner representation of the deceased: one that is both frozen in time and timeless, immortalized and lost simultaneously. Schafer (1968) regards the bereaved's inner representation of the deceased as persisting unmodified and, therefore, as inaccessible to secondary process—that is, to rational, reflective thinking.

Fenichel (1945) thought of mourning in terms of an introjection to be made before the object could be given up. A first step in grief was that the mourner hypercathected the lost object; the survivor was preoccupied with thoughts about the dead person. Hypercathexis was understood to be a prelude to decathexis, in which the dead person was held closer early in grief so he or she could be given up at the end of grief (Dietrich & Shabad, 1989; Furman, 1984; Jacobson, 1965; Rochlin, 1959; Schafer, 1968; Wolfenstein, 1973).

There have been minority voices within the psychoanalytic dialogue. In 1974 Pincus wrote that successful resolution of bereavement involved the mourner's identifying with aspects of the deceased and incorporating these aspects into a new sense of self that develops in the process of adapting to the loss. This brings about the diminution of the dependence on the external presence of the deceased: "The bereaved can draw on memories, happy or unhappy, and share these with others, making it possible to talk, think or feel about the dead person" (p. 127). Once this dialogue can take place, the internalization is not a static phenomenon.

Tahka (1984) has expanded psychoanalytic theory in the direction of the theory supported by this book. The limited circulation of the *Scandinavian Psychoanalytic Review*, however, seems to have prevented widespread use of his work by other scholars. Tahka provides for an ongoing element of the lost object after the process is complete in the form of a "remembrance formation," which is neither identification nor introjection. The remembrance formation is a third form the inner representation of the dead can take. The question is whether the object is internalized prestructurally (preverbally) or poststructurally (verbally). The difference between the two is that in the prestructural level, there is no distinction between inner and outer, self and other. At the prestructural level, as in the borderline personality, internalizations are experienced as empty anxiety or hypochondriacal symptoms. "Since the self and the object presuppose each other . . . even a temporary loss of the object becomes a threat to the existence of the self" (p. 26). At the poststructural level Takha thinks it is possible to work though identification so that "once these feelings and experiences have become conscious, endured and worked through, they will become part of the remembrance object with corresponding reductions in the introject" (p. 24). The remembrance formation, he says,

> represents an entirely different form of internalization: building and integrating the representation of the lost object into a remembrance of him as he was really experienced during a common period of life. Once it has been established, its later calling back to mind, reminiscing about it and dismissing it again from the mind, are invariably experienced as activities of the self taking place exclusively on the subject's own conditions. Although it is experienced as a fully differentiated object representation, no illusions of its separate and autonomous existence are involved. In contrast to fantasy objects possessing various wish-fulfilling functions, it includes the awareness that nothing more can be expected from it and therefore, in its fully established forms it has chances for becoming the most realistic of all existing object representations. (p. 18)

Pincus and Takha, as well as a few others, have suggested that psychoanalytic theory be revised in a way that allows more forms of healthy ongoing bonds with the dead. At this time, however, their critiques do not seem to have been incorporated into the mainstream of psychoanalytic thinking on grief.

Bowlby's attachment theory of grief (1969–1980) was a central part of his attempt to totally revise psychoanalytic theory. Bowlby continued the model that the purpose of grief is to sever the bond with the dead. Late in his life, Bowlby recognized the fullness of the grieving process, but that recognition was not used by Bowlby's followers (Klass, 1987). Bowlby grounded psychological theory in the actual events of childhood, not in the psychic trauma (largely the Oedipal conflict), which was at the center of psychoanalytic theory. Bowlby thought progress in psychology "would be possible only if we have far more systematic knowledge about the effects on a child of the experience he has within his family" (1981, p. 244).

As a postwar consultant to the World Health Organization on the needs of homeless children, Bowlby discovered the ill effects of maternal deprivation. His initial theories of grief derived not from the experiences of people after a death, but from children deprived of their mothers under traumatic conditions. Bowlby adopted the idea of attachment behavior as a way of understanding these children. Attachment is "regarded as a class of social behavior of an importance equivalent to that of mating behavior and parental behavior. It is held to have a biological function specific to itself" (1969, p. 179). Its purpose is to keep the mother in close proximity.

In his early papers on this process, the final stage that Bowlby described was labeled adaptation, a conceptualization that could be consistent with the thesis of this book. But soon adaptation was defined as detachment. He identified a distinct and unvarying sequence of behaviors that can be identified in children separated from their mothers: protest, despair and yearning, and detachment.

> Each of the phases is related to one or another of the central issues of psychoanalytic theory. Thus the phase of protest is found to raise the problem of separation anxiety; despair that of grief and mourning; detachment that of defense. (1973, p. 27)

Bowlby excluded identification, or internalization, from the themes he would investigate in his 1961 paper, "Processes of Mourning." Perhaps this was due to the youthfulness of his first subjects, but he was quite conscious of his decision to exclude identification. "To some a discussion of mourning that omits identification will seem like Hamlet without the Prince," Bowlby wrote (1961, p. 319). It was the nature of his data that they "do not seem to lend themselves readily to the study of identificatory processes and their deviations," though he was "inclined toward the view that the role of identification amongst processes of mourning may become easier to discern after some of the problems to be tackled here have been clarified" (1961, p. 319). Rewriting that paper in the third volume of *Attachment and Loss*, he added identification to the list of themes, but "in the upshot, the role given to identificatory processes in the theory advanced here is a subordinate one: they are regarded as occurring only sporadically and, when prominent, to be indicative of pathology" (1980, p. 30).

Bowlby's attachment theory proved very popular among child development scholars and led to many important studies on parent–child bonding. Bowlby's ideas on grief were carried forward by his compatriot Parkes, who in the early

1970s, along with his colleagues, solidified the dominant model of grief in their analysis of their findings from studies of widows (Glick, Weiss, & Parkes, 1974; Parkes, 1972, 1975a, 1975b; Parkes & Brown, 1972; Parkes & Weiss, 1983). Bowlby followed Parkes and his colleagues' work closely using their theory and data in the final volume of his three-volume study on attachment and loss (1969–1980).

Parkes' theory of grief was ethological—that is, grief was understood as a preprogrammed series of behaviors cued by a specific environmental stimulus. In this respect, grief was like nest-building behavior in birds. Parkes seems to have been influenced in his interpretation of his data by the attachment theory with which he began. In his study of London widows, Parkes found that experiences of the presence, or visual and auditory hallucinations, are a function of the searching behavior, which is one of the early behaviors activated by separation from the attached object. "It is postulated that maintaining a clear visual memory of the lost person facilitates the search by making it more likely that the missing person will be located, in fact, to be found somewhere within the field of search" (1972, p. 49). Thus,

> Searching fills the gap between aim and object. . . . The goal-situation to which these behavior patterns normally give rise is the optimum proximity of the loved person. When this is achieved the appetitive behavior ceases. But if the loved person is permanently lost, appetitive behavior will tend to persist and with it the subject discomfort that accompanies unterminated striving. This is what is experienced as frustration. (p. 54)

Parkes understands the interaction with the inner representation of the dead to be an important element of the early stage of grief, for it functions to repeatedly frustrate the survivor and opens the way for the survivor to relinquish the attachment to the deceased. He sees no useful place for interaction with the dead after grief is resolved. He sees the necessity of widows taking on the practical roles of their husbands, such as monitoring the automobile repairs. Parkes finds no resolution in widows taking more symbolic aspects of their husbands into themselves. "Getting through" the grief means breaking the attachment. He finds that only a minority of the widows

> . . . were conscious of coming to resemble or contain the dead spouse. . . . There was nothing to suggest that identification is a necessary part of the process of recovery. It seems, rather, that identification with the lost person is one of the methods that bereaved people adopt to avoid the painful reality of loss; as such it may delay acceptance of the true situation, but, like most other coping mechanisms, it is only intermittently effective. The sense of the husband 'inside' is a transient phenomenon. . . . Episodes of comfortable 'closeness' are followed by periods of grieving and loneliness, and it is only intermittently that identification occurs. The London widows seemed, rather, to find their new identity emerging from the altered life situations which they had to face. (1972, p. 105)

As the studies progressed Parkes and his colleagues' data began to show that the widows were maintaining a continuing bond with their husbands. Glick, Weiss, and Parkes (1974) write in a footnote, "We are unable to give reliable figures regarding the incidence of the sense of the husband's presence. Direct questions were not at first asked on this subject, since we had not anticipated the phenomenon" (p. 146).

They did not change their theory to fit their unanticipated data. In their descriptions they did not distinguish between the widow forgetting that the husband is dead (i.e., when the widow feels that the husband is about to arrive home at dinner time), and an ongoing sense that the husband is present and available for consultation on important matters in their lives. Nor did they change their definition of the resolution of grief in a way that would make the experiences a part of the resolution instead of just being a part of the experience of loss. They report that

> In contrast to most other aspects of the reaction to bereavement, the sense of the persisting presence of the husband did not diminish with time. It seemed to take a few weeks to become established, but thereafter seemed as likely to be reported late in the bereavement as early. (p. 147)

They explain that such attachment is not incompatible with the withdrawal of attachment from the lost object and reinvestment in new objects that their theory defines as healthy resolution of grief. They say that the widows were comforted by talking to the dead spouse and the "feeling" that they were being listened to (p. 154). They found that, for many widows, the sense of presence was comforting, and the widows invoked the presence when they were unsure or depressed. However, Parkes and his colleagues do not follow up the issue of the continuing role of such comforting solace in the widows' lives. They also found that a year after the death, 69% of the widows agreed with the statement "I try to behave in ways he would have wanted me to," or "I think as he would have wanted me to." After 2 to 4 years, 83% of those whose spouse died suddenly still agreed with the statement, as did nearly half of those who had forewarning of the death. Because they do not shift their theoretical framework, Parkes and his colleagues are not able to distinguish the functions of the inner representations of the dead husbands in the processes of the widows' grief, nor in the ongoing lives of the widows after the resolution of grief. They cannot explain the role of the comforting sense of presence and the moral function of using the husband as a standard of self-judgment in the widows' ongoing lives.

In the final volume of his work on attachment and loss, Bowlby (1980) recognizes the data gathered by Parkes and his colleagues as he tries to understand why observations about a continuing bond with the deceased is largely ignored or overlooked. He uses the data to point out that Freud was wrong. He does not use the data to amend his own earlier theory about the resolution of grief.

> Failure to recognize that a continuing sense of the dead person's presence, either as a constant companion or in some specific and appropriate location, is a common fea-

ture of healthy mourning has led to some confused theorizing. . . . Indeed, findings in regard both to the high prevalence of a continuing sense of the presence of the dead person and to its compatibility with a favorable outcome gives no support to Freud's well-known and already quoted passage: "Mourning has a quite precise psychical task to perform: its function is to detach the survivor's memories and hopes from the dead." (p. 100; see Peskin, 1993, and Stroebe, Gergen, Gergen & Stroebe, 1993, for a recent controversy on the correct interpretation of Bowlby on this point.)

Those who follow the Bowlby/Parkes theory continue to define the resolution of grief as severing bonds rather than as establishing a changed bond with the dead person. Raphael (1983) retains Freud's earlier idea of hypercathexis to the dead in the early part of grief. Any interaction with the deceased is, for her, a hallucination.

Thus the bereaved may believe he hears the return at a familiar time, sees the face in a familiar place, feels the touch of a body, smells a familiar perfume, or hears a familiar sound. These perceptual misinterpretations reflect the intense longing and, like dreams are a source of a wish fulfillment. (1983, p. 40)

Raphael says that eventually the behaviors directed toward the deceased "become extinguished, and new attachment bonds are formed, or it may be that in some instances the relationship persists in altered form in fantasy" (1983, p. 69). For her the fantasy serves no useful purpose except to shield the person from reality, and she believes the fantasy serves to prevent the survivor from making meaningful attachments in the present.

Family systems theorists have adopted this model of grief from the psychoanalytic school that they rejected. Walsh and McGoldrick (1991) define therapeutic goals with a family after a death as shared acknowledgment of the reality of the death, shared experience of the loss and revising the family narrative to include the death, reorganizing the family system, and reinvesting in other relationships (p. 54). At one point they write that part of revising the narrative means that family members "reclaim and incorporate aspects of the lost person's part in the family narrative" (p. 62). Such reclaiming seems to be a reassignment of roles, rather than the inclusion of the inner representation as a continuing family member. They see a danger in one member holding on to the bond with a dead child by keeping the child's clothes and regularly visiting the grave because it is "compulsive repetitions, tying up family energy, so that family members are never free to make new commitments" (p. 64). Some of their case material notes "linking objects" that may be kept (p. 13), but such activities are neither examined in the text nor incorporated into the theory.

Some brutal techniques, similar to Volkan's regriefing, grow out of family systems theory. Rosen (1988) defines the problem of grief in a family where a child has died as the withdrawal of the "identified mourner" (p. 193) from the family system. Hence, the goal of treatment was the "reentry of the mourner" (p. 195) into the family system. We can ask what the actual intervention with the family would be in this theory of families after a death. Although the authors do not say it clearly, the answer would appear to be that instead of sharing the inner representation of the dead within the family system, the therapeutic task is to force the identified mourner to give up the dead in exchange for acceptance within the living family.

Gradually, in the last few years, the weight of evidence began to infiltrate the dominant model of grief, so we have seen some attempts to modify the theory to accommodate the data. In the revision of his book on grief therapy, Worden (1991) rephrases the final task of grief. In the first version he stated the last task is to reinvest in new relationships. In his revision, he writes that the last task is "to emotionally relocate the deceased and move on with life" (p. 16). Nonetheless, he phrases this task in such a way that it seems by continuing to care for the deceased, the mourner cannot develop other relationships.

Sanders (1989) notes that sensing the presence or actually seeing the dead person "brought a sense of comfort," but she understands the experience to be the "cognitive counterpart of yearning" (p. 70). She is saying interaction with the inner representation of the dead is wish fulfillment rather than a positive element in resolution.

In Rando's 1991 presidential address to the Association for Death Education and Counseling (1992), we see the cognitive difficulty of attempts to expand the dominant model of grief to accommodate to the idea of an ongoing bond. She said that "developing a new relationship with the deceased" was part of moving "adaptively into the new world without forgetting the old" (p. 45). Yet three lines later, she defined pathology as the attempt to maintain relationships to the deceased:

> In all forms of complicated mourning, there are attempts to do two things: (1) to deny, repress, or avoid aspects of the loss, its pain and the full realization of its implications for the mourner; and (2) to hold onto, and avoid relinquishing, the lost loved one. (p. 45)

AUTONOMY OR INTERDEPENDENCE

The model of grief that began with Freud is based on a view of the world that stresses how separate people are from each other. As Chapter 2 of this volume shows, there is a consistent basic understanding of the nature of the self and the nature of the self's bonds to others at the heart of the common 20th-century model of grief. This model is an artifact of Western modernity (also see Hepburn, 1994), and is not the operant model in human societies in other times and places (Doi, 1973; Sullivan, 1987). A central feature in the modern Western world view is the value placed on autonomy and individuation. Autonomy is the stated goal of human development (Erikson, 1963; Miller, 1986). Independence, rather than interdependence, is prized. Being dependent is judged as "bad." Relationships with others are viewed instrumentally; an individual enters into relations with others to have "needs," such as security or intimacy, met. When a relationship no longer provides instrumental satisfaction to the individual, as in the case of an unsatisfactory marriage or a death, the relationship is severed. There is little place in this model for any idea of individuals as interdependent and living in a web of relationships. In this modern view humans are understood to have a limited amount of energy for any one type of relationship. To have a new relationship we need to give up the old one (Silverman, Campbell, & Patti, 1994).

The idea that people can have only one relationship at a time—that is, one love, one mother, and so forth—is exemplified most vividly in the practice of adoption in this century. Birth parents were instructed to surrender their child and to carry on with their lives as if they had not had this baby (Silverman, 1981; Winkler & Van Keppel,1984). Adoptive parents were told to act as though this baby had been born to them. The baby's birth certificate was changed to conform to the new "fact" (Kirk, 1985; Sorosky, Baran, & Pannor, 1978). Birth parents who found that they could not meet these expectations were told that continuing interest was a sign of psychological disturbance (Deykin, Campbell, & Patti, 1984; Silverman, 1981). Adoptees who asked about their birth origins were similarly dismissed (Fisher, 1973; Lifton, 1981). Treatment in both instances was to close off these questions so that the patients could get on with their lives. This model is still vigorously defended. The Uniform Adoption Act proposed by the National Conference of Commissioners on Uniform State Laws in 1994 recommends that all contact between adoptees and birth parents be banned even in cases of older children who have existing relationships with their birth parents. Adoptees' and birth parents' testimony about their ties to each other were ignored.

Relationships are so stylized that we have no model for considering that a child could love two mothers, albeit each in a different way. Yet, it is clear in practical experience that to care, to be involved in more than one relationship at a time, is part of the human condition whether the other people in the relationship are present, absent, or dead. To insist on a separateness that keeps very clear boundaries between people requires a mechanistic view of human functioning that fails to appreciate the importance of connection and relationship. Separateness predominates in modern Western cultures. The myth of rugged individualism associated with the United States and the concept of individuality that played itself out in the development of the western frontier springs from the same modern understanding of self—in spite of the actual historical situation on the frontier, which was one of cooperation and communal ties (see Coontz, 1992). This understanding of the self and the self's relationship to others is all-pervasive today, and without philosophical examination has made its way into clinical psychological practice (Bellah, Madsen, Sullivan, & Tipton, 1985). People are instructed to stand on their own feet, to pick themselves up by their bootstraps. Individuals find they can clarify their world when they can say, "That's your problem." Feeling good about the self is an antidote to internalized voices that make demands for more social responsiveness. In this world view, it is legitimate to ask for help if one has a diagnosed illness, for the concept of illness carries with it the possibility of cure; an illness is a short-term interruption in normal healthy functioning. From this point of view, bereavement was easily made into an illness, for then it is possible for the bereaved to ask for and receive help, which in most other societies would be automatically forthcoming.

We can see the consequences of valuing autonomy in the criteria for what has been called pathological grief. In the dominant model of grief, dependence has often been seen as a condition for "pathological" grief. While admitting her lack of data, Raphael (1983) assumes that dependent personalities are more prone to pathological grief:

> Although no specific risk factors have been demonstrated, it may be suggested that people with personal characteristics that lead them to form dependent, clinging, ambivalent relationships with their spouses are at greater risk of having a poor outcome. (p. 225)

Parkes and Weiss (1983) are more certain.

> Some people may feel compelled to engage in perpetual mourning as tribute to the dead or to make restitution for some failure or sense of guilt. . . . There is some confirming evidence from systematic studies that both ambivalence and over-dependence predispose individuals to chronic grief. (p. 19)

The difficulty has been confounded because in the modern West, when autonomy for men was asserted, all dependent behavior was ascribed to women and other lower status groups (Coontz, 1992). The pathology of grief was associated with the stereotype of feminine behavior.

ANOTHER PARADIGM

It is clear by now that the model of grief put forward in this book is quite different. In this book, rather than judging dependence as undesirable, we accept the way people feel themselves to be involved in each other's lives. In the model of grief we propose, interdependence is sustained even in the absence of one of the parties. The data presented by the contributors to this book suggest that the bereaved remain involved and connected to the deceased, and that the bereaved actively construct an inner representation of the deceased that is part of the normal grieving process.

"Internalization" as used by the psychoanalytic school of thought does not accurately describe the process occurring in the experiences reported on in this book. What we observe is more colorful, dynamic and interactive than the word "internalization" suggests. For example, among bereaved children the inner representation of the parent was neither buried in the unconscious nor stable over time. The child was aware of the inner representation and that representation seemed to change with time as the child developed.

Bereaved parents, more inhibited and self-conscious than children, were reluctant to talk of their interactions with their deceased children in the presence of people for whom their experiences seemed "crazy." When the experiences are normalized in settings such as self-help group meetings, they eagerly share the experiences as good parts of their lives (Klass, 1984, 1988). As the parents' lives continue, the children remain a taken-for-granted part of their inner lives, and a good part of those social systems in which they feel most at home.

Adoptees, typically in their late adolescence and early adulthood, experience relief when they first hear other adoptees talk about their preoccupation with birth parents: "Why did they give me up? What were they like? Do I look like them?" The recent growing number of adoption reform organizations has vastly helped adoptees who previously believed that their inner lives marked them as abnormal in some way. Some use the phrase "coming out as an adoptee" as they identify with others whose stories they have heard (Lifton, 1994). Birth parents have similar experiences (Campbell, 1979; Silverman, 1981; Silverman, Campbell & Patti, 1988).

Robert Anderson, the playwright, used the word relationship to more accurately describe his experience of the deceased (Anderson, 1974). He wrote after the death of his first wife, "I have a new life. . . . Death ends a life, but it does not end a relationship, which struggles on in the survivor's mind toward some resolution which it never finds" (p. 77). Memorializing, remembering, knowing the person who has died, and allowing them to influence the present are active processes that seem to continue throughout the survivor's entire life. Rubin (1985) observed that there is a direct link between the bereaved's comfort and fluidity in relating to representations of the deceased and the bereaved's ability to cope effectively with the loss. Shuchter (1986) found that in the first years after their spouses' death, widowed people maintained an active connection to the deceased through their dreams, through feeling "watched," by having a sense of their presence, and by talking to them. Shapiro (1994), who sees grief as a family process, suggests that the restoration of a living, evolving image of the deceased becomes a supportive resource for ongoing family development. While the intensity of the relationship with the deceased may diminish with time, the relationship does not disappear. We are not talking about living in the past, but rather recognizing how bonds formed in the past can inform our present and our future.

Rizzuto (1979) observed that the process of constructing inner representations involves the whole individual, and that these representations are neither static nor unchanging but something that grows and changes with the individual's development and maturation. Rizzuto observed the importance of the role of others, as well, in the construction of inner representations of significant people in her subjects' lives. Construction, she suggests, is partly a social activity. The family and institutions in the larger society are involved.

Rosenblatt and Elde (1990) point to the importance of the family in maintaining connection in Western societies. They studied a group of bereaved families and found that grief work done by these families included maintaining connections with memories of the deceased. Mourners kept these memories "alive" while integrating them into the present and into relationships with others. A helpful family environment has positive facilitating effects. While individual family members have their own "internalization" or inner representation of the deceased, the family as a whole may also have communal or shared representations, which become integrated into their relationships with each other. These may be experienced by individual members as existing or proceeding from outside the self. These can be altered as people and relationships change. Klass (1988) made a similar observation about the importance of others in aiding bereaved parents to actively maintain "relationships" with their dead children.

An analogous situation can be found in adopted children, when the fact of adoption is disclosed to a child who was placed in infancy (Nickman, 1985). How well adoptive parents were able to remain in touch with the children's developing internal representation of birth parents can impact on the children's self-esteem, personality development, and overall level of functioning. How well parents can help their adopted children build a realistic representation of the birth parents that is compatible with the children's changing ability to understand is also a factor. With later-adopted children the experience is similar to that of bereaved children because they are old enough to remember their birth parents.

We propose that it is normative for mourners to maintain a presence and connection with the deceased, and that this presence is not static. The young adoptee faces the question, "How could they give me up?", and deals with the birth parents' motivation over a period of years. The bereaved child must deal with how and why the parent died and what the presence of the parent might have been like had it continued over time. Bereaved parents recognize the reality of their children's death and still maintain the love they have for the children and a role for them in their lives.

One cannot deal with a loss without recognizing *what* is lost. When someone dies, as for example a spouse or a parent, what is lost is more than the person, it is also a social role. The self in that role and the role itself are lost as well (Silverman, 1988). Even parents with several children report that there is a specific part of their self that is devoted only to parenting the dead child. In the same way, they reported, there are parts of themselves that are devoted only to parenting each of their living children. The construction of an inner representation of the deceased, while in part a continuation of the old relationship, in large part must be by its very nature a different relationship (Marris, 1974; Silverman, 1981, 1988).

We are suggesting a process of adaptation and change in the postdeath relationship and the construction and reconstruction of new connections. In taking these findings into consideration, our understanding of the bereavement process shifts. We cannot look at bereavement as a psychological state that ends and from which one recovers. The intensity of feelings may lessen and the mourner become more future- rather than past-oriented; however, a concept of closure, requiring a determination of when the bereavement process ends, does not seem compatible with the model suggested by these findings. We propose that rather than emphasizing letting go, the emphasis should be on negotiating and renegotiating the meaning of the loss over time. While the death is permanent and unchanging, the process is not.

The concepts of identification and introjection are insufficient to describe what we have observed. Survivors construct a sense of the deceased and develop an inner representation of that person. The bond with the deceased may include, at either a conscious or an unconscious level, becoming like that person. Identification in the sense of merging our self-representation with the representation of another is characteristic of bonds we have with living persons as well as with the deceased. Such identification may be considered psychologically healthy or pathological; but the health or pathology of such identification is judged by criteria other than whether the other person is living or dead. In the same way as in the bond between living persons, one person can be introjected, and their representation held as a "frozen" entity in the psyche. In family systems as well, a person may be held in a rigid role, especially when that role supports pathologies in other parts of the system. However, such rigidity and dissociations within the self do not depend on the living or dead status of the other, but depend on wider factors that facilitate health or reinforce pathology.

The studies in this book suggest that we need to consider bereavement as a cognitive as well as an emotional process that takes place in a social context of which the deceased is a part. The process does not end, but in different ways bereavement affects the mourner for the rest of his or her life. People are changed by the experience; they do not get over it, and part of the change is a transformed but continuing relationship with the deceased.

Accommodation, in its full Piagetian sense, may be a more suitable term than recovery, closure, or resolution. Accommodation in this context is not a static phenomenon. People do not change in some time-limited bereaved condition and then remain unchanging until their next bereavement. Accommodation is a continual activity, related both to others and to shifting self-perceptions as the physical and social environment changes and as individual, family, and community developmental processes unfold. It is a continual process because individuals and communities continually construct meaning in the interchanges between themselves and their world. Accommodation does not disregard past relationships, but incorporates them into a larger whole. In this process, people seek to gain not only an understanding of the meaning of death, but a sense of the meaning of this now dead or absent person in their present lives.

The idea of meaning-making as a continuous process requires that we develop a more adequate language for talking about and to the deceased (Klass, 1993a, 1993b). As the modern Western world has moved toward a more and more autonomous and individualistic definition of the self, it has tended toward valuing "reality-based" behavior that precludes acknowledging any ongoing relationship with the deceased. Most other cultures in the history seem to have supported the notion that the deceased continue to live in some form after death, and they provide mourners with rituals to sustain an appropriate relationship (Silverman & Silverman, 1979). In some cultures the spirits are not necessarily seen as benevolent. Rosenblatt and his colleagues (1976) identified some cultures in which tie-breaking ceremonies are quite elaborate. In these societies the power of the deceased is feared and must be neutralized and contained for the survivor to carry on. The deceased are endowed with supernatural powers that can be harmful. Even here, there is a continuity between this life and the next. The relationship is acknowledged and the mourner provided with rituals for developing an appropriate place for the deceased in their lives. The need for such ritual is less acknowledged in the contemporary West.

Critical to the development of a new language are the family's and community's rituals that legitimate the construction of an inner representation of the deceased. Many of the studies in this book show how individuals and communities, when they found no rituals for maintaining contact with the deceased, developed such rituals on their own (Klass, 1982). We may need to look anew, in the historic Western traditions and in the traditions of other peoples, for rituals that facilitate continuing bonds with the dead and absent. In the model of grief we propose, we would find a new language to talk not only about loss and the person who is gone, but about connections in general.

The contributors to this book have identified ways in which mourners maintain a connection to the deceased. These studies challenge the traditional clinical practice of encouraging the bereaved to disengage from the deceased. In the parallel experience of adoptees, studies suggest that it is critical to adoptees' well-being that their need to "know" the birth parent(s) be acknowledged. In the experience of children of divorce, the inner connection they maintain with the absent parent should be recognized and made a part of their social reality as well as a part of their inner reality (Tessman, 1978). The focus in facilitating mourning needs to be on how to change connections, to hold the relationship in a new perspective rather than on how to separate.

QUALITATIVE VERSUS QUANTITATIVE METHODS IN THE STUDY OF GRIEF

If grief is about construction and reconstruction of a world and of our relationships with significant others, what research methods are appropriate to investigate it? After we had received drafts of their chapters from the contributors to the book, we were surprised to find that there was a good deal of methodological consistency among them. Most of those who had identified a continuing relationship with the deceased had used qualitative, not quantitative, research methods.

It seems to us that the link between these findings and the method of study was no accident. Empirical research methods in the social sciences have their roots in the modern world view that focuses on individualism and separateness. The idea of individual autonomy is fundamental to the philosophy of logical positivism as espoused by John Stuart Mill and the English school of empiricism.

This school of thought has dominated Western thinking and psychological research in this century. Kuhn (1962) pointed out that science is not value free. Rather, it reflects and is often designed to support the view of the world held by the dominant group in the society. Science is influenced by the culture in which it is embedded (Valsinaar & Winegar, 1992). In the positivist model of science, detachment and independence were attitudes valued both in the scientist and in the world that the scientist defined. Especially important was the separation of the researcher from the subjects, for "objectivity" demanded noninvolvement. In the positivist view, the physical and the social world is seen as an object to be mastered and thus controlled.

Empiricism sees a rational order in the world, with one fact leading to another. By finding certain truths, empiricists believe it will be possible to discover general laws that explain how the world operates. Their concern is with prediction and verification based on external observable phenomena that can be objectively measured. Consciousness and meaning-making are not observable, but behavior is. Behavior is reduced to discrete, observable acts that can be verified in controlled conditions. This reductionism loses sight of the complex social and historical context in which human behavior takes place (Seely et al., 1956). Bruner (1990) described the conventional aims of a positivist science as the "trinity" of reductionism, causation, and explanation. He writes that this mechanistic view of science and of the world permeates all aspects of the psychological sciences. This approach dismisses the subjective experiences of people and minimizes the importance of relationships in the human experience because these are difficult to study in their model. What are valued are the reports of objective observers; internal states such as belief, desire, and intention are often dismissed as personal bias (Bruner, 1990). Bruner says that in the dominant research view, acceptable explanations of behavior could only be made by experts based on their "objective" findings. It is left to the expert to assess what a person is experiencing and what these experiences mean. There is no way that findings can be corrected by personal, subjective experiences because these are seen to contaminate the data. Bruner writes that

> To insist upon explanation in terms of causes simply bars us from trying to understand how human beings interpret their worlds and how we interpret their acts of interpretation. . . . Are not plausible interpretations preferable to causal explanations that force us to artificialize what we are studying to a point almost beyond recognition as representative of human life? (1990, p. xiii)

Bruner observes that there are, in fact, socially accepted relationships between the meaning of what people say and what people do in given circumstances, and these meanings govern how individuals and communities conduct their lives. He talks of the need to attend to what he calls "folk psychology," which is grounded in asking how people make meaning: People are assumed to have world knowledge that takes the form of beliefs and are assumed to use that world knowledge in carrying out any program of desire or action (1990, p. 40).

It is difficult, using a positivist approach to social science, to ask how people make meaning and to try to understand the social context in which they live. Wittgenstein (1953) observed that behavioral sciences cannot follow the model of classical physics. Rather, they need to see the world as composed of processes, and that the systematic study of these processes should be acknowledged as appropriate to contemporary science.

It is no accident that most of the chapters in this book describe research that uses a nonpositivist research paradigm. The contributors to this book have undertaken to describe what people are experiencing in their own words and have understood their own roles as actors in the research enterprise (Garfinkle, 1967; Glaser, 1978; Glaser & Strauss, 1967; Mead, 1934; Reinharz, 1992; Strauss, 1987). Researchers applying qualitative methods do not set out to verify a hypothesis or to prove a preconceived theory. They are instead reporting on what people experience and the way people make meaning out of their experiences. Using this method, it is possible to hear and legitimate the web of relationships in which the bereaved are involved, including that with the deceased.

We are developing a model of grieving that focuses on the complexity of human relationships and the ways in which people remain connected to each other in life and in death. In so doing, we need to shift our paradigm not only about the nature of the resolution of grief, but also about how to conduct research on grief.

CONCLUSION

This book revisits the way we talk about the resolution of grief. When we discuss the nature of resolution of grief, we are at the core of the most basic questions about what it means to be human, for the meaning of the resolution of grief is tied to the meaning of our bonds with significant people in our lives, the meaning of our membership in family and community, and the meaning we ascribe to our individual lives in the face of absolute proof of our own mortality.

The book challenges the idea that the purpose of grief is to sever the bonds with the deceased in order for the survivor to be free to make new attachments and to construct a new identity. Although there are many differences among the book's contributors, the constant message of these contributions is that the resolution of grief involves continuing bonds that survivors maintain with the deceased and that these continuing bonds can be a healthy part of the survivor's ongoing life.

This chapter outlines the model of grief in general use and shows how this model of grief was developed in the face of data that suggested its inadequacy. We suggest that the dominant model of grief is based on inadequate assumptions about the nature of the self and is based in inappropriate social scientific methodology used to study bereavement. We note that because the model is based in the unexamined assumptions of our age, the model shows remarkable resiliency in the face of data. In a more positive way, the chapter suggests the direction we should move to develop a more adequate model of how people cope with their grief, though a fuller sense of the new model emerges throughout the other chapters in the book.

We are not certain about the shape of a new model, though we think it is implicit in the contributions to this book. As we read the chapters when they came from the authors, we found ourselves in conversations with each author through his or her article and then among ourselves about what he or she said. Often our discussions ended with more questions than answers. We hope readers find the same spirited dialogue in their minds and with their colleagues as they read the book, including this first chapter. If this book leads to further discussion and conversations on the subject, then we have succeeded. This book grew out of extended conversations and correspondence among the editors and many of the contributors to the book. We hope by bringing these scholars into one volume, that we have opened and focused the conversation for others.

REFERENCES

Abraham, K. (1927). A short study of the development of the libido, viewed in the light of mental disorders. In D. Brian & A. Strachey (Eds.), *Selected Papers* (pp. 248–279). London: Hogarth Press.

Anderson, R. (1974). Notes of a survivor. In S. B. Troop & W. A. Green (Eds.), *The patient, death and the family*. New York: Scribner.

Baker, P. (1991). Socialization after death: The might of the living dead. In B. Hess & E. Markson (Eds.), *Growing Old in America* (pp. 539–551). New Brunswick, NJ: Transaction Publishers.

Batson, G. (1980). *Mind and nature*. New York: Bantam Books.

Belanky, M., Clinchy, B., Turale, J., & Goldberger, N. (1986). *Women's ways of knowing*. NewYork: Basic Books.

Bellah, R. N., Madsen, R., Sullivan, A. S., & Tipton, S. M. (1985). *Habits of the heart; Individualism and commitment in American life*. Berkeley: University of California Press.

Black, M. (1962). *Models and metaphors*. Ithaca, NY: Cornell University Press.

Bowlby, J. (1961). Processes of mourning. *International Journal of Psychoanalysis, 42*, 317–340.

Bowlby, J. (1969–1980). *Attachment and Loss*, Vols. 1–3: *Attachment*, Vol. 1, 1969; *Separation: Anxiety and anger*, Vol. 2, 1973; *Loss: Sadness and depression*, Vol. 3, 1980. New York: Basic Books.

Bowlby, J. (1981). Psychoanalysis as a natural science. *International Review of Psychoanalysis, 8*(2), 243–256.

Bruner, J. (1990). *Acts of meaning*. Cambridge, MA: Harvard University Press.

Buchsbaum, B. C. (1987). Remembering a parent who has died: A developmental perspective. *The Annual of Psychoanalysis, 25*, 99–112.

Campbell, L. (1979). The birthparents' right to know. *Public Welfare, 37*(3), 22–27.

Clayton, P. J., Desmarais, L., & Winokur, G. (1968). A study of normal bereavement. *American Journal of Psychiatry. 125*, 168–178.

Coontz, S. (1992). *The way we never were: American families and the nostalgia trap*. New York: Basic Books.

Deykin, E., Campbell, L., & Patti, P. (1984). The adoption experience of surrendering parents. *American Journal of Orthopsychiatry, 54*, 271–280.

Dietrich, D. R., & Shabad, P. C. (1989). *The problem of loss and mourning: Psychoanalytic perspectives*. Madison, CT: International Universities Press.

Doi, T. (1973). *The anatomy of dependence* (John Bester, Trans.). Tokyo: Kodansha International.

Edelstein, L. (1984). *Maternal bereavement: Coping with the unexpected death of a child.* New York: Praeger.

Erikson, E. H. (1963). *Childhood and society* (2nd ed.). New York: W. W. Norton.

Fenichel, O. (1945). *The psychoanalytic theory of neurosis.* New York: Norton.

Fisher, F. (1973). *The search for Anna Fisher.* New York: Arthur Fields.

Freud, E. L. (Ed.). (1960). *Letters of Sigmund Freud.* (J. Stern & T. Stern,Trans.). New York: Basic Books.

Freud, S. (1961a). Mourning and melancholia. In J. Strachey (Ed. and Trans.), *The standard edition of the complete psychological works of Sigmund Freud* (Vol. 14, pp. 243–258). London: Hogarth Press. (Original work published 1917)

Freud, S. (1961b). *Civilization and its discontents.* (J. Strachey, Trans.). New York: W.W. Norton. (Original work published 1917)

Furman, E. (1984). Children's patterns in mourning the death of a loved one. In H. Wass & C. Corr (Eds.), *Childhood and death* (pp. 185–203). Washington, DC: Hemisphere Press.

Garfinkle, H. (1967). *Studies in ethnomethodology.* Englewood Cliffs, NJ: Prentice-Hall.

Gergen, K. J. (1985). The social constructionist movement in modern psychology. *American Psychologist, 40*(3), 266–273.

Glaser, B. (1978). *Theoretical sensitivity.* Mill Valley, CA: Sociology Press.

Glaser, B., & Strauss, A. (1967). *The discovery of grounded theory.* Chicago: Aldine.

Glick, I. O., Weiss, R. S., & Parkes, C. M. (1974). *The first year of bereavement.* New York: John Wiley & Sons.

Hepburn, A. (1994, November–December). What do we really know about grief counseling? Exploring the contemporary challenges of multiculturalism, postmodernism, and imaginal psychology, *The Forum Newsletter,* pp. 7, 8, 13–18.

Hofer, M. A. (1984). Relationships as regulators: A psychobiologic perspective on bereavement. *Psychosomatic Medicine, 46,* 183–197.

Hogan, N., & DeSantis, L. (1992). Adolescent sibling bereavement: An ongoing attachment. *Qualitative Health Research, 2*(2), 159–177.

Homans, P. (1989). *The ability to mourn: Disillusionment and the social origins of psychoanalysis.* Chicago: University of Chicago Press.

Horowitz, M., Wilner, N., Marmor, C., & Krupnick, J. (1980). Pathological grief and the activation of latent self-images. *American Journal of Psychiatry, 137*(10), 1157–1162.

Jacobson, E. (1965). The return of the lost parent. In M. Schur (Ed.), *Drives, affects, and behaviors* (Vol. 2, pp. 193–211). Madison, CT: International Universities Press.

Jackson, E. N. (1957). *Understanding grief: Its roots, dynamics, and treatment.* New York: Abingdon Press.

Jones, E. (1957). *The life and work of Sigmund Freud.* Volume 3. New York: Basic Books.

Kegan, R. (1982). *The evolving self: Problem and process in human development.* Cambridge, MA: Harvard University Press.

Kirk, D. (1985). *Adoption kinship: A modern institution in need of reform.* Port Angeles, WA: Ben Simon.

Klass, D. (1982). Self-help groups for the bereaved: Theory, theology and practice. *Journal of Religion and Health, 21*(4), 307–324.

Klass, D. (1984). Bereaved parents and The Compassionate Friends: Affiliation and healing. *Omega, Journal of Death and Dying, 15*(4), 353–373.

Klass, D. (1987). John Bowlby's model of grief and the problem of identification. *Omega, Journal of Death and Dying, 18*(1), 13–32.

Klass, D. (1988). *Parental grief: Solace and resolution.* New York: Springer.

Klass, D. (1993a). Solace and immortality: Bereaved parents' continuing bond with their children. *Death Studies, 17,* 343–368.

Klass, D. (1993b). The inner representation of the dead child and the world views of bereaved parents. *Omega, Journal of Death and Dying, 26*(4), 255–272.

Knapp, R. (1986). *Beyond endurance: When a child dies.* New York: Schocken.

Kuhn, T. (1962). *The structure of scientific revolution.* Chicago: University of Chicago Press.

Lamm, M. (1969). *The Jewish way in death and mourning.* New York: J. David.

Lifton, B. J. (1981). *Lost and found.* New York: Bantam.

Lifton, B. J. (1994). *Journey of the adopted self:A quest for wholeness.* New York; Basic Books.

Lopata, H. Z. (1973). *Widowhood in an American city.* Cambridge, MA: Schenkman.

Lopata, H. Z. (1979). *Women as widows, support systems.* New York: Elsevier.

Marris, P. (1974). *Loss and change.* London: Routledge and Kegan Paul.

Matchett, W. F. (1972). Repeated hallucinatory experiences as a part of the mourning process among Hopi Indian women. *Psychiatry, 35,* 185–194.

Mawson, D., Marks, I. M., Ramm, L., & Stern, R. S. (1981). Guided mourning for morbid grief: A controlled study. *British Journal of Psychiatry, 138,* 185–193.

Mead, G. H. (1934). *Mind, self and society.* Chicago: Chicago University Press.

Miller, J. B. (1971). Children's reactions to the death of a parent: A review of the psychoanalytic literature. *Journal of the American Psychoanalytic Association, 19*(6), 697–719.

Miller, J. B. (1986). *The new psychology of women.* Boston: Beacon Press.

Mogenson, G. (1992). *Greeting the angels: An imaginal view of the mourning process.* Amityville, NY: Baywood Publishing.

Moss, M. S. & Moss, S. Z., (1980). The image of the deceased spouse in remarriage of elderly widows(er)s. *Journal of Gerontological Social Work, 3*(2), 59–70.

Moss, M. S., & Moss, S. Z. (1984). Some aspects of the elderly widow(er)'s persistent tie with the deceased spouse. *Omega, Journal of Death and Dying, 15*(3), 195–206.

Nickman, S. L. (1985). Losses in adoption: The need for dialogue. In A. Solnit, R. Eissler, & P. Neubauer (Eds.), *The psychoanalytic study of the child* (Vol 40, pp. 365–378). New Haven, CT: Yale University Press.

Offner, C. B. (1979). Continuing concern for the departed. *Japanese Religion, 11*(1), 3–16.

Parkes, C.. (1972). *Bereavement: Studies of grief in adult life.* New York: International Universities Press.

Parkes, C. M. (1975a). Determinants of outcome following bereavement. *Omega Journal of Death and Dying, 6*(4), 303–323.

Parkes, C. M. (1975b). Psycho-social transitions: Comparison between reactions to loss of a limb and loss of a spouse. *British Journal of Psychiatry, 127,* 204–210.

Parkes, C. M., & Brown, R. J. (1972). Health after bereavement: A controlled study of young Boston widows and widowers. *Psychosomatic Medicine, 34*(5), 449–461.

Parkes, C. M., & Weiss, R. (1983). *Recovery from bereavement.* New York: Basic Books.

Peppers, L. G., & Knapp, R. J. (1980). *Motherhood and mourning.* New York: Praeger.

Peskin, H. (1993). Neither broken hearts nor broken bonds. *American Psychologist, 48*(9), 990–.

Piaget, J. (1954). *The construction of reality in the child* (M. Cook, Trans.). New York: Basic Books.

Pincus, L. (1974). *Death and the family.* New York: Pantheon Books.

Pollock, G. H. (1975). On mourning, immortality, and utopia. *Journal of the American Psychoanalytic Association, 23*(2), 334–362.

Rando, T. A. (Ed.). (1986). *Parental loss of a child.* Champaign, IL: Research Press.

Rando, T. A. (1992). The increasing prevalence of complicated mourning: The onslaught is just beginning. *Omega, Journal of Death and Dying 26*(1), 43–59.

Raphael, B. (1983). *The anatomy of bereavement.* New York: Basic Books.

Rees, W. D. (1975). The bereaved and their hallucinations. In B. Schoenberg et al. (Eds.) *Bereavement: Its psychosocial aspects* (pp. 66–71). New York: Columbia University Press.

Reinharz, S. (1992). *Feminist methods in social research.* New York: Oxford University Press.

Rizzuto, A. M. (1979). *The birth of the living god: A psychoanalytic study.* Chicago: University of Chicago Press.

Rochlin, G. (1959). Loss and restitution. *The Psychoanalytic Study of the Child, 8,* 288–309.

Rosen, E. J. (1988) Family therapy in cases of interminable grief for the loss of a child. *Omega, Journal of Death and Dying, 19*(3), 187–202.

Rosenblatt, P., & Elde, C. (1990). Shared reminiscence about a deceased parent: Implication for grief education and grief counselling. *Family Relations, 39*, 206–210.

Rosenblatt, P. C., Walsh, R. P., & Jackson, D. A. (1976). *Grief and mourning in cross-cultural perspective.* Human Relations Area Files, Inc.

Rubin, S. S. (1985) The resolution of bereavement: A clinical focus on the relationship to the deceased. *Psychotherapy, 22*(2), 231–235.

Sanders, C. M. (1989). *Grief: The mourning after.* New York: John Wiley & Sons.

Schafer, R. (1968). *Aspects of internalization.* New York: International Universities Press.

Schafer, R. (1976). *A new language for psychoanalysis.* New Haven, CT: Yale University Press.

Seeley, J., Sim, R. A., & Loosley, E. W. (1956). *Crestwood Heights: A study of the culture of suburban life.* New York: Basic Books.

Shapiro, E. R. (1994). *Grief as a family process.* New York: Guilford Press.

Shuchter, S. R. (1986). *Dimensions of grief: Adjusting to the death of a spouse.* San Francisco: Jossey-Bass.

Silverman, P. R. (1966). Services for the widowed during the period of bereavement. In *Social work practice.* New York: Columbia University Press.

Silverman, P. R. (1981). *Helping women cope with grief.* Newbury Park, CA: Sage Publications.

Silverman, P. R. (1986). *Widow to widow.* New York: Springer.

Silverman, P. R. (1988). In search of new selves: Accommodating to widowhood. In L.A. Bond and B. Wagner (Eds.) *Families in transition: Primary programs that work.* Newbury Park, CA: Sage Publications.

Silverman, P. R. (1989). The impact of the death of a parent on college age women. *Psychiatric Clinics of North America, 10*(33), 387–404.

Silverman, P. R., Campbell, L., & Patti, P. (1988). Reunions between adoptees and birth parents: The birth parents's experience. *Social Work, 33,* 523–528.

Silverman, P. R., Campbell, L., & Patti, P. (1994). Reunions between adoptees and birth parents: The adoptive parents' view. *Social Work, 39*(5), 542–549.

Silverman, P. R., Nickman, S., & Worden, J. W. (1992). Detachment revisited. *American Journal of Orthopsychiatry, 62*(4), 494–593.

Silverman, P. R., & Worden, J. W. (1992). Children's reactions to the death of a parent in the early months after the death. *American Journal of Orthopsychiatry, 62*(4), 93–104.

Silverman, S. M., & Silverman, P. R. (1979). Parent-child communication in widowed families. *American Journal of Psychotherapy, 33,* 428–441.

Smilasky, S. (1987). *On death: Helping children understand and cope.* New York: Peter Lang.

Smith, R. J. (1974). *Ancestor worship in contemporary Japan.* Stanford, CA: Stanford University Press.

Sorosky, A., Baran, A., & Pannor, R. (1978). *The adoption triangle.* Garden City, NY: Doubleday/Anchor Press.

Strauss, A. L. (1987). *Qualitative analysis for social scientists.* Cambridge: Cambridge University Press.

Stroebe, M. (1992). Coping with bereavement: A review of the grief work hypothesis. *Omega, Journal of Death and Dying, 26*(1), 19–42.

Stroebe, M., Gergen, M. M., Gergen, K. J., & Stroebe, W. (1993). Hearts and bonds: Resisting classification and closure. *American Psychologist, 48*(9), 991–992.

Sullivan, L. E. (1987). Death, afterlife, and the soul. Selections from *The encyclopedia of religion* (M. Eliade, Ed.). New York: Macmillan.

Tahka, V. (1984). Dealing with object loss. *Scandinavian Psychoanalytic Review, 7,* 13–33.

Tessman, L. H. (1978). *Children of parting parents.* New York: Jason Aronson.

Valisiner, J. & Winegar, L. T. (1992). Introduction: A cultural historical contest for social "context." In L. T. Winegar & J. Valisiner (Eds.), *Children's development within social context* (pp. 1–14). Hillsdale, NJ: Lawrence Erlbaum.

Volkan, V. D. (1981). *Linking objects and linking phenomena.* New York: International Universities Press.

Volkan, V. D. (1985b). Psychotherapy of complicated mourning. In V. D. Volkan (Ed.), *Depressive states and their treatment* (pp. 271–295). Northvale, NJ: Jason Aronson.

Volkan, V., & Showalter, C. (1968). Known object loss, disturbance in reality testing, and "re-grief" work as a method of brief psychotherapy. *Psychiatric Quarterly, 42,* 358–374.

Walsh, F., & McGoldrick, M. (Eds.). (1991). *Living beyond loss: Death in the family.* New York: W.W. Norton.

Weisman, A. (1972). *On dying and denying: A psychiatric study of terminality.* New York: Behavioral Publications.

Weizman, S. G., & Kamm, P. (1985). *About mourning: Support and guidance for the bereaved.* New York: Human Service Press.

Wilber, K. (1995). *Sex, ecology, spirituality: The spirit of Evolution.* Boston: Shambhala.

Winkler, R., & Van Keppel (1984). *Relinquishing mothers in adoption* (Monograph 3). Melbourne, Australia: Institute of Family Studies.

Winnicott, D. W. (1953). Transitional objects and transitional phenomena. *International Journal of Psycho-Analysis, 34,* 89–97.

Wittgenstein, L. (1953). *Philosophical investigations* (G.E.M. Anscombe, Trans.). New York: Macmillan.

Wolfenstein, M. (1973). The image of the lost parent. *The Psychoanalytic Study of the Child, 28,* 433–456.

Worden, J. W. (1991). *Grief counseling and grief therapy: A handbook for the mental health practitioner.* New York: Springer.

Yamamoto, J., Okonogi, K., Iwasaki, T., & Yoshimura, S. (1969). Mourning in Japan. *American Journal of Psychiatry, 125,* 1661–1665.

Part Two

Setting the Stage

The chapters in this section introduce several themes critical to understanding the meaning of continuing bonds in the lives of the bereaved. They also place grief in an inclusive framework involving social, cultural, historical, philosophical, and psychological factors. Specifically, they bring into the conversation the place of time, identity, and culture in the bereavement process and the relative nature of our thinking about these elements. They move us to a postmodern view of the world that ceases to see things in dualities. All the chapters focus on the many layers of behavior guiding us and indicate very clearly that life is not lived in a straight line.

We really cannot intellectually define the spirit of an age until the age is past, because only then can we look at it from the outside. Modernity is passing. The chapter by Margaret Stroebe, Mary Gergen, Kenneth Gergen, and Wolfgang Stroebe sets the model of grief that calls for severing bonds with the deceased within the world view of modernity. The authors note that modernity is characterized by a machinelike model of the self. Modernity is a reaction against romanticism, which valued deep interpersonal bonds that could not be broken by death. These authors argue that a postmodern view of grief will recognize the continuing bond.

The need for a shift in mourners' sense of personal identity is often one of the consequences of loss. For example, the wife can change "widow" to "formerly married woman," relinquishing those aspects of the self that were defined within the relationship to her husband. A new identity more suited to her new situation can evolve. But identity is formed within a broad framework. Identity is rooted in the cultural meanings into which a person is born. The self has been defined differently in different historical and cultural epochs. As the self is defined differently, the meaning of bonds between people and within communities is defined differently. As the cultural meaning of bonds change, the meaning of those bonds after death change. To have a new identity does not necessarily mean giving up the old. If, as some postmodernists think, identity can be seen as many selves that form in many different relationships, we might ask: In what way is the past incorporated into a new identity after a death? As we cope with death, we change. But how do the changes in various aspects of our identity relate to each other?

The issue of closure (i.e., when does grief end?) has been an issue in the model of grief in modernity. In the modernist view, people were expected to "recover," to "put the past behind them," and "to get on with their lives." Employers typically give a funeral leave of two or three days when a member of the immediate family dies. Leaves for other deaths are counted as "personal days." Some researchers have defined the end of grief as little as 6 weeks after the death. Is it possible to be both bereft and to move on at the same time? Can the deceased both be here and not be here?

Paul Rosenblatt challenges the whole idea that there is an end to grief and that it can be resolved. He reviews data from his studies of 19th-century diaries, from his study of couples who have miscarried, and from his study of families of farm accident victims. In all these data he finds that what are called grief reactions occur for many years after the death. These findings led him to reassess the basic concepts that have guided the discussion in recent scholarship.

The death of an individual may, in fact, be a series of losses and changes in status of many interconnected members of the immediate social network. Rosenblatt moves to question the whole concept of grief work. His critique of the grief work hypothesis is somewhat different from the previous chapter; Rosenblatt locates the issue in the reality of loss over time and in the nature of continuing bonds with the deceased.

In the section's third chapter Dennis Klass studies grief in a cultural perspective by showing how rituals of Japanese Buddhism and, to a lesser extent, Shintoism provide a framework for maintaining the presence of the deceased in the lives of survivors. We see that the idea of closure is not present in a tradition that keeps an active interaction with the deceased for 30 to 50 years, and makes the deceased part of the spirit of the family after that. As we begin to give form to a new model of grief resolution, it would serve us well to look to Western religious traditions to see what types of rituals we have overlooked in our psychological theory. In Judaism, for example, tradition dictates that at least four times a year memorial prayers are said for the dead in the synagogue and that a memorial candle be lit at the home for each deceased member of the family. On these occasions, the living are to remember the dead and consider the meaning of the deceased in the survivors' lives. The memorial prayer for the wife, to choose an example, reads: "I find solace in the memories of our years together. . . . In tribute to my dear one who brought me cheer and joy, may I, through acts of loving kindness, bring cheer into the lives of others."

P. R. S.

S. N.

Chapter 2

Broken Hearts or Broken Bonds?

Margaret Stroebe, Mary Gergen, Kenneth Gergen, and Wolfgang Stroebe

Have I forgot, my Only Love, to love thee,
Severed at last by Time's all-wearing wave?
—Emily Brontë

One of the chief characteristics of psychological inquiry in the present century has been the search for robust laws of human nature. In their attempts to emulate natural scientists' claims to broad covering laws, psychological researchers have aimed at formulating general principles of human functioning. This universalizing tendency is strongly evident in all domains of psychology, including the mental health professions. Both researchers and practitioners have used their observations to support claims of the broadest scope, hoping to generate insight into the "basic" processes of depression, drug dependency, stress disorders, and the like, and to establish optimal treatment programs of various forms of dysfunction.

Although such a universalizing approach is highly optimistic in its promise of incremental knowledge and reliable programs of counseling or treatment, there has been recurrent doubt about its basic assumptions (Foucault, 1965; Rose, 1985). Specialists in community mental health, family therapy, and social work, in particular, have drawn increasing attention to the ways in which various problems, including the very definition of the problematic, are generated in particular social milieus or conditions (see McNamee & Gergen, 1992). These conclusions strongly suggest that patterns of action, including their meanings and significance, are, at least in part, socially constituted, and thus subject to historical and cultural change. Similar conclusions have been reached in many investigations across the social sciences (Badinter, 1980; Carrithers, Collins, & Lukes, 1985; Corbin, 1986; Shweder & Miller, 1985). For example, on the basis of her review of the cross-cultural literature on depression, Lutz (1988) proposed that the disorder is not universally recognized and in some cultures does not appear to exist.

Although sensitivity to culturally constructed components of dysfunctional behavior and ameliorative action is increasing, the relevance to specific mental health practices is far less apparent. What implications does viewing dysfunc-

This chapter is reprinted from *American Psychologist,* October 1992, Vol. 47, No. 10, pp. 1205–1212. Copyright © 1992 by the American Psychological Association. Reprinted by permission.

tional behavior as culturally and historically contingent have for matters of daily practice and policy development within the mental health professions? Are caregiving strategies and therapeutic practices subject to historical and cultural limitations? Does each new generation require new forms of support and treatment? If people of one subculture or generation consider a given form of action appropriate and acceptable, are those who fail to share their views justified in viewing such action as a problem in need of attention? All such questions gain focal significance in this context.

These issues are complex and multifaceted. In this chapter we explore the dimensions of one particular area of central concern to many health care researchers and therapists—reactions to the loss of a loved one, and the associated processes of grieving. In so doing we both demonstrate the concrete significance of a cultural constructionist view and suggest a possible alternative to currently prevailing practices.

We first consider the predominant Western view of grief and grief intervention strategies that are embedded in what we view as *modernist* practices. This view is contrasted with evidence from other cultures and then with the *romantic* conception of grief, which was most popular in the previous century but is still a mainstay of cultural life. As we argue, the romantic view is threatened by modernist practices. At the same time, theory and results from recent research and analysis challenge the modernist orientation, and are used to demonstrate ways in which the romantic view can be sustained. Finally we consider this conflict in a postmodern context.

BREAKING BONDS IN THE 20TH CENTURY

Scholars frequently have used the term *modernist* to characterize the cultural zeitgeist of contemporary Western society, in contrast with that of the preceding century, which has often been described as *romanticist*. Among the chief attributes of cultural modernism are an emphasis on reason and observation and a faith in continuous progress (K. J. Gergen, 1991). The modernist approach to life is one that emphasizes goal directedness, efficiency, and rationality. In psychology, modernism has given rise to the machine metaphor of human functionality. When applied to grief, this view suggests that people need to recover from their state of intense emotionality and return to normal functioning and effectiveness as quickly and efficiently as possible. Modernist theories of grief and related therapeutic interventions encourage people who have experienced loss to respond in just this way. Grieving, a debilitating emotional response, is seen as a troublesome interference with daily routines, and should be "worked through." Such *grief work* typically consists of a number of tasks that have to be confronted and systematically attended to before normality is reinstated (for more detailed discussions of the grief work hypothesis, see Stroebe & Stroebe, 1991; M. Stroebe, 1994). Reducing attention to the loss is critical, and good adjustment is often viewed as a breaking of ties between the bereaved and the dead.

The belief in the importance of severing ties from a deceased loved one found early and important expression in Freud's (1917) work. Freud conceptualized love as the attachment (cathexis) of libidinal energy to the mental representation of the loved person (the object). When the loved person dies, the libidinal energy remains attached to thoughts and memories of the deceased. Because the pool of energy is limited, the cathexis to the lost object has to be withdrawn in order for the person to regain these energy resources. The ties to the loved object are severed by a process of energy detachment that Freud termed *hypercathexis.* Freud saw the psychological function of grief as freeing the individual of his or her ties to the deceased, achieving gradual detachment by means of reviewing the past and dwelling on memories of the deceased. This process is complete when most of the energy is withdrawn from the lost object and transferred to a new one. Those who fail to hypercathect remain emotionally stunted.

A more fully developed modernist view was offered by John Bowlby. Consider his reaction to C.S. Lewis's (1961) classic case study, *A Grief Observed.* Lewis described his overwhelming feelings of grief and frustration as he attempted to make sense of the death of his wife. Just two years after the book's publication, Lewis also died. By contemporary standards of mental health, Lewis's reactions seem excessive; his preoccupation with the loss of his wife may have even hastened his own demise. As Bowlby (1980) wrote, Lewis's account

> suggests a man whose feeling life had become . . . inhibited and suppressed during childhood and who had grown up, as a result, to be intensely introspective. . . . His frustration (was) . . . due to the systems mediating his attachment behavior having become deactivated after his mother died when he was nine. (pp. 241–242)

In Bowlby's view, grief is conceptualized as a form of separation anxiety, the motivation for which is to restore proximity to the lost object. In the case of death, a permanent separation, the attempt to restore proximity is inappropriate or nonfunctional. The dysfunctionality does not prevent the attempts from occurring, and only gradually do they become extinguished. This takes place through a sequence of phases, sometimes alternating from protest and anger through to despair when hope that the lost person will return is gradually abandoned (Bowlby, 1971, 1975, 1980).

Like psychoanalytic theory, which focuses on the importance of relinquishing ties, Bowlby's work suggests that bonds with the deceased need to be broken for the bereaved to adjust and recover. Relevant counseling or therapy programs are designed to help achieve this process of withdrawal. Those who retain ties are considered maladjusted. This general assumption that ties with the deceased need to be severed is referred to in this chapter as the *breaking bonds* hypothesis.

Other modernists have written of the need for a grieving person to gain a new identity; again, the theme is one of achieving independence from the deceased. The title of an article by Golan (1975), "Wife to Widow to Woman," expressed this succinctly. More elaborate is the title of Judith Viorst's (1986) volume, *Necessary Losses: The Loves, Illusions, Dependencies and Impossible Expectations That All of Us Have to Give Up in Order to Grow.* Parkes (1972/1986) has written at length on processes of identification in bereaved people, particularly widows, pointing out how the old identity that relies heavily on the deceased person gradually dissolves and is replaced by a new and different one. Sanders (1989) described the task of "letting go" of the tie to the loved one as a necessity for the resolution of grief work, and for the "rebuilding of a life with new rewards and reinforcements" (p. 94). Sociologist Helena Lopata (1975, 1979, 1988) has written extensively on the need for widows to develop new identities.

The breaking bonds hypothesis receives further support from the literature on counseling and therapy for the bereaved (for a recent review, see Raphael & Nunn, 1988). Principles of grief counseling and therapy follow the view that, in the course of time, bereaved persons need to break their ties with the deceased, give up their attachments, form a new identity of which the departed person has no part, and reinvest in other relationships. People who persist in retaining a bond with their deceased loved one are in need of counseling or therapy. Worden (1982), a leading authority on grief intervention, maintained that the bereaved may need counseling or therapy to achieve emotional withdrawal from the deceased and reinvest in other relationships. In his view, one of the major hindrances to the completion of grief is holding on to the past attachment rather than letting go and forming new ones. Even more extreme are two syndromes described by Gorer (1965), *mummification* and *despair,* wherein grief remains intense and sometimes permanent. Cases of mummification are characterized by an incessant dwelling on the deceased and retention of the life routine as it was before that person's death. Despairing grief is said to be accompanied by "flat" emotion and social isolation; the tie to the deceased may be clung to in the absence of alternative social relationships.

In line with both theoretical formulations and counseling practices, researchers consistently identify "relationship to the spouse" as one of the major risk factors for poor bereavement outcomes. Parkes and Weiss (1983) described two major causes of pathological grief which stem from problematic marital bonds. One of these, following Freud, is called the *ambivalent grief syndrome.* This refers to a relationship in which elements of love and hate coexisted, conflicts were frequent, and divorce or separation may have been contemplated. After loss the bereaved may still be attached to the deceased, but insecurely so. Another syndrome, called the *chronic grief syndrome,* follows the termination of a relationship characterized as highly dependent or clinging.

It is noteworthy that aspects of a closely bonded marital relationship have been identified not only as a cause of pathology, but as a major contributor to poor adjustment among the bereaved in general. Lopata (1973, 1979) found disorganization in widowhood to be related to previous marital roles. Those widows who had been intensely involved in their husband's lives and who were psychologically as well as socially dependent on them had greater problems in adjustment than those who were more autonomous.

As we see, the prevailing view of grief within the professions emphasizes the importance of breaking bonds and the problematic implications of deeply dependent relationships.[1] Proper bereavement requires that ties with the deceased be relinquished, and counseling and therapy programs are designed to further this breaking of ties. From this it follows that those persons who are independent and autonomous in marriage will encounter less difficulty in breaking their bonds and thus will have a less problematic experience of grief.

GRIEF IN OTHER CULTURES

Although the breaking bonds orientation appears from a modernist perspective to have implications of universal scope, its spatiotemporal limitations become apparent when it is viewed in cultural contrast. A brief survey of non-Western cultures reveals that beliefs about the value of continuing bonds with the deceased vary widely. In sharp contrast with Western conventions, the maintenance of ties with the deceased is accepted and sustained by the religious rituals of Japan. Yamamoto, Okonoji, Iwasaki, and Yoshimura (1969) compared the courses of grief among a small sample of Japanese widows with those of British counterparts. Adjustment among the Japanese widows was comparatively better. The authors attributed this to the belief in both the Shinto and Buddhist religions (to which most of the Japanese widows belonged) that contact should be maintained with the deceased. In both religions the deceased join the ranks of one's ancestors. As Yamamoto (1970) explained, "The ancestor remains accessible, the mourner can talk to the ancestor, he can offer goodies such as food or even cigars. Altogether the ancestor "remains with the bereaved" (p. 181). This cultivation of continued contact with the deceased is facilitated by the presence in nearly all homes of an altar dedicated to the family ancestors. Offering food at the altar of a loved one would be classified as pathological by most Westerners, who would fear that the bereaved was fixated in the grief process and had failed to relinquish the tie to the deceased. However, in the Japanese case, such practices are fully normal.

In sharp contrast with both the Japanese and the Western patterns of grief are those of certain Native American tribes. Among the Hopi of Arizona, for example, the deceased are forgotten as quickly as possible, and life is carried on much as usual. As Mandelbaum (1959) explained, the bereaved may well feel the pain of loss, but "they give themselves over to no overt transport of grief" (p. 201). This habit is congenial with their beliefs about the afterworld. The Hopi believe that contact with death brings pollution, and they are afraid of death and of the dead person, whose spirit becomes a depersonalized entity. Supernatural spirits are not Hopi and do not have the characteristics of deceased relatives or friends.

[1]It should be noted that seldom do the writings of a single author remain consistently tied to a period of paradigm. Thus, within the works of Parkes, Gorer, Worden, and Raphael, for example, romanticist concepts and opinions are sometimes voiced as well.

They are greatly to be feared. As Mandelbaum described, "The Hopi go to great lengths to make sure that the dichotomy of quick and dead is sharp and clear. Many rites having to do with spirits conclude with the ritual device which breaks off contact between mortals and spirits" (p. 202). Mandelbaum gave a vivid illustration of Hopi attitudes toward the deceased. He had taken a photo of a young girl, whom he later learned had died. On a subsequent visit to the village he presented her mother with an enlarged copy, and was surprised to have his gift returned. As he later learned, the reason for the return was that the photo reminded the woman too much of her daughter. As Mandelbaum (1959) described it, "The sovereign desire is to dismiss the body and the event" (p. 203).

Detailed descriptions of differing cultural prescriptions and their effects on grief are found in the recent work of the Norwegian anthropologist Unni Wikan (1988, 1990). In an insightful analysis, Wikan has explored the experiences and expressions of grief in two Muslim societies, in Bali and in Egypt. That grief is debilitating is clearly accepted in both societies, but Wikan described entirely different ways by which the two come to terms with loss. In Egypt, the bereaved are encouraged to dwell profusely on their grief, surrounded by others who relate similarly tragic accounts and express their own sorrow. They show their compassion and love for the bereaved by ceaseless mournful tirades and emotional outpourings. Wikan pointed to the "cathartic significance" of such recurrent tales. One can conclude that, among Egyptian Muslims, little attempt is made to block memories or to break ties with the deceased. In Bali, the pattern of grieving is entirely different. The bereaved are enjoined to contain their sorrow, even to laugh and be joyful. They may be made to feel that they are doing others an injustice if they do not do so. Generally speaking, no overt signs of retained bonds with the deceased are evidenced, but should they be, they are harshly judged. One Balinese man who expressed his grief in an "excessive" manner was stigmatized as mad (*gila*) and was ridiculed each time the incident was discussed.

The picture that emerges from these cultural descriptions is far different from prevailing 20th century Western culture. In none of the cases described above (and there are many more) do we find evidence of Western forms of "proper grieving." In some cultures people hold tight to those who are dead: in others they try quickly to relinquish all ties. In all cases the result, in general, is normal adjustment within the culture.

GRIEF IN THE ROMANTIC AGE

Given broad cultural differences in patterns of grieving and adjustment, further questioning of our own patterns is appropriate. Is it possible that the breaking bonds orientation, naturalized and universalized by Western practices of research and therapy, is largely a product of contemporary times? And if the prevailing view is the product of the modern age, what is being overshadowed? If alternative views of death and mourning have previously proved rich resources in the culture, does not the hegemony of the present view threaten their existence? To the extent that the professional view of proper mourning becomes accepted as normal, then previous orientations become irrelevant—if not deviant.

This possibility gains significant credibility when one begins to survey cultural reactions to death even a century ago. In bold contrast with the modernist modes, the romantic view of life held sway. Whereas modernists hold scientific rationality as the critical ingredient of successful human functioning, romanticists believed in the centrality of "the deep interior"—mysterious forces or processes, beyond consciousness, somewhere toward the center of one's being and one's life (K. J. Gergen, 1991). Many felt that the deep interior was occupied by the human spirit or soul, the source of love, creative inspiration, and the powers of genius. Romanticists placed love at the forefront of human endeavors, and praised those who would abandon the "useful" and the "functional" for the sake of a loved one. Romanticists saw marriage as a communion of souls, a family as bonded in eternal love, and friendship as a lifetime commitment.

Within the romanticist context, the concept of grief was far different from the modern one. Because close relationships were matters of bonding in depth, the death of an intimate other constituted a critical point of life's definition. To grieve was to signal the significance of the relationship, and the depth of one's own spirit. Dissolving bonds with the deceased would not only define the relationship as superficial, but would deny as well one's own sense of profundity and self-worth. It would make a sham of a spiritual commitment and undermine one's sense of living a meaningful life. In contrast with the breaking bonds orientation of modernism, in romanticism valor was found in sustaining these bonds, despite a "broken heart."

Some of the most expressive indicators of the broken heart mentality are found in 19th century poetry. For William Barnes, the memory of his deceased wife was constantly present:

> In every moaning wind I hear thee say
> sweet words of consolation . . .
> I live, I talk with thee wheree'er I stray.
> (Stallworthy, 1973, pp. 361–362)

And echoing a common theme in romanticist writings, he concluded,

> Few be my days of loneliness and pain
> Until I meet in love with thee again.

For Emily Dickinson, these impassioned memories were borne out in actions. As she wrote,

> The grave my little cottage is,
> where "keeping house" for thee
> I make my parlour orderly
> And lay the marble tea.

Then, echoing again the belief in a spiritual reuniting, we find:

> For two divided, briefly.
> A cycle, it may be,
> Till everlasting life unite
> In strong society.
> (Johnson, 1970, pp. 706–707)

Poetic writings of the time provide some of the most dramatic expressions of the broken heart mentality; another glimpse of its manifestations in daily life is given in Paul Rosenblatt's (1983) volume *Bitter, Bitter Tears: Nineteenth Century Diarists and Twentieth Century Grief Theories*. Rosenblatt examined accounts of grief as revealed in 56 diaries from the 19th century. As these diaries indicated, not only was there little evidence of breaking bonds, but the prevailing attempt was to hold fast to the departed loved one. This holding fast was accomplished in numerous ways. There are many instances in the diaries of striving to sense the presence of the deceased; some dreamed of the lost person, whereas others had compelling impressions of the deceased actually being present, as of old, in habitual settings. As Rosenblatt noted, the "sense of presence, like sorrow and other aspects of grief, can return repeatedly" (p. 126). Praying for someone dead maintained the same caring relationship that was present before the loss. Similarly, prevalent references to a reunion in heaven reflected a continuing aspiration to resume, rather than break, contact with the deceased. Some families used child naming as a way of bringing back the presence of the deceased. Rosenblatt also found evidence of a phenomenon that we report on later in the context of 20th-century bonds with the deceased, namely using the wishes of the lost one as a guide to action. Finally a common recourse for the grieving was to try to retain ties through spiritualism. The belief that one could communicate with the spirits of the dead through seances and spirit mediums became popular in the mid-19th century, and many diarists recorded taking part in these rituals.

It should also be noted that these attempts to maintain the relationship with the deceased were not merely the expressions of an appropriately delimited period of mourning. Rather, they continued for long durations. As Rosenblatt (1983) concluded from this study of diaries, grief was felt "quite possibly as long as one lives" (p. 59).

UNRELINQUISHED RELATIONSHIPS IN CONTEMPORARY SOCIETY

Do inhabitants of 20th century Western culture, although dominated by modernist views, continue a romance with romanticism? Surely there is much in popular culture—in film, television, music, and the like—to suggest that this is so. And do those who retain ties to romanticism confront more severe problems of adjusting to grief, as might be suggested by the breaking bonds orientation? The

Tubingen Longitudinal Study of Bereavement (see M. Stroebe & Stroebe, 1989, 1991; W. Stroebe, Stroebe, & Domittner, 1988) has provided evidence relevant to these questions. Among this sample of young widows and widowers, it was evident that many demonstrated romanticist tendencies to maintain their ties, despite the modernist emphasis on breaking bonds. Even after two years, more than two thirds of the sample planned to continue in their previous (prebereavement) lifestyles as much as possible, and only a handful of respondents reported looking ahead to changes in their lives. Likewise, only a small minority (17%) said they were seeking a new partner. These results indicate that many of the widowed persons were not planning a major break with their pasts, rather that they were integrating the loss experience into their life-styles and trying to carry on much as before.

More specific information about the persistence of ties with the deceased was also available. When asked about the perceived presence of the deceased, nearly one third of the sample agreed that they still sensed their spouses' presence, and searched for them even after two years. The extent to which the deceased partner was used as a model for decision making and other behaviors was assessed. These results indicated that the deceased continued to have strong psychological influences over the way the widowed organized and planned their lives. For example, well over half "consulted" the deceased when having to make a decision. One widow said, "I gain great comfort knowing that this is exactly what Paul would have wanted me to do."

Very similar results have recently been reported by Shuchter and Zisook (1993) for an American sample. These authors detailed a number of ways in which the relationship to a deceased spouse is cherished and even nurtured. Just as was found in the Tubingen Longitudinal Study, these authors concluded that ties are not broken, but strongly held:

> The empirical reality is that people do not relinquish their ties to the deceased, withdraw their cathexis, or "let them go." What occurs for survivors is a transformation from what had been a relationship operating on several levels of actual, symbolic, internalized and imagined relatedness to one in which the actual ("living and breathing") relationship has been lost, but the other forms remain or may even develop in more elaborate forms. (p. 14)

Silverman and Worden (1993) noted similar attempts by children who have lost a parent to maintain a sense of the deceased in their current life, and to connect with the parent by talking to him or her, keeping mementos, visiting the grave, and thinking about the parent.

These observations suggest that romanticist styles of attachment remain robust in significant sectors of the adult population and that the broken heart orientation to loss seems no more or less conducive to poor adjustment than are dispositions more congenial to breaking bonds. One may argue, of course, that these results are specific to a population in a specific culture—that is, that they are both historically and culturally limited. But to argue this is simply to underscore our central thesis: The grieving process is indeed embedded within cultural traditions, and to approach the therapeutic or counseling setting with a universalist (and more specifically a modernist) preference for breaking bonds is not only to undermine existing patterns of culture, but to throw into question the normalcy or emotional adequacy of an otherwise unproblematic segment of the population.

Additional support for the pervasiveness of the romantic or broken heart reaction of maintaining ties, and its relationship to adjustment to loss, comes from a different culture. Consider recent findings from a study of parents of sons who died during two Israeli wars, 4 or 13 years previously (Rubin, 1993). Although adverse effects characterized the bereaved for many years following loss, difficulties associated with functioning and overt areas of behavior subsided over time; the bereaved parents went about their daily activities much as usual, somatic complaints were no longer excessive, and their psychological adjustment seemed normal. However, on a deeper level, the parents remained very involved with their sons. The picture Rubin painted is one of the intense involvement and strong valuation of the bereaved parents with this private relationship, often to the detriment of relationships they had with living children, relatives and friends. For example, the parents idealized the lost son in ways that were not apparent among a control group of parents whose sons were still alive but had recently left home. Thus, despite apparent adjustment, the effect of loss on the inner lives of the parents did not subside. Rather, there was a persisting preoccupation and retention of very close ties even when there was a reduction in the more overt signs of grieving and problems of functioning. As Rubin concluded, bereaved parents of adult sons show virtually no change in their preoccupation with the deceased over the years.

By current standards, these parents failed to break their bonds properly, and the result appears to be a life preoccupied with the dead, at the expense of the living. From the modernist perspective, the tragedy of death is compounded: Not only are the sons lost to them, but in significant ways, their families are as well. However, for those who retain a romanticist world view, the breaking of bonds would approximate sacrilege. It would be to degrade the significance of their son, the cause for which he died (their cause as well), and the significance of their relationship with him. To be sure, it is a suffering, but it is a suffering that validates the very significance of their lives. Is this pathology or purpose? It depends on the sociocultural setting.

BEREAVEMENT IN POSTMODERN PERSPECTIVE

To return to the more general issue, inquiry into grieving suggests that diverse groups of people engage in different patterns of action and share different meaning systems within which their actions are understood. Thus, actions deemed aberrant, maladjusted, or pathological in one cultural milieu may be fully acceptable in another. We have seen how the repetitious reciting of mournful stories, weeping, and wailing are normal reactions in one culture, whereas smiling and making jokes in the face of a loss are acceptable reactions in another. Treatment designed in one culture to "correct" or "repair" the actions of the other would at best appear to be insensitive, and at worst a form of cultural (or historical) imperialism. What are the implications of this line of reasoning for research and therapy concerned with grief? Are there forms of therapy that are more sensitive to cultural and social variations? Are there means by which attention can be focused on the better strategies for helping someone in distress?

The present account grows out of a newly developing consciousness, which may be termed *postmodern*. That is, when the relativity of the modernist perspective is recognized (here against the backdrop of romanticism), modernism loses its power of persuasion. In effect, we thus move beyond the modernist commitment and recognize the possibility of multiplicity in perspective. This shift toward multiplicity of voice is hardly unique to the present analysis, and by most standards would be considered a constituent feature of postmodern consciousness more generally (see analyses by Connor, 1989; K.J. Gergen, 1991).

However, recognition of the possibility of variations in perspectives does not itself lead to unequivocal conclusions concerning the future of grief research and therapy. At the outset we find that any evaluation of research and therapeutic outcomes can only be made from within some cultural framework. Thus, the negative functions of holding on to a relationship with the dead are fully compelling as long as one remains in the modernist perspective. Within this tradition, retaining ties may be symptomatic of emotional problems and mental illness, and may even lead to premature death: Building a life around a broken heart is contraindicated. Yet, from within the romanticist framework, there is much to be said on behalf of retaining ties. Parents of the Israeli war dead reveal the ennobling aspects of keeping strong ties to the dead, even if difficulties are incurred in their relations with the living. Each perspective yields its own outcomes, and suffers its own limitations. Therapeutic outcomes would be similarly affected.

If definitive resolution is beyond our grasp, what alternatives then lie before us? Let us consider three possibilities. First, attention may be given to means of *conceptual integration*. That is, rather than sustaining the disparate conceptions of grief—along with their accompanying theories and practices—we might seek means of integrating or combining them in some fashion. There are good precedents for such syntheses. Psychoanalytic theory borrowed heavily from romanticism in its conception of unconscious forces, and combined it with a theory of ego functioning, a mainstay of subsequent modernism. The result was a more enriched and compelling theoretical edifice. It is not our attempt, in the present context, to offer an integrative theory of bereavement. However, for purposes of illustration, consider the implications of Mary Gergen's (1987) conceptual analysis of "social ghosts." Social ghosts are defined as real or fictitious persons with whom individuals conduct imaginal interactions over time; they are the cast of characters with whom we engage in imaginal dialogues. Gergen detailed a variety of positive functions that these relationships play in people's lives. For example, social ghosts provide models for action, offer attitudinal perspectives, and lend esteem and emotional support to those who engage with them.

Romanticists may favor the concept of social ghosts, which suggests that it is both normal and emotionally sustaining to retain and nurture images of the deceased. Similarly, in their concern with social efficacy, modernists may also find the view sustaining. In this case the concept of social ghosts expands the range of significant others with whom relations should be effective, adding an internal dimension of the social world. In addition, the existence of social ghosts may have useful outcomes for ongoing interaction. Also supportive of this conclusion is Rosenblatt and Meyer's (1986) discussion of internal dialogues with a deceased person. As they argued, such dialogue serves the positive function of helping the bereaved clarify thoughts, deal with unfinished and emergent relationships, and prepare for the future.

A second outcome of postmodern consciousness for theory and therapy is an invitation toward *culturally embedded practices.* That is, rather than attempting conceptual integration, one may approach the culture with an appreciation for its rich texture of possibilities. Thus, researchers would not attempt to generate conclusions of universal proportion; even the attempt to characterize a culture as a whole may be considered too generalized. Rather, researchers might profitably be concerned with the enormous variations in forms of bereavement. Rather than attempting to generalize, they would search for an appreciative understanding of grief in all its varieties. On the therapeutic level, this would mean curtailing the search for ideal therapeutic procedures and focusing instead on tailor-made treatments. This would require a highly sensitive receptivity—an open listening to the client voice, for the reality and values of its sustaining subculture. At the same time, this option would invite educating for alternatives. It might prove desirable to teach clients that there are many goals that can be set, many ways to feel, and no set series of stages that they must pass through—that many forms of expression and behavioral patterns are acceptable reactions to loss. The stoic widower may need to learn to cry out over his loss at times, and the weeping widow to put her husband's wishes aside as she becomes the financial manager of her estate. The key concepts are growth, flexibility, and appropriateness within a cultural context. Awareness of a need for such multiplicity is just beginning to penetrate the field of bereavement research (cf. M. Stroebe, Stroebe, & Hansson, 1993). We support this endeavor.

Finally, a postmodern orientation toward grief theory and therapy invites an *expansion of responsibility.* A psychologist committed to either the romantic or the modernist view has a sense of moral or social responsibility that is constrained by a particular set of practices. The sense of choice is muted. A therapist committed to a Rogerian interpretation need not worry about the morality of not choosing to practice as a Freudian or behaviorist. In this sense, as the psychologist develops a postmodern consciousness, the range of viable perspectives is vastly increased (Anderson & Goolishian, 1992). One becomes aware that assumptions of health and adjustment are by-products of cultural and historical processes. Similarly, one realizes that theories of personal deficit harbor implicit systems of value, favoring certain ideals over others. More generally, theories and therapeutic practices favor certain forms of cultural patterns over others. For good or ill, they move the society toward or away from certain ends. Effectively, this is to urge a substantial broadening of self-reflective dialogue within the field.

REFERENCES

Anderson, H., & Goolishian, H. (1992). The client is the expert: A not knowing approach to therapy. In S. McNamee & K. J. Gergen (Eds.), *Social construction and the therapeutic process* (pp. 117–1346). London: Sage.

Badinter, E. (1980). *Motherlove, myth and reality*. New York: Macmillan.

Bowlby, J. (1971). *Attachment and loss: Vol. 1. Attachment*. Harmondsworth, England: Pelican Books.

Bowlby, J. (1975). *Attachment and loss: Vol. 2. Separation: Anxiety and anger*. Harmondsworth, England: Pelican Books.

Bowlby, J. (1980). *Attachment and loss: Vol. 3. Loss: Sadness and depression*. London: Hogarth.

Carrithers, M., Collins, S., & Lukes, S. (Eds.). (1985). *The category of the person*. Cambridge: Cambridge University Press.

Connor, S. (1989). *Postmodernist culture: An introduction to theories of the contemporary*. New York: Basil Blackwell.

Corban, A. (1986). *The foul and the fragrant*. Cambridge, MA: Harvard University Press.

Foucault, M. (1965). *Madness & civilization* (R. Howard, Trans.). New York: Vintage Books.

Freud, S. (1917). Trauer and Melancholie (Grief and melancholy). *Internationale Zeitschrift fur Artztliche Psychoanalyse, 4*, 288–301.

Gergen, K. J. (1991). *The saturated self: Dilemmas of identity in contemporary life*. New York: Basic Books.

Gergen, M. M. (1987, August). *Social ghosts: Opening inquiry on imaginal relationships*. Paper presented at the 95th Annual Convention of the American Psychological Association, New York.

Golan, N. (1975). Wife to widow to woman. *Social Work, 20*, 369–374.

Gorer, G. D. (1965). *Death, grief and mourning in contemporary Britain*. New York: Doubleday.

Hochschild, A. R. (1979). Emotion work, feeling rules, and social structure. *American Journal of Sociology, 85*, 551–75.

Johnson, T. J. (Ed.). (1970). *Emily Dickinson: The complete poems*. London: Faber & Faber.

Lewis, C. S. (1961). *A grief observed*. London: Faber.

Lopata, H. (1973). *Widowhood in an American city*. Morristown, NJ: General Learning Press.

Lopata, H. (1975). On widowhood: Grief work and identity reconstruction. *Journal of Geriatric Psychiatry, 8*, 41–55.

Lopata, H. (1979). *Women as widows: Support systems*. New York: Elsevier.

Lopata, H. (1988). Support systems of American urban widowhood. *Journal of Social Issues, 44*, 113–128.

Lutz, C. A. (1988). *Unnatural emotions*. Chicago: University of Chicago Press.

McNamee, S., & Gergen, K. J. (1992). *Social construction and the therapeutic process*. London: Sage.

Mandelbaum, D. G. (1959). Social uses of funeral rites. In H. Feifel (Ed.), *The meaning of death*. New York: McGraw-Hill.

Parkes, C. M. (1986). *Bereavement: Studies of grief in adult life*. London: Penguin. (Original work published 1972)

Parkes, C. M., & Weiss, R. (1983). *Recovery from bereavement*. New York: Basic Books.

Raphael, B., & Nunn, K. (1988). Counseling the bereaved. *Journal of Social Issues, 44*, 191–206.

Rochlin, G. (1965). *Griefs and discontents: The forces of change.* Boston: Little, Brown.

Rose, N. (1985). *The psychological complex: Politics and society in England 1869–1939.* London: Routledge & Kegan Paul.

Rosenblatt, P. (1983). *Bitter, bitter tears: Nineteenth century diarists and twentieth century grief theories.* Minneapolis: University of Minnesota Press.

Rosenblatt, P., & Meyer, M. (1986). Imagined interactions and the family. *Family Relations, 35,* 319–324.

Rubin, S. (1993). The death of a child is forever. The life course impact of child loss. In M. Stroebe, W. Stroebe, & R. O. Hansson (Eds.), *Handbook of bereavement.* New York: Cambridge University Press.

Sanders, C. (1989). *Grief. The mourning after.* New York: Wiley.

Shuchter, S., & Zisook, S. (1993). The course of normal grief. In M. Stroebe, W. Stroebe, & R. O. Hansson (Eds.), *Handbook of bereavement.* New York: Cambridge University Press.

Shweder, R. A., & Miller, J. G. (1985). The social construction of the person: How is it possible? In K. J. Gergen & K. E. Davis (Eds.), *The social construction of the person* (pp. 42–72). New York: Springer-Verlag.

Silverman, P., & Worden, W. (1993). Children's reactions to the death of a parent. In M. Stroebe, W. Stroebe, & R. O. Hansson (Eds.), *Handbook of bereavement.* New York: Cambridge University Press.

Stallworthy, J. (Ed.). (1973). *Penguin book of love poetry.* New York: Penguin Books.

Stroebe, M. (1994). Coping with bereavement: A review of the grief work hypothesis. *Omega, 26,* 19–42.

Stroebe, M., & Stroebe, W. (1989). Who participates in bereavement research? A review and empirical study. *Omega, 20,* 1–29.

Stroebe, M., & Stroebe, W. (1991). Does "grief work" work? *Journal of Consulting and Clinical Psychology, 59,* 57–65.

Stroebe, M., Stroebe, W., & Hansson. R. O. (Eds.). (1993). *Handbook of bereavement.* New York: Cambridge University Press.

Stroebe, W., & Stroebe, M. (1993). Determinants of adjustment to bereavement in young widows and widowers. In M. Stroebe, W. Stroebe, & R. O. Hansson (Eds.), *Handbook of bereavement.* New York: Cambridge University Press.

Stroebe, W., Stroebe, M., & Domittner, G. (1988). Individual and situational differences in recovery from bereavement: A risk-group identified. *Journal of Social Issues, 44,* 143–158.

Viorst, J. (1986). *Necessary losses: The loves, illusions, dependencies and impossible expectations that all of us have to give up in order to grow.* London: Simon & Schuster.

Wikan, U. (1988). Bereavement and loss in two Muslim communities: Egypt and Bali compared. *Social Science and Medicine, 27,* 451–460.

Wikan, U. (1990). *Managing turbulent hearts.* Chicago: University of Chicago Press.

Worden, W. (1982). *Grief counseling and grief therapy: A handbook for the mental health practitioner.* New York: Springer-Verlag.

Yamamoto, J. (1970). Cultural factors in loneliness, death, and separation. *Medical Times, 98,* 177–183.

Yamamoto, J., Okonoji, K., Iwasaki, T., & Yoshimura, S. (1969). Mourning in Japan. *American Journal of Psychiatry, 126,* 74–182.

Chapter 3

Grief That Does Not End

Paul C. Rosenblatt

Many Americans still seem to think that grief can be finished. Would-be support-ers of the bereaved often talk about getting over the grief and offer suggestions and help to facilitate achieving this goal. Self-help literature is still being pub-lished for bereaved people telling them that they can and should reach a point where they do not feel grief. There are also writings in the contemporary profes-sional/scholarly literature that are based on the idea that grief felt too strongly for too long is pathological and that there are things one can do to help a bereaved person to get beyond such grief (e.g., Jacobs, 1993). By contrast, there are cul-tures where the expectation is that people bereaved for certain losses will grieve very intensely for many years, if not a lifetime (e.g., Wikan, 1980). Research and personal experience have led this author to believe that many Americans grieving major losses will not ever reach a time when they completely stop grieving. The expectation that they can and should reach the end of their grief is based on a misunderstanding of normal grieving and does them a disservice (Rosenblatt, 1993).

This chapter defines *grief* as the blended emotional and cognitive reactions to a loss (in agreement with the Balinese studied by Wikan, 1990, that feelings and thoughts are not separable, at least when it comes to reactions to loss). The reactions to a loss that are most frequently part of grief in the United States in-clude sorrow, anger, depression, anxiety, fear, unpleasant feelings of confusion, disorientation, and other "down" emotions. But they may also include virtually any "up" emotion, with the obvious ones being relief that a long and difficult ill-ness has ended and joy at someone's entry to heaven. Grief can be seen as typi-cally an amalgam of differing feeling/thought blends, with the amalgam different for different bereaved persons and different losses, and with the amalgam chang-ing from time to time for any specific person bereaved for a specific loss.

When it is said that many Americans grieving major losses will not ever reach a time when they completely stop grieving, this does not mean that their grief will be continuous. Grief is probably not continuous beyond the first few days or weeks, even after a major loss. But the evidence from this author's re-search indicates that strong feelings of grief for major losses will recur over a lifetime. Another author (Parkes, 1975) called recurrent surges of grief "pangs." This chapter presents evidence that strong feelings of grief can recur over a life-time, discusses how and why this may be so, and discusses some of the implica-tions of this author's findings and interpretations. Finally, the focus returns to

American cultural notions that a grief that never ends is pathological, to explore whether and how the recurrent grief discussed here is actually incongruent with those notions.

EVIDENCE OF GRIEF RECURRENCE

Grief in 19th-Century Diaries

The research that first led me to believe that grief can recur over a lifetime was a study of grief over deaths and separations in 19th-century U.S. and Canadian diaries (Rosenblatt, 1983). Diaries seemed an ideal medium for investigating grief over time, because people provide information about themselves repeatedly in a diary without being affected by a researcher's questions or, ideally, by the intrusion of anyone into their private account of their thoughts and feelings. Another reason to study grief in 19th-century diaries was the desire to read what people had to say about their feelings and thoughts before 20th-century psychology added notions of grief work and ego defenses to the culture.

As it turned out, studying diaries was not that simple. Some diarists chose not to deal with loss or with feelings; some diaries were not private; many published diaries and at least some unpublished diaries had been edited (often to remove precisely what was of interest—more personal material), and many diaries were kept only sporadically and not necessarily over a long time. Still, some of the diaries provided what seemed at the time to be striking evidence of long-term grieving. Here are two of the diary excerpts that helped to persuade me.

> I was alone at Eve, fearfully alone, Ma, and you cannot come back. It was cruel to take you so, so soon. (Diary of Corwin R. Snow, unpublished manuscript, quoted by permission of the University of Iowa Libraries (Iowa City), entry of July 4, 1896, 29 months after his wife ("Ma") died.)

> Have been reading over some of my old letters to my beloved husband, & been ready to long that the bond may be sundered wh. holds me to earth, & detains me from *him*. . . . Reading those letters (a thing wh. I have never trusted myself to do before) seems to have revived all the exclusiveness & intensiveness of my love for him I once called *husband*. I am so filled with a sense of the fearfulness of my loss & the awful chasm made in my heart & affections that all one earth seems a void without him. "'I sit alone as a swallow upon the house top." My heart turns away from all human helpers. Oh how bitter was that cup of trembling wh. God put into my hands! (Diary of Susan Mansfield Huntington, unpublished manuscript, John Trumbull Papers, Manuscripts and Archives, Sterling Memorial Library, Yale University, entry of June 26, 1822, 34 months after her husband had died.)

Diary entries like these two were persuasive, at first, that grief could recur indefinitely in people bereaved for major losses, but the study had many limitations. Perhaps the greatest limitation was the study's focus on grief in the first 3 years following a loss, so little evidence was gathered about the recurrence of grief over a lifetime extended decades beyond a loss. Even before the diary book was published, it seemed clear that data were needed from many years beyond a loss. That led to a first study of loss due to miscarriage, stillbirth, or infant death.

Long-Term Grieving over Perinatal Loss

With an interest in finding evidence for or against the idea that some people grieve over a lifetime, with an interest in documenting the problems created by American downplaying of miscarriage as an important event in a person's life, and with an interest in studying grief in a representative sample, this author and Linda Hammer Burns set out to study grief over miscarriage, stillbirth, or infant death (Rosenblatt & Burns, 1986). At the time the study was planned, there were estimates that 20 to 25% of pregnancies end in loss (Peppers & Knapp, 1980). That seemed a high enough percentage so that a simple random sample of individuals or households would be feasible in generating a sample of people to be interviewed. In fact, randomly sampling from the community directories of a mixed blue-collar and middle-class urban neighborhood and a well-to-do suburb, 18% of the householders contacted reported at least one perinatal loss. Interviews were carried out with 31 people who had experienced a perinatal loss two or more years previously.

Among the 31 informants, 55 perinatal losses had been experienced. The losses had occurred from 2 to 46 years prior to the interview. Most people who were interviewed provided a fine grain of detail in describing the loss event, including where they were, what happened, how they felt, and who did what. That seemed to mean that a perinatal loss was not a trivial experience in the lives of most people. Two people describing experiences with an infant death and five describing experiences with one or more miscarriages reported occasional or frequent pangs of grief continuing up to the present. Some pangs seemed to be intense, even decades after the loss. For example, 42 years after her 2-month-old son died, one woman said:

> It isn't that deadly, aching thought you have at the beginning. It's a pleasant thought. Well, I just feel that we were fortunate to have him. . . . Oh, you feel a definite loss, and you feel an anger, not an anger, a sorrow. . . . I'll tell you why I think it's harder now. You see, we didn't have any more children. . . . Each day, you know, you look at these happy young men around, and you think, "I wonder if he would have looked like that." (Rosenblatt & Burns, 1986, pp. 243, 244)

Another woman, talking 26 years after a miscarriage, said, "The sad feelings of loss, you're going to have that for the rest of your life" (Rosenblatt & Burns, 1986, p. 243).

In the diary study, there had been plenty of evidence that different people grieve different aspects of their loss and that the same person may grieve different aspects at different times. But we had not done anything with that information, because one could never tell whether a diarist wrote all that she or he was thinking and feeling or only bits of it. In the perinatal loss study it seemed easier to determine, at least with some people, what they had grieved initially and what they grieved more recently. What they grieved seemed to be not always, or not only, the child. Sometimes, for example, it seemed to be the loss of what the child could have become, sometimes the loss of parental role, and sometimes the loss of full husband support in time of need. If we are ever to make sense of long-term grieving, one part of it must be to understand what people grieve. We cannot presume, for example, that every widow's loss is the same. Using a single term, *grief*, for a diversity of feeling/thoughts makes it harder for us to realize how much diversity there is in the feeling/thoughts of different people or of the same person for different losses or even the same loss over time.

From the perinatal loss study, there seemed to be evidence for long-term grieving, but the fact that only seven people talked about grief extending over many years could be seen as a challenge to those of us who believe grief for major losses extends over a lifetime. However, some women and most men seemed not to have had strong feelings of grief about a miscarriage even at first. Also, there were experiential factors unique to perinatal loss that seem to have blocked some people from grieving over a long term. One of those factors was subsequent fertility. With a miscarriage, the birth of a subsequent child muted grief for some people, perhaps particularly when the subsequent child was only born because the miscarriage had occurred. (For example, the subsequent child was conceived during the time the woman would have been pregnant with the miscarried child, or a couple would not have planned to have the child they had if a previous pregnancy had not ended in miscarriage.) With miscarriages, and perhaps even with other perinatal losses, people often said that the loss had been treated at the hospital as only a medical event, not a personal or couple tragedy, and the community at large often did not acknowledge the perinatal loss or support grief extended beyond the first days or weeks following the loss. These factors may have pushed some people to construct meanings for a loss and for their feelings that blocked them from grieving over the long run or from labeling feelings as grief that others would label grief. At the same time, others who have studied perinatal loss have reported long-term grieving—for example, Peppers and Knapp (1980), who called it *shadow grief,* and Gilbert and Smart (1992), who found shadow grief continuing for a few respondents, although lessening in frequency and intensity for most. The upshot of all this is that even though only seven people reported long-term grieving, I believe that Burns and I had generated persuasive evidence.

Believing that long-term grief was a fact (although the evidence discussed so far is not necessarily convincing), I have assumed in all subsequent interview studies of grief that anybody who has experienced a major loss, no matter how long since the loss, has recent grief feelings and might well feel strong pangs of grief during the interview. One recent example of interviewing with the assumption of long-term grieving is a study of farm families bereaved for a family member killed in a farm accident.

Grief Following a Fatal Farm Accident

The farm accident study (Rosenblatt & Karis, 1993, 1993-94) involved interviews of 39 people in 21 families. The losses had occurred up to 50 years prior to the time of the interview. Although the project focused on family dynamics, there was plenty of evidence concerning long-term individual grieving. All the people who were interviewed had lost a close relative, typically a father, son, or daughter. Quite a few people became teary-eyed and showed other expressions of grief during the interview. For example, a woman who had lost a 7-year-old child 11 years before the interview cried as she told about the accident:

> She was pinned like from the waist, from the waist down. And uh (crying) I guess it bothers me (can't understand one or two words). I haven't talked about it, you know, for a long time. And don't worry that it bothers me, because maybe it's good for me to get it out.

She cried again when talking about the reactions of her other children to the death of their sister.

> I'm sure if you go in their room now, they (crying again) have things of hers in the drawer.

The woman's 17-year-old son, brother of the deceased, also became emotional as he replied to a question about his grief.

> **Rosenblatt:** *If I wanted to write things for families that had kids who were around the age you were when it happened, to help them deal with the problems or the things that might affect their kid . . .*
>
> **17-year-old** (interrupting): *Oh, it's more of a problem for them later than it is when it first happens. Tell them that right now. They think more, more of it when they get older (becoming teary-eyed) than they ever did when they were young (voice shaking).*

A man who was interviewed talked, with shaking voice, about the death of a 12-year-old brother. He concluded the description of the accident by saying,

> The rest is just a nightmare from that point. It's just like, it's been 17, almost 20 years, 19 years now. So, it's still hard.

Like the man quoted immediately above, others also talked about grieving recurrently years after the loss. A man whose son was killed in a farm accident 5 years before the interview said,

Sometimes when you go through something like this, if something else happens, it just seems like, you know it's not true, but it seems like in your mind that everything is going wrong, you know, and ah, it takes you a long time. It took me until, I'm still getting over it, which I, you'll never totally get over it, but I'm still learning to handle different things.

HOW AND WHY GRIEF
CAN RECUR OVER A LIFETIME

A Loss Is Often a Series
of Losses or of Realizations

Family and community pressure to be over grief may be based on a number of false assumptions about grief. Some people may not realize that attachments endure and that some losses are so big and so painful that one cannot ever get to a place where grief has ended. The pressures for people to get over grief also seem to be based on a very simple view of what a loss is. Although the American short-hand way of thinking about a loss may be that a loss is a single event, it typically is not. Consider a woman in the farm accident study. Interviewed 6 years after the death, she talked about an experience a few weeks before the interview:

> I started crying about when I mentioned [my husband's] name, and somebody said, "Boy, you know, it's been a long time. You should be over that by now."

What should she be over? Judging by what she said in the interview, she loved her husband dearly. She told stories of dancing with him in the barn, of coming home during her lunch break at work to check on him and eat with him, of taking delight in his delight in children, and so on. His death was a tremendous blow to her. But his death was not the only blow. The way he died was quite grue-some, so she was haunted not only by his death but by his dying. Following his death, her other losses included having to give up dairying and sell the milk cows and heifers, some of which were like pets or even friends for her. Another loss was that she had to sell her house. She also had to deal with estrangement from her two stepsons and with a lawsuit filed by them to stop her from selling the farm. One of her own sons came home to live with her (despite the dream of rural tranquility, rural Minnesota is dangerous enough so that it is inadvisable for a widow to live alone). Having her son come home created other losses for her—his leaving school and his loss of direction. So when this woman grieved, her grief was not only for the death of her husband but for much more, including losses that only began or were only perceived years after his death.

Most times with a death or other major loss, all that is lost is not concen-trated at the time of loss. There is, instead, a sequence, perhaps extending over one's lifetime, of new losses or new realizations of loss. Some of those new realizations or new losses are developmental (Johnson & Rosenblatt, 1981); they are only present or perceived when one has developed to the point where one would need what has been lost. Consider the 17-year-old, quoted above, who talked about his sister. Based on things he said during the interview, he had only come recently to grieve aspects of his sister's death that were related to his recently developed understanding of death and to his recently developed awareness of girls and young women as vital individuals.

Another case where developmental factors were obviously involved in a sequence, spread over years, of newly experienced losses related to a death was that of a woman whose father had died when she was an infant. She described herself as recurrently coming to deal with her father's death and with things associated with it throughout her lifetime. The following describes one of the matters that arose, apparently decades after the death:

> I . . . went through some stuff where I feel I caused the death, and that was really, really deep stuff, because I, it was, I couldn't verbalize it. It made no sense to me . . . but I think in searching, I had this sort of replacement idea, that once you had a birth you automatically had a death. And I got born so he died, you know. Why me? And, sort of, so it's been a huge issue, just taking the right to be alive. . . . When I was 24 I was in a car accident, and looking . . . back on it, I'm sure it was a veiled suicidal kind of thing.

With farming fatalities, the unfolding nature of loss was related in part to the nature of farming. With the death of a family member whose work was crucial to the farm economically, some people had to give up farming and the farm (Rosenblatt & Karis, 1993). So for some, there were economic losses, the loss of home, the loss of a way of life, and the loss of a desired occupation to grieve. These losses did not all occur at the time of the death but were spread out. For example, surviving family members might try to farm for a year or two after the death and only then realize that they could not maintain the farm economically. They might rent out the farm for a few more years, continuing to live on the farmstead, but then it might be financially necessary to sell the entire farm and to move elsewhere. Some of the farm widows who were interviewed realized that losses are compounded, not unitary, with a husband's death. Some of those widows seemed to choose to spread out some of their losses over a matter of years, rather than concentrate many losses at one time. Thus, it may be that grief for major losses is long term partly because some people prefer not to deal with many secondary losses at the time they first begin to deal with a major death.

With the first significant loss in one's life, if not before, comes a realization of one's own mortality and of the human incapacity to stop death or to reverse it. That can make the first significant loss in one's life much more challenging (Rosenblatt et al., 1991). It can also mean the recurrent grief following one's first major death may include grief for mortality (one's own, that of others), for human limitations in contending against death, and for loss of the innocence one had when death seemed irrelevant to one's own life.

Another way in which the losses related to a death may first begin at some time after the death has to do with the ways that grief is a familial or relationship phenomenon (Rosenblatt, 1993). Individual grief does not occur in a relationship vacuum but in the context of close relationships. When family members or others with close relationships share a loss, they may find that in some sense they lose one another as their individual griefs are preoccupying, depressing, or debilitating. And these losses of others may only occur later on, as one turns to others for attention, sympathy, understanding, or something else. To illustrate, one of the women interviewed in the farm accident study talked about a note she received from one of her children a few months following the death of another of her children:

> [My oldest daughter] at that time had wrote me a note, and I still have that note. She said, "I not only lost a sister. I lost a mother also." When I got that note, I couldn't help her, 'cause I couldn't help myself.

Thus, one may lose a specific family member at one point in time and then lose other family members over a substantial period of time as their grief preoccupies them, depresses them, or otherwise affects them. A family member who is aware of being unavailable to other family members may, like the woman quoted immediately above, grieve her unavailability as well the loss that is at the focus of the family grief. And each recurrence of grief in one family member may create loss for all other family members. The issue is even more complicated because in grief one may be particularly needy, so the losses of other family members who are grieving may be especially upsetting because one wants so much to receive what one thinks they should be able to provide (Rosenblatt et al., 1991). Moreover, the grief of one family member may remind other family members of their loss or may set off empathic grief feelings that both reflect the initial loss and express the sorrow, pain, etc., of knowing that another family member is grieving.

The Nature of Grief Work

Grief work can be understood as a cognitive process of coming to terms with a loss through confronting the loss and restructuring thoughts about the deceased, the events of the loss, and the world as it is without the deceased (Stroebe, 1992–93). Grief work is a foundational concept in writings about grief. But in writing about grief work, it is important to be aware of the challenging questions that Stroebe (1992–93) has raised about misuse of the concept of grief work and about assertions of the universality and necessity of grief work.

As Freud described grief work, it cannot be done all at once, but by fits and starts (Freud, 1954). The endpoint of the process may be understood as an emotional neutralizing of one's relationship to the deceased. However, it may also be understood as an identification with the lost person (Peskin, 1993). Grief work, as

Freud understood it, cannot be done all at once, partly because people have mixed feelings about reducing the intensity of their connections to the person they have lost. Mixed feelings arise for people who experience the carrying out of grief work as like killing a deceased person again, like being disloyal, like giving up memories of good times, like saying they do not care about the deceased, and like other actions that deny the value and importance of the deceased and of personal connections to the deceased (see Brice, 1991, for a brilliant account of the ambivalence of bereaved mothers toward grief work). So one reason to expect grief to be spread out over time and to come and go is that there is a holding back from grief work that reflects ambivalence.

In the face of ambivalence, a major challenge to the grief work process (assuming there is such a process) is to come to terms with a loss while honoring and perhaps even holding on to the meanings, memories, investments, and identities connected to the deceased. As Marris (1974) persuasively argued, a grief process that leads to turning one's back on the meanings, investments, and so on of a significant relationship will block one from investing in other relationships and will make for a meaningless life. Thus, part of the grief work process, and something that would undoubtedly be a long-term project, is to transform one's understandings of meanings, investments, and so on connected to the deceased in such a way that the past is validated.

A further complication in the grief work process is that death often does not end one's relationship with the deceased. The most familiar expression of that in the grief literature is the sense-of-presence experience, the sense many bereaved people have of still being in contact with somebody who has died (e.g., Marris, 1974; Parkes, 1975; Rosenblatt, 1983; Rosenblatt, Walsh, & Jackson, 1976). Moreover, there are bereaved people who feel a continuing relationship with the deceased (Rosenblatt & Elde, 1990). For them, there may be a holding back of grief because aspects of the relationship have not ended, at least not at the time of death. Also, for them, there will be recurrent opportunities to interact with the deceased, yet when those interactions seem limited in some way (for example, the deceased does not provide what is requested), there are new opportunities to grieve.

As Freud described it, grief work also demands enormous amounts of energy. Because of this, one reason for grief to be spread out over time and to occur in fits and starts is that people do not have the energy to carry out grief work continuously. In fact, even if they did have such energy, the demands of other aspects of their life (work, dependents, self-maintenance, getting from one place to another, etc.) would pull them away from grieving.

Freud described grief work as a process of hypercathecting each memory and hope connected to the deceased. By hypercathexis he meant a kind of emotional neutralizing of each memory and hope, not a forgetting (Rosenblatt, 1983). To carry out that neutralizing, one must bring a relevant memory or hope to mind. It is in the nature of human thought that not all memories or hopes can be thought of at once or thought of at will. Consciousness is so focused and hopes and memories in close relationships are so numerous that a person can deal with memories and hopes only bit by bit. One can go many years without thinking of a specific memory or hope. For that reason alone, we would expect grief work to be played out over a substantial period of time. A person would only be able to grieve and hypercathect a memory or hope when something sets off thoughts about that memory or hope.

After the first few days of loss, many of the diarists who provided the data for the diary study would write, in entries describing feelings of grief, statements about what set off their grief. Almost invariably grief was set off by some sort of reminder, something that focused consciousness on memories or hopes connected to the deceased. Among the many reminders mentioned were a visit from another person, the sight of someone who looked like the person who had died, an event (a storm, a celebration, a trip to town), something someone said, a date, finding a piece of memorabilia, visiting a place that was linked in memory with the deceased, and reading a poem, biblical passage, or news account that reminded one of the death or of the person who had died. Among the striking things about these reminders is that many of them cannot be anticipated, most are out of one's control, and many occur in the family setting. Thus, one cannot know in advance when one will experience a grief recurrence, one typically cannot block what sets off the recurrence even if one would choose to do so, and one's own family members are important in setting off recurrent grief and are in the best position to know when it occurs. That family members are important in setting off grief adds a bittersweet element to family gatherings, particularly the first ones after a significant family loss, as people welcome the connection but feel the sorrow, preoccupation, and so on of freshly set-off grief. For a death in a long-term relationship, it is easy to imagine that decades after the loss one would still be encountering reminders that would set off new hypercathexis. Moreover, one of the most significant reminders of previous loss is a new loss. Thus, the fresh grief for a new loss may often be entangled in grief for other losses, and, quite possibly, each recurrence of grief for one loss may set of grieving for other losses.

IMPLICATIONS OF GRIEF RECURRENCE

One implication of grief recurrence is that after one's first major loss, one will never be completely free of grieving. Without wearing mourning clothing appropriate in other cultures or other times, we are a nation, in fact a species, of mourners. However, since grief is not continuous, at any one time there may be many people who have experienced major losses who are not grieving. Their freedom from grief may be temporary, and their temporary distance from grieving may make them vulnerable to shock, disorientation, and depression as their capacity to focus on work or driving or a relationship, their ability to sleep easily, and much else are lost to bouts of renewed grieving.

A related implication of grief recurrence is that grief can sneak up on one. One may feel finally finished with grieving for a specific loss, and even announce that to others, and then be surprised by a new pang of grief for that loss. Perhaps part of the challenge of recurrent grieving is dealing with that surprise. For people who do not expect grief to recur, the fact of recurrence may itself be a source of grief. Also, for others who are close to the bereaved person, recurrence may come as a surprise, and they too may be distressed and perhaps disappointed to see evidence of a grief that had seemed to be finished.

It would be a mistake to think of grief as necessarily a bad thing. People may often welcome grief recurrence, and even if there is a sad or bitter side to it there may also be a sweet, affirming, and to-be-cherished side. The positive elements of grief may include memories of how important the person who died was to one or memories of a particularly joyous or profound time together. A widow or widower may remember times of intense passion, of youthful play, of caresses and kind words. A bereaved parent may remember a child's laughter, the tender feelings of holding a sleeping infant, or a child's creative mischief. Thus, recurrent grief is not like recurrent illness. It can be a link with the best of life, an affirmation of light and joy. This is not to say that recurrent grief is not difficult for many people but to say that there is much more to it than sorrow.

The idea that grief is set off by reminders suggests that one can, to some extent, control grief recurrence. One can dispose of memorabilia, avoid others who could remind one of the deceased, and stay away from places that were significant in one's relationship with the deceased. In the diary study, there were diarists who did just that, hoping to feel less of the pain of grief. People who do that possibly miss some grieving, but it is more likely that their efforts to avoid grief create additional grief (grief for the lost memorabilia, grief over the home that they moved from in order to avoid feeling grief, grief over lack of contact with the living who are being avoided, and so on). It is also likely that grief work cannot be put off indefinitely, that an avoidance of certain reminders of a loss makes it likely that one will grieve later on, as one encounters still other reminders that set off the process of dealing with emotionally charged memories and hopes.

The idea that controlling reminders controls grief recurrence suggests that some people might seek out reminders, perhaps to facilitate the grief work process but also to assess the nature of what was lost or to acknowledge and symbolize the importance of what was lost. People might, for example, review a family photo album or return to an old neighborhood as a way of reminding themselves of how significant a relationship ended by a death was.

AMERICAN CULTURAL NOTIONS ABOUT GRIEF RECURRENCE

It is possible that the American cultural notion about finishing grief in a defined period of time is not as incongruent with the idea of recurrent grieving as it seems. Recurrent grief is not constant grief. Even if the memories and pain are still inside of one and can still be brought to the surface recurrently, it is not grief if it is not currently felt, thought, or expressed. Even if the pangs of recurrent grief are quite intense and even if some pangs last days, weeks, or perhaps even longer, a grief that comes and goes can still be understood as a lessened grief. There may be other, less overtly emotional expressions of continuing grief—for example, continuing idealization of the deceased (Lopata, 1981) or an unwillingness to change life patterns that began with the onset of bereavement—but the gaps between emotional/cognitive bouts of grieving may be consistent with the cultural notion that people should get over a loss.

America is a land of many cultures, yet there are efforts to medicalize and routinize grief therapy in ways that are grossly insensitive to cultural differences (Averill & Nunley, 1993; Rosenblatt, 1993). Cultures differ enormously in how grief is understood, how much long-term grieving is desired and nurtured, and how much it is considered pathological to grieve or not to grieve over the long-term. Thus, even though people who study grief have been moving to the position that some aspects of grief work never end (Shuchter & Zisook, 1993), just as it seems a mistake to define long-term grieving as necessarily pathological, it may be equally a mistake to define culturally prescribed, time-limited grieving as pathological.

There seems to be a movement away from a scientific perspective on grief that assumes there is a human nature in which can be discerned basic principles of grieving. The movement seems toward a postmodern sensibility in which the diversity of realities is acknowledged (Chapter 2, this volume). In a postmodern approach, assertions about grief must be understood as framed in a specific perspective and relative to that perspective. Thus, the question of whether grief is timeless or not has no meaning unless placed within a perspective. If one is working within a scientific perspective that makes sense of trying to understand human nature, one can ask whether lifetime grieving is common or not, associated with various dispositions considered pathological or not, makes sense or not from the perspective of various principles of psychology, and is or is not consistent with the norms of some culture. However, if one is working within another perspective, the issue of lifetime grieving may be meaningless in itself. If it has any meaning at all, it may only be as a side issue to questions that are considered of real importance. Those other questions might concern how one can maintain a satisfactory relationship with the deceased, how one can hold on to precious memories, or how one can find acceptance and understanding for one's feelings no matter what those feelings are.

It may suffice, for this chapter and this book, to address the modernist, scientific question of whether lifetime grieving is normal, common, understandable, and healthy. It may also be useful, within that framework, to explore the functions of long-term attachment. One can turn, for example, to the Moss and Moss (1984–85) analysis of the social functions of long-term attachment in widowhood. One may then explore how recurrent grieving might be related to personal commitment to the deceased, to the place of relationship with the deceased in personal identity, and the persistence of affection beyond a person's death. But it is also important to keep track of other perspectives in which those questions are irrelevant and to be open to the questions about long-term grieving that matter from those other perspectives. Effective counseling, practice, grief support, friendship, spiritual collaboration, and functioning as individuals, family members, and community members will depend on our being able to see the importance of those questions and on being able to think in terms of them. One then might have to address such questions as, How does one honor a long-term grief? In what ways might a deceased person affect one's artistic work or parenting? If this book lays to rest the notion that grief ends, or should end, and that the end of grief should come fairly soon (one year, two years) after a death, there are still many questions about long-term grieving to address.

REFERENCES

Averill, J. R., & Nunley, E. P. (1993). Grief as an emotion and as a disease: A social-constructionist perspective. In M. S. Stroebe, W. Stroebe, & R. O. Hansson (Eds.), *Handbook of bereavement* (pp. 77–90). New York: Cambridge University Press.

Brice, C. W. (1991). What forever means: An empirical existential–phenomenological investigation of maternal mourning. *Journal of Phenomenological Psychology, 22,* 16–38.

Freud, S. (1954). Mourning and melancholia. In *Collected papers of Sigmund Freud: Vol 4. Papers on metapsychology, papers on applied psychoanalysis* (pp. 152-170). New York: Basic Books.

Gilbert, K. R., & Smart, L. S. (1992). *Coping with infant or fetal loss: The couple's healing process.* New York: Brunner/Mazel.

Jacobs, S. (1993). *Pathologic grief: Maladaptation to loss.* Washington, DC: American Psychiatric Press.

Johnson, P. A., & Rosenblatt, P. C. (1981). Grief following childhood loss of parent. *American Journal of Psychotherapy, 35,* 419–425.

Lopata, H. Z. (1981). Widowhood and husband sanctification. *Journal of Marriage and the Family, 43,* 439–450.

Marris, P. (1974). *Loss and change.* New York: Pantheon.

Moss, M. S., & Moss, S. Z. (1984–1985). Some aspects of the elderly widow(er)'s persistent tie with the deceased spouse. *Omega, 15,* 195–206.

Parkes, C. M. (1975). *Bereavement: Studies of grief in adult life.* New York: Penguin.

Peppers, L. G., & Knapp, R. J. (1980). *Motherhood and mourning.* New York: Praeger.

Peskin, H. (1993). Neither broken hearts nor broken bonds. *American Psychologist, 48,* 990–991.

Rosenblatt, P. C. (1983). *Bitter, bitter tears: Nineteenth century diarists and twentieth century grief theories.* Minneapolis: University of Minnesota Press.

Rosenblatt, P. C. (1993). Grief: The social context of private feelings. In M. S. Stroebe, W. Stroebe, & R. O. Hansson (Eds.), *Handbook of bereavement* (pp. 102–111). New York: Cambridge University Press.

Rosenblatt, P. C., & Burns, L. H. (1986). Long-term effects of perinatal loss. *Journal of Family Issues, 7,* 237–253.

Rosenblatt, P. C., & Elde, C. (1990). Shared reminiscence about a deceased parent: Implications for grief education and grief counseling. *Family Relations, 39,* 206-210.

Rosenblatt, P. C., & Karis, T. A. (1993). Economics and family bereavement following a fatal farm accident. *Journal of Rural Community Psychology, 12*(2), 37-51.

Rosenblatt, P. C., & Karis, T. A. (1993-94). Family distancing following a fatal farm accident. *Omega, 28,* 183-200.

Rosenblatt, P. C., Spoentgen, P., Karis, T. A., Dahl, C., Kaiser, T., & Elde, C. (1991). Difficulties in supporting the bereaved. *Omega, 23,* 119-128.

Rosenblatt, P. C., Walsh, R. P., & Jackson, D. A. (1976). *Grief and mourning in cross-cultural perspective*. New Haven, CT: Human Relations Area Files Press.

Shuchter, S. R., & Zisook, S. (1993). The course of normal grief. In M. S. Stroebe, W. Stroebe, & R. O. Hansson (Eds.), *Handbook of bereavement* (pp. 23–43). New York: Cambridge University Press.

Stroebe, M. (1992–93). Coping with bereavement: A review of the grief work hypothesis. *Omega, 26*, 19–42.

Wikan, U. (1980). *Life among the poor in Cairo*. London: Tavistock.

Wikan, U. (1990). *Managing turbulent hearts*. Chicago: University of Chicago Press.

Chapter 4

Grief in an Eastern Culture: Japanese Ancestor Worship

Dennis Klass

Ancestor worship in Japan is an elaborate set of rituals, supported by a sophisticated theory, by which those who are living maintain personal, emotional bonds with those who have died. The deceased remain individual spirits, available to the living for 35 or 50 years. Ancestor worship is an important element in Japanese culture and the predominant feature of Buddhism in Japan. At critical points in Japanese history, the power of the rituals of ancestor worship have been put in the service of political power, so we need to give some historic and philosophical background as a context. But at its core, ancestor worship is an expression of the human community that cannot be separated by death. This chapter: first, traces the role of ancestor worship in historical Japanese politics and family structure; second, examines the nature of the spirits of the dead and relates those spirits to Buddhist beliefs and practices; and third, gives an account of the rituals of ancestor worship showing how the rituals provide a vehicle by which resolution of grief is accomplished.

DEFINITION

The Japanese term *sosen sūhai* translates to "ancestor worship" (Gorai, 1984; Offner, 1979; Plath, 1964; Smith, 1974). The word *sūhai* means a deep, respectful feeling toward another person; it may be translated as admiration, adoration, idolization, or veneration, as well as worship. *Sūhai* may be used to refer to respect toward highly esteemed living persons as well as toward the dead. *Sosen* are the objects of veneration. Some are lineal ancestors, that is, individuals from whom the family is descended. The important lineal ancestors are owed the same kind of respect as are living patriarchs and matriarchs. But also included are deceased children, relatives outside the formal hereditary line (including those by adoption or marriage), and nonrelatives such as a respected teacher, friend, or lover. Deceased people who have no one else to care for them, that is, no family to perform the rituals, may also be included in a family's ancestors. Other *sosen* are ancestors of origin, that is, the mythical deity from whom the family is descended, as the emperor's family is descended from the Sun Goddess. There is not, however, a sharp distinction between lineal ancestors and ancestors of origin because mythical deities may once have been extraordinary humans, and as we

59

shall note, the goal of the rituals of ancestor worship is to transform the dead from a human (*shirei*) to a god (*kami*).

HISTORY

The history of ancestor worship in Japan is intertwined with Japanese political power and kinship bonds. There has been a link between ancestor worship and political power at least since the Nara era (8th century), when the reverence for imperial ancestors was linked with reverence for one's own family ancestors. During the Nara era, the indigenous gods (*kami*) were incorporated into Buddhism, which had been imported from China. Contemporary Japanese people are especially aware of two important historical political meanings. First, at the beginning of the Tokugawa period (1603–1868) everyone was required to register as a parishioner of a Buddhist temple, where the main emotional and ritual connection was the ancestor rites. The historical membership continues as people return to their family's historic temple for funerals and subsequent rites. Second, in the Meiji Restoration (1868) an attempt was made to establish Shinto (which is the religion devoted to the indigenous gods) as the national religion, that is, State Shinto. That was not successful, partly because Buddhism's ancestor worship was so deeply integrated into the social fabric. But at that time, there was a link made between Shinto emperor worship *tennō sūhai* and Buddhist ancestor worship *sosen sūhai*. State Shinto ended in 1945, though it remains as a latent conservative political force. When World War II dead were enshrined as *kami*, there was a great deal of controversy.

Ancestor worship was important in kinship bonds in Japan because a person's place in the family was defined by who a person's ancestors were and what ritual duties a person had to the ancestors. A common way of dividing Japanese households was into "succeeded houses" and "created houses." A succeeded house was headed by a successor to the previous head, usually the oldest son. The successor inherited the property as well as the duty to care for the ancestors. A created house was headed by a nonsuccessor such as a second son who has no duty to care for ancestors except when he returned to his parents' house. When someone in the created house died, that person became the first ancestor of the new house, thus setting the stage for further divisions in successive generations. So ancestors defined the individual's place in the family system.

Japanese society underwent a series of radical changes after World War II, so the meaning of ancestor worship is more ambiguous. At the end of World War II the tie between ancestor worship and loyalty to the emperor was officially severed. The end of the war also signaled a change in the family patterns as households were replaced by conjugal families, that is families based on the marriages with self-chosen partners. Yet the rituals continue to be observed in virtually all families.

The historic centrality of ancestor worship should remind us that the theories about grief and the social forms through which grief is expressed are never apart from larger cultural meanings nor from economic and political power. The concept of the individual as the center of a collection of temporary attachments, which are broken when they no longer instrumentally meet the individual's needs in the present, is just as integral to the social power of business corporations in consumer capitalism as was ancestor worship to imperial power. In the same way, the modern Western theories of grief and the social forms by which grief is expressed are as connected to the nuclear family and serial monogamy that characterizes the modern family system as was ancestor worship to the traditional household system. Just as we are defined in consumerism by the temporary satisfactions of products we buy, the dominant theories of grief in modernity define us by the attachments that serve us in the present. We wish to cut the bonds with the dead in the same way adolescents wish to cut the bonds with their family of origin in order to found their own family, which consists of a living pair bond and their children. We need to sever the bonds with a spouse after both death and divorce so we can be free to enter a new monogamous pair bond, the basis of which is emotional investment, and the success of which is supposed to provide individual personal fulfillment.

WESTERN PSYCHOLOGY AND JAPANESE RITUAL

Yanagawa and Abe (1983) note that Japanese religion has traditionally been communal; that is, the core of religion is ritual, which symbolically reinforces kin group interactions and national identity. At the same time, however, there is also a strong personal element. Individuals undertake the disciplines of Buddhist meditation and people put their individual concerns on the prayer papers at Buddhist temples or buy charms for their personal problems at Shinto shrines. Most studies of Japanese religion focus on the communal. But in this discussion, we will bracket many of the historical/communal issues so we can see how ancestor worship facilitates the bond between those who have died and those who survive. Just as there is an individualistic element in other aspects of Japanese religion, there has always been a more personal element in ancestor worship. This personal element has received far less attention from scholars, partly because the communal aspect is much easier to observe, and partly because the communal allows Japanese people to talk about what they share, not about differences that make them feel uncomfortable.

The personal element is difficult to study in Japanese culture. To ask the direct question is to invade privacy most impolitely. In Japan, one is supposed to be so attuned to the other that important meanings need not be spoken. To ask the Western question "How do you feel about that?" is only to prove that the questioner cannot understand. It is especially impolite to ask about matters having do with religion, because there is a great deal of diversity in the various Japanese religions and talk of religion may bring out conflicting opinions, which is uncomfortable to Japanese.

We can use beliefs, customs, and rituals to understand the personal sphere on which Western studies of grief have focused. As Jung (1938) wrote, what we in the modern West feel as internal and psychological is, in other societies, external and objective in the form of rituals and myth. Kaneko (1990) makes the same point with consummate Japanese tact when he says that perhaps the rituals of Japanese religion comprise "a more complicated and differentiated extrinsic religiosity than that seen in the West" (p. 3).

THE NATURE OF THE SPIRITS OF THE DEAD

The ancestors are those who can be reborn. The point in the various meditation practices of Buddhism is to escape rebirth. The aim is nirvana, which means "to be blown out," as the wind blows out a candle. Nirvana in esoteric practice is achieved in life, for example, in the enlightenment of Zen, or becoming a "Buddha in the body" in Shingon. To achieve nirvana is to realize one's Buddha nature. Rebirth can cease because there is no karma left to pass on. If one is not to be reborn, it will be known within 7 days after death. If one, however, is to be reborn, it will happen within 49 days after death. In Japanese Buddhism, the spiritual elite strive for nirvana in this life. But ordinary people become a Buddha only when they die. "This gave a new and appealing meaning to the concept of nirvana, and the Japanese began to conceive of their ancestors as living in peace in the Pure Land or Western Paradise of the Amida Buddha" (Smith, 1974, p. 51). Hence, the largest Buddhist sects are now Pure Land, relying on the merit and compassion of Amida Buddha to insure the individual's entrance into the Pure Land after death.

But the Pure Land is not a separate realm as Heaven is often conceived in Christianity. The wall between the world of the dead and the world of the living is much more permeable in Japan. Only equivocal phrases can describe the world of the dead:

> Spatially it is both here and there, temporally both then and now. The departed and ancestors always are close by; they can be contacted immediately at the household shelf, the graveyard, or elsewhere. Yet when they return "there" after the midsummer reunion they are seen off as for a great journey. They are perpetually present. Yet they come to and go from periodic household foregatherings. (Plath, 1964, p. 308)

Spirits of the dead are available for interaction. They may be in the mountains, but usually they are thought of as at the grave or on the altar where they are venerated. So the spirit may be contacted in this world by addressing the stone or tablet, and may be called back in the Bon festival. Some of the dead go on to become gods (*kami*). To some extent this is a function of where and by which rituals they are venerated (Buddhist or Shinto). The easiest way to become *kami* is to die in war or be a shogun or emperor. But for most people, the movement is slower and occurs at the end of the funeral rituals, which is either 35 or 50 years after the death. Practically, then, the spirits of those who have died are available for active interaction for the remaining lifetime of those who knew them.

> Between a person's last breath and the final prayers said on his behalf, his spirit is ritually and symbolically purified and elevated; it passes gradually from the stage of immediate association with the corpse, which is thought to be both dangerous and polluting, to the moment when it loses its individual identity and enters the realm of the generalized ancestral spirits, essentially purified. (Smith, 1974, p. 69)

The names by which the dead are called shows this progression:

shirei — spirits of the newly dead
nī-hotoke — new buddhas
hotoke — buddhas
senzo — ancestors
kami — gods (Smith, 1974, p. 56)

The spirit of the dead, at whatever its stage in this progression, is not an entity with individual existence. That is, the spirit of the dead in Japan does not have substantial existence as does the soul in Christian doctrine. The spirit is not an independent element that enters the body at some point before birth and exits the body at death. Rather, just as there is no self (*anatman*) in the living, there is no self in the dead. In Hinduism, the religion from which Buddhism emerged, *atman* is the true self, that piece of Brahman, or God, which is the essential part of every person. The most important Buddhist teaching is that there is no *atman*, no self, hence, *anatman*. Some scholars (Smith, 1974) have interpreted the Japanese myth of an afterlife as an abandonment of true Buddhism. But clearly a millennium of highly developed Japanese Buddhist scholarship, which has disagreed enough to break into many sects and schools, has not reached that conclusion (see Kapleau, 1965, pp. 155–157). The Buddhist doctrine of no self (*anatman*) easily includes the spirit of the dead as a Buddha that stays as an entity to which one can relate for as long as a survivor's memory lasts. Long (1987) notes that Sakyamuni Buddha (the one most Westerners think of as "the Buddha") redefined reincarnation from the idea of a substance that passed through various lives.

> The human being or personality, therefore, is not to be understood essentially as an integral and enduring mind–body organism, but rather the manifestation of a highly complex succession of psychosomatic movement propelled along the temporal continuum by the force of *karman*. (p. 141)

The individual self is an interaction of the five *skandhas* (bundles): form (physical shape), feelings (our responses to forms), perceptions (the picture the mind makes from sense perceptions and feelings), complexes (our historically conditioned ways of responding), and background consciousness. The self so defined is an interaction of the physical, the affective, the cognitive, and the cultural. The great mistake the unenlightened make is to think this self has an independent concrete existence. It does not; it is merely a temporary interaction. Hence the teaching is, "There is nothing that transmigrates and yet there is rebirth." How can this be? The question grows out of a misconstruing of the nature of *karman*, which is not an independently existing entity that moves from life to life as a person would put on one coat after another:

> Rightly understood, *karman* is the life process itself, the blending of energy and form that coordinates an unending flow of life moments. That is, the myriad clusters of factors that constitute the universe at any given moment are nothing more than the product of all its pasts. . . . Birth and death, then, are to be construed as nothing more than dramatic interruptions or exceptional innovations in the ongoing life process. (Long, 1987, p. 142)

The individual who has died gradually merges with the generalized group of all those in the family who have died—that is, the *shirei* takes on the character of the *hotoke* and then the *kami*. Eventually the spirit of the individual melds into the family as an ancestor. And the family *kami* is part of the clan, community, and finally the nation. But this nonsubstantial and nonindividual nature is not unique to the spirits of the dead. A true understanding of both the living and the dead is that there is no self. To be in touch with the dead, then, is to be in touch with many transcending realities, and to understand the nature of the ancestor's being is to understand our own.

HOME ALTARS AND MEMORIAL TABLETS

The focal points for ancestor worship in the home are the *butsudan*, the Buddha altar, and to a lesser extent, the *kamidana*, the Shinto god shelf. The Buddha altar is a cabinet with the implements of a Buddhist temple—incense burner, bell, candles—in which the *ahai* (memorial tablets) for departed spirits are placed. Each morning Buddhist worship is performed in front of the Buddha altar. Even though the central image on the altar is a more famous Buddha—usually Kannon, Bodhisattva of Mercy—the basic reason for having a Buddha altar in the home is veneration of spirits of the dead. The god shelf is the household shrine before which Shinto worship is performed. When the dead becomes a *kami*, 35 or 50 years after the death, in some places the tablet is moved from the Buddha altar and a substitute is placed on the god shelf.

Traditional memorial tablets are upright lacquered wood plaques 4 to 6 inches high. Another type of tablet is unlacquered wood in a small container shaped like a small altar. Recently, rather than having tablets, some families keep a book on the altar with all the names of the deceased family members. Tablets are not always made for children and other minor members of the household. Sometimes temporary tablets for children are set adrift or burned; but some people keep tablets for children on the altar for many years. Written on the tablet is a posthumous name (*kaimyo*). The name usually includes one character from the person's name in life, an indication of the age group the person belonged to when he or she died, and a reference to the person's qualities which is often stereotyped, but is occasionally highly personalized. The death date is written on the face of the tablet. The reverse side has the person's name in life and age at death and often includes the relationship of the person to the head of the household. Typically, photographs of the dead are also kept on the Buddha altar for up to several years after a person dies.

What is going on in the lives of people as they are in the presence of their ancestors on the Buddha altar? Offner (1979) did a survey asking the purpose and motivation of the people performing the rites before the home altars. Results were as follows:

	An important element	Most important element
Comforting/cheering	81%	44%
Expressing gratitude	65%	29%
Maintaining tradition	34%	10%
Reporting on the family	31%	
Showing respect	30%	8%
Sense of personal satisfaction	23%	6%
Fulfilling responsibility	12%	
Petitioning for favors	12%	
Apologizing	7%	
Averting punishment	5%	

The survey list was designed by a Christian and some respondents added elements not on his survey:

Eliminating one's own evil karma
Self-reflection
Opportunity for family fellowship, probably fellowship with the dead.

Expressing gratitude, showing respect, fulfilling responsibility, and reporting are expressions of *amae*, the attitude of dependence proper for a family member to have toward others in the family, especially important others (Doi, 1973). Comfort and cheering would seem to be similar to the Western idea of solace or consolation (Klass, 1988, 1993). A Japanese woman whose 2-year-old daughter died 17 years ago talked about the daughter's tablet: "I have it because I want to keep her near at hand" (Smith, 1974, p. 130). A woman visiting the succeeded family home said it was good to be back. The researcher asked her why; the building was new, not the one she grew up in, and all her siblings were gone.

> She turned to the *butsudan* and said it was because of all the people in there, especially her father. Then she turned to another wall of the room and began pointing out

photographs of the ancestors, explaining to me which of them had tablets in the butsudan. She obviously felt warm and close to the altar and to the tablets it contained. (Smith, 1974, p. 131)

Plath (1964) quotes a novel about an illegitimate daughter who returned to her father's house as a widow, for there was nowhere else for her to go. She was treated badly. She comforted herself with the dreamy memory of her father and would sometimes speak to his photograph, which was on the Buddha altar (p. 309).

Yamamoto et al. (1969, p. 1664; first discussed in Chapter 2) said the altar with its tablets was a transitional object (see also Winnicott, 1953). The phrase was first used to describe things like a child's security blanket. Volkan (*1981*) noted that such transitional objects are common in grief. He called them "linking objects," and says they evoke the presence of the dead. But the concept of linking objects does not convey the lively, personal relationship between the living and the dead. Yamamoto and his colleagues (1969) give us a sense of the living relationship in ancestor worship.

> The family altar would be your "hotline" (to the ancestors). As such, you could immediately ring the bell, light incense, and talk over the current crisis with one whom you have loved and cherished. When you were happy, you could smile and share your good feelings with him. When you were sad, your tears would be in his presence . . . the relationship would be continuous from the live object to the revered ancestor. (p. 1663)

The dead are addressed in the same language and with the same emotion as when they were living. Smith (1974) tells of a nearly deaf old man with whom he often passed time. Smith was away when the old man died; when Smith returned, he came to the man's house and asked if he could burn incense at the family altar. The wife of the house was pleased. She put one of the cakes Smith had brought on a dish and took it to the altar. She knelt and said loudly, "Grandfather, Mr. Smith is here" (p. 143).

Many of the interactions in front of the Buddha altar are continuations of the bond that was there before the person died. Offerings on the altar are often foods or flowers that the deceased liked (Plath, 1964). Smith (1974) gives a report of a widow who, at a death anniversary ritual, had a chocolate cake—her husband's favorite—with decorative inscription saying "Happy Anniversary." The first slice was placed at his tablet on the altar and the rest served to guests. Smith constructs a composite story of a young man about to take college entrance exams going to the altar where his mother's tablet is and there asking for her to look after him as he takes the exam. If he passes, he may say, "Thanks to you, everything went well. Thank you." If he fails, he will apologize and promise to try harder next time. Smith notes that these interactions are entirely within the developmental phase-appropriate son–mother relationship, for if the mother were living, getting him to pass the exams would be consuming most of her energy and so be the central focus of their relationship at that time in his life.

The dead still care for the living, not by granting favors like Western saints, but in the sense that the dead share the joys of any positive achievement of a family member, and indeed may be given credit for the success. In a TV drama about a recently widowed woman and her 20-year-old daughter, the daughter waits for a letter telling her she has been hired for a job she really wants. When the letter arrives, she opens it and

> clasps the letter to her breast, beams tearfully to her mother, and hurries into the living room. There she kneels before the altar, opens its doors, holds up the letter to her father's photograph and tablet, and bows low. The camera pans to the mother's tear-streaked face. (p. 142)

If the dead can support and encourage, they can also be a potent force in guiding behavior. Plath (1964) quotes a sociology book written in the early 1960s, which assumes it is a common experience to be

> dragged by dad or mom to the front of the household shelf and asked "Do you think you can give any excuse to the ancestors for doing that?" The shelf is associated with the household and with society, so that rebelling before it is like rebelling against the whole world; and that is why a lecture in front of the shelf has such potency. (p. 312)

A Japanese psychologist related to the author that when children have been bad, instead of being sent to their room as in America, they may be sent into the room with the Buddha altar and told to sit there and reflect on their behavior in the presence of their ancestors.

GRAVES

Although the stones in the "cemeteries" around Buddhist temples or among the rice fields remind us of Western graveyards, they are quite different. Each grave is for a family. There is a wide variation in the complexity of each grave, but each has an upright stone on which is carved the family name. Names of individuals may be inscribed on the side or back of upright stone, or on stones set along the sides of a small area in front of the upright stone, but sometimes only the family stone marks the place. Near the front of the grave is a stone incense burner. Behind each grave there is a stand for holding "stupas," boards about 8-feet-high with the top cut in the shape of a Buddhist stupa, on which is written the name of the dead and the date, and on the back, who gave the board. Stupas are placed there as part of the funeral rites. Bodies are cremated (the Japanese say "burned"). In old-style cemeteries, no bones are in the graves. In the newer-style there is a large pit in which bones of all the family members are put. This grave is primarily a ritual site. This is where visits are made and where prayers are said. The grave is cleaned at *O Bon,* the festival described below, and at the equinoxes. Ordinarily, flowers are offered and water is poured over the stone.

On a walk through a cemetery attached to a temple, the author's guide, whose grandmother had died a few months earlier, pointed to the stone slab in the ground and said her grandmother was "here." She then bowed with her hands together, the same gesture made in front of Buddhist statues and at Shinto shrines. When asked what they are doing, Japanese who speak English say they are "praying." When this guide was asked what the prayer was, the answer was that there are no words. The ritual, it seems, is the communication.

Although the graves are the focal points at *O Bon*, at the temple where we stayed there was a steady stream of visitors to the cemetery. We saw old people, a teenager on his way home from school, and an assortment of people of many ages. People would take a bucket from a rack, fill it with water and wash the grave, described in Japanese as "cooling the spirit." Then they would bow and burn incense. Usually they brought a gift or flowers. As are the offerings on the Buddha altar, the gift on the grave is often something the person liked when alive. Canned drinks ranged from beer to carrot juice. Most of the burners at the graves had stubs of incense sticks and many had gifts and flowers—evidence, it seemed, of recent visits. An old woman explained,

> For us old people, visiting the graves is like going to the pictures and so on for the youngsters. You go and meet your dead; you can see their faces in your mind's eye and you can talk to them. You don't get any reply, of course, but it feels good. (Plath, 1964, p. 309)

RITUAL TIME: *O BON*

O Bon, the major summer festival in Japan, celebrates the temporary return of the dead to visit the living. Spirits of the newly dead, *shirei*, people who have died since the last *O Bon*, have a special place in the ceremony. The newly dead are welcomed back in some places with, "You must be very sad," indicating that the family understands that it is as hard for the dead to leave the world of the living as it is for the survivors who are left behind. The dead loosen their ties with the physical world at the end of their first *O Bon*.

The rituals' purpose is the welcoming of spirits of the dead into the village (Smith, 1974).

> The periodic merging of the two worlds (living and dead) strengthens the sense of continuity of the house and reassures the dead of the living's continuing concern for their well being. Neither death nor time can weaken or destroy the unity of the members of the house. (p. 104)

Smith quotes answers to a survey on people's thoughts at *O Bon*. A 63-year-old woman said, "Maybe they come and maybe they don't: I feel that they are here" (p. 150). A 67-year-old man said, "I live in their presence and make a welcoming fire early and a sending-off fire late at *bon*, so that the ancestors will stay longer" (p. 150).

Currently, in many places the public parts of *O Bon* are hardly celebrated. So the ceremony has become privatized. This is part of the decline in the household family in favor of the modern conjugal family. That means, it would seem, that the ceremony takes on a more psychological character, because the remaining reason for the rituals are in the personal relationship with the dead. We will describe the traditional ceremonies. There is a great deal of local variation, but we can describe a typical one (see Gilday, 1993, Smith, 1974).

The festival takes place over 3 days in late summer. It is preceded by a period of preparation. Wildflowers are gathered, paths to graves sites are cleared, and graves themselves are washed and decorated. Fresh flowers, incense, water, and lanterns are readied at the grave site for the first evenings. After sunset on the first day, lanterns at the family grave sites are lit and incense burned to invite the spirits home. The color of these lanterns varies depending on whether a family has lost a member during the preceding year; if so, white, otherwise, red or blue/green. There is one lantern for each deceased member still remembered by someone in the household. Fires are lit at the doorway of the house to guide the spirits. In some areas the entire village forms a torchlight procession, singing and dancing through the village to those homes that have lost a member in the previous year.

In some places, a temporary spirit shrine is built outside the house as a shelter for these spirits during their visit. In other places, this temporary shrine is placed inside the home; in some families, the Buddha altar is thought to hold and shelter the spirits. In early evening, family members gather to welcome back the spirits of the dead, who are greeted very formally, just as honored guests would be.

On the second day of *O Bon*, people visit the grave again, and may go to temple. A Buddhist priest makes rounds to each family in the parish, offering brief prayer at each house, but the day is a family affair and the priest may not even be invited in.

On the third day, the spirits depart. There is a large gathering and a dance in which the spirits are entertained before their departure. "Many of the songs that accompany the dance are laments, expressing the community's regrets that the visit is drawing to a close" (Gilday, 1993, p. 296). And then the spirits return to the *kami* realm. In some places, the gathering just disbands, so it seems the dead can find their own way back. In other places, lanterns are lit by individual families to send the spirits off. Formal farewells are said with expressions such as, "Come back next year." In some areas, a candlelight procession moves

> toward the river where one by one representatives of each household place small boats, bearing the candles, into the current. As far as the eye can see the flickering flotilla plies on. When the candle goes out, it is said, the spirit has been released to the other world. (Gilday, 1993, p. 296)

CONCLUSION

Ancestor worship in Japan is a central part of the culture. When we take out the communal functions of the rituals, that is, those aspects that symbolically reinforce kin group interactions and national identity, we find that ancestor worship is an elaborate set of rituals, supported by a sophisticated theory, by which those who are living maintain personal, emotional bonds with those who have died. The deceased remain individual spirits, available to the living for 35 or 50 years, which in practical terms, is for the lifetime of those who knew them. At critical points in Japanese history, the power of the rituals of ancestor worship have been put in the service of political power, but at its core, ancestor worship is an expression of the human community that cannot be separated by death.

REFERENCES

Doi, T. (1973). *The anatomy of dependence* (John Bester, Trans.). Tokyo: Kodansha International.

Gilday, E. T. (1993). Dancing with the spirit(s): Another view of the other world in Japan. *History of Religions, 32*(3), 273–300.

Gorai, S. (1984). Folk religion and the cult of the ancestors. *Japanese Religions, 13*(2), 26–32.

Jung, C. K. (1938). *Psychology and religion.* New Haven, CT: Yale University Press.

Kaneko, S. (1990). Dimensions of religiosity among believers in Japanese folk religion. *Journal for the Scientific Study of Religion, 29*(1), 1–18.

Kapleau, P. (1965). *The three pillars of Zen: Teaching, practice, enlightenment.* Boston: Beacon Press.

Klass, D. (1988). *Parental grief: Solace and resolution.* New York: Springer.

Klass, D. (1993). Solace and immortality: Bereaved parents' continuing bond with their children. *Death Studies, 17,* 343–368.

LaFleur, W. R. (1992). *Liquid life: Abortion and Buddhism in Japan.* Princeton, NJ: Princeton University Press.

Long, J. B. (1987). Reincarnation. In L. E. Sullivan (Ed.), *Death, afterlife, and the soul* (pp. 138–145). New York: Macmillan.

Offner, C. B. (1979). Continuing concern for the departed. *Japanese Religions, 11* (1), 1–16.

Plath, D. W. (1964). Where the family of god is the family: The role of the dead in Japanese households. *American Anthropologist, 66* (2), 300–317.

Smith, R. J. (1974). *Ancestor worship in contemporary Japan.* Stanford, CA: Stanford University Press.

Volkan, V. (1981). *Linking objects and linking phenomena: A study of the forms, symptoms, metapsychology, and therapy of complicated mourning.* New York: International Universities Press.

Winnicott, D. W. (1953). Transitional objects and transitional phenomena. *International Journal of Psychoanalysis, 34,* 89–97.

Yamamoto, J., Okonogi, K., Iwasaki, T., and Yoshimura, S. (1969). Mourning in Japan. *American Journal of Psychiatry, 125,* 1661–1665.

Yanagawa, K., & Abe, Y. (1983). Cross-cultural implications of a behavioral response. *Japanese Journal of Religious Studies, 10*(4), 289–307.

Part Three

Bereaved Children

In the previous section, Paul Rosenblatt asked what long term grieving is. So much energy has been spent on how the bereaved need to give up the deceased that we have little sense of what an ongoing connection might look like, and by inference, what long-term grief might look like. It seems appropriate to begin this discussion with chapters on children's grief.

Many misconceptions about bereaved children exist. We will discuss bereaved siblings later, but here we talk about children whose parents died. One misconception is that children will quickly complete their mourning. Studies of children who have lost parents have often focused on outcome. The studies assume that at some time the children should have x, y, or z qualities to indicate that the children have completed their grief and are either psychologically damaged or psychologically healthy as a result. If they are in a healthy state, researchers assumed their grief was completed. If they were in some perceived state of damage, the focus was on how to prevent long-term sequelae. There was general agreement that it was desirable to prevent long-term damage after the death of a parent. By their very nature, children are always changing and there are always long-term sequelae, for the past is always prologue. The sequelae, however, may be positive as well as negative.

It is interesting that the desire to prevent any lasting interruption of the child's life after the death of a parent came into being just as the word "orphan" was dropped from common usage. Being an orphan is a permanent condition. A child might be taken in, or even adopted, by surrogate parents, but the orphan label recognized the reality of the change in the child's life. The studies reported in these chapters show that even as the adult world tries to deny it, if a child loses a parent, there is no way the child's life can be reconstituted as it was before. The children know that. We begin to appreciate children's capacity to cope, to be creative, and to prevail as we let them speak for themselves.

Another common perception of children was that they were simply bereft. They were viewed as passive recipients of their fate. Their loss and their way of dealing with it was often not considered in detail, or was viewed as pure pain, pure absence, or pure defense. As these chapters indicate from the very beginning, whether we are talking to a child or to an adolescent, we find them engaged in a process of trying to make sense of the experience. One of the ways they do this is by finding a way to carry the deceased parent with them. Like Oliver Twist, the fictional orphan, they evoke the presence of the parent they once had even as they negotiate the often-harsh realities of their changed world.

The first two chapters in this section, Chapter 5 by Phyllis Silverman and Steven Nickman and Chapter 6 by Claude Normand, Phyllis Silverman, and Steven Nickman, use data from the MGH/Harvard Medical School Child Bereavement Project. These chapters begin to flesh out our understandings of how bonds with deceased parents develop, are sustained, and change over time. The process has cognitive, interactive, and emotional aspects. In Chapter 7, Betty Buchsbaum illustrates this process clearly. Focusing on cognitive aspects of the process, she demonstrates how the bond with the deceased parent changes over time. The children develop and hold images of their dead parents in a manner appropriate to their age and developmental stage. Therefore, the images change and mature as the children mature and grow. Chapter 6 supports the idea with which Betty Buchsbaum closes her chapter, that resolution is associated with an understanding of who the deceased was as a person. Again, this connection is not a static phenomenon. As we study children retroactively and prospectively, we begin to understand the long-term meaning of the loss. Throughout their lives, children will work on the meaning of the death, albeit intermittently.

In Chapter 8, Kirsten Tyson-Rawson reports on the lives of college-age women whose fathers have died. Her findings are similar to the findings with younger children. She reminds us that the death of a parent requires the bereaved to rediscover meaning by formulating new representations of the self, the surviving others and the deceased; but most important, we need to keep in mind that the shift is in the relationship between them.

We begin to see that the meaning of continuing bonds with the deceased is not clearly defined. All the authors in this section do not define the same activity as examples of the continuing bond. Active remembering and self-invented rituals can be seen as defensive techniques or as ways of maintaining connections. These chapters agree, however, in the call to look again with new appreciation at the consequence of the child's ability to have inner conversations with the deceased in which the child plays both roles. In the same way, we need to look carefully at the data that identify children who actively distance themselves from their memories and from connections with their deceased parent. Like Normand et al., Tyson-Rawson found a more negative theme in a small subsample where images of the parent and of the parent's death are intrusive and disturbing, and like Normand et al., she raises questions about the nature of their relationship before the parent's death. As we develop a model of grief that includes continuing interactions with the dead, we need to be open to both the positive and negative consequences of this activity.

These chapters also remind us that surviving parents, as well as other significant adults in children's lives, can play an active role in facilitating children's connections and in giving them information they need to vitalize their memory. To do so, adults need to be comfortable with their own bonds with the deceased.

P. R. S.
S. N.

Chapter 5

Children's Construction
of Their Dead Parents

Phyllis R. Silverman and Steven L. Nickman

This chapter describes how children construct connections to their deceased parents. It utilizes data primarily from the Massachusetts General Hospital/Harvard Medical School Child Bereavement Study, a longitudinal, prospective study of the impact of a parent's death on children from ages 6 to 17. Both children and their surviving parents were interviewed in their homes approximately 4 months after the death and then 1 and 2 years later. This is a community sample from the greater Boston area, recruited through the funeral directors that served the bereaved families. Interviews with these respondents included many open-ended questions, thus allowing them to tell their stories in their own words (Silverman & Worden, 1992). To provide a cross-cultural perspective, some data were utilized from a parallel study conducted in Israel in the greater Haifa area. Families were recruited through the school system, shortly after a parent's death.

Analysis of data from the Child Bereavement Study called our attention to the way children were talking about the deceased. They seemed to be maintaining relationships to their dead parents rather than letting go (Silverman, Nickman, & Worden, 1992; Silverman & Worden, 1992). This did not seem to be connected to their yearning for the deceased or wishing that he or she would return. Instead, we found that children had sets of memories, feelings, and behaviors that, as they saw it, brought them closer to their deceased parents. We called these activities "constructing" the deceased. This inner representation or construction led the children to remain in relationship with the deceased. We further noted that this relationship seemed to change as the children matured and as the intensity of their grief lessened. We postulated that this relationship seemed to be part of the normal bereavement process, in contrast to what we understood from traditional bereavement theory, which advocated the need to divest oneself of the emotional energy invested in the relationship with the deceased. We have been taught that only then could grief be "resolved." Instead, we saw that the construction seemed

This study was sponsored by Harvard Medical School's Department of Psychiatry at Massachusetts General Hospital. It was co-directed by Phyllis R. Silverman and J. William Worden and funded by the National Institute of Mental Health, the National Funeral Directors Association, and the Hillenbrand Foundation. A similar study conducted at Haifa University in Israel was directed by Phyllis Silverman, Anita Weiner, and Nava El Ad and funded by the Littauer Foundation.

to provide the children with comfort and seemed to facilitate their coping with their grief. These findings were consistent with those of other researchers working with bereaved adult populations (Klass, 1988; Rubin, 1984; Shuchter, 1986). Our own thinking about the grieving process was that coping did not involve recovery or resolution but a process of adaptation and change (Silverman, 1966, 1986, 1988). This process involved negotiating anew the meaning of the loss coincidental with other changes in the life cycle (Silverman, 1989). Based on these observations from the Child Bereavement Study, we suggest that learning to remember and finding a way of maintaining a connection to the deceased, consistent with the child's cognitive development and family dynamics, are also normative aspects of the accommodation process that allows the child to go on living in the face of the loss.

We came to see this construction of the lost person as an ongoing cognitive process. The nature of the construction of the deceased in children was connected to a child's developmental level with particular reference to children's typical changing ability to know themselves and to know others (Kegan, 1982; Piaget 1954). For example, a critical developmental shift takes place when children move from seeing others in terms of how these others can meet their needs to seeing others as people with needs of their own and with whom some reciprocity is required for a relationship to be sustained. While the deceased does not change, the child's ability to understand a given set of data about this person will change as the child matures. Adult behavior can be characterized as changing and developing as well (Kegan, 1982), so that we saw similar changing constructions of the deceased in the surviving parents. The inner representation of who died changes as mourners move through the life cycle and their sense of self and other continues to evolve (Belanky et al., 1986; Kegan, 1982; Silverman, 1988).

The word "construction" derives from the Latin *struere*, to make something out of component parts; to construe is to analyze or set out logically the figurative aspects of a thing. In the psychological literature, constructivism refers to a theoretical position that regards persons or systems as constituting or constructing their own reality (Gergen, 1985). In this context the mourner's attempt at maintaining a connection to the deceased or lost parent can be seen as an active effort to make sense out of his or her experience and to make it part of his or her reality.

Children's cognitive processes include their ability to experience complex feeling states as well as inborn qualities and their intellectual and social development. Piaget has observed that development involves a push toward greater mastery of one's situation (Piaget, 1954). In Kegan's view (1982), mastery emerges as children and/or adults construct and reconstruct their world to find greater coherence and new meanings: These can unify memories and feelings into a temporary coherent whole that prevails until the child or adult moves to the next stage of development. Calling up memories of specific events, abstractions concerning the nature of past interactions, and on the highest level, descriptions of the deceased's personality, likes, and dislikes will depend on the individual's level of development.

This process cannot be separated from the interaction in the family system. We see the role of the surviving parent as important in enhancing the children's ability to construct a relationship to the deceased.

THE STUDY POPULATION

A total of 70 families with 125 children were interviewed in the Child Bereavement Study. There are an almost equal number of boys and girls in the sample, with an average age of 11.6 years. Among the children, 74% lost a father and 26% a mother. The average age of the surviving parent was 41 years, with a range of 30 to 57 years for the surviving mothers and 33 to 50 for surviving fathers. Fifty-eight percent ($n = 72$) of the children experienced the death of their parent from a long illness. Seventy percent of the study population were Roman Catholic, reflecting the large concentration of Catholics in the greater Boston area.

In the parallel study of Israeli Jewish children's grief, 43 children in 23 families were interviewed. Families where the death was war related were not included. There are no significant differences between these samples, in ages and gender of surviving parent, ages and gender of the children, or in whether the deaths were sudden or anticipated. Israeli children, like their American peers, constructed a relationship with their dead parent. Therefore, where appropriate, examples from these children's experience will be included to provide a cross-cultural perspective.

Data presented in this paper were taken from semistructured research interviews with these bereaved children and their surviving parents. A subset of 24 families, with children between the ages of 11 and 13, was identified and submitted to further in-depth analysis. This subset was used to determine how the children's view of the deceased changed over time (see Chapter 6, this volume). In this chapter, we use this subset of the data to look at how the parents' response affected the children's developing connections to the deceased.

All the interviews were taped, and when they were not transcribed we listened to the tapes. Areas covered in these interviews included questions about the death, mourning behavior, and thoughts about the deceased, in part informed by one author's prior research with bereaved children (Silverman, 1989; Silverman & Silverman, 1979). Additional qualitative data were drawn from the children's responses to the Child's Understanding of Death questionnaire (Smilansky, 1987). The analysis of data followed that recommended by Strauss (1987), leading to a development of theory that is grounded in the data (Glaser & Strauss, 1967). In this instance we were trying to develop theory related to the bereavement process. We studied a group of interviews in order to identify themes and to verify the existence of the construction, and then we read additional records to see if the same themes were present (Strauss, 1987). In the remainder of the chapter, we will describe the elements out of which a connection is made.

FINDINGS

Understanding the Finality of the Death

An important issue that needed to be reviewed before we could proceed was whether the children's efforts at connecting with the deceased were the consequences of a faulty understanding of the concept of death. Findings from research with nonbereaved children raise questions about the age at which a child understands the irreversibility and finality of death (Lonetto, 1980). If these children did not understand the finality and irreversibility of death, then we would have no basis for our formulation. However, findings from the Smilansky questionnaire about their understanding of death indicated that these bereaved children, regardless of their age, seemed very aware of the finality and irreversibility of death. For example, one 7-year-old girl had no doubt about the finality of her father's death: "Sometimes I want to talk to him, but I go to sleep fast so I won't think about his being gone." A 10-year-old said, "He's not with me and it hurts."

It was with great difficulty that these children accustomed themselves to the fact that their parents were dead. The contrast between presence and absence often seemed too difficult for them to contemplate and their discomfort was very apparent. A 10-year-old boy said in response to the standardized question, "What does it mean when someone dies?", "I can't think about that." It seemed impossible to think that his father was gone. Some talked about the shock they felt when they heard the news. This was especially true for children whose parents died suddenly. An Israeli child said she had to go outside to look at the sun. She could not understand how anything could be the same when she was told that her father was dead.

Their new reality required an understanding of death not typical for nonbereaved children of the same ages. A 12-year-old girl whose mother died after a long illness said that she could not talk about her mother because it "simply hurts too much." She added, "However, I don't want her to come back and be in such pain." When asked how he felt after the death, one 13-year-old boy said plaintively, "I don't know . . . I just know he's not here anymore." The connection to the deceased cannot be dismissed as merely a way of denying the finality of the loss. The special tension in these children was very clear. While being very aware that their parents were dead, they experienced the parents as still existing in themselves and in their world, sometimes attributing living qualities to their parents' spirits. This duality caused cognitive dissonance for some and may have accounted for some of the inarticulateness seen shortly after the loss.

Strategies of Connection

Children engaged in five types of activities that seemed to lead to their maintaining a connection to the deceased parent during this period. The activities were (1) locating the deceased, (2) experiencing the deceased, (3) reaching out to the deceased to initiate a connection, (4) remembering (waking memories), and (5) keeping something that belonged to the deceased (linking objects). The majority of the children reported some activity in each of these areas. There seemed to be no significant relationship between the type of death or the gender or age of the children and any of these responses. The construction of connections to their dead parents was also part of the experience of Israeli children. However, there was some variation in where they located the deceased. Each aspect is exemplified below with anecdotal data from interviews with the children.

Locating the Deceased   When asked where they thought their parent was presently, most of the children were able to locate the deceased. Seventy-four percent ($n = 92$) believed in a place called "heaven". American children were more likely to think of their parent as being in heaven, while Israeli children when asked where they thought their parent was now, often answered "in the grave." Some Israeli children did refer to their parents as being in heaven or in the "Garden of Eden." Consistent with their concept of heaven, American children are more likely, in contrast to Israeli children, to feel watched by their dead parent (chi-square $[1, N = 168] = 7.17, p > .001$). There was no relationship between a child's age and his/her belief about an afterlife, nor was there any relationship between belief system or country and how frequently children dreamed or thought about their parent. Although 70% of our American sample was Roman Catholic, and Catholic theology encourages these children to believe in the existence of heaven and in a life after death, there was no statistical relationship between the children's expressed beliefs and their religious background. Many non-Catholic children shared a similar belief system in which their parent had some form of existence in a place called heaven. Even children in their early teens, who were otherwise developmentally and cognitively sophisticated, did not always make a distinction between the state of being of the spirit and the body. Many continued to endow the deceased, now residing in heaven, with concrete attributes of a living person, e.g., that dead people see, hear, feel and move. Others recognized that there was a difference between the body that was buried and the soul that was in heaven; nonetheless, they endowed the soul with living qualities of vision, hearing, and mobility. By contrast, matched nonbereaved control children were less likely to endow a deceased person, talking hypothetically, with living attributes. Locating the deceased in a distant place (heaven) seemed to help the bereaved children make sense of their experience—although the deceased cannot see, feel, and move here, they may be able to do so in another location (where I cannot see).

The words of a 14-year-old Catholic boy whose father died reflected this:

> I want my father to see me perform. If I said a dead person can't see then I would not be able to have my wish that he see what I am doing. I believe that the dead see, hear, move. Don't ask me how, I just believe it. Heaven is a mysterious place. My father is with all the other relatives that died.

Belief in heaven allowed this boy to maintain a sense that his father was still in his life. Two years after her father died, a 17-year-old American Jewish girl was very clear about the permanency and finality of death, as would be expected given her age. The concept of heaven or an afterlife is not an important part of her religious orientation. However, in her response to a question about whether or not the dead can see or hear, she said, "Yes, the dead can see and hear. It's what I would *like* to think, so he could hear comforting words and . . . that maybe he can see significant events in my life." A similar cognitive construction was made by a 15-year-old girl who both saw her father in heaven and recognized that some of what she was experiencing was of her own making: "I think heaven is not a definite place. . . . I know I'm not imagining him . . . it's not as if I actually see him standing there, but I feel him and, like, in my mind I hear his voice."

Experiencing the Deceased   Believing that their dead parents were watching them was an extension of this construction of the parent in heaven and provided these children with yet another way of connecting with their dead parents. Eighty-one percent ($n = 101$) of the children felt that their parents were watching them, and of those who felt watched, 57% ($n = 71$) were "scared" by this. For these children, their uneasiness was related to a fear that their parent might not approve of what they were doing.

> I sometimes think he is watching me. It scares me because sometimes he might see me do something he wouldn't like. Like, it's weird . . . it's not scary . . . like if you're doing something, like if someone's watching you, you don't do it, if it's bad. You don't do it if someone's watching.

This 11-year-old child saw his father in the role of disciplinarian and his feelings about his father included experiencing him as a helpful external control to supplement his incompletely formed superego. A teen-aged girl talked about how important good grades were for her mother. She almost playfully said she could "imagine my mother yelling in heaven if I didn't do well in school."

In contrast, a child who did not have a good relationship with her father pictured him in a dream with a mean facial expression. She could not make out his attitude toward her with any certainty. The dream frightened her and seemed to reflect an aspect of their relationship before the death that was not affirming of the child. Whether the parent was disciplinarian, nurturer, or one whose response might be unpredictable, these children experienced the parent in a way that reflected aspects of their relationship before the death.

Some children experienced their parent as communicating with them in a benevolent way that reflected the parent's status as a spirit. One 9-year-old boy saw flashing colored dots in his bedroom at night, and told us he liked to think that it was his mother trying to be in touch with him. He asked his father if this was possible. His father allowed the possibility and did not try to rationalize the experience away. An adolescent girl noticed a puff of wind blowing open the door of a restaurant where both she and her mother had worked. She thought of the wind as her mother's presence coming to visit. This became a standing, good-natured joke between herself and the others working in the restaurant. A 7-year-old Israeli girl talked, a year after her father's death, about his watching her. She said, "He looks at me from his star and I say hello to him. When he talks to me the star changes color."

Another way of experiencing the deceased was through dreams. Many children (55%, $n = 69$) dreamed about their parents and for almost all of these children ($n = 63$), the parents were alive in the dreams: "I dreamed he met me on the way home from school and that he hugged me. When I woke up I felt so sad that I won't have that anymore."

Even though there was sadness when faced with the fact that it was only a dream, some children found these dreams comforting: "When I wake up from these dreams, I know she's gone but when I dream, it feels like she is there and it's reality"; "I'm not sure but I hear his voice at night. It's probably in my dreams. He tells me he likes what I did, that I did real good." Experiencing the deceased in this way tempered the pain and provided an occasion for the child to get parental approval: "It feels good to remember, to feel that he is still part of the family."

Children who found the deceased parent available to them in this way attributed some initiative to the parent and saw themselves as recipients. At some level, they knew that this construction was probably coming from something within themselves. This may be similar to what Weisman (1972) has called "middle knowledge": a partial awareness of the reality of death that forms the best compromise between an unpleasant truth and a wished-for state of events.

Reaching Out to the Deceased   Children also took some initiative to keep a connection. Visiting the cemetery was one way of actively seeking a place where they could "find" the deceased. For many this was the place where they had the last contact with the parent. A 12-year-old girl whose mother died said, "I go to the cemetery when I feel sad and I need someone to talk with. Going to the cemetery makes me feel close." A 15-year-old boy passed the cemetery on the way home from school: "I don't talk about it much, but I stop by to visit about once a week. I tell him about my day and things I've done."

Speaking to the deceased was another way of bringing the parent into the child's life. Fifty-seven percent ($n = 71$) spoke to the deceased parent. The initiative to choose the place was clearly with the child. A teen-aged girl said, "I say, 'Hi, how are you' when I go by her picture in the house." A 10-year-old boy reported, "In my mind, I talk to him, I tell him what I did today, about the fish I caught and that I did real good."

While 43% ($n = 29$) of these children, mostly younger, felt they received an answer, they were not usually able to tell us what their parent said. A 15-year-old girl said, "It's not that I hear him, but in my head I felt he said, 'You'll be O.K. Carry on.'" A 10-year-old Israeli girl said that she talks, in her heart, to her mother. A 16-year-old described her experience a year after her mother died, "My mother was my friend. I could talk to her about anything. I talk to her but she can't respond. She doesn't tell me what to do, but like she helps me—I can't explain it."

The ability to take an active role in relation to the death of their parents was reflected in children's answers to the question: "What advice would you give another child who had lost a parent?" There were children who could not answer this question, saying "I don't know" or "I can't think of anything." These were the same children who did not dream about the deceased, and who did not talk to the deceased. They did not seem to have a place, as yet, for the deceased in their lives. The majority of children, however, did have suggestions and most counseled fortitude. They said they would advise another child "to not let it get you down all the time," and that "it's possible to carry on." This included the advice, "It's best to think about the person who died and to remember the good times that you had"; "Just think of them as often as you can"; "It helps to go to the cemetery a lot to let him know." These responses reflected the ability of some children to organize their experiences and to reflect on what would be helpful to others in the same plight.

Waking Memories   The dead parent was present in the children's waking thoughts as well. These waking thoughts involved both reflection and memory. At the 4-month interview 90% ($n = 99$) of the children were still thinking about their parents at least several times a week. When asked what they thought about, most children remembered in fairly literal and concrete terms what they did with their parents. A 15-year-old girl whose mother died said, "I think about the stupid little things we did together." A 7-year-old remembered her father: "I think about all the things that he used to bring me and how he used to flip me over."

It would seem logical to consider this new construction as building on the preexisting introject of the parent as it existed in the child during the parent's life. A 12-year-old described her father as she remembers him, "If you were ever in trouble he would help you out, no matter what. He would try to help out, whatever you did. When I needed an operation he was the one who stayed with me." We see the current construction as an intensification, fortification, or other modification of this introject to render it more serviceable to the child, and more accessible to consciousness in the parent's absence. This same child talked about her current relationship to her father:

> I keep my room nice and tidy now, that's the way he had everything. Before I would just throw stuff down. Now every morning I pick everything up. I know it would please him. He'd understand if I screwed up in school. Mom would get real mad. So now when I get a bad grade I "talk" to him about it.

The process of identification is clearly involved here but we see it as a conscious, changing process.

A few children reported that they still could not believe the death was real and sometimes they forgot their parent had died. Others, reflecting on their new reality, thought about how hard it was to get along without their parents and wished for them back. An Israeli boy, age 9, said, "Every time I open the door, I wait 5 minutes to feel that something is moving. I am sure that my father is here. I need and want my father to come back, but it doesn't happen." Such reflections were painful and contrasted to the comforting memories that some children counseled a hypothetical bereaved child to call upon.

Linking Objects   Having an object belonging to the deceased was an important means of maintaining a link to him or her. Linking objects, a term used by Volkan (1981), refers to an aspect of the relationship or an object from that relationship that keeps the mourner living in the past. A more positive link or connection can be found in the concept of a "transitional object"—one that connects one realm of experience with another (Winnicott, 1953; Worden, 1991). These transitional objects provide comfort while one is engaged in the initial mourning process. Seventy-seven percent ($n = 95$) of the children had something personal that belonged to their dead parents. Children acquired these objects in different ways. Often it was something the deceased had given them or something belonging to the deceased that the children had taken after the death. Sometimes the surviving parents had given the objects to them or told them they could take what they wanted from the deceased's possessions. For the most part, children kept these items either on their person or in their room. One teen-aged girl said, "It makes me feel good to wear his shirt to school." Another girl said, "I carry his key chain, it makes me feel good . . . the way some people use crystals or whatever."

As the first year of mourning progressed, some of these transitional objects had become less powerful for the children and took on more of the characteristics of a "keepsake" (Worden, 1991). A 13-year-old boy took his father's baseball hat and his cologne right after he learned that he was dead. He did not understand why but just reached out and took what was there and put it in his room. A year later, both were still in the room. The hat now hung in a remote corner rather than on the bedpost. Two years after the death, he was not sure what had happened to the hat. However, he described feeling very reassured by his feeling that his father was always with him, making sure that "I am safe and stuff."

Role of the Surviving Parent

We see the process of constructing a connection to the deceased as part of an ongoing family dialogue. Surviving parents have also experienced a loss and are grieving: a part of this grief work may be the development of an inner representation of the deceased for themselves. For example, a mother of three reported that, "There have been times when I have felt he has been close by . . . watching over us." Another mother reported, "I go to the cemetery to talk to him when I feel that things are too much for me. I talk to him about the kids, the Red Sox, the elections."

Thus, helping children to carry out a similar process may be a natural outgrowth of the parents' grieving. They generally saw the need for such memorial activity that kept the deceased's presence alive in the family although they did not always articulate it in so many words. Even when they themselves saw their marriage as troubled or felt negatively about their spouse, some were able to foster their children's remembering the deceased in a positive way: "We have to remember Daddy as he was smiling in the sun." This is what one mother told her 10-year-old boy whose sadness was very clear and who could not talk about his father. This boy told the interviewer what his mother told him about how to remember his father:

> She says we'll pray every night for Daddy and that he'll be able to see me. She says we have to remember Daddy outside in the sunshine laughing, not like he looked when he died. I asked if Daddy can help me now, if he'll always be with me. Mom said "yes."

On the other hand, ambivalence can in the long run render a surviving parent unhelpful to the child. For example, one father felt that his deceased wife had been more involved in the community than in their home or with their marriage. He reported that the children forgot how angry they were with her for not being available a good deal of the time. He did not miss her as much as he thought he would. He reported asking his teen-aged daughter, from time to time, in the first months after the death if she wanted to go to the cemetery: "We've gone three or four times. I ask her if she wants to go. She will always say yes, but she never asks me. We just stand and say a prayer."

Within the year this changed. The child reported that her father forgot that he had promised to take her to the cemetery on the anniversary of the death and that the father would not talk to his children about their mother, which made his daughter very uncomfortable about sharing her feelings or dreams with him. He remarried within the year. His daughter reported how she remembered and cried in the privacy of her room. She made herself a scrapbook of pictures of the mother that comforted her when she looked at it. She was beginning to withdraw when she discovered that she could talk with her older sister and her friends who knew her mother. This was very helpful as they talked about the mother and what she had done. (This confirms the need for others to facilitate this process. When the parent is not available, significant others in the child's network can play this role.)

On the other hand, some parents were eager to talk but were met with resistance on the part of the child: "I know my father would listen but I don't want to talk." This same boy one year later said, "Talking makes me sad, but it is better than thinking about it alone. My father listens and it really helps."

Children seemed to be comforted by their ability to remember. The comfort does not necessarily have to come from direct conversation with the surviving parent. One 14-year-old, although he did not share his reaction with his mother, commented, "It makes me feel good when I hear my mother talking to someone about how nice my father was."

Specific Parental Contributions to Remembering

There were a number of ways in which parents contributed to the formation, in the child, of a continuing inner representation of the deceased parent. They talked about the deceased with the children. For example, one mother told the interviewer,

> There are things that will remind us of him. When I see the family, when we are together and we'll say, "Dad would like that." It comes up like that, either myself or one the children brings it up. We talk about something he would like or dislike. Then we would become quiet and some of us would laugh; others would take it sad, depending on what's said. My daughter is most ready to talk. Usually at night when she had the last operation [she has a chronic orthopedic problem], I had her sleep with me. We would be in bed and we'd be talking about him . . . he had always been with her when she needed surgery before . . . and how she missed him. And then we would start laughing and then she would fall asleep.

Parents provided the children with opportunities to participate in activities that memorialized the deceased. A 12-year-old boy said, "Me and my father went to Mass, in memory of her."

A mother of a 12-year-old girl said,

> I always invite her to go to the cemetery with me. We go on holidays to put flowers on the grave. We live near the cemetery. I know she also goes by herself. She used to skate near there with her father. I think it is good, it seems to comfort her.

Surviving parents gave children mementos of the deceased (belongings, photographs, jewelry, articles of clothing): "I let the children pick out what they wanted. I thought they needed to have something of him."

Surviving parents often were alert to children's feelings about the deceased as they were communicated verbally and nonverbally. For one mother, her children left no doubt how they felt when she tried to give away all of her husband's clothes. She had the flexibility to stop when the children got really angry with her and let them take what they wanted. She had given her daughter the father's rosary beads, which the daughter now keeps with her at all times. The mother had not thought they would care about his clothes.

The father of an 11-year-old was aware that sometimes his son's silence about his mother was because the boy was trying to protect his father. In the first year, the father had cried whenever they tried to talk about the mother. At the end of the second year, he now says,

It's becoming easier to talk about my wife at home. Quite often I try to wait for my boy to bring it up. But I do initiate some conversation. I try to bring it up in a natural way. I jut try to bring up a similar situation when my wife was alive, or I ask, "What do you think Mom would have done if this happened?" I'll ask him if he's thinking about his mother. At a particular time of the year I ask if there is something special that he used to do with Momma that he wants to do now.

Surviving parents helped their children to find language to express their feelings. One mother of two sons, ages 11 and 13, recognized that the older boy never talked to her about his father. She tried to find ways of encouraging him: "Sometimes I try to explain how other people feel. I ask if that applies to him. I figure maybe if I give him some words, that would help."

Some parents showed the child directly that they valued the deceased and also valued the child's relationship to the deceased. This same mother of two sons told one, "That sounds like something Dad would say."

Several parents used humor to modulate the pain of the loss when thinking about the deceased. One family laughed together at Thanksgiving: "I told them that if Dad is watching he'd be pleased. We did his job of cutting vegetables and we did it like he would have liked."

Changes Over Time

There were children at the first interview who did not dream and seemed to have little or no connection with the deceased. By the second interview some of these children found it easier to remember. An 11-year-old girl reported during the first interview that she did not dream about her mother and could not describe her to the interviewer. She was unable to concentrate at school because of her thoughts about her mother's absence. She did not have anything that belonged to her mother. Her sadness was palpable. She could not talk about her feelings, and she did not feel close to anyone in the family with whom she could talk about her mother. By the end of the first year she began to dream. She wanted to keep the dreams private but said they went back to before her mother died. She visited the cemetery, where she talked to her mother and said she could hear her mother's voice in her head, giving her good advice. She took some of her mother's jewelry and kept it in her room. School improved and her sadness seemed less pervasive. She talked to her friends and her father about her mother and what she was like:

This Christmas was hard but I got through it, because I got used to it. Just looking at her picture is hard because I miss her. I think about whether or not she can see me and she can hear me. Is she happy? I hear her voice in my head telling me it's okay. I talk to my friends I can trust and to my dad because he loved her too and understands what I am going through.

It is not clear if this child became more able to confront the loss and tolerate sad feelings because she found a way of connecting with her deceased mother or whether being able to tolerate her feelings enabled her to connect with her mother.

DISCUSSION

We have described an aspect of the bereavement process in children: the establishment of a set of memories, feelings, and actions having to do with the deceased that we have called "constructing" the deceased. We have presented some examples of this process from another country in recognition that this is a phenomenon that is common in other cultures as well. This inner representation or construction leads the child to remain in a relationship with the deceased and this relationship changes as the child matures and as the intensity of the grief lessens. The concept of identification is insufficient to describe what we have observed. The child may construct a sense of the deceased and develop an inner representation of that person that does not involve (at either a conscious or an unconscious level) becoming like that person. Memorializing, remembering, and knowing who died are active processes that may continue throughout the child's entire life. Rubin (1985) observed that there seemed to be a relationship between the comfort and fluidity with which the bereaved can relate to the representations of deceased and their ability to cope effectively with the loss. While the intensity of the relationship with the deceased must diminish with time, it does not disappear. We are not talking about living in the past, but rather recognizing how the past informs our present.

On taking these findings into consideration, our understanding of the bereavement process shifts. We cannot look at bereavement as a psychological state that ends if and when one recovers. The intensity of feelings may lessen and the child become more future- rather than past-oriented, but a concept of closure that requires a determination of when the bereavement process ends does not seem compatible with the view suggested by these findings. We propose that rather than emphasizing letting go, the emphasis should be on negotiating and renegotiating the meaning of the loss over time. While the loss is permanent and unchanging, the process is not. Our data suggest that to facilitate this process, we need to consider bereavement as a cognitive as well as an emotional process that takes place in a social context of which the deceased is a part.

Accommodation may be a more suitable term than recovery or closure for what takes place as a result of a death in the family. However, accommodation in this context should not be viewed as a static phenomenon either. Accommodation is rather a continuing set of activities related both to others and to shifting self-perceptions, as the child's mind and body change, that affect the way the child constructs meaning. In this process the child seeks to gain not only an understanding of the meaning of death, but a sense of the meaning of this now dead parent in his or her life. This requires the development of a language in the family for talking about the death and the person who died.

In conclusion, we have identified ways in which the child maintains a connection to the deceased parent. We see these data as challenging the traditional clinical practice of encouraging the bereaved to disengage from the deceased. The focus in facilitating mourning may need to be on how to change connections and give the relationship a new perspective rather than on how to separate.

REFERENCES

Belanky, M., Clinchy, B., Goldberger, N., & Tarule, J. (1986). *Women's Ways of Knowing*. New York: Basic Books.

Gergen, K. J. (1985). The social constructionist movement in modern psychology. *American Psychologist, 40*(3), 266–273.

Glaser, B., & Strauss, A. (1967). *The discovery of grounded theory*. Chicago: Aldine.

Kegan, R. (1982). *The evolving self: Problem and process in human development*. Cambridge, MA: Harvard University Press.

Klass, D. (1988). *Parental grief: Solace and resolution*. New York: Springer.

Lonetto, R. (1980). *Children's conceptions of Death* (Volume 3). New York: Springer.

Piaget, J. (1954). *The construction of reality in the child* (M. Cook, Trans.). New York: Basic Books.

Rubin, S.S. (1985). The resolution of bereavement: A clinical focus on the relationship to the deceased. *Psychotherapy: Theory, Research, Training and Practice, 22*(2), 231–235.

Shuchter, S. R. (1986). *Dimensions of grief: Adjusting to the death of a spouse*. San Francisco, CA: Jossey-Bass.

Silverman, P. R. (1966). Services for the widowed during the period of bereavement. In *National Conference on Social Welfare, Social Work Practice* (pp. 170-189). New York: Columbia University Press.

Silverman, P. R. (1986). *Widow to widow*. New York: Springer.

Silverman, P. R. (1988). In search of new selves: Accommodating to widowhood. In L. A. Bond and B. Wagner (Eds)., *Families in transition: Primary programs that work* (pp. 200–220). Newbury Park, CA: Sage Publications.

Silverman, P. R. (1989). The impact of the death of a parent on college age women. *Psychiatric Clinics of North America, 10*, 33, 387–404.

Silverman, P. R., Nickman, S., & Worden, J. W. (1992). Detachment revisited. *American Journal of Orthopsychiatry, 62*(4), 494–593.

Silverman, P. R., & Worden, J. W. (1992). Children's reactions to the death of a parent in the early months after the death. *American Journal of Orthopsychiatry, 62*(4), 93–104.

Silverman, S. M., & Silverman P. R. (1979). Parent-child communication in widowed families. *American Journal of Psychotherapy, 33*, 428–441.

Smilansky, S. (1987). *On death: Helping children understand and cope*. New York: Peter Lang.

Strauss, A. L. (1987). *Qualitative analysis for social scientists*. Cambridge: Cambridge University Press.

Volkan, V. D. (1981). *Linking objects and linking phenomena*. New York: International Universities Press.

Weisman, A. (1972). *On dying and denying: A psychiatric study of terminality*. New York: Behavioral Publications.

Winnicott, D. W. (1953). Transitional objects and transitional phenomena. *International Journal of Psycho-Analysis, 34*, 89–97.

Worden, J. W. (1991). *Grief counseling and grief therapy: A handbook for the mental health practitioner*. New York: Springer.

Chapter 6

Bereaved Children's Changing Relationships with the Deceased

Claude L. Normand, Phyllis R. Silverman, and Steven L. Nickman

In Chapter 5, Silverman and Nickman described how children, shortly after the death of one of their parents, construct a connection to the deceased that facilitates their coping with that parent's death. They questioned whether their connections to the deceased would be sustained by these children over time, and if modified with time, what these changes would look like. In this chapter, we describe the analysis of data that was undertaken to answer these questions. Findings from this analysis show that relationships with the deceased were sustained over the first 2 years after the death of a mother or father; they were not static but evolved and changed, in both form and content.

This chapter uses data from the Massachusetts General Hospital/Harvard Medical School Child Bereavement Study. The findings reported here are based on an analysis of the responses of a subsample of 24 children interviewed as part of the study. These children were 10, 11, and 12 years of age at the time of the death of one of their parents. This age group was chosen in part to ensure a level of verbal ability allowing for potentially more elaborate responses than younger children might provide, while at the same time providing diversity and movement due to the cognitive transition that typically takes place in early adolescence. These 24 children were chosen so that there would be an equal number of boys who had lost their mother and girls who had lost their mother, and an equal number of boys who had lost a father and girls who had lost a father, at each of those ages (Normand, 1994).

The semistructured interview schedule used in the study provided sufficient material to allow for qualitative analysis of the responses. The methodology used was an application of grounded theory (Glaser & Strauss, 1967; Strauss & Corbin, 1990) and narrative approaches (Polkinghorne, 1988). The questions were sufficiently open-ended so that the children's responses formed a narrative about the bereavement experience. The interviews with the children and their surviving parents were thoroughly read and reread to learn as much as possible about each child's story. We listened for themes that would tell us how children represented and related to their dead parents in order to expand on the findings of the earlier analysis. We were able to identify discrete clusters of responses and

This chapter is based on Normand's unpublished doctoral dissertation.

could thus discern several different ways in which children constructed a connection to their dead parents. These clusters were categorized into *types* of connections. Each child's responses could be typified by one of these types at a given time. By looking at each of the three interviews with these children and assigning a type of connection to the children's narratives, we were able to identify patterns of change in the way the child constructed a connection to the deceased over time. These changes seemed to follow some order and several trajectories were identified.

We concluded that our original hypothesis was correct—that is, that children's inner representation of their deceased parents does change over time, that the intensity of this representation may continue undiminished with time, and that it provides the child with comfort and solace.

In the first part of this section we will describe the several different ways in which children constructed a connection to their deceased parent and the particular characteristics of each of these connections. In the second part we will describe the trajectories we identified that reflect how children, over time, shift the way in which they remain connected to the deceased.

TYPES OF CONNECTIONS

The analysis pointed to four types of relationships that children constructed between themselves and their dead parents. It was possible to identify these four types from differences in the way these children maintained a connection to their deceased parents on the five parameters described in Chapter 5. These parameters are (1) locating the deceased, (2) experiencing the presence of the deceased, (3) reaching out to the deceased, (4) remembering the deceased, and (5) keeping linking objects. Each cluster of responses was given a name that seemed to reflect the main activity of the cluster: Seeing the Parent as a Visiting Ghost, Holding on to Memories from the Past, Maintaining an Interactive Relationship, and Becoming a Living Legacy. Each of these is described below, with examples from each of the five elements that placed the child in this particular cluster.

Dealing With a Ghost

In this cluster, children conceived of their deceased parent as a ghost whose presence was frightening, unpredictable, and out of their control. These feelings were sustained for the first year after the death. The children perceived themselves as passive and their connections to their parent seemed to be largely the ghost's doing. Most notably, these children located the deceased as being "right beside me," unlike all the other children in the sample who located their deceased parent either in heaven or were uncertain about his/her location.

Unlike any of the other children in the sample who reported feeling watched by the deceased, these children were frightened by the idea. At the 1-year interview, 12-year-old Justin explained,

Like, it's just quiet, and I think that she's right there behind me and she's gonna. . . .
Like when I look in the mirror in the morning, like to comb my hair, I always think
that she's gonna pop up behind me and scare me.

The two children in this cluster were not comforted by the fact that they thought
their parent was watching over them or could see what they were doing. Their
dreams of their mother left them feeling fearful as well. The content of the
dreams they reported, however, did not seem frightening to the reader. Their fear
seemed to come not from the content of the dream but from their feelings when
they woke up. Most other children reported feeling sad when they woke from a
dream about the deceased as they realized that the parent was truly not there.
Sometimes they felt glad that they were given this opportunity to be reunited
with their dead parent in a dream, if only for a brief time. Children who experienced their parent as a visiting ghost did not feel sad or glad, only frightened.

These children talked to their dead parents. For Justin, this left him feeling
uneasy. He feared he would activate his mother's ghost. He said, "It bothers me
to think that she might hear me, 'cause . . . sometimes when I'm alone, I get
scared." Sasha, an 11-year-old girl, when talking about her mother reported that
she heard noises in the house. "Just the other day I was watching a movie with
my neighbor and I was just thinking about her and, um, all of a sudden that cellar
door just slammed shut."

These children said they "never" cried during the first year after the death.
All the other children in the sample said they cried every day or at least several
times a week at that time. Neither of these children talked about the deceased, to
avoid getting "all upset and everything." They did so reluctantly if the conversation was initiated by other family members. There were other children in the
sample of 24 who said that they did not talk about the deceased, but not that they
made a deliberate effort to not communicate. These children visited the graves—
with the rest of their families—and found it unpleasant. In addition, they saw no
resemblance between themselves and their deceased parents.

These two children both described their parents as ghostlike and reported
feeling angry or wishing their parent had not died whenever they thought about
the deceased. In contrast, for most children thinking about the deceased brought
back memories of good times or they asked themselves how their parent was doing. The most important similarity between these children is the representation of
the deceased as an unpleasant ghost out of the child's control. This distinguishes
them from the other children, especially at the first interview. Only in this group
did the children believe that the parent was nearby and that this presence was
frightening. Another distinguishing quality was that these children reported that
when they thought about their parent, they did not cry.

One interpretation of this construction of the deceased as a ghost is that this
is an expression of the children's desire to negate the death. Hence, they strive to
maintain and perceive the dead to be as close to them as possible. However, this
does not account for the negative consequences of the image they have con-

structed. Their fear could be explained by psychoanalytic theory as a projection of the anger and ambivalence felt by the bereaved toward the deceased (Yates & Bannard, 1988). Alternatively, traditional folklore would explain the phenomenon as arising from the belief that spirits who roam among the living are evil (Bennett, 1987; Rosenblatt, Walsh, & Jackson, 1976). We cannot ignore their other behaviors; they avoided crying or talking about the deceased. It may be more reasonable to conclude that the roots of their behavior may be in their prior relationship with the deceased and their current relationship with their surviving parent (Nickman, Silverman, & Normand, 1995).

PRESERVING MEMORIES OF THE DECEASED

In another type of construction we identified, children used the five activities in such a way as to allow them to maintain a fragile connection to the deceased based on their reminiscences of the past when the parent was alive. In other respects, their dead parents seemed very absent from their current lives.

In this construction most children believed their deceased parents were in heaven. Some were less certain about where to place them. In contrast to the construction of the deceased as unreachable, unpredictable ghosts, the maintenance of the memory of the deceased did not evoke feelings of fear. These children, whose connection to the deceased revolved around preserving their memories, still felt the presence of their parents watching over them, but this did not frighten them. However, unlike the children who developed interactive relationships with their lost parents, the children who focused on remembering did not attempt to enter into communication with their parents by talking or praying to them. None heard the voices of their dead parents. They were also less likely to dream about the deceased or to visit the grave.

Their connection to the deceased seemed to rely mostly on their memories of the past relationships and their preservation of things that used to belong to the parents. These children told the interviewers that they reached back to the past where they had been happier, when they had two parents to care for them. They said that they thought and talked about "the good times." For example, Annie, who lost her mother at age 13, reported during the first interview that she and her father "talk about, like, times we had—Canobie Lake, the cottage, when we went to the Rocky Mountains or something like that" and that it feels good. They also thought about how life would be now, if the death had not occurred. Quincy, whose father died suddenly of a heart attack when Quincy was 12, thought about his father 4 months after the death, "Well, if he was here, it would be a lot easier moving, and stuff like that."

Children who relied mostly on thoughts about the deceased to maintain the connection with their parents were not likely to talk about the deceased with other members of their family or with friends. When they did, these conversations centered around "what we used to do."

Only four children out of the 24 sampled stated that they were most like their surviving parents at the time of the first interview, and these children were in the group that maintained connections by preserving memories. The majority of the other children sampled thought of themselves as more like the deceased.

For children who relied on memories and mementos, the parents seemed truly "lost", except for what was left of the past. This is not to say that these children were living in the past. Their memories and linking objects serve as the bridge between the world with and the world without one parent. They evoke feelings of comfort, consolation, and continuity (Chapter 7, this volume; Moss & Moss, 1989) in a time of great sadness, as reflected by the advice these children said they would give others: "It doesn't get easier right away," or "Take it one day at a time," or "You have to be strong." There were a few children who maintained this type of connection in all three interviews, showing almost no movement toward finding greater solace.

MAINTAINING AN INTERACTIVE RELATIONSHIP WITH THE DECEASED

In a third cluster we found children who developed an elaborate array of strategies through which they felt connected to their dead parents. They seemed to be maintaining relationships in which they were not only active in reaching out to the spirit of the deceased, but they also perceived the deceased to be active spirits in their lives. They were involved with a number of activities designed not only to preserve but also to continue developing relationships between themselves and their dead parents. We perceived these children as maintaining interactive relationships with the deceased. This was the most common pattern of continuing relationships with dead parents. At all three interviews, it was possible to identify children involved with the deceased in interactive relationships.

Invariably, children who maintain interactive relationships with their dead parents told the interviewers that their deceased parents were presently in heaven. When they were not sure, they said the parents were "probably in heaven." In our view, being able to locate the deceased, be it in one's mind, memory, heart, heaven, the clouds, or the cemetery, is an important cognitive activity and a prerequisite to the development of an ongoing relationship. All children who developed this type of connection felt watched by their dead parents. By locating the deceased in heaven it is then easier for the children to feel that their parents are watching over them as they go about the business of daily life. The bereaved saw this observing presence as a motivating factor to act in ways that would please the deceased. This was true for all but one of the interacting children.

The most distinguishing theme in these children's stories is that they all talk to their dead parents, either by sharing their feelings, jokes, or events of the day, or by praying to them. Moreover, the majority heard their parents talking to them or answering back when addressed. The answers took many forms, including making wishes come true, or simply reassuring the child. "Sometimes at night, I talk to her when I say my prayers, and I cry, she just tells me not to cry and that, maybe someday I'll see her." This reflection was made by an 11-year-old girl who lost her mother a year earlier. In a similar vein, a 12-year-old boy confided, "Sometimes I pray to her to wish me good luck on a test" and then "I do good." A year later, the same boy was asked if his mother answered him when he talked to her. "No" he replied, "She just helps." Others simply tell their parent "I love you" or "I miss you" without expecting an answer. The older the children, the less likely they were to report that their parents answered them. Instead, they tended to report that the answer came from within themselves.

Dreaming about the deceased, which is a common mode of experiencing a dead loved one, was also more frequent in this type of connection than in others. Visiting the grave can be seen as an expression of active reaching out by children to their deceased parents, but such a visit is often dependent upon the surviving parents' behaviors—that is, whether or not they visit the grave. However, since many of the parents were buried in town cemeteries, some children were able to visit alone without other family members always being aware they were doing so. Thus, almost all of these children did visit the cemetery, alone or with their surviving parents.

Nearly all of the children who developed this type of connection reported talking about the deceased with others—another activity that helped to keep the parents "present" within the families. The theme of thinking about the deceased was also present in nearly all of these children's accounts, as was identification with the deceased. These children named the deceased as the parents they were "most like." Often the resemblance rested on physiognomy, but they also said they were alike in personality or in their choice of certain behaviors.

Keeping objects that used to belong to their dead parents, or which they associated with them, was common for most of these children. Sometimes they had taken this shortly after the death or it was given to them by the surviving parents.

This type of connection has many elements of Bowlby's (1980) second stage of grieving, in which yearning for the dead is accompanied by searching for them. Here, however, the search seemed fruitful, to a certain degree. These stories tell of ways in which these children sustained interactive relationships with the spirits of the deceased, in which both the children and the dead were believed to be participants. These children had a good awareness of the finality of death. By their actions they are not trying to undo the finality of the death, but to mitigate the pain (Silverman & Silverman, 1979).

In this construction the deceased seem to be playing the same roles they played in the children's lives (Silverman & Worden, 1992). Thus, sometimes the dead become guardian angels, protectors, authority figures, or granters of wishes and prayers. Albeit altered, these roles have been created by the children for the dead parents in their lives. The reciprocal and comforting nature of the continuing relationships with the deceased was easy to identify. The spirits' activity, mostly talked about in terms of the watching presence or as interlocutors, was at least welcome, if not plainly solicited.

Becoming a Living Legacy

A fourth type of connection only became apparent in the last interview with some children, 2 years after the death of their parents. These children reported a type of connection to their deceased parents that had dimensions not seen earlier. In their narratives these children showed signs of having internalized the deceased's values, goals, personalities, or behaviors as a way of remaining connected to the forever absent parents. They saw this as a legacy from their parents and cherished these qualities in themselves as a way to immortalize the dead. This type of representation seemed to be a natural progression for those children who previously had interactive relationships with the deceased. They were no longer seeking out the spirit of the deceased. They seemed less preoccupied with the deceased, whose spirits seemed to have lost some concreteness, appearing more as abstract ideas rather than as external yet very present spirits. Most noticeably, in the accounts illustrating this type of connection children reported that they were no longer talking to their deceased parents. However, all other activities present in the interactive relationships remained.

The idea of the deceased residing in heaven remained constant, as did the experience of feeling watched. Although sometimes still present, dreams were less frequently remembered and recounted. In comparison to the previous types of connection to the dead, the more concrete aspects of relating to the deceased had decreased in importance or intensity. Most striking perhaps was the observation that these children had stopped addressing their parents in talk or prayer. Visits to the cemetery were also less frequent.

Thoughts and talking about the deceased occurred less frequently and were less painful. The remembering activities were more comforting. Reminiscences appeared to be focused on good memories and to bring more solace than before. Many said it was now easier to talk about the deceased, and even comforting. Cathy, age 13, said that sometimes she and her mother talked about "what he'd [her deceased father] do in certain situations when we watch Red Sox games, or when something good happens." Annie and her best friend, who spent a lot of time with Annie's mother, talk about the "times we [all three] had together, and how she [mother] was."

The frequency of crying also decreased, as did the intensity of the pain of grief. Two years after his father's death when he was 9, Jeremy stated, "I was a lot sadder then than I am now." This was corroborated by the advice that these participants were offering to hypothetically bereaved children. They emphasized that it was more difficult at first and that time had a healing quality: "It will get better" (Cathy, age 13, who lost her father at age 11).

While feelings of sadness and crying decreased, their description of the deceased increased in detail. The children identified many ways in which they resembled their parents. They saw themselves as having adopted many of their parents' interests, behaviors, or personality characteristics. They also were more likely to consider how their behavior might further their parents' ideals and would have earned them their parents' approval. For example, when 12-year-old Julian thinks about his mother, he thinks, "Like if I did something good, she'd be proud of me or something." Similarly, Sylvia, age 14, developed an interest in sports her father used to like, and she performed her chores to please him. She said it made her feel good because "[she] never did [her] chores when he was around."

Mementos seemed fairly stable—that is, the rule in this type of relationship was apparently that no new acquisitions were made or old objects discarded. However, as illustrated by Jeremy at age 11, his relationship to objects left him by his father was less intense 2 years later. A watch that used to sit on his dresser was now in his closet and he was not using the fishing rods every day anymore; they were stored in the basement.

For the children in this sample, seeing themselves as a living legacy was not always a conscious choice; it was something that happened. Lori, 14 years old, explained it clearly. After having given the interviewer a detailed list of personality and behavioral attributes in which she was most like her deceased father, she was asked by a misunderstanding grown-up, "Why do you think you chose to be like your father in these things?" Vehemently, she replied, "I didn't choose them! It just happened. You know, it's like the way everybody says I look like, my eyes look like my father, you know. I didn't choose that my eyes look like my father's eyes. It just happened that way." This same girl said, "I try to do the best I can. I mean, I don't do it because I think my father would approve of it or disapprove of it. I just do what comes naturally to me." On the other hand, some children were more deliberate in their behavior. They felt good about those things they did that they knew would have made their parents proud or pleased.

In summary, we have identified four types of ongoing connections maintained by bereaved children with their deceased parents. For some the connection took the form of an interactive relationship with the spirit of the dead; for others, it resembled a chaotic relationship with a ghost. Yet others remained connected to their deceased parents by reviving memories from the past, while for some the connection gained an abstract quality by internalization of the deceased's spirits. We see a persistence of this connection over time that changes in its qualities and intensity. It cannot be explained away as searching behavior as described by Bowlby (1980), nor it is frozen in time as implied by Furman (1974).

TRAJECTORIES OF CONNECTIONS TO THE DECEASED

It was possible to identify in most children a progression over time, from one type of construction to another. Those children dealing with ghosts out of their control seemed to move on to the preservation of a memory. Other children moved from preserving memories to maintaining interactive relationships. These children initially tended to hold on and revive the good memories they had of the times spent with the now absent parents, as though this was truly all that was left of the deceased. With time however, they developed a more elaborate representation of the deceased as a spirit with whom they could communicate and therefore with whom they could maintain relationships. This type of connection provided a comfort that was not evident earlier. Still others moved from interactive relationships to seeing themselves as living legacies. This modification took the form of internalization of the deceased parents' values, beliefs, interests, ideals, personality traits, or behaviors.

Change was not invariable. For seven of these children, the construction was the same over the 2 years. Five of the children whose relationships to the deceased did not evolve were primarily children who simply preserved memories associated with the deceased. Two additional children were categorized as constructing interactive relationships throughout the 2 years. The examples below describe the nature of the change and its direction. It is possible to talk now of trajectories of change.

From Dealing with Ghosts to Preserving Memories

The two children who had reportedly exhibited a connection with the deceased that was characterized by fear of the deceased's ghosts eventually constructed a connection in which the ghosts seemed to have disappeared. They began to preserve memories from the past.

In time, the deceased were understood to retreat to heaven. Two years after her death, Justin conceived of his mother in "a park up in heaven and she'd be sitting on a bench with [his] grandmother." Meanwhile, Sasha told her brother (and the interviewer, at the 1- and 2-year interviews) that she thought of her mother as being "on a big cloud, in bed, with a remote control in her hand and a TV in front of her . . . and a bunch of quilts on her . . . watching TV, watching Oprah, or Donahue or something . . . doing her nails." The ghost has now become a benevolent spirit of the deceased.

By the end of the first year after his mother's death, Justin's fear was accompanied by sadness. By the second anniversary of her death, Justin did not feel his mother's presence watching him any longer. Neither did he talk to her or hear her in his mind anymore. Both Sasha and Justin stopped dreaming about their mothers. They rarely visited the grave, did not talk to the deceased anymore, and did not hear the deceased talking to them. The ghosts seemed to have vanished from their lives and simultaneously the door opened to their sadness and they were able to remember.

The most noticeable change we observed in this trajectory was that these children were now thinking about and remembering the deceased. Whereas Justin used to distract himself and tried not to think about his mother at first, he thought about her "once a day" 2 years later, a frequency that was most common in the early interviews of other children. However, his thoughts about his mother had yet to bring him solace. When asked to describe his thoughts, he began to cry. "I never said 'I love you' to her. . . . Maybe when she died, she didn't know that I loved her. I didn't want her dying thinking that." Meanwhile, Sasha thought about her mother "a few times a week. . . . Some are good things about her and some are bad things."

A critical aspect of this trajectory is the increase rather than decrease in sadness over time. For example, in the first interview Justin said he had "stopped crying," whereas at the third interview he reported crying "maybe once every 3 or 4 months because [he] just lies in bed and thinks." In fact, he was one of the most tearful children of this sample during the last interview.

The fear that previously immobilized these two children so that they held back their tears and did not think about the deceased seems to have gone. (Perhaps as a result of never having had an actual and frightening encounter with their ghosts). There remain, however, certain indicators of the possible ambivalence of their relationships, which can be seen as an explanation of their previous connection to their deceased mothers. For example, Justin's tears at the thought that his mother may not have known that he loved her, or Sasha's comment that if her mother were to come back to life, she "would be in much trouble" seem to point to a certain uneasiness or unfinished business with the deceased.

Given that there were only two children who demonstrated this trajectory, any conclusion can only be tentative. Nevertheless, it is noteworthy that in both instances the trajectory was the same, that is, from dealing with a ghost to preserving memories of the deceased. Another eminent feature is the increased expression of grief as they move from one type of connection to the other, which suggests a movement from a certain negation of the death to experiencing their sadness and despair. This movement points to a positive development, a positive transition, and adaptation to life without the deceased.

From Memory to Relationship

Dennis's story serves as a paradigm case for the shift from a preservation of memories to the development of an interactive relationship. He was 11 when his father died of cancer. A few months after the death, Dennis' representation of his father centered around the belief that his father was watching over him, although he was uncertain as to where his deceased father was located. He thought his father "was the best," and he did not cry "too often." Neither did he dream of his father, talk to him, or talk about him with his friends or family.

One year after the death, he increased the ways through which he related to his dead father. He was now definite about his father being in heaven, whereas at first he was unsure. This possibly allowed him to say not only that his father was watching him from above like before, but that now he talked to his father sometimes. He told his father "I wish you were here." He also entertained the possibility that his father might be able to answer back, although he was not aware of his doing so. When asked, "Does he answer you?", Dennis replied, "Not that I know of."

One year after the death, he said that he remembered dreams about his father, whereas he did not before. He could talk to his friends about his father, especially if they had "lost" their fathers to divorce. He accompanied his mother to the cemetery, but unlike his account of the first 4 months after the death, he had also gone to visit the grave on his own with some friends. "I went with my friends, you know. I went with them a couple of times. And I went with my mom a couple of times, so I go often, you know? But not a lot, you know?"

He thought about his father often; sometimes it made him feel good, sometimes sad. And although when asked which parent he was most like, he replied, "I'm like both of them put together," he was now able to recognize ways in which he was more like his father. He said,

I usually say stuff that he would probably say. . . . Sometimes, if I'm in a situation or something he would probably do the same—well, if he was in the situation that I was, he would probably do the same that I did.

Two years after his father's death, Dennis was now 13 years old and his relationship to the spirit of his deceased father had further increased in intensity. Not only did he remain very active in the ways he connected to the spirit of his dead father, but he seemed to relate to his father in more ways now than ever. He visited the grave more often; he said he went "once every week or two." There, he would talk to his father "in [his] mind." He prayed for him and others. His mother reported that it was "comforting to [her children] to go to the cemetery."

Dennis talked about his father more often, especially with his brother and friends, and he thought more frequently about his father. He said he thought about his father often: at the cemetery, lying in bed, when something on TV reminded him, in the places where they went with him before. He felt sad thinking that he could not see his father except in pictures. With the growing social cognitive abilities that accompany adolescence, he wished he had a chance to get to know his father better and had him around to confide in. Nevertheless, he was able to confide in his father by talking to his spirit regularly about what was going on in his life (not just how much he missed him like he did a year earlier). For the first time, he reported being able to hear his father's voice in his mind, answering his questions. Whereas he could not name any specific object belonging to his father that he had in his possession at the end of the first year, he now could point to cufflinks that he had inherited, although they were still in his mother's custody. He was even explicit about how by being nice to other people he would be like his father. He was moving toward seeing himself as a living legacy of his father. He said, "I'm nice to anyone who's nice to me. This is something to remember him by." This suggests that although much of his connection to his father took the form of an interactive relationship, Dennis was on his way to internalizing the teachings of his deceased father.

Dennis' experience of grief and continuing connection to his father illustrates how memories of the deceased can evolve into a representation that brings solace to the child. Like any construction, it takes time to build; and with time, instead of reviving the pain of loss, relating interactively with the deceased brought a sense of presence and continuity of caring.

An increase in the ability to talk to the deceased was an important component in this trajectory. According to the surviving parents, talking about the deceased became increasingly easy to do. This was corroborated by the children. As their connection to the deceased changed, the children's descriptions reflected a fuller sense of who the deceased were. Children following this trajectory showed greater attachments to the mementos they had.

Until approximately age 12, Piagetian theory would have us expect children to reason at a concrete operational level. It is interesting to note that it is only a year or more after the death that half of these children developed interactive relationships with concrete spirits of the deceased. Until then, what was left for them seemed to be only the memories. Relying on memories and objects of the past can perhaps be considered concrete connections to the deceased. The children's beliefs in some form of afterlife and their sense of presence of the dead parents watching over them are also concrete representations of death. Transforming these into relationships with more abstract spirits of the deceased would follow the predictable course of cognitive development. However, the dead continued to be described in very concrete terms with concrete sensory functions like hearing and seeing.

This trajectory, then, could stem from sources other than children's cognitive development alone. The question remains as to whether a younger or older sample, whose cognitive development would fit preoperational or formal stages of reasoning respectively, would develop similar connections with deceased parents, moving from the preservation of memories to interactive relationships with their representation of the deceased. Evidence from widowed adults in our culture indicates that this trajectory is not dependent entirely upon one's cognitive level of reasoning. Adults, who supposedly can think formally or abstractly, maintain similar concrete relationships with the dead. (See other chapters in this volume.)

Another interpretation then, is that all these activities are a part of the process of searching for the lost love object, the second stage of grieving according to Bowlby (1980). For searching to end, Bowlby suggests, it is required that the mourner accept the reality of the death. However, according to our data, while accepting the fact that a person is really dead, the bereaved may refuse to accept that a dead person is really gone. In the process of searching for the lost loved one, the bereaved locate the deceased, visualize a form the dead may take, and attribute a purpose to the spirit of the dead. All of these come out of our culture's longstanding belief in afterlife (Bennett, 1987; Rosenblatt, Walsh & Jackson, 1976). One function of preserving memories of the deceased for children may be to attenuate the pain and defer facing the full reality of the death. However, these memories provide them with some comfort. From our data we see that as they move toward the greater acceptance of the reality, they give a new form to the deceased as spirits. These spirits now have additional purpose in the lives of the survivors, beyond attenuating their pain. The deceased now play roles in the bereaved's lives by becoming, for example, protectors, helpers, supporters, or confidantes. From this position, some children move to a more abstract and internalized connection to the deceased; that is, the interactive relationship is transformed as described in the next section.

From Interactive Relationship to Becoming a Living Legacy

Cathy's story illustrates how the frequency and intensity of her interaction with the spirit of her dead father decreased and changed over the course of the first year after his death. She seemed more identified with her father and had internalized her experiences so that her construction of her father led her to become what we have called a living legacy.

Cathy was 11 years old when her father died of encephalitis. A few months following his death she had constructed an elaborate representation of him and of their continuing relationship. She and her mother described her relationship to her father as very close, the closest of the three children in their family. Cathy described her father in a very positive light; she said, "He was kind, courageous. He was nice to everyone. It was fun being with him." She also described him as an authority figure and a disciplinarian. She said, "The days that I was supposed to do the dishes, I'd hide and he would always yell at me. He would get angry a little, then he would always laugh."

At the time of the first interview, she was crying several times a week and thought about her father every day. "All the things we did together. See the Red Sox games on TV." She believed he was in heaven and that the dead had the properties of the living, only they were in heaven. She believed that he was watching her from above.

She took on her father's household chores and she identified many ways in which she was like her father in her physical appearance, in her interest in sports, and in her intelligence. To put it her way: "I look like him. We liked the Red Sox. I don't like to say I'm smart, but people say I'm smart like him." Cathy talked to her father. She told him "just that I wish he was here and I miss him and stuff." She dreamt about him. She recounted, "One day I came home from school, I don't know but my dreams are always weird but I went to the hospital and he was there in his room. My mother came in and she was all happy and crying." It made her sad to wake up and find that he was not there.

She was given her father's rosary beads and Red Sox hat by her mother. She kept them in her room as reminders of him. She talked about him with her friends and sister. "We remember what we did with him. He used to take us places and do a lot of stuff with us. It was fun." She talked to her mother also, but their talk was more focused on how she felt about her father's death. "She just asks me how I feel. I feel sad." She visited the cemetery with her mother "a lot," after her mom would come home from work. Her mother visited the cemetery daily. She had other relatives buried there. Every day, Cathy said, she reminisced about the good times she had spent with her father, and she would not miss a Red Sox game on television.

A year after the death she cried less often and thought about him less. She thought about the things they used to do, "like over the weekends we used to play games and watch baseball." She still felt as though her father was watching her, but she did not talk directly to him anymore. She had stowed the baseball hat away in her closet "because it was getting all dusty." Nevertheless, she still visited the grave regularly (in her estimation, about once a month).

She talked about the "good old days" with her sister; "we just remember . . . like when we were little, things we did." She had stopped talking to her friends about her father. "Nobody, like, I don't feel, I don't know, my friends don't really like to talk about it." She did not seem to identify with her father as intensely anymore. All she could think of that they had in common was her interest in baseball.

At the end of 2 years after the death, Cathy's continuing relationship to her deceased father seemed to have changed in other ways. There seemed to be an increase in the internalized aspects of the connection. She described her father in idealized terms. "Smart, like, a good person, tried everything and didn't give up anything; gave everyone a chance." She could not come up with any bad points to counterbalance her description of him: "[We] got along very well. Spent a lot of time together, playing games, watching TV."

Her mother explained that when her husband first came home from the hospital with encephalitis, Cathy would not leave the house. Her mother felt that since Cathy was the closest to her father of the three children, she felt the loss the most. Cathy identified many qualities that she had in common with her father. She also acted in ways to please him and make him proud. "I try out things, at school and in sports. I'm not as smart as he was. I like sports just to please him. I want him to be proud of me."

The most distinguishing characteristics of this particular trajectory is the lessening of activities that involved reaching out to the deceased. The direct communications with the spirit of the deceased (e.g., talking to and receiving an answer), the dreams, the cemetery visits, the talks about the deceased, the attachment to linking objects, the preoccupation with thoughts about the deceased, the reviving of good memories, all seem to decrease in frequency and/or intensity. This pattern follows that described by Moss and Moss (Chapter 10, this volume) in regard to widowed persons' connection to the deceased. They wrote, "There is a range of ways in which the widowed person maintains intimacy with the deceased spouse, from talking with the deceased, to thinking about what the deceased would have thought or done, to internalizing the orientation of the deceased (Bowlby & Parkes, 1970)" (p. 166). In a similar vein, Volkan (1981) considers grief work ending when the bereaved "no longer has a compulsive need to cling to the representation of the dead person. Meanwhile, however, paradoxically, the mourner identifies with certain aspects of the dead and comes to resemble him

[sic] in these particulars" (p. 67). However, we differ with Volkan in that the bereaved in our data still maintain an active and changing representation of the deceased that they may carry with them for the rest of their lives.

We suggest that the process of adaptation to loss is similar to the learning process described by Vygotsky (in Berk, 1991). Children learning a new task or encountering a challenging one first recite instructions out loud, before internalizing the steps required to perform the task. This "communication with the self" serves the purpose of self-guidance and self-direction. Perhaps it is in a similar fashion that recently bereaved children first talk out loud, or in their prayers, in order to relate to the deceased, while they are faced with the challenge of adapting to the absence of the parent and the meaning of death. Alternatively, one can turn to Cooley's argument that "imaginary conversations with significant others are a primary source of our notions of self and the basis of self-control" (Baker, 1991, p. 540). Another way to explain this trajectory is by the behaviorist principles of extinction (Rosenblatt, 1983). A bereaved child may find herself talking out loud to a parent who is now forever absent as a result of years of conditioning—that is, years of confiding or asking for help or advice. After the death, these habitual behaviors are likely to "reoccur" spontaneously, but lacking the reinforcement of receiving a response from the parent, the child was left to create this response in her mind. With time, the absence of an external reinforcer leads to the extinction of the behavior. As Nickman, Silverman, & Normand (1995) have suggested,

> The bereaved is accustomed to dealing with the deceased multiple times on a daily basis and in addition is accustomed to dealing with the internalization of the deceased, or "introject" on a daily basis as well, though this may be generally out of awareness . . . the inner representation or introject provides a transitional way of experiencing the deceased.

Yates and Bannard (1988) propose that children are more prone to hallucinations because of their cognitive immaturity. They would resolve the conflicts of grieving through a perceptual mode, whereas cognitively mature adults can use an ideational mode of resolution. The perceptual mode seems to correspond with what we have labeled the interactive relationship pattern of connecting with the deceased, whereas the ideational mode would better fit the living legacy pattern. (We want to exercise caution here; the reference to hallucinations does not in any way belittle or delegitimate these children's experiences). Elsewhere, Buchsbaum (Chapter 7, this volume) discusses an intervention she used with a bereaved child 8 ½ years of age who had hallucinations of his deceased father. By allowing the child to express his sadness and reminisce, the visual hallucinations subsided and were replaced by functional memories of his deceased father. If again we postulate a continuum including the "sense of presence" phenomenon, the dialogues with the deceased, and hallucinations, then we can argue that the progression described in this therapeutic setting serves to corroborate the "natural" progression observed in this sample for those children whose connection became that of a living legacy. It also lends support to the fact that we did not find this type of connection in the earlier interviews, since it seems to require prior expression or experience of the emotional pain and the formation of clear and reliable memories of the deceased as an independent person (Buchsbaum, 1986; Chapter 7, this volume). Two children who moved from an interactive relationship to becoming a living legacy in fact seemed to indicate an awareness that they were "making up" this whole "spirit business," these voices—they could not fall prey to their own construction anymore. As Sebastian laughingly said, "Not really. Not in reality" did he hear his father's voice answering him, after having candidly reported so at the first interview. Julian, who in the second interview said "it's nice to know" that his mother was watching him, now clarified that she was "not really" watching him, but that she "knows [his] movements."

Although one may not want to get rid of the transitional objects entirely, they do not replace the parent in any way, and so they can be stored away, like the memories, only to be brought out occasionally. Moreover, as Raphael (1983) would predict for "healthy" grieving, the positive or even idealized memories are sometimes interspersed with more negative ones. For example, a number of children reminisced about the good times they had shared with their deceased parent, but also at times recalled the pain caused by the death. Similarly, in their description of the deceased, children were more likely in the third interview and in this particular type of connection to be willing to include a few "bad points" along with the deceased's "good points" that had been more easily shared with the interviewer. After talk focused on the deceased and the loss, these children could more freely and willingly go on to other topics. Although these activities gave life to memories and may at times have created a lifelike presence, in the end none of these activities brought the dead back to life. The dead are nowhere to be found, except deeply within oneself. Rather than a continuous search for the spirit of the dead in the external world, there was an increasing awareness on the part of these bereaved children that the most precious legacy of the deceased was within themselves. They are what is left of the deceased. Therefore, it becomes important to keep certain personal qualities of their parent alive not only within, but in their behavior, personality, values, and physical traits as well. There would still be inner dialogue with this representation. This is an ongoing conscious process, with the child in charge.

REVOLVING WITHIN A SINGLE TYPE OF CONNECTION TO THE DECEASED

The children in this cluster seemed to maintain the same type of connection over the 2 years since the death. Five continued to preserve memories of the deceased at all three interviews and two others pursued interactive relationships throughout this period.

Holding on to Fragile Memories

There were five children who, over the course of the first 2 years of bereavement, maintained a connection to their deceased parents that was centered around their preservation of memories of the deceased, and there was very little, if any, activity of reaching out. Instead of experiencing greater solace as they reminisced, they seemed to become either more numb or more sad. In this sense there was change. In fact, there was little preserving of the memories other than not forgetting the deceased.

Contrary to the vast majority of the children sampled who believed their dead parents to be in heaven, these children were less certain about the location of their deceased parents. Tanya, for example, who was 11 when her mother died, could not specify where her mother was. At the third interview, another 11-year-old was explicit that he did not want to think about where his deceased mother might be. Not knowing where someone is could understandably be a strong impediment to the development of an intense, interactive relationship with him or her, especially at a stage of cognitive development where concreteness is often key to understanding.

It was as though these children did not know how, where, or whom to reach out to. While it was not universal, several of these children seemed to feel limited in their connection to the deceased. They experienced a decrease in feeling that the deceased was watching over them, in dreaming about the deceased, and identifying with the deceased. They all visited the graves with their surviving parents, but did not necessarily relate to the dead at the cemetery.

There is some indirect evidence for the hypothesis, based on previous studies and theories, that it may be some ambivalence or conflictive history in their relationships that is preventing them from moving on to other types of connections to the deceased. If they were able to move on, this might indicate a better adaptation or transition to life without the loved one (Bowlby, 1980; Crenshaw, 1990; Worden, 1991). Jackie's mother, for example, had a long history of mental illness and committed suicide. In another situation, the mother of the three children said that the daughter in our sample had the most conflictive relationship with her father. The fact that only two of these five children could identify similarities between themselves and the deceased during the first two interviews suggests again that they may not have felt particularly close to the deceased.

Most striking about the stories that come together in this "trajectory" is the quality of their grief, even 2 years after the death. These children were the only ones who reported they never cried at 4, 12, or 24 months after the death, or they were the ones who cried most frequently at the end of 2 years after the death.

Their pervasive sadness is exemplified by Mike, aged 13, who told the 2-year interviewer that he would like his mother to be around "'cause I wouldn't miss her and I wouldn't be upset all the time." This is in contrast to children who saw themselves as becoming the living legacy of their deceased parents and mostly wished their parents to be around so that they could show them their accomplishments and share their new interests—in brief, so that their parents could be proud of and perhaps even rejoice in the life they had made for themselves despite the death.

These children were also less likely to talk about their deceased parents, especially as time went on. This contrasts with the other families from this sample who generally found it easier to talk about the deceased with time, even though they did so less often, as the months unfolded. Two years after his mother's death, Mike, 13, said he did not talk to his siblings about their mother "'cause I don't know how they would react."

The reviving of memories was not reported to bring solace. Rather, it brought pain back to the surface. A year after her father's death, Ashley, now 12, explained, "It's not that I want to forget, I just want to get on with my life." For her part, Tanya was explicit in saying that death hurt more after 2 years. In contrast, children whose connection shifted so that they saw themselves as the living legacy of their dead parents were saying that it hurt less at 2 years than it had in the past.

These stories all give the impression that these children's grief was so intense that they blocked it out in order to carry on with their daily lives. It seemed to be wavering among the stages of numbness, yearning, and protest (Bowlby, 1980). These children tried to keep their thoughts to themselves, lest they get too emotional or upset others. As mentioned in the discussion of the preservation of memories as a type of connection to the deceased, the parents, for these children, seem truly lost, except for whatever remains of the past. But even those past memories cannot bring them the comfort and solace as they do for other children. This is not to say that they never will. Perhaps as the surviving parents become more able to help and support their children in their grieving process, there is no reason to believe that their connections to their deceased parents will not evolve into another form later. Nonetheless, for now, the lack of fluidity, the lack of transformation of the connection, and, especially, the lack of comfort that it seems to bring to the grieving points to an unfinished process, a transition incomplete (Rubin, 1985; Silverman, 1966; Silverman & Silverman, 1979). There seems to be some danger of their becoming stuck.

Staying in a Relationship

For two children, their very active relationship with the deceased in the early months did not become an internalized relationship, or living legacy, over the 2 years of the study. In the case of Laura, who lost her mother to cancer at the age of 11, and that of Kim, who lost her father at 13, the interactive relationship to the deceased parent seemed to have in fact increased in intensity, without becoming noticeably internalized.

At the first interview, Laura was not sure where her mother might be. By the end of 2 years after her mother's death, although she still was not definite about where her mother might be, she said, "I feel she's with me sometimes. She's with the people she wants to be with." In contrast, Kim believed her father to be in heaven, and she also believed that the dead can see, "'cause they say that, uh, dead people watch over their loved ones" and they can hear, "because everybody says to pray to the person. If they couldn't hear you, why would they say to pray to them?" Interestingly, she believed that the dead can rise from the dead. "It happened to Christ, it could always happen." She also expected to see her father when she came home from school for many months following his death. Laura did not believe that death was final or irreversible either. "When I'm mad, I like to think she's away and she's going to come back." This sentiment, not uncommon in other children's accounts during the early months of bereavement, was expressed 2 years after Laura's mother's death.

These children's beliefs in an afterlife, where the deceased have been transformed into supernatural beings who can remain near the living or eventually come back to life, is critical to their maintaining an interactive relationship to their dead parents. In Laura's case in particular, she shares similarities with the stories of children who were dealing with the ghosts of their parents. To a certain extent, since death is not believed to be final, it keeps them from acknowledging and accepting the reality of the loss, a primordial task in the process of grieving according to most theorists (Bowlby, 1980; Crenshaw, 1990; Furman, 1974; Parkes, 1986; Rubin, 1985; Worden, 1991). As will be elaborated below, this externalized spirit seems related to their wishing that this parent would eventually materialize in order for family life to return to normal. It may also feed their refusal to accept the death, which in turn keeps them from really internalizing the deceased's legacy, since he or she is present in the child's external reality. There may be elements here that might lead a clinician to suggest that detachment from the dead is critical in the resolution of grief.

In both cases, the children described a number of strategies they used to reach out to the deceased and many ways in which they felt the deceased's presence. Most striking perhaps is the fact that they talked to the deceased when they felt they could not talk to anyone else about certain things. For example, Laura would visit her mother's grave by herself to confide to her the problems she was having in school. She "knew" her father would get mad at her for not doing well. Kim tells a similar story. She talks to her father about "anything. You know, if I ever have a problem, stuff like that. If there's anything that I can't go to my mother with, like what's going on at school and stuff." According to her, her mother would "freak out" if she learned that her daughter obtained a 70% on a test. Even while he was alive, she felt she could talk more easily with her father.

Despite her saying that she felt close to her father, Laura still needed her mother and wanted to keep their relationship alive as it was in the past. In Kim's family, it was understood that Kim had always been closest to her father. However, when it came to identifying which parent they were most like, these girls saw little resemblance with the deceased at first, but as time went on, they became increasingly able to find more and more ways in which they actually were more like the deceased than the surviving parent.

In both instances, the attachment to the deceased was apparently very strong, and the surviving parents alone could not provide all the support that these children needed. Therefore, they created these intense relationships with the spirits of the deceased—connections that did not decrease in intensity as one would expect from simple extinction principles, but rather, became more elaborately defined over time. In Laura's case, this need for her mother may have been exacerbated further by the fact that her father started dating steadily during the second year of bereavement and that her older sister left the house that same year as a result of her constant arguing with their father.

Furthermore, Laura interpreted her dreams of her mother as visits from her mother's spirit, and said she saw her mother coming into her classroom at school, and could feel her mother's presence around her constantly. A psychiatric study of three nonpsychotic children within the same age range (i.e., 9 to 14) who experienced visual or auditory hallucinations of a dead relative led the authors to conclude that the unavailability of the surviving parent and/or the deceased can be tempered by the arrival of a visible and audible companion providing both a source of connection and of comfort (Yates & Bannard, 1988).

We can speculate that for Laura what appeared to be such an intense relationship with her dead mother was likely the result of a lack of support from her immediate family. She visited the grave by herself, every other Friday, when she had a free half day, or "when I felt sad and when I needed someone to talk to." Her father likely became less available when he began dating than he had been during the previous year, when he and his daughter reportedly became closer than they had been prior his wife's death. Her older sister leaving the house on bad terms with their father probably made her less readily available as well—not to mention the fact that this left Laura as the only female in the house. According to Yates and Bannard (1988), what they call hallucinations in children point to a conflict between internal need and environmental deprivation. Clearly, this criterion could apply to almost any bereaved child in various degrees, deprived by death of a family member. The feeling of being watched might even be placed along the same continuum, qualifying as a less severe "hallucination" followed by hearing the deceased in one's mind, then seeing the deceased, as was the case with Laura (the only reported visual hallucination in our sample).

Kim and Laura's interviews also share a certain element of fear about being watched by the deceased. "It's scary when you're doing something you're not supposed to. Like, I know she'd say something to me," said Laura. As for Kim, she reported that feeling watched by her father was "scary sometimes. Like having someone looking over your shoulder. It makes me really nervous. But not all the time. It's not constant or anything." So, although these are reminiscent of the stories of children who were dealing with the ghosts of their mothers, in these instances, the fear appears to be less pervasive, less constant, and it seems to have a defined object, a legitimate motive. Another difference is that Laura's dreams of her mother, for example, did not make her feel sad or scared, but, like children who maintained an interactive relationship with the deceased, her dreams brought her solace, because she was able to visit with her mother.

Another similarity these children share with the stories of children who experience their dead parents as ghosts is the anger that they feel and still express 2 years after the death. Her father reported that Laura carried a picture of her mother around the house, from room to room, and she would tell her how she felt. "I tell mother how I'm doing, and how mad I am she's not there." On the other hand, Kim said that conversations about her father still made her feel angry 2 years later. "I still have that anger, still in me. To this day I still have that anger. I'll probably have anger until the day I die! Till I figure out why it [the illness] happened to my father."

As was the case for the children whose connection to the deceased did not evolve from the preservation of memories, these children's accounts reveal a grief that is still very raw. They prefer not to talk about the deceased, for fear it would upset their surviving family members, or that their friends would not understand. Kim said, "I'm afraid it's [sharing feelings about her father's death] gonna get them all sad and everything so I just mostly keep my mouth shut . . . I mean, if my family wasn't like close to my father and stuff, I would be able to go to them. They were too close to my father and if I go to them it's going to get them sad, too. I mean I don't want that." It seems, however, that these children express their grief more (they reported crying more often and shared their feelings more willingly with the interviewers) and to some extent seemed less numb, with their feelings more available to themselves. Their yearning is evident, and so strong that they hold on to this construction of the spirits with whom they can interact, even though reason would have us believe that the spirits cannot respond and satisfactorily provide for their needs.

It may well be that over time when children feel less supported by the living, they turn to the deceased for support, making such a connection functional and adaptive to a certain extent. Eventually, it may become too unsatisfying and Kim and Laura might then find more gratifying and tangible support from those living around them. However, were they to remain unchanging, their ties to their deceased parents would correspond in many ways to what for Rubin (1985) qualifies as an indication of unhealthy grieving. When the deceased is idealized in a shallow fashion, when the relationship is inappropriately intense, when the deceased is still used to provide gratification in lieu of the living, and the preoccupation with memories of the deceased is almost constant (frequent cemetery visits, reminiscing, inability to get rid of deceased's belongings), then the connection is viewed as problematic, as a detriment to the well-being of the bereaved.

GENERAL SUMMARY OF THE TRAJECTORIES

In summary, the trajectories of these bereaved children's connections to their deceased parents seem to follow a sequence that could be likened to the stages of the grieving process proposed by Bowlby (1980). As long as the bereaved are still in shock, or have yet to acknowledge the reality of the death, they yearn and search for the deceased in the memories that they have of them. As the permanence and irreversibility of the death become more real for the children, then the search for the deceased becomes more externalized and the deceased take the form of spirits with whom the bereaved can pursue their relationship. This interactive connection to the deceased has great potential to bring comfort and solace. By the end of the second year, some children had internalized this relationship by what is being called "becoming the living legacy" of the deceased. This transformation may be taken as a sign of reorganization. This would be the final stage of grieving according to Bowlby's framework. It also has strong parallels with Furman's (1974) final task of identification with the deceased. Detachment from the dead does not seem to be a prerequisite for adaptive grieving. However, the nature of the attachment is not static and is more complex than any process of identification. Further adaptation is an ongoing process, so we use the words "end of bereavement" advisedly. All these children whose connections to the deceased evolved into ever-changing relationships showed no signs of pathology. However, the children whose connections to the deceased did not change significantly over the course of the first 2 years of bereavement do raise some concerns. Unless their trajectory is simply delayed or slower, we need to consider that these bereaved children are holding on to the past, or forever searching for the deceased, probably because they lack the support in their environment that facilitates their transforming their relationship to the dead parents.

The deceased have a place in people's lives, but they cannot replace the living. The movement from one type of connection to another may be a clear indication of the quality of the bereaved's adaptation in the face of loss, their transition to life without the loved one as a living partner, but with the loved one as inner representation.

CONCLUSION

Our classifications are attempts to capture the fluidity of the process of developing continuing attachments to the deceased by way of taking snapshots of the children's inner representations at given points in time. However, children's accounts did not necessarily fit tightly into a single type. Rather, the stories told tended to reflect mostly a preservation of memories, or mostly an interactive relationship, and so forth. The direction of the trajectory, on the other hand, created a predictable superimposition. The interactive relationship included the connective activities of preserving memories, but not vice versa. To become a living legacy includes some interactive communication and some preservation of memories, but it is heavily weighted with identification indices. The most exciting discovery in this study is probably the uniformity with which the representations and connections to the deceased followed the trajectory of memories to relationship to identification.

Death robs us of a present and future with our loved one, but it has no firm grip on the past. Therefore, memories are probably the most precious gifts that survivors are left with. They are the most prominent and accessible links the bereaved have to the deceased. They need not be created, only revived. By reminiscing, children are demonstrating their beginning acceptance of the loss. Talking about the deceased and thinking about him or her in the past makes the death real. It brings forth the reality that the past is all that there is left of a father or mother. Reminiscing also serves to bring solace in the face of despair and loneliness. By reviving happy memories, children are able to generate the positive affect associated with the deceased, relieving themselves temporarily of the pain of loss. It would seem, however, that for concrete thinkers such as children in this age group, this is a somewhat unsatisfying way to maintain their dead parents in their lives. Deep-rooted and widespread beliefs in some form of afterlife may facilitate the transformation of the representation of the deceased from a memory to spirits with whom survivors are free to interact. When a child maintains such an active, two-way relationship with his or her dead parent, she has acknowledged the fact that he or she is really dead—that is, belongs in another world, in another form. Yet, the dead and living are able to communicate and pursue their relationship. The dead parent maintains his or her role of authority figure, helper and supporter, and/or confidante. This may be interpreted as the family system's attempt to return to homeostasis (Rosenblatt, 1983). An alternative interpretation would relate to the Vygotskian notion of speech for self. In their effort to make sense and adapt to living without one of their parents, bereaved children may need to resort to a form of private speech externalized (which they later can internalize).

A transformation occurs for some children within the first 2 years of bereavement whereby their relationship to the deceased becomes more internalized. The pain of grieving has subsided somewhat. The search for the dead parent, the disorganization, and the despair also appear to be less intense or frequent. Now the child carries more than memories of a past with the lost parent, she carries an awareness of and seems to act upon the deceased's beliefs, values, wishes, style, physiognomy, interests, and personality. She has made them her own and recognizes these as gifts from the deceased, as well as a link to him or her. By connecting with the deceased in this way, she can maintain his presence in her life today, and in the future. They can grow together, as she learns more about the deceased and becomes more cognitively aware of who her parent was.

The representation of the deceased as a ghost, a scary presence, is more difficult to explain. At first glance, it may seem like a variation on the theme of an interactive relationship with the spirit of the deceased. However, both the affect and the trajectory of this particular connection has made us classify it as a separate type. The children who offered these stories appeared very distraught. After 2 years, they had only just begun to shift their connection to their dead parents toward a preservation of memories. Despite the small number of indicators, we favor the interpretation that the parent–child relationship prior to the death must account in part for this representation. The media promotion of ghosts and the cultural beliefs in afterlife probably further contribute to the development of this type of connection.

Clearly, the world of the dead is not so remote from the world of the living. The dead influence our lives, and their impact may be felt especially by children whose parents have entered the otherworld. Grieving children do not simply let go of their ties to their parents forever gone from earthly life, but rather, create new bonds that are likely shaped by their former relationships while the parents were alive, as well as their beliefs in afterlife and their need for this continuity. This continuing connection seems to be part of a functional adaptation to, not a denial of, life without the mother or father. It evolves following the changing experiences of the pain of loss. Since grief has no end, then likewise parents become immortal within the hearts and minds of their bereaved children, not only as memories, but as witnesses and as guides for living.

REFERENCES

Baker, P. M. (1991). Socialization after death: The might of the living dead. In B. Hess & E. Markson (Eds.), *Growing old in America* (4th ed.) (pp. 539–551). New Brunswick, NJ: Transaction.

Bennett, G. (1987). *Traditions of belief: Women, folklore and the supernatural today.* London: Penguin Books.

Berk, L. E. (1991). *Child development* (2nd Ed.). Boston: Allyn and Bacon.

Bowlby, J. (1980). *Attachment and loss: Vol. 3. Loss: Sadness and depression.* New York: Basic Books.

Buchsbaum, B. C. (1986). Remembering a parent who has died: A developmental perspective. *The Annual of Psychoanalysis, 15*, 99–112.

Crenshaw, D. A. (1990). *Bereavement: Counseling the grieving throughout the life cycle.* New York: Continuum.

Furman, E. (1974). *A child's parent dies. Studies in childhood bereavement.* New Haven, CT: Yale University Press.

Glaser, B., & Strauss, A. (1967). *The discovery of grounded theory.* Chicago: Aldine Publishing.

Moss, M. S., & Moss, S. Z. (1989). The death of a parent. In R. A. Kalish (Ed.), *Midlife loss: Coping strategies* (pp. 89–114). Newbury Park, CA: Sage.

Nickman, S. L., Silverman, P. R., & Normand, C. L. (1995). Children's construction of their deceased parent: The surviving parent's contribution. Manuscript submitted for publication.

Normand, C. L. (1994). *A longitudinal analysis of bereaved children's continuing relationships to their deceased parents.* Unpublished Ph.D. dissertation, Waterloo University, Waterloo, Ontario, Canada.

Parkes, C. M. (1986). *Bereavement: Studies of grief in adult life* (2nd ed.). London: Tavistock.

Polkinghorne, D. E. (1988). *Narrative knowing and the human sciences.* New York: State University of New York Press.

Raphael, B. (1983). *The anatomy of bereavement.* New York: Basic Books.

Rosenblatt, P. C. (1983) *Bitter, bitter tears. Nineteenth-century diarists and twentieth-century grief theories.* Minneapolis: University of Minnesota Press.

Rosenblatt, P. C., Walsh, R. P., & Jackson, D. A. (1976). *Grief and mourning in cross-cultural perspective.* New Haven, CT: Human Relations Area Files, Inc.

Rubin, S. S. (1985). The resolution of bereavement: A clinical focus on the relationship to the deceased. *Psychotherapy, 22*, 231–235.

Silverman, P. R. (1987). The impact of parental death on college-age women. *Psychiatric Clinics of North America, 10*, 387–404.

Silverman, P. R. (1966). Services for the widowed during the period of bereavement. *Social Work Practice: Selected Papers*, 93rd Annual Forum.

Silverman, P. R., Nickman, S. & Worden, J. W. (1992). Detachment revisited: The child's reconstruction of a dead parent. *American Journal of Orthopsychiatry, 62*(4), 494–503.

Silverman, S. M., & Silverman, P. R. (1979). Parent–child communication in widowed families. *American Journal of Psychotherapy, 33*, 428–441.

Silverman, P. R., & Worden, J. W. (1992). Children's reactions in the early months after the death of a parent. *American Journal of Orthopsychiatry, 62*(1), 93–104.

Strauss, A., & Corbin, J. (1990). *Basics of qualitative research.* Newbury Park, CA: Sage.

Volkan, V. (1981). *Linking objects and linking phenomena.* New York: International Universities Press.

Worden, J. W. (1991). *Grief counseling and grief therapy* (2nd ed.). New York: Springer.

Yates, T. T., & Bannard, J. R. (1988). The "haunted" child: Grief, hallucinations, and family dynamics. *American Academy of Child and Adolescent Psychiatry, 27*, 573–581.

Chapter 7

Remembering a Parent Who Has Died: A Developmental Perspective

Betty C. Buchsbaum

The Institute of Medicine report *Bereavement: Reactions, Consequences and Care* (1984) lists three basic requirements in order for mourning to occur: (1) an understanding of the concept of death, (2) the ability to form a genuine attachment, and (3) possession of a mental representation of the attachment figure. This chapter will concentrate on the third prerequisite by exploring the parental memories of bereaved children between 3 and 16 years of age. The aim is thus to elucidate the developmental patterns that shape the parental image over time. As these patterns are delineated, further insight into the mourning process may be achieved.

MEMORY AND ADULT MOURNING

Before considering memory in childhood, let us review the ways in which recollections serve the bereaved adult. Memory plays a prominent role for adults in four separate situations. First, memories appear soon after the occurrence of a death has been comprehended. At this time, associations, images, and even hallucinations inundate the bereaved individual. Parkes (1972) has written about the vivid recollections reported to him by widows and widowers following the demise of a spouse. In this phase, memory serves as an anchor from which attachments to the deceased can gradually be relinquished. As Freud (1917) has observed, emotional bonds are released "bit by bit . . . while the existence of the lost object is continued in the mind" (p. 154). Once affective detachment is achieved, the "ego becomes free and uninhibited again" (p. 154), available to new relationships. Memories of the deceased serve as an essential bridge between the world with and the world without the loved person.

After the acute phase of mourning has abated, recollections become more neutral. The image of the lost person can be apprehended, then, as part of the past, entering consciousness at the command of the bereaved, providing a sense of consolation, continuity, and inner enrichment. The quality of the recollected relationship to the deceased has been highlighted by Rubin (1984). After behavioral adaptation to bereavement has been achieved, he stated, the "intrapsychic

This chapter is reprinted from *The Annual of Psychoanalysis*, Vol. XV, pp. 99–112 (1987).

process of relating to the memory of the deceased continues" (p. 340). Resolution of the loss is defined by Rubin with reference to the "comfort and fluidity with which one can relate to the representation of the deceased" (p. 340).

A third occasion for the emergence of memories of the dead is associated with anniversary reactions. Family events, birthdays, or the period around the anniversary of the death serve as reminders of loss. Pollock (1970) has reported the frequency of anniversary reactions occurring in unconscious, pathological forms. The recurrence of relatively brief episodes of mourning at times when the loved person would be acutely missed is described by Johnson and Rosenblatt (1981) as a normal phenomenon, distinct from unresolved mourning.

A fourth mode of remembering occurs when symbolic representations of the deceased find expression in works of art, literature, philosophy, or science, as well as in religious and social rituals. In exploring the impact of loss on the creative process, Pollock (1978a) observed that a successful outcome of mourning often results in a work that "may itself stand as a memorial" (p. 272). As an example, he described (Pollock, 1978b) how James Barrie's *Peter Pan* preserved the image of Barrie's "lost" brother (who had died in childhood) while yielding him up to a never-never land in which only magic powers could sustain survival.

MEMORY, MATURATION, AND CHILDHOOD BEREAVEMENT

The extent to which memory participates in the mourning process of adults is more than matched by the role of memory following the death of a parent during childhood. As Furman (1974) states, should a young child suffer the death of a parent the resulting vacuum can reach self-destructive proportions. Recollections of the parent would serve as links to object ties required for the narcissistic nurturance essential to development. The goal of affective detachment from the image of the deceased parent is thus a questionable one for the very young child. It may be more reasonable (especially before latency) for the child to retain an attachment to whatever representation of the parent is available to him/her until the needs it serves are met. As development proceeds, the urgency of the parental presence diminishes. Concomitant with growing emotional independence is the child's maturing capacity to perceive who the parent is or has been. Just as loss has a special meaning for each phase of emotional development, its impact varies with cognitive maturation as well. The fragmented, egocentric, and often contradictory images of the preschooler provide a much more tenuous ballast than do the consolidated, objective, and multidimensional recollections of the adolescent.

The young child's unstable, subjective view of the parent may further impede the work of mourning. To accomplish the necessary disengagement from the parental image, the bereaved individual would require a clear, reliable picture of the deceased. For children, the emergence of this image is not an all-or-nothing phenomenon, but is characterized by phase-appropriate alterations over time.

Though mourning is distinct from the act of remembering, it is intimately bound to the transformations of the memory function.

Given the interdependence of maturation and the bereavement response, Pollock's (1978) view that mourning has its own line of development is a helpful one. It implies that mourning is possible in childhood, but must be defined in terms of a child's affective, defensive, and cognitive capacities. As maturation proceeds, the mourning process would more closely approximate Freud's goal of emotional distancing from the love object. In essence, once a loss occurs the child has an ongoing task that will be completed only as adulthood is approached. The work of mourning, then, is not time-limited. It is, rather, an open-ended endeavor requiring mature affective and cognitive structures for its completion.

In addition to participating in the mourning process, parental memories contribute to the bereaved child's personality development. As the works of Spitz (1957), Emde (1983), and Mahler, Pine, and Bergman (1975) have demonstrated, the interactions between parent and child are essential in the achievement of both social and self-definition. Disruption of the child's continuous, taken-for-granted exchanges with the parent can result in an inner sense of fragmentation, confusion, and disjointedness. Clinical literature has amply demonstrated the negative impact of parental loss on a young child's life (Bowlby, 1980; Furman, 1974; Kliman et al., 1969). The availability of early parental memories may permit an essential form of psychic survival, providing the continuity required for the coherent development of the sense of self.

Unfortunately, memories of the parent are not uniformly retained by the bereaved child. Externally imposed prohibitions against talking about the parent can inhibit thoughts that would otherwise emerge, or children themselves may lack the cognitive or psychological capacities required for the articulation of verbal memories. Should loss occur during infancy, for example, experiences with the parent would not have registered in a verbal, consciously retrievable form. Older children, using defenses to contain affective responses to mourning, may distort or repress parental images (Cryan & Ganter, 1992; Yates & Bannard, 1988). Elsewhere it has been suggested that early modes of remembering, dominant at the time of bereavement, may persist long afterward (Buchsbaum, 1985). The following vignette of a patient's treatment, previously reported (Buchsbaum, 1985; Kliman et al., 1969), illustrates how the memory function was itself compromised while a primitive form of parental recall was employed.

Richard was 5½ years old when his father died of cancer. Three years later, following the death of his maternal grandfather, he was referred for therapy. He was receiving poor grades and was restless and inattentive at school. Memory difficulties were prominent, and Richard stated that he "got mixed up a lot." He evidenced many slips of the tongue when speaking about illness or death and also forgot school-related material.

When Richard did recall emotionally significant content he often did so in an immature mode—that is, in a visually oriented context. For example, he frequently projected the percept of a man's arm onto a tree branch that could be seen from the office. Once Richard was momentarily confused when he thought that a man who resembled his father was, in fact, his father. Richard also reported that he sometimes saw things as appearing smaller and more distant than they were, as well as larger and closer than he knew them to be. The feeling of distance was associated with the notion of people leaving or dying. When the therapist speculated about Richard's wish for his father to be alive again, he revealed that he had once seen an image of his father, who had appeared as a "very small man in the kitchen cabinet."

The treatment process supported Richard in tolerating his sadness as he remembered his father. By reminiscing, it was hoped that visual imagery could gradually be exposed, decathected, and replaced by age-appropriate memories. After 16 months, Richard's functioning improved both at school and on the Wechsler Intelligence Scale for Children. His progress was understood in terms of his diminished need to use his memory as a wish-dominated vehicle that retained his father's image. Memory, as an ego function, was becoming increasingly autonomous.

Richard was one of three patients whom this author knew to have described hallucinations of a deceased parent. Pollock (1961) and Kliman (1965) have also noted illusory meetings between patients and a parent who has died. The fact that these individuals experienced loss at or before the age of 6 years suggests that developmental issues were pertinent to their response.

MEMORY AND COGNITIVE DEVELOPMENT

Having noted the importance of both memory and development to childhood bereavement, let us state the main question addressed by this chapter: How do children at different developmental phases recall a parent who has died? Both content and organization of memories will be considered with respect to age. A secondary question this chapter will address is how the time interval between the age of loss and the age of report affect parental recall. Are early memories incorporated into an age-appropriate mode or do they retain the features characteristic of the age when loss occurred? Limitations in data prevent an answer at this time, but some speculations will be offered.

These issues will be examined within the framework of Piaget's cognitive theory. Piaget's work suggests that memories become transformed from the vague sensations of infancy (sensorimotor phase) through emotionally bound, self-referential experiences of early childhood (preoperational) to relatively objective recollections (operational) after 8 years of age. In adolescence, more abstract, coordinated, and generalized elements of experience are remembered (formal operations) (Piaget & Inhelder, 1973). Piaget and Inhelder have documented the progression of both intellectual functioning and memory. They have linked the course of memory development to the patterns observed generally in cognitive growth. Specific to memory, however, are the following observations:

1   From infancy to about 2 years, remembering can be demonstrated through recognition. A baby, for example, reveals familiarity by becoming animated when he sees his mother's face.

2   After 2 years, overt behavior, such as imitation of experiences, reflects the child's ability to reconstruct a memory. Finally, recall is available without the aid of external cues, props, or actions.

3   By the age of 3 years, the child can verbalize or fantasize about past events. At this age play, integrating both words and fantasy, still remains a prominent form of recall.

4   After about 5 years, children tend to use auditory or visual percepts in order to remember. Thus, imagery is typically associated with verbal reports of past events.

Kosslyn and Kagan (1981) have corroborated Piaget's notion that only later, at about 8 years of age, do propositional or verbally dominant ideas begin to replace images. The dependence on visual imagery may account for the persistence of illusions or hallucinations noted earlier. For the 8-year-old, there is a transition from the use of images to verbal ideas in representing the past. As Kosslyn and Kagan (1981) have noted, this shift is not totally stable since emotional factors play a role in determining the form a memory takes. They have reported, for instance, that chocolate cake is imaged by children, and sexual experiences tend to be recalled visually by adults. Rosenbach, Wapner, and Crockett (1973) have also shown that a subject reports his impressions of a person at a lower level of integration than usual when he is emotionally involved with that person. In a clinical context, the case of Richard, described earlier, exemplifies the profound influence of affect on the memory function. The sadness associated with the father's image at times inhibited recall and at other times contributed to a regressive form of remembering.

PERSON PERCEPTION

Supplementing Piaget's studies of the sequential organization of memory is the work done on person perception. A child's description of another person appears to parallel the pattern of remembering delineated by Piaget. According to Shantz's (1975) summary, very young children tell about others in an action-oriented, personalized manner. The 7-year-old tends to elaborate details, such as hair and eye color, aspects that are easily perceived. By 8 or 9 years, children can include more covert, inferred content, such as personality traits. These portrayals would rely more on verbally mediated concepts than would earlier responses. The adolescent can construct an increasingly complex description, referring to external circumstances, for example, in reconciling contradictory features of a personality.

DEVELOPMENTAL PATTERNS OF PARENTAL MEMORIES

Let us now examine some preliminary data with reference to the developmental expectations just outlined. Presented below are examples of parental memories of seven children who were interviewed as part of a pilot study. All of the children were living at home with the surviving parents. They were of at least average intelligence and none had been in psychotherapy prior to bereavement. Four of the children were currently in treatment for mild adjustment difficulties; none was known to the author before the time of the interview. Subjects were told that they would be asked questions about memories and thoughts of their deceased parents and that their answers would help in understanding other children who had experienced the death of parents.

In discussing excerpts from the interviews, features relevant to the child's phase of maturation will be stressed. The patterns reflected here may then be more systematically explored and validated through future research. The accounts that follow are designed to illustrate the quality of parental memories reported by the seven subjects at five different points in development.

The youngest child seen was Bobby, $3^1/2$ years old, whose father had jumped to his death from the window of his apartment a few months before the interview. Bobby spent most of our time together placing toy soldiers on the bottom hinge of a door, pushing them off the hinge, and pronouncing them dead. About halfway into the session, Bobby was able to answer direct questions concerning his father's activities. He replied that his father played with toy soldiers, hit a baseball, and went to the playground with him. When the interview appeared to have ended, Bobby announced that he wanted to talk about his father, as though he had not already done so. He then informed me that somebody had pushed his father (to his death). Bobby's mother, who was present, commented about her son's difficulty in comprehending the suicide about which she had informed him. The distortion he reported seemed a reasonable compromise in dealing with the difficult task of understanding a suicide at Bobby's age.

Bobby's soldier play was viewed as a condensation in which he recalled an activity shared with his father but used it to imitate his father's suicidal behavior. It was through motoric and fantasy enactment with actual objects that Bobby could first associate to his father's death. Following his play, verbal recollections could be elicited. In addition, the opportunity to reminisce about his father seemed to prompt his effort to describe verbally his version of the traumatic loss. It is possible that the process of recollecting permitted Bobby's ideas about his father to move from a motoric to a verbal dimension. (Bobby had himself attempted to jump from a window soon after being told of his father's death. This imitative impulse, usually interpreted as identification with the parent, may also be viewed as an expression of learning and assimilating information—a method characteristic of his age.)

Bobby's reactions typified those of the preschool child. Words, play, and fantasy were all employed primarily to express and, possibly, to reinforce the attachment between father and son. Words used to describe and objectify his father were not yet accessible.

Ted, a 5-year-old boy, was able to speak directly about his father who had died the previous year of a heart attack. After a period of exploration and spontaneous play in the office, Ted readily participated in the interview. Among Ted's recollections were those of his father going to the beach and taking him into the water. His father also went with Ted to the park and put him on the slide. When questioned directly about his father's appearance, Ted answered that he had brown hair. Inquiry into dreams and thoughts about his father elicited the following: "Sometimes when I open my eyes . . . I thought about him outside in the cold, out of my house, out in the snow. Then I closed my eyes, opened them," and, he implied, the thought went away. Ted further noted, "When I was not a little bit good I think he's alive." At those times he just looks up in his head (to see his father), and Ted rolled his eyes upward to demonstrate. When questioned, Ted revealed that he has never forgotten that his father is dead.

Ted's active engagement in the interview permitted us to observe his capacity to report spontaneously the activities he and his father had shared. Explicit, descriptive comments were offered only after inquiry. While Ted did not depend on playing out the associations to his father, unsolicited verbal content was still confined to shared behavior. The emergence of imagery could be observed—in the service of his conscience. Reality testing was sufficiently intact to permit Ted to distinguish the self-generated image of his father from the actual sight of him.

Seven-year-old Jonathan was interviewed 6 months after his father died of cancer. Without prompting, Jonathan easily recalled that his father had gigantic glasses, a wiggly tooth, and he worked in an office. Remembered activities included his father cutting the lawn and picking up Jonathan's toys. Verbal descriptions were further elaborated, combining subjective reactions with objective facts. For example, memories of what he had liked about his father included being picked up and thrown around by him as well as the fact that his father always used to fix things. In his thoughts, his father appeared visually, in color, saying, "Hi, Jonathan." Sometimes, when Jonathan went into his mother's room, he forgot that his father had died, assuming that the "snoring bump on the bed" was his father instead of his mother. He had also been confused when he passed somebody with the same hair color that his father had. When the man turned around, Jonathan would say, "Whoops, that's not my Dad!"

Jonathan's responses coincided with the expectations of a 7-year-old who is just reaching the stage of concrete operations. He could describe his father as a separate person with characteristics relatively free of reciprocal interactions with himself. Visual and auditory perceptions occurred as a form of deliberate thought. Confusion of other people with his father seemed to replace the illusory experiences of younger children. Furthermore, these errors were immediately and spontaneously corrected. The content of Jonathan's descriptions highlighted concerns about physical impairment. It is difficult to determine whether Jonathan's psychosexual phase or the bereavement response itself best accounts for the focus.

The following interview was conducted with a 10-year-old girl who had clearly established logical, operational thought. Ruth was 5 years old when her father died after a brief illness. She remembered her father as being tall and happy. He had worked as a rabbi in a synagogue. He used to teach and he loved books. What she had liked best about him was that

> He used to drive places with us. I have lots of relatives, and we would visit them when I was a baby. A lot of times he'd come home from work and give me presents for my birthday. He got a necklace for me. He used to love to buy presents for my mother. Once I hid the present for Mother's Day [and] I forgot where I hid it but he didn't get mad.

Ruth readily described her father as an independent individual with qualities that referred to his temperament, interests, and pleasures. Shared activities were described objectively, with references to time and place included. The ability to report covert qualities, such as his love of books, is consistent with Shantz's report (1975) regarding children over 8 years of age. One could speculate that the content of Ruth's memories, in contrast to their formal qualities, reflects the issues significant to her at the time of her father's death. This notion requires further research for validation.

Mary was 11 years old when her father died by drowning. She was interviewed 4 months later. As a preadolescent whose contact with her father had been recent, she could describe his physical appearance, including his height and hair color. She thought of him as "nice" because "he helped you when you needed help; he would take you where you wanted to go." She specified that he had worked as a computer programmer. The formal organization of her responses resembled that of Ruth's memories, more objectively detailed than the responses of early-latency children, such as Jonathan.

Let us next consider the ways in which memories are reported and employed at adolescence. During this period the ability to perceive and coordinate a variety of perspectives is developing. Thus, information derived from earlier years can be used to consider how parents' attitudes and reactions might apply to ongoing events in the child's life. In addition, the growing capacity for abstract thought and symbolic imagery offers the adolescent a chance to speculate about a deceased parent in ways not previously possible. Feelings and recollections may now take the shape of mature creative works. At this stage, too, the novel ability to integrate diverse views permits an increasingly realistic, coherent picture of the parent to emerge.

Excerpts from interviews with two 15-year-old girls illustrate the advances in parental recall achieved by the adolescent. Carol was seen 1½ years after she had learned of her mother's fatal accident. The suddenness of death, as well as the ensuing dislocation of family members, undoubtedly contributed to the heightened intensity of the bereavement response. Nevertheless, the relative completeness of character delineation obtained is not unique to this situation. Carol stated that she remembered everything about her mother. She and her mother had been very close and got on well. Her mother was popular, sociable, was on the PTA board, did ceramics, and used to exercise at a workout studio. Carol admired most her mother's supportive and understanding attitude, but had not liked her stubbornness. Carol's thoughts turn to her mother at family barbecues and get-togethers where her presence is painfully missed. Then Carol might daydream, visualizing her mother outside, standing against a background of trees or sky. She also speculates about how things would have been if her mother were here now—how the family would not have fallen apart.

Barbara's father had died unexpectedly of a heart attack 1½ years before the interview. She portrayed him as an intellectual, who enjoyed his work as a lawyer; he was part of a cultural community, and the activities he shared with his family had an "educational bent." She recounted the pleasure he experienced in religious services as well as his love of travel. Though it was difficult to confine her comments to one thing, Barbara liked best her father's concern with and involvement in everything that was happening. She liked least his need for everyone to be quiet when he was working, and his occasional temper flare-ups. When she is alone, Barbara thinks about how her father might have reacted to things she is currently doing.

Barbara and Carol were both able to integrate the backgrounds, values, and pursuits of their deceased parents. In depicting their parental relationships, they could still objectify the rest of their parents' lives. Positive and negative attributes were noted in an unbiased manner. Conjecture about what the responses of the parent would be if he or she were alive have appeared as one of the repeated concerns of the bereaved adolescent. By means of hypothetical formulations, the teen-ager can build a new kind of parental contact. Advances in role-taking and conceptual skills can thus solidify the link to the past while allowing the individual to remain oriented to the present, and even to the future. A 16-year-old girl, for example, had considered how strict her deceased father would have been, applying this notion to the limit testing she was currently engaged in with her mother. Career and marital choices might also be validated in this way. The knowledge of parental values and preferences can thus be used by the adolescent in a supportive and confirmatory manner.

Subjects older than 16 years have not been included in this study. By late adolescence one would expect that a fairly comprehensive, realistic construction of a parent can be achieved and remembered. By this stage, personal needs and traits would determine the response to loss, dominating cognitive issues.

DEVELOPMENTAL ARREST AND PARENT LOSS

Longitudinal data would be valuable in tracing the transformation of memories with maturation. Ruth is the only child presented who had lost a parent as long as 5 years before the interview. Her statements, at the age of 10 years, suggest that the organization of her memories was developmentally appropriate. On the other hand, the content of her responses contained themes pertinent to the age at which she was bereaved. The implicit idealization of her father may have been further reinforced by the affective needs pressuring Ruth near puberty. One of the tasks for future research would be to examine the vicissitudes of content with respect to the age of loss and the age of report. The quality of the recollected relationship and its alterations may reveal the level of object relations the child has achieved with the deceased parent. Such data would be pertinent to the question of developmental arrest raised by Fleming and Altschul (1963). They found that object relations in adult patients who had lost a parent as late as adolescence remained arrested at the stage attained at the time of the parent's death. From this observation, Wolfenstein (1966) reasoned that "the child needs the continuing relation with the parent in order to advance in his development" (p. 108).

On the other hand, might not children be informed about their deceased parents in ways that upgrade the internal parental image? Once normative data are obtained, they could be used by adults to communicate information about the parent in synchrony with a child's changing capacities and needs. The poor fit that often occurs between adults' reports about a parent and a child's understanding of them is sadly noted by Troyat (1967) (Tolstoy's biographer):

> The harder little Leo tried to remember his mother (who had died when he was two years old) the more she eluded him. He tried to identify her by questioning those who had know her, but in vain. They told him she was good, gentle, upright, proud, intelligent, and an excellent storyteller, but he could not attach a face to this assortment of qualities, and as though to deepen the mystery, there was not a single portrait of her in the house. Only a silhouette cut out of black paper, showing her at the age of ten or twelve. His whole life long Leo Tolstoy tried to instill life into this frustrating profile. He grew older, but his mother remained a little girl. Driven by his need for love, he finally came to think of her as a mythical being to whom he had recourse in time of distress and upon whom he relied for supernatural assistance. (p. 24)

Possibly, successive elaborations of his mother might have provided Tolstoy with a transforming image to which he could have anchored his love. In addition to offering a focus of attachment, the parental descriptions permit a changing concept of the parent–child relationship to evolve. The perspective provided by available memories and the elaborations of others might prevent the freezing of early interactions, facilitating a more objective understanding of the parent and the self.

PRACTICAL IMPLICATIONS

The views expressed here can be applied to the ongoing life of the bereaved child. Following the death of a parent, the child's play, fantasies, and any other references to the deceased parent should be accepted as part of the work of mourning. These productions may be viewed as analogous to the flood of memories observed in adults (Parkes, 1972). Only destructive acts or dangerous forms of identification require limits. Help in concretizing the child's past experiences with the parent would be useful. In this context, the function of anniversary reactions may be extended. It is possible that as a child reaches a new cognitive level, more complete and complex constructions of the deceased parent would be sought. A widow observed that her 14-year-old daughter was talking about her father 2 years after his death as though she were newly bereaved. We may assume that it was a maturational push that prompted this young teen-ager to review, once again, the memories of her father, reorganizing them in terms of more mature concepts and emotional concerns.

The clinical implications of this study are consistent with the usual process of psychotherapy. That is, the child's unique modes of representing a parent are identified and incorporated into treatment. As affective and cognitive issues are clarified, memories of the parent may become increasingly ordered and objectified (Zambelli & Clark, 1994). The therapist must be attuned to the many ways in which a young child refers to the parent. Aspects of the parent embedded in fantasy and metaphor are subtly, secretly, and often unconsciously retained. For example, a 7-year-old boy was prompted by Halloween to think about tombstones and ghosts. These notions were ultimately connected to the guilt experienced when his father died.

The ways in which symbolic communications are interpreted must defer to the cognitive constraints of a given age. The forms of recall suggested by this chapter provide a framework both for therapeutic interventions and for consolidating an age-appropriate parental image.

SUMMARY

This chapter has outlined different ways of recalling a deceased parent as a child matures. The intellectual capacities available at adolescence are considered to be necessary for the retention of stable, coherent memories. These memories, in turn, are believed to be essential for the mourning process to be concluded. It has been suggested that younger children will mourn in an incomplete manner, just as their personality development is incomplete. The final phase of mourning has been associated by Wolfenstein (1966) with the achievement of a separate and autonomous sense of self. The resolution of mourning would also be characterized by a view of the parent as a self-contained. independent person whose unique identity is preserved in the mind of a bereaved son or daughter.

REFERENCES

Bowlby, J. (1980). *Attachment and Loss: Vol. 3. Loss: Sadness and depression.* New York: Basic Books.

Buchsbaum. B. (1985). Memory and the child's ability to mourn. In S. Gullo, P. Patterson, J. Schowalter, M. Tallmer, A. Kutscher, & P. Bushman (Eds.), *Death and children: A guide for educators, parents and caregivers* (pp. 109–118). Dobbs Ferry, NY: Tappan Press.

Cryan, E., & Ganter, K. (1992). Childhood hallucinations in the context of parental psychopathology: Two case reports. *Irish Journal of Psychological Medicine, 9*(2), 120–122.

Emde, R. (1983). The prerepresentational self and its affective core. *The Psychoanalytic Study of the Child, 38,* 165–192. New Haven: Yale University Press.

Fleming, J., & Altschul, S. (1963). Activation of mourning and growth by psychoanalysis. *International Journal of Psycho-Analysis, 44,* 419–431.

Freud, S. (1917). Mourning and melancholia. *Collected Papers,* Vol. 4, pp. 152–170. London: Hogarth Press, 1953.

Furman, E. (1974). *A child's parent dies.* New Haven: Yale University Press.

Institute of Medicine (1984). Bereavement during childhood and adolescence. In *Bereavement: Reactions, consequences and care* (pp. 99–141). Washington, DC: National Academy Press.

Johnson, P., & Rosenblatt, P. (1981). Grief following childhood loss of a parent. *American Journal of Psychotherapy, 35,* 419–425.

Kliman, G. (1965). *Psychological emergencies of childhood.* New York: Grune & Stratton.

Kliman, G., Feinberg, D., Buchsbaum, B., Kliman, A., Lubin, H., Ronald, D., & Stein, M. (1969, April). Facilitation of mourning during childhood. Paper presented to the American Orthopsychiatric Association, New York.

Kossylyn, S., & Kagan, J. (1981). "Concrete thinking" and the development of social cognition. In J. Flavell & L. Ross (Eds.), *Social cognitive development* (pp. 82–96). New York: Cambridge University Press.

Mahler, M., Pine, F., & Bergman, A. (1975). *The psychological birth of the human infant.* New York: Basic Books.

Parkes, C. (1972). *Bereavement.* London: Tavistock.

Piaget, J., & Inhelder, B. (1973). *Memory and intelligence.* New York: Basic Books.

Pollock, G. H. (1961). Mourning and adaptation. *International Journal of Psycho-Analysis, 42,* 341–61.

Pollock, G. H. (1970). Anniversary reactions, trauma and mourning. *Psychoanalytic Quarterly, 34,* 347–371.

Pollock, G. H. (1978a). Process and affect: Mourning and grief. *International Journal of Psycho-Analysis, 59,* 255–276.

Pollock, G. H. (1978b). On siblings, childhood sibling loss and creativity. *This Annual, 6,* 443–481.

Rosenbach, D., Wapner, S., & Crockett, W. (1973). Developmental level, emotional involvement and the resolution of inconsistency in impression formation. *Developmental Psychology, 89,* 120–130.

Rubin, S. (1984). Mourning distinct from melancholia: The resolution of bereavement. *British Journal of Medical Psychology, 57,* 339–345.

Shantz, C. (1975). The development of social cognition. In E. M. Hetherington (Ed.), *Review of child development* (pp. 257–323). Chicago: University of Chicago Press.

Spitz, R. (1957). *No and yes.* New York: International Universities Press.

Troyat, H. (1967). *Tolstoy.* New York: Dell.

Wolfenstein, M. (1966). How is mourning possible? *The Psychoanalytic Study of the Child, 21,* 93–123.

Yates, T., & Bannard, J. (1988). The "haunted" child: Grief, hallucinations and family dynamics. *Journal of the American Academy of Child and Adolescent Psychiatry, 27*(5), 573–581.

Zambelli, G., & Clark, E. (1994). The constructive use of ghost imagery in childhood grief. *Arts in Psychotherapy, 21*(1), 17–24.

Chapter 8

Relationship and Heritage: Manifestations of Ongoing Attachment Following Father Death

Kirsten Tyson-Rawson

The way in which human beings experience the world, and themselves, is shaped, moderated, and reciprocally influenced by the relational contexts within which they live. This network of relationships is primary in the development of the individual's understanding of the meaning of the death experience and the nature of the self. The late adolescent period of the life cycle is a time fraught with challenges and opportunities. It is the time when individuals forge new relationships, renegotiate and renew old ones, and begin to move toward a new sense of self within the context of the adult world. When the death of an important family member occurs, the intricate web of relationships that helps to define the self is disrupted, creating opportunities for new understanding as well as threats to the individual's ability to function in the world.

The study reported here (Tyson-Rawson, 1993) sought to discover how late adolescent women perceived the deaths of their fathers in terms of the effect on both their individual and relational worlds. The study was designed to identify and investigate factors, and categories of factors, that the subjects perceived as significantly influencing their bereavement experience. Results of the study focused on outcomes within three contexts: the family, the self, and peers. Of primary interest here is the family context, specifically the nature of the daughter's relationship with her father preceding and following his death.

The first section of this chapter addresses the nature of bereavement in terms of how the death of an important person in the individual's life creates demands for change. The second section provides an overview of the tasks of bereavement as they interact with those of late adolescence. The study design is described in the third section and the findings of the study are reported in the fourth. Finally, some conclusions are offered regarding the results of the study.

BEREAVEMENT, RELATIONSHIP, AND MEANING

A primary assumption of the study presented here was that the bereavement process is experienced within a relational context. It is within this context that the individual who has lost an important person to death grieves and attempts to come to a resolution of grief. Carse (1987) states that, as a result of bereavement, "our own lives lose their meaning . . . grief has power in that it drives us to the formidable task of reassembling a new universe" (p. 5). The death of an important person causes a break in the network of relationships and a concomitant loss of meaning previously derived from interactions with the other.

Bereavement requires a change in one's "internal working model" (Bowlby, 1980), developed in early life and used to govern the nature and quality of attachments throughout the life span. The internal working model has been defined by Belsky and Pensky (1988) as:

> affectively-laden mental representations of the self, other, and of the relationship, derived from interactional experiences, which function (outside of conscious awareness) to direct attention and organize memory in a way that guides interpersonal behavior and the interpretation of social experience. (p. 198)

The death of an important person creates a demand for the bereaved to rediscover meaning by formulating new representations of the self, the other survivors, and the deceased—and of the relationships among them. A significant death begets a life crisis, "a situation that is so novel or major that habitual responses are insufficient" (Moos & Schaefer, 1986, p. 9). The personal disorientation that accompanies loss points to the need to construct new guidelines for behavior and understanding of experiences in the world of social interaction—a new internal working model.

The creation of this new model of relational meaning is necessary if the bereaved person is to reestablish stability and order in his or her life. The state of being characterized by stability following the crisis of death has typically been termed "resolution," literally "re-solving" of the dilemma presented by loss of someone important.

Bereavement Resolution

The outcomes of this task of rebuilding a model of the relational world—and the processes through which that resolution is reached—have occupied the attention of bereavement researchers for many years. Studies of the effects of bereavement on individuals are numerous and have provided a strong foundation for understanding the bereavement experience. Areas investigated include the effects of parent death on young children (Berlinsky & Biller, 1982; Denes-Raj & Ehrlichman, 1991; Elizur & Kaffman, 1986), adolescent responses to sibling death (Balk, 1981, 1991; Hogan & DeSantis, 1992; Martinson & Campos, 1991) or to the death of a peer (Schachter, 1991–92), parental reaction to the death of a child (Klass, 1988; Miles & Crandall, 1986), and the responses of surviving partners to the death of a spouse (Parkes, 1972; Parkes & Weiss, 1983; Silverman, 1970; Silverman, MacKenzie, Pettipas, & Wilson, 1974).

Bereavement in the individual has been linked not only to emotional distress and disturbances in mental health, but also to problems in social relationships, cognitive functioning, self-esteem, and physiological problems (Bowlby, 1972; Dura & Kiecolt-Glaser, 1991; Osterweis, Solomon, & Green, 1984, 1987; Parkes, 1987-1988). In addition to acute problems, bereavement has the potential to result in chronic patterns of grieving that may block successful functioning and the attainment of a satisfying life for the individual (Parkes, 1972; Parkes & Weiss, 1983; Zisook, 1987).

Although bereavement may create problematic outcomes, it may also serve as the catalyst for the development of richer meanings, more satisfying relationships, and greater individual maturity. The potential for a positive outcome of bereavement-an internal working model that meets the needs of the bereaved individual—is reflected in a statement from Parkes (1972): "Just as broken bones may end up stronger than unbroken ones, so the experience of grieving can strengthen and bring maturity to those who have previously been protected from misfortune" (p. 5).

The important question then becomes: "What is necessary for a successful resolution of bereavement?" The conventional wisdom in the field of bereavement studies has been a process of orientation, the outcome of which is to redirect the "emotional energy" previously expended in relationship with the deceased in a new relationship that replaces the old (Worden, 1991). One bereavement researcher (Raphael, 1983) summarizes this position when she states "the bonds binding the bereaved to the dead partner may gradually be relinquished, freeing the emotional investment for ongoing life and further relationships" (p. 187).

In contrast, the research of Klass on parental bereavement (1988) highlights the importance of an additional element in the resolution of bereavement. Klass finds that resolution includes not only the establishment of social equilibrium by investment in new relationships and tasks, but also incorporation of an "identification" with the deceased within the survivor's self-image. Klass states, "The resolution of grief is . . . not a return to life as it was before, for there is no going back. The resolution of bereavement is a sense of a new self" (1988, p. 120).

While Klass speaks of changes within the self of the individual, Silverman's findings in a study of parental death among college women (1987) raise important questions regarding the ongoing relationship between deceased and bereaved. She asks, "Are some bereaved telling us instead that although they recognize that they must change their relationship to the deceased, they do not necessarily break the connection?" (p. 403).

The work of these scholars points to a component of bereavement resolution that requires further inquiry. Klass's inclusion of a "new sense of self" and Silverman's emphasis on the continuation and renewal of connection to the deceased are especially salient when considering the tasks, both individual and family-related, facing the late adolescent college student. The context within which an individual experiences bereavement includes the psychosocial demands that impact her or his life concurrent with the death. Because of the psychosocial tasks facing the late adolescent college student during this phase of the life cycle, the need to integrate the loss into the internal world may be particularly relevant. In the case of the bereaved college student, the pressures to separate from the nuclear family and form new, more intimate, peer relationships—issues to which attachment and loss are salient—continue to exert influence during the grieving process.

LATE ADOLESCENT BEREAVEMENT

The major focus of research and model building efforts in the area of bereavement has been on increasing our understanding of the adult grief response at the death of a child or spouse. Since 1981 there has been a significant increase in the amount of research on adolescent bereavement (Balk, 1991; Corr & McNeil, 1986; Fleming & Adolph, 1986; Hogan & DeSantis, 1992). Although some scholars (Balk, Tyson-Rawson, & Colletti-Wetzel, 1993; LaGrand, 1981, 1985; Silverman, 1987) have explored the effects of bereavement on college-age students, most research on child or adolescent response to death has focused on subjects 18 years old or younger. In general, the experience of bereavement during late adolescence has been underexplored, although there are distinct and unique qualities to bereavement during this period.

The myth of the carefree college student permeates our culture. In contrast, recent surveys of college campuses indicate that from 40 to 70% (Balk, 1990; La-Grand, 1981; Segal & Figley, 1988; Zinner, 1985) of traditionally aged students will experience the death of an important person during their college years. College students are typically geographically separated from their families of origin. When a death occurs in the family, these individuals are usually required to experience the long-term bereavement process away from other family members and within an environment that may not validate their experiences and provide support for grieving. The combination of geographical separation, the possibility of a lack of support in the immediate environment, and the interaction of bereavement and psychosocial tasks can increase the intensity of the crisis experienced because of the death of someone important.

Late Adolescent Development and Parent Death

Bereavement during adolescence has been described as the time when "conflicts of grieving collide with those of ego development" (Fleming & Adolph, 1986, p. 103). Late adolescents are involved in the negotiation of new, more adult relationships with their families of origin, especially with their parents, as well as addressing issues related to the formation of intimate relationships that will be the basis for their own future families. The death of a parent during late adolescence creates challenges to an internal working model that is already in a state of growth and change. Bereavement and adolescence not only require that the individual cope with the loss of the person but also "both involve coping with changed inner and external realities, and both must encounter the ambivalence and conflicts inherent in the phases of separation and loss: protest/searching, disorganization, and reorganization" (Fleming & Adolph, 1986, p. 102).

Late adolescents can be conceptualized as having achieved some degree of emotional and physical autonomy with regard to their parents. They are in the process of creating distinct personal and social identities based upon the work of earlier developmental phases. The struggle of this period is defined by the conflict between intimacy and distance. Inherent in intimacy is the risk of being overwhelmed and losing one's autonomy. Distance from others holds the threat of being left alone—abandoned. This process, described as individuation, focuses on the development of a sense of "mature connectedness . . . not concerned exclusively with separation or autonomy but rather with the continuing embeddedness of the individual in relationships with others" (Gavazzi & Sabatelli, 1990, p. 501).

The death of a parent may create difficulties in both separation and intimacy tasks (Fleming & Adolph, 1986; Houser & Greene, 1990; Preto, 1989). Difficulties in separation tasks may occur because the individual may feel pulled back into the nuclear family in order to ameliorate the distress experienced by other family members. Separation may also be complicated because one of the key family members from whom the individual is trying to separate is no longer able to participate in the renegotiation of the relationship. In the case of death of a parent, intimacy tasks—including the selection of an opposite-sex partner—may become more complicated because of the initial sense of abandonment by a significant gender role model.

Although the experience of bereavement may interfere with completion of the developmental tasks of late adolescence/young adulthood, the outcome of bereavement and the grieving process may also create a sense of greater maturity and increased closeness to important others (Gordon, 1986). As in other populations, the possibility of another type of relational outcome is reflected in Silverman's (1987) work on college women who experienced parent death. Silverman conceptualized the college women she interviewed as "growing up before their time" (p. 393), an idea reminiscent of Elizur & Kaffman's (1986) finding of "accelerated maturity" among bereaved young children of a kibbutz in Israel.

STUDY DESIGN

The College Women and Father Death study reported here was completed between 1992 and 1993. It was developed as a response to questions arising from a longitudinal study at Kansas State University of the effect of social support interventions on the bereavement experiences of college students (Balk et al., 1993). The approach to research design was based upon the "grounded theory" paradigm as explicated in the work of Glaser and Strauss (1967) and Strauss and

Corbin (1990). Grounded theory is theory that has been discovered from analysis of data; it is therefore theory that is "grounded" in the data. It is an inductive reasoning process as contrasted with the deductive process used when hypotheses derived from an existing body of theory are tested. The grounded theory approach is focused on the discovery of plausible concepts and hypotheses relevant to the specific area under study. Theory grounded in data has the advantage of being relevant to the area under study such that its findings are directly applicable to the issues of most salience to the subject group. For the purposes of the present study, the models of bereavement found in the literature did not reflect what seemed to be the most significant concerns of the group. Using a grounded theory approach minimized the damage that can be done when theory of "dubious fit and working capacity" (Glaser & Strauss, 1967, p. 4) is used as the basis for empirical research.

Subjects

Twenty women between the ages of 18 and 23 were interviewed for the study during 1992 and 1993. Ten of the women attended Kansas State University (KSU) in Manhattan, Kansas, and ten were undergraduate students at East Carolina University (ECU) in Greenville, North Carolina. All subjects had experienced the deaths of their fathers and had living mothers.

The study was focused on the exploration of the women's bereavement experiences during the late adolescent phase of the life cycle but was not limited to subjects whose fathers had died during that phase of their daughters' lives. Rather, the focus of research was on the interaction between their understanding of the deaths of their fathers and the tasks that faced them during this period of their lives. Of the total sample, 60% ($n = 12$) of the subjects had their fathers die during the late adolescent phase, between the ages of 18 and 23 years old. Another 30% ($n = 6$) of the total sample experienced the deaths between the ages of 14 and 16 years old. The final 10% ($n = 2$) of the sample lost their fathers at the age of 9 years. The ECU and KSU subsamples ($n = 10$ each) differed in that two more of the ECU sample experienced the loss during the late adolescent phase of the life cycle (70%) than did those in the KSU population (50%). For the total sample ($N = 20$), the range of time elapsed since death was from 3 months to 14 years. Fifty percent ($n = 10$) of the sample experienced the death within 1 to 4 years before the time of the interview and an additional 20% ($n = 4$) of the fathers died a year or less prior to the interview time. In general, the subjects in this study showed remarkable similarities in ethnic background, religious orientation, and marital status of parents at the time of the father's death.

The study was restricted to female subjects based upon the state of theory in the field of bereavement studies. Unlike other areas of research in the social sciences in which primarily males have been studied, models of bereavement are typically based upon the female experience of loss by death. Using women in this study allowed a sense of continuity with previous research and made overt the gender-specific nature of bereavement models developed to date.

A decision was made to focus on the death of a father, rather than the death of either parent, because the research literature indicates gender-specific differences in relationships between adolescent daughters and their mothers and fathers (Greenspan & Pollock, 1990; Isay, 1990; Youniss & Smollar, 1985). Additionally, given that a primary task of the late adolescent period is the formation of cross-sex, intimate relationships, it was thought that the death of a father could create specific issues for women related to this task. Specifically, recent research on identity development has suggested that identity is, for women, more closely linked with interpersonal connectedness than it is for their male counterparts (Chodorow, 1978; Gilligan, 1979; Josselson, 1987; Miller, 1976).

Data-Collecting Instrumentation

Personal interviews that included a genogram procedure (McGoldrick & Gerson, 1985) and a structured questionnaire were used to gather data from the subject group. The genogram is a graphic assessment procedure designed to reveal the family structure and family history of individuals in order to gain a better understanding of multigenerational influences on current functioning (Bowen, 1991; McGoldrick & Gerson, 1985; Rolland, 1991).

The "long-interview" format (McCracken, 1988) structured questionnaire was based on concepts drawn from a review of theoretical models and the literature in adolescence, bereavement, and family stress and coping. The primary categories addressed in the interview were

1   circumstances of the death and related events,
2   individual psychosocial factors,
3   family factors, and
4   experiences in the college environment.

The questionnaire was used to establish "channels for the direction and scope of discourse" (McCracken, 1988, p. 24) such that the general, open-ended questions led to the accomplishment of the overall research objectives rather than generating an excessive amount of information unrelated to research objectives. In addition, this approach insured that all subjects were presented with the same questions, allowing comparability of subject responses. All interviews were tape-recorded and transcribed verbatim onto computer disk.

Data Analysis

The analytic methodology used in this study of the bereavement experience of late adolescent women was the "constant comparative method" developed by

Glaser and Strauss (1967). This method of qualitative data analysis and theory building consists of joint coding and analysis of data. It uses specific coding/analysis procedures to systematically generate substantive theory that closely reflects the data from which it was drawn. The term "constant comparison" refers to the ongoing process by which statements, incidents, or events appearing in the data are continually examined for similarities and differences in order to develop categories.

Categories are defined in this method as classifications or groupings of concepts where concepts are "labels placed on discrete happenings, events, and other instances of phenomena" (Strauss & Corbin, 1990, p. 61). The grouping of concepts represented by the category is "discovered" in the process of comparing concepts with one another and determining that they apply to the same or a similar phenomenon. The placement of concepts within a single category creates a more abstract level of understanding represented by the category.

Subcategories within each category represent "clusters" of concepts that apply to a particular issue within the larger category. Within subcategories, themes that represent differing views of the phenomenon under study may be delineated in order to clarify the nature of the subcategories.

This chapter discusses one subcategory within the Family Relationship Process Context: Emotional Relationship with Father After Death. The defining dimension of this subcategory is the nature of the relationship, characterized as either "attached" to the father or "detached" from the father. Each of these two positions, attached and detached, will be discussed in terms of two themes that represent two different outcomes of the bereavement process in the area of relationship to the deceased. Figure 1 is a graphic representation of the relationship of subcategories and themes discussed in this chapter.

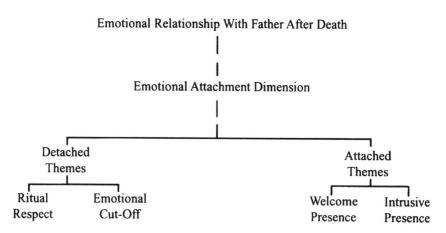

Figure 1 Emotional relationship with father after death: subcategory, dimension, and themes.

EMOTIONAL RELATIONSHIPS AFTER DEATH

Before addressing the bereavement experience in terms of subjects' perceptions of relationships with the deceased after their deaths, it is important to understand the nature of these relationships prior to the deaths.

Seventy percent ($n = 14$) of the subjects indicated that, at the time of the deaths, their fathers were among the people in their families to whom they felt closest. These women reported three primary ways they knew they were close to their fathers: shared activities, protection, and emotional support. One woman, age 22, described the emotional nature of her relationship with her father: "He was my best friend, absolutely. I told him everything and he did everything for me." Women often described shared activities as settings within which they experienced emotional closeness with their fathers:

> We were always really close . . . I loved to go out and cut corn with him and do farm things and so he kind of had a companion. You know there was that bond. . . . Me and dad . . . would just be quiet a lot, we just understood each other, I guess. We were the serious ones in our family.

They reported sharing activities with their fathers in ways that were unique to their dyad and so distinguished the father–daughter relationship from other relationships in the family: "We used to watch basketball games together. He'd be sitting with me eating—pretzels and cheese—that was our big thing." Another instance of shared activities was: "Playing basketball is when I felt closest to him . . . Dad would say like, 'Hey, she's on my team.' Course I was too little but it didn't matter."

Other women emphasized the personally supportive nature of the relationship: "He was there when I had a problem. He helped me figure things out," and "My father always made me feel I was special and talented." Some of the women described how their fathers' expectations for them helped them judge their own performances: ". . . he'd get mad when I didn't do very well and I knew I could have done better—so when I mess up now I get mad at me, too." Another example of support emphasized the way in which a woman's father conveyed his belief in her abilities: "I wanted to take a year off before college and try to be a dancer . . . Dad just said, 'You do what you think is best for you.' He was disappointed 'cause he wanted me to go to college but he still supported me."

Protection was another way in which daughters saw themselves being connected to their fathers prior to their fathers' deaths. Perceptions of their fathers as protectors included setting standards in social situations:

> Dad was always very specific about who I went out with . . . I really felt embarrassed at times. I never told him but I really appreciated it. I mean there were times I just wanted to go home and it was a great excuse to like say "Well, my dad'll kill me if I'm not home" by a certain time.

Fathers were also protective through being problem-solvers: "All my friends would come and talk to him about their problems. . . . So even though I didn't have trouble like some of them, I knew he would do it for me too if I asked." Several women pointed out that their father's presence in the home was a source of security for them: "I knew I was safe when I went to sleep. When he went out of town on business I thought, 'There'll just be women in this house, what if someone breaks in?' and then I couldn't sleep."

Not all subjects reported feeling close to their fathers. Thirty percent ($n = 6$) of the subjects did not select their fathers as a person to whom they felt emotionally connected prior to his death. Of those 6 subjects, 4 reported either a mildly conflictive relationship or one characterized by nonconflictive detachment: "I liked him. He made me laugh, that's what I remember most. But I didn't talk to him about anything." Eight months after her father's death, another woman remembers: "Well, he was a—good dad. This sounds bad but we just weren't that close. I mean I loved him, he was my daddy, but as people we were real different. I wish I'd known him better." A second woman reported that she remembered her father primarily as a disciplinarian: "He was the one—when I messed up Mom would say 'Wait til Dad gets home' . . . I remember watching TV with him. I don't know why it still bothers me so much that he died. That doesn't sound very good, does it?"

Representative of some was the statement of one woman whose response to the illness that led to her father's death was influential in her sense of emotional distance:

> When he was dying I just got farther and farther away. Like, you know, he wasn't great to be around, not real angry or anything, just sick you know. We fought some. I felt bad about that later. Not that we were close before but being sick didn't help . . . I just kind of tried to stay out a lot.

The subjects with the most ambivalence about their relationships with their fathers were those whose parents had divorced prior to the death. For example, one subject stated, "He just wasn't part of my life until he got sick and then he moved back to town . . . I got to know him some in that year . . . But you know a year's not very long after 10 years away."

Although the majority of subjects (70%) described their relationships with their fathers before the fathers' deaths as emotionally supportive, close, and protective, this position was not representative of all of the women interviewed. Thirty percent of the subjects described their predeath relationships with their fathers as emotionally detached or conflictive.

The Attachment Dimension

Women's statements about relationships with their deceased fathers were classified as representing one of the two ends of a continuum of attachment. At one end is the emotionally connected or "attached" position, indicative of an "ongoing attachment" (Hogan & DeSantis, 1992). The alternate "detached" position indicated the subjects' perceptions that they no longer had a relationship with their fathers because of their deaths. These terms were chosen to characterize relationships because of the centrality of the concept of attachment in the field of bereavement studies. The loss of an important loved one, and the consequent distress of the bereaved, can be attributed to the severing of an attachment that required rebuilding of the internal working model used by the individual to negotiate the relational world. The results of this study indicated that the "re-created" model could include ongoing attachments to the deceased. However, it should be remembered that neither the attached nor the detached position necessarily guaranteed a "positive" outcome emotionally. That is, being attached to the father following his death was not viewed by all subjects as comforting, desirable, or helpful. Conversely, a detached position could not be interpreted as representing emotional distress in all cases.

In this, and later discussions of themes, the numbers of women reporting specific themes are provided to give the reader a sense of how frequently particular ideas were encountered. However, this practice is not intended to indicate that the women who made these responses never questioned or felt ambivalent about the ideas they expressed. Statements were categorized according to the predominant themes or ideas expressed. For example, women who made statements about ongoing relationships with their deceased fathers typically also stated that they were keenly aware of being physically separated from them. There was not a sense that the subjects found these two states to be incompatible. Nor did all women who stated that they did not have ongoing relationships with their deceased fathers necessarily report that their fathers had no impact on their current lives. However, statements were not categorized as attached unless the subject stated that she believed she had an ongoing relationship with her deceased father.

Emotionally Attached Relationships

The responses to questions about present relationships with the deceased father were classified according to whether or not the subject expressed a sense of her father's continuing presence in her life. The key question determining ongoing attachment was, "How has your relationship with your father changed since his death?" Some of the subjects answered the question directly, accepting the underlying assumption that a relationship with a deceased person was a possibility. Another group questioned the assumption of the inquiry, asking for explanation or stating that the fact of their fathers' deaths made the question irrelevant. Of the total sample, 70% ($n = 14$) of the subjects reported an ongoing attachment to the deceased, indicating a continuing bond with the important person who died (Klass, 1988).

The data revealed two primary ways ongoing attachment was expressed in the bereavement experience of the late adolescent women. Each theme expressed a type of relationship as well as the subjects' responses to that perceived presence. Attachment to the deceased was expressed as either (a) a Welcome Presence or (b) an Intrusive Presence.

Welcome Presence   The Welcome Presence theme was typically expressed as a perception that the deceased continued to affect the subjects' lives in positive ways. 10 of the 14 subjects in the "attached" group (70%) stated that their fathers' presences were welcome in their lives although they initially had experienced some anxiety about such presences. Rather than responding to the portion of the question that asked about change in the relationship, some of the women described interactions with their fathers in which they spoke with the deceased or sensed his presence in the physical environment. One woman whose father had died when she was 14 stated,

> When I was up at school, about a month ago, I had this real weird dream that he was alive and he was talking to me. I freaked out, I woke up and I thought it was real. I thought I had talked to him. It was so cool. And then I realized it wasn't true and I started bawling . . . but I think it was real after all, 'cause I did better after that. Now sometimes I just talk to him and I know he's there to hear me.

The effect of these experiences was sometimes mixed and yet the response of many of the women who had these experiences indicated they were welcome and even sought after.

> Sometimes I just know he's around, you know. And other times I don't. But when I do think that he is it's such a strong feeling that I'm sure of it. . . . But it could be a lot to do with how much I want him to be there. And I think if my dad only shows up at times of stress so I think that it's that I want him to be there so bad. And yet I think, "Well, he just knows I'm having a stressful time."

Many of the women who reported sensing an actual presence, even years after the death, revealed their fears of being thought of as "being ready for the loony bin," "psycho," "fruity," or "just plain weird." Yet, they were willing to describe these experiences specifically for the interviewer and all reported they had talked about them with at least one friend or family member.

Two examples of responses to the question, "How has your relationship with your father changed since his death?" provided a bridge between the experience of actually sensing the presence of the deceased and other ways in which women experienced their fathers' presence in their lives. These responses focused on the aspect of change in the relationship:

> In a way I feel closer to him 'cause now I feel like maybe he knows how I feel and before he didn't . . . because I always felt like I never told him and now I do tell him. Like about my bulimia . . . Now he knows, but he also knows that I've done some-

thing really good about it. So when I have a slip, or want to, I talk to him in my mind and he understands. Now he understands.

Well, I'm older now and I think he probably really appreciates what I've become. We had some fights, not real big or anything but typical teenage stuff, and I said things I shouldn't have, you know like "I hate you." But I'm more mature and it makes me feel good to realize he's proud of me and understands that the arguing and talking back weren't how I felt about him.

Final examples of a welcome presence involved the influences daughters felt their fathers had on their lives and their characters—essentially, their fathers' heritage as incorporated into the selves of the bereaved women, into their new working models of the relational world. One woman said, "So now I realize that he can't take care of me in the world. But he does take care of me in that he's in me now . . . in everything I do." Another woman reported how her father influenced her college work: "I know he's so proud. So that makes me want to keep going and prove to him that I can . . . the fact he died has tons to do with it because the fact he died means I can't quit school." These responses were clearly related to what Klass (1988) has described as the development of a "new sense of self" following the death. One final example demonstrates how the beliefs of the father, incorporated into the self of the daughter, can influence and moderate future primary relationships:

Well, I see how the people I used to go out with must have looked through his eyes. Since his death it's easier for me to use what he's taught me about how to know who's . . . a good person, I guess. When I start to date now I always think that my father is with me, looking at this person, helping me make choices about this man.

The women who welcomed the presence of their fathers in their lives experienced the ongoing attachment in one or more of three different ways. Some women reported that there was an actual presence of the other in the physical environment with which they could interact. The second type of welcome presence was reflected in changes that the subjects reported in the relationships with their fathers. In this instance, the relationship change was tied to changes the women perceived in themselves. They discussed the changes in terms of their fathers' expected responses to the new behaviors, abilities, or characteristics of the daughter. Finally, subjects talked about how they had incorporated their fathers' ideas, beliefs, and values into their view of the relational world and their own achievements. In all cases, the subjects discussed the possibility of interactions with the self of the deceased parent and the possibility for growth and change in the dyadic relationship.

The women whose responses revealed a welcome presence of their fathers in their current lives were more likely to report that they viewed themselves as having reached some resolution of their grief than were those who did not have this experience. Typical statements about resolution from women in this group were

I don't think you ever get over it, really. But yes, I think I've resolved it somewhat . . . It doesn't make me happy that he died, I think I'll always miss him . . . but I'm content with what I have now.

And,

There are times when something happens and I want to call him up . . . But it doesn't stop me from anything and sometimes now I feel happy thinking about good memories or telling someone I like about him. I guess that's some resolution, huh?

The responses of these women were characterized by a reflective quality. It was apparent that they had thought their relationships with their fathers were congruent with their view of themselves, relationships, and the world as a whole.

Intrusive Presence   In contrast, a second group of four women, representing 30% of the group whose responses fell toward the attached end of the dimension, reported qualitatively different experiences with the presence of their fathers in their lives. These women's responses had a desperate, struggling quality although their expressions of grief were no more powerful than those of the first group. Their statements described what was labeled an intrusive presence, typically expressed in nightmares, intrusive thoughts, and high levels of anxiety that debilitated the subject in one or more areas of functioning.

After he died, I was so depressed that I couldn't go to school or sleep or anything. So they put me on an antidepressant for a while. Lately, I've been feeling that way again. I have these dreams, nightmares, and I can't stop thinking about him dying. I think he's mad at me . . . I don't know why, no, I think I feel this way because I never said good-bye to him. I knew he was dying and all that time I just stayed away, went to someone else's house.

Anxiety and guilt were commonly reported by the women whose relationships with their fathers were experienced as intrusive presences: "I really got crazy after he died. . . . Now I'm quieter, but I have these dreams that he's there and I'm supposed to do something. I feel guilty and I don't know why. I loved him so much"; "After four years I still can't study, like, I keep getting scared and jumpy, like there's someone outside the door. I can't be alone since he died"; "I'm just so nervous all the time. I keep expecting him to show up . . . I know it's only been four months but I don't know if he'll ever go away," and, "I don't know what's the matter with me. Sometimes I think I'm crazy and other people just can't see it."

The symptoms described in the above passages could be expected from people who had recently experienced a bereavement (Parkes, 1972). The nightmares, anxiety, inability to concentrate, depression, and problems with sleeping are fairly common in recent bereavement. In fact, 90% ($n = 18$) of the total sample reported one or more such symptoms during early bereavement. However, the women who reported an intrusive presence had lost their fathers from 4 months to 4 years prior to the time of the interview.

The common factor that united the experience of these four women was a sense of "unfinished business" (McGoldrick, 1991). Each reported thinking that she had not been able to effect closure in the relationship with her father. Two of the subjects reported that they had avoided interacting with their fathers during a prolonged illness that led to his death. The second 2 subjects had highly conflictive relationships with their fathers, characterized by cutoff from contact and minimal interaction. In comparison to those who welcomed their fathers' presence in their lives, those who experienced an Intrusive Presence were unanimous in reporting no sense of having resolved their grief.

Emotionally Detached Relationships

The two faces of emotional attachment to the deceased—welcome and intrusive—provided a contrast to the women whose responses fell toward the detached end of the continuum. Data analysis revealed that 30% ($n = 6$) of the total sample demonstrated detachment from the deceased. In some cases, the face of detachment seemed less passionate than that presented by subjects with attached relationships. This outcome was designated ritual respect. In other cases, it was more passionate. The second outcome is represented by the term emotional cutoff.

Ritual Respect   The term *ritual respect* was chosen to represent the less passionate of the detached responses to the question "How has your relationship with your father changed since his death?" Inherent in these subjects' answers was respect for their deceased fathers and indications that they thought about their fathers as unique individuals with specific strengths that the subjects valued. Often, the respectful quality of the subjects' attitudes was revealed by ritually related practices such as maintenance of the deceased's belongings, or memorial practices: "I look at things I've kept—a hat, a watch, a couple of plants he had that he liked—and I take care of those. It feels good."

Sometimes, the subjects included descriptions of what their relationships might be like if their fathers were still alive. For example, "I would like to think that now if he was alive I would tell him . . . things and talk to him more." However, this type of response never referred to the idea that the father–daughter relationship continued or could change and grow. These responses typically included a disclaimer that a relationship could continue after death but acknowledged a lasting influence on the lives of the subjects: "Well, he's dead, so there's no relationship. Oh, I mean, I have a lot of his qualities. He wasn't judgmental and I'm not judgmental . . . my dad had such a good business mind. And I have to have some of that somewhere. But, I don't know."

The tenor of the responses of women in this group was, in general, positive in terms of their feelings about remembering their fathers: "He's real well remembered in the community. Everybody came to the funeral—everybody in the town came to the funeral. That was real important to me. I think about that when I feel sad." The responses of women in this group were both similar to and different from those of women in the Welcome Presence group. Both groups of subjects reported that their fathers had a positive influence on their lives. However, the women in the Ritual Respect category tended to view that influence as part of the past, rather than as a part of the present and future.

Emotional Cutoff   Two (33%) of the subjects in the group that displayed attitudes characterized by emotional detachment did not fit into the group that displayed Ritual Respect. These 2 subjects' responses revealed a sense of intense, emotional distress at the severing of the relationships with their fathers. This theme has been designated emotional cutoff. One woman stated,

> I feel the same about him now as I did when he was alive but I don't feel connected anymore . . . It's hard 'cause there's times like things will happen and, "Oh gosh, I need to talk to him about it," and then it's like whenever something good happens I just want to phone him up and tell him and that's one of the hardest things, is not being able to share things with him.

The second woman in this group revealed her struggle to keep distressing feelings at bay by pushing them aside:

> Well, I just keep telling myself that it's not such a big deal now. He's gone and I've just got to get used it. When I start to feel bad I say like, "Cut it out," you know. But it keeps coming back and sometimes I get real worn down.

As at the attached end of the continuum, there were two outcomes possible from an emotionally detached position. The women who displayed Ritual Respect toward their fathers reported that they continued to miss them and also appeared to have achieved a greater sense of resolution than those whose responses evinced emotional cutoff. Women in the Emotional Cutoff group expressed greater distress and little or no sense of resolution of their grief.

Bereavement Resolution

It should be noted that none of the subjects equated resolution of grief with "getting over" their fathers' deaths. Rather, those who reported a sense of having resolved the loss to some degree, described resolution as (a) coming to terms with the death in the sense of its having meaning, (b) an increased individual ability to function effectively, and (c) a sense of acceptance of the loss as a part of their life histories. All of these descriptors can be seen as indications of changes in the internal working models for relationships. Women who stated they had not resolved their grief were those who felt they were prevented from effective functioning by having lost their fathers. They continued to see the event as incompatible with their lives to that point and found the death unexplainable and mystifying.

The four types of resolution previously mentioned were not conceptualized as being permanent endpoints. Nor were these themes interpreted as stages in the resolution process. Although the subject pool contained women who had experienced the deaths of their fathers from 3 months to 14 years prior to the time of the interviews, there was no indication that the time since death was associated with one or more specific themes. This statement, however, is not meant to imply that the passage of time does not affect the bereavement process. Subjects for whom longer periods of time had elapsed since the deaths tended to express these themes more clearly, as though they represented an outcome of bereavement they viewed as more or less permanent. In contrast, women who had more recently experienced the deaths of their fathers expressed these themes more tentatively— that is, they were likely to indicate that they were not sure that their current perceptions would persist. They viewed their relationships with the deceased parents as less stable and characterized by a greater degree of ambiguity.

Perceiving themselves as having achieved resolution, or as moving toward that state, was conceptually tied by the subjects to having several kinds of information available. First, information about the circumstances of a death, particularly about accidental death, or about the disease process and its cause, was linked to reports of resolution of grieving. Second, there needed to be open access to information about emotional responses to the death. Information about how the subject and the family members most significant in her life were feeling and what they were thinking in response to the loss was key in the degree to which subjects reported they had been able to begin the resolution process.

The transmission of information was facilitated by an open attitude among family members toward sharing information about the deceased and the circumstances of his death. This description of availability and quantity of information available to the women shares a conceptual base with the concept of social support (McCubbin et al., 1982; Pearlin & Schooler, 1982). Social support within the family unit was perceived by female subjects as being present to the degree that they had access to information about the factual circumstances of a death and that they were connected to a family system that also shared information about emotional states of its members.

Resolution and Family Relationships

Continued attachment to the deceased was presented as a welcome, supportive presence or as a presence that was perceived as intrusive, disruptive, and disquieting. The difference between these two themes was that subjects who reported a welcome presence were those who also reported that their families in general, or one member in particular, were supportive, were understanding, and valued their beliefs and experiences of bereavement.

Within the domain representing detachment from the deceased, those subjects describing a stance of ritual respect also reported that they experienced their families as supportive, although they did not report an ongoing attachment to the deceased. In contrast, those who took a position of emotional cutoff from their fathers, despite their attempts to avoid grieving, displayed emotional uneasiness about the fact of the death and their relationship to the parent who had died. Subjects who reported emotional cutoff also stated that their families were not an important part of their grieving process, did not know or understand the subjects' responses to their fathers' deaths, and shared little information either factual or emotional. These subjects' relationships with their families were most likely to be characterized by conflict avoidance. Relationships with family members characterized by dependency between or among two or more members were typically also characterized by an intrusive presence.

It is clear from these findings that neither an attached nor a detached position insured the resolution of grief among subjects. Similar patterns emerged in relationships to the deceased and in relationships to surviving family members. However, those positions that were characterized by the least distress and highest levels of acceptance of the loss were also characterized by high levels of information within the family, a sense of resolution, and an attached position. The subjects who reported the greatest levels of distress, and reported little if any degree of resolution, were those whose responses have been categorized as intrusive presence and emotional cutoff in reference to their fathers and who indicated either a conflict-avoiding or immature dependence on surviving family members. Occupying the middle position, in terms of reported distress, resolution, and available information, were those whose responses reflected a ritual respect with regard to their deceased fathers.

CONCLUSION

In essence, the death of an important person creates a demand, experienced as distress, that the bereaved construct new "affectively laden, mental representations of the self, other, and the relationship"—a new internal working model of attachment (Belsky & Pensky, 1988, p. 198). These new or revised representations will determine how significant relationships will be emotionally experienced, cognitively valued, and behaviorally enacted in the future. In this formulation, the distress of bereavement is ameliorated or resolved only when the bereaved has been able to create a new representational structure within the internal working model. Within this framework, the outcomes reported by women in this study can be thought of as reflecting the degree to which the subjects had been able to revise their models of attachment and create order in their relational worlds.

A working hypothesis derived from the results of this study is that women who report the greatest sense of resolution will be those who are able to revise or restructure their internal working models to accommodate the fact of the death in a way that ameliorates their distress. For example, women who reported ongoing attachments to their deceased fathers did not perceive that death had ended their relationships. Daughters who reported a welcome presence believed that their fathers continued to influence their lives and development in two ways. First, the father—and the fact of his death—was experienced as being an integral part of the woman's development of a new sense of self. Second, the father was perceived as a separate presence with whom the woman could interact and from whom she received emotional support and guidance. These women reported that they had, in varying degrees, resolved their distress regarding the deaths of their fathers. In contrast, those women whose responses were classified in the subcategory Intrusive Presence did not report incorporation of the father into the daughter's sense of herself, nor did they perceive that they had achieved a sense of resolution regarding the death. In fact, these women perceived that the disturbing presence interfered with their ability to resolve the loss.

A contrast was also found among those women who reported that the father–daughter relationship ended with the death. Women in the Ritual Respect group, who stated that they felt they had achieved some resolution of the death, appeared to have created a place for their fathers in their internal working models. For them, the memory of their fathers was reverently held and nurtured, yet was set apart from daily life and their own individual development. Whereas women in this group reported being comforted by ritualized, memorial practices, women in the Emotional Cutoff group were unresolved regarding the meaning of the loss of their fathers and the significance of them in their lives.

Thinking about the resolution of bereavement from the standpoint of understanding changes in individuals' working models of relationships gives direction to practitioners involved with the bereaved. Understanding that a continuing attachment to and relationship with a deceased loved one is possible and can have positive effects can lead professionals to explore potential forms of resolution that are unique to the needs of the clients with whom they work. Focusing on the dynamic, relationship-making characteristics of the process of resolution empowers the bereaved person to validate the significance of his or her own experience of loss.

REFERENCES

Balk, D. E. (1981). *Sibling death during adolescence: Self-concept and bereavement reactions*. Unpublished Ph.D. dissertation, University of Illinois, Champaign, IL.

Balk, D. E. (1990). The self-concepts of bereaved adolescents: Sibling death and its aftermath. *Journal of Adolescent Research, 5*(1), 112-132.

Balk, D. E. (1991). Death and adolescent bereavement: Current research and future directions. *Journal of Adolescent Research, 6*(1), 17–27.

Balk, D. E., Tyson-Rawson, K. J., & Colletti-Wetzel, J. (1993). Social support as an intervention with bereaved college students. *Death Studies, 17*, 427–450.

Belsky, J., & Pensky, E. (1988). Developmental history, personality, and family relationships: Toward an emergent family system. In R. A. Hinde & J. Stevenson-Hinde (Eds.), *Relationships within families* (pp. 193–219). New York: Oxford Universitiy Press.

Berlinsky, E. B., & Biller, H. B. (1982). *Parental death and psychological development.* Lexington, MA: D. C. Heath.

Bowen, M. (1991). Family reaction to death. In F. Walsh and M. McGoldrick (Eds.), *Living beyond loss: Death in the family* (pp. 79-92). New York: W. W. Norton.

Bowlby, J. (1972). Foreword. In C. M. Parkes, *Bereavement: Studies of grief in adult life* (pp. 7-8). New York: International Universities Press.

Bowlby, J. (1980). *Attachment and loss: Vol. 3. Loss, sadness, and depression.* New York: Basic Books.

Carse, J. P. (1987). Grief as a cosmic crisis. In O. S. Margolis, H. C. Raether, A. H. Kutscher, J. B. Powers, I. B. Seeland, R. DeBellis, & D. J. Cherico (Eds.), *Acute grief: Counseling the bereaved* (pp. 3–8). New York: Columbia University Press.

Chodorow, N. (1978). *The reproduction of mothering.* Berkeley: University of California Press.

Corr, C. A., & McNeil, J. N. (Eds.) (1986). *Adolescence and death.* New York: Springer.

Denes-Raj, V., & Ehrlichman, H. (1991). Effects of premature parental death on subjective life expectancy, death anxiety, and health behavior. *Omega, 23*(4), 309-321.

Dura, J. R., & Kiecolt-Glaser, J. K. (1991). Family transitions, stress and health. In P. A. Cowan & M. Hetherington (Eds.), *Family transitions* (pp. 59-76). Hillsdale, NJ: Lawrence Erlbaum Associates.

Elizur, E., & Kaffman, M. (1986). Children's bereavement reactions following death of the father. In R.H. Moos (Ed.), *Coping with life crises: An integrated approach* (pp. 49–58). New York: Plenum Press.

Fleming, S. J., & Adolph, R. (1986). Helping bereaved adolescents: Needs and responses. In C. A. Corr & J. N. McNeil (Eds.), *Adolescence and death* (pp. 97-118). New York: Springer.

Gavazzi, S. M., & Sabatelli, R. M. (1990). Family system dynamics, the individual process, and psychological development. *Journal of Adolescent Research, 5*(4), 500-519.

Gilligan, C. (1979). *In a different voice.* Cambridge, MA: Harvard University Press.

Glaser, B. G., & Strauss, A. L. (1967). *The discovery of grounded theory.* New York: Aldine De Gruyter.

Gordon, A. K. (1986). The tattered cloak of immortality. In C. A. Corr & J. N. McNeil (Eds.), *Adolescence and death* (pp. 16-31). New York: Springer.

Greenspan, S. I., & Pollock, G. H. (Eds.) (1990). *The course of life: Volume IV. Adolescence.* Madison, WI: International Universities Press.

Hogan, N., & DeSantis, L. (1992). Adolescent sibling bereavement: An ongoing attachment. *Qualitative Health Research, 2*(2), 159–177.

Houser, S. T., & Greene, W. M. (1990). Passages from late adolescence to early adulthood. In S. I. Greenspan & G. H. Pollock (Eds.), *The course of life: Volume IV. Adolescence* (pp. 377-405). Madison, WI: International Universities Press.

Isay, R. A. (1990). The second separation stage of adolescence. In S. I. Greenspan & G. H. Pollock (Eds.), *The course of life: Volume IV. Adolescence* (pp. 453-467). Madison, WI: International Universities Press.

Josselson, R. (1987). *Finding herself: Pathways to identity development in women.* San Francisco: Jossey-Bass.

Klass, D. (1988). *Parental grief: Solace and resolution.* New York: Springer.

LaGrand, L. E. (1981). Loss reactions of college students: A descriptive analysis. *Death Education, 5,* 235-248.

LaGrand, L. E. (1985). College student loss and response. In E. S. Zimmer (Ed.), *Coping with death on campus* (pp. 15-27). San Francisco: Jossey-Bass.

Martinson, I. M., & Campos, R. G. (1991). Adolescent bereavement: Long-term responses to a sibling's death from cancer. *Journal of Adolescent Research, 6*(1), 54–69.

McCracken, G. (1988). *The long interview.* Beverly Hills, CA: Sage.

McCubbin, H. I., Cauble, A. E., & Patterson, J. M. (Eds.) (1982). *Family stress, coping and social support.* Springfield: Charles C. Thomas.

McGoldrick, M. (1991). The legacy of loss. In F. Walsh & M. McGoldrick (Eds.), *Living beyond loss: Death in the family* (pp. 104-129). New York: W. W. Norton.

McGoldrick, M., & Gerson, R. (1985). *Genograms in family assessment.* New York: Norton.

Miles, M. S., & Crandall, E. K. B. (1986). The search for meaning and its potential for affecting growth in bereaved parents. In R. H. Moos (Ed.), *Coping with life crises: An integrated approach* (pp. 235–244). New York: Plenum Press.

Miller, J. B. (1976). *Toward a new psychology of women.* Boston: Beacon Press.

Moos, R. H. & Schaefer, J. A. (1986). Life transitions and crises: A conceptual overview. In R. H. Moos (Ed.), *Coping with life crises: An integrated approach* (pp. 1–28). New York: Plenum Press.

Osterweis, M., Solomon, F., & Green, M. (Eds.) (1984). *Bereavement: Reactions, consequences and care.* Washington, DC: National Academy Press.

Osterweis, M., Solomon, F., & Green, M. (1987). Bereavement: Reactions, consequences and care. In S. Zisook (Ed.), *Biopsychosocial aspects of bereavement* (pp. 3-19). Washington, DC: American Psychiatric Press.

Parkes, C. M. (1972). *Bereavement: Studies of grief in adult life.* New York: International Universities Press.

Parkes, C. M. (1987-88). Research: Bereavement. *Omega, 18*(4), 365-377.

Parkes, C. M., & Weiss, R. M. (1983). *Recovery from bereavement.* New York: Basic Books.

Pearlin, L., & Schooler, C. (1982). The structure of coping. In H. I. McCubbin, A. E. Cauble, & J. M. Patterson (Eds.), *Family stress, coping, and social support* (pp. 109-135). Springfield: Charles C. Thomas.

Preto, N. G. (1989). Transformation of the family system in adolescence. In B. Carter & M. Mc-Goldrick (Eds.), *The changing family life cycle* (2nd ed.). New York: Allyn & Bacon.

Raphael, B. (1983). *The anatomy of bereavement.* New York: Basic Books.

Rolland, J. S. (1991). Helping families with anticipatory loss. In F. Walsh & M. McGoldrick (Eds.), *Living beyond loss: Death in the family* (pp. 144-163). New York: W. W. Norton.

Schachter, S. (1991–92). Adolescent experiences with the death of a peer. *Omega, 24*(1), 1–11.

Segal, S. A., & Figley, C. R. (1988). Stressful events. *Hospital and Community Psychiatry, 39*(9), 998.

Silverman, P. R. (1970). The widow as caregiver in a program of preventive intervention with other widows. *Mental Hygiene, 54,* 540–547.

Silverman, P. R. (1987). The impact of parental death on college-age women. *Psychiatric Clinics of North America, 10*(3), 387-404.

Silverman, P. R., MacKenzie, D., Pettipas, M., & Wilson, E. (1974). *Helping each other in widowhood.* New York: Health Sciences.

Strauss, A., & Corbin, J. (1990). *Basics of qualitative research: Grounded theory procedures and techniques.* Newbury Park, NJ: Sage.

Tyson-Rawson, K. J. (1993). *College women and bereavement: Late adolescence and father death.* Unpublished dissertation study. Kansas State University, Manhattan, KS.

Worden, J. W. (1991). *Grief counseling and grief therapy: A handbook for the mental health practitioner* (2nd ed.). New York: Springer.

Youniss, J., & Smollar, J. (1985). *Adolescent relations with mothers, fathers, and friends.* Chicago: University of Chicago Press.

Zinner, E. S. (Ed.) (1985). *Coping with death on campus.* San Francisco: Jossey-Bass.

Zisook, S. (Ed.) (1987). Unresolved grief. In *Biopsychosocial aspects of bereavement* (pp. 23-24). Washington, DC: American Psychiatric Press.

Part Four

Spousal Bereavement

The chapters in this section describe how people whose spouses have died retain and modify their bonds with the deceased. Widowhood is the expected status of later years. However, death does not respect age, and the bereaved children described in the prior section all were living with widowed parents who were young. All widows and widowers have to deal not only with death and its attendant personal, social, and financial changes, but also with the loss of their social roles as spouses and the sense of self that was formed within their marriage. Typically, especially for the younger widowed person, remarriage was used as an indicator that they had successfully completed their grief work (i.e., they had let go of the past and could now move ahead).

The following chapters note that among tasks the widowed face is how to negotiate transformations to new roles while at the same time maintaining bonds with the deceased spouses. As Helena Lopata reminds us in Chapter 9, widows must find ways to acknowledge their prior marriages and the roles of the deceased spouses in the restructured families. In Chapter 10 Sidney and Miriam Moss write that a spouse's death and the surviving spouse's remarriage does not end the feeling that the dead spouse is still part of the family. Caring does not end, nor does the active sense of a person's essence.

In Chapter 11, Roberta Conant reminds us that adults may be self-conscious about any relationships they have with the deceased. This is because they are more aware of the attitudes in the larger society and are more cautious about associating themselves with any behavior that might be considered deviant or defined as abnormal. In the face of a society that provides them with few socially acceptable ways of acknowledging and legitimating their connection to their dead spouses, widowed people do so anyway. In her chapter, Lopata describes in detail how widows idealize or sanctify their deceased husbands. She finds differences in the widows she studied based on age, race, and education, and demonstrates how these variables impact on memory construction. Memorializing and remembering are ways of maintaining a bond. As Moss and Moss point out, memory and recollections are links to the past requiring that an image of the deceased be maintained.

Conant notes that for some widows, the continuing bond to the dead spouse is in the form of a sense of real presence. These widows feel protected and watched over; their self-esteem is given a boost. With this sense of presence, they experience a "gentle touching of the mind" that is, consciously or subliminally, always with them. Given the strong social sanction against this sense of presence, and given the lack of legitimizing beliefs and rituals to facilitate the sense of presence, it is surprising how often widows and widowers report the sense of presence. One of the challenges of future research on widows and widowers is to listen carefully to how the sense of presence functions in their inner life and in their interactions with others.

Two of the three chapters in this section focus on the experience of widows. Would the findings be different if men's voices were included? Using data from other sections in this book, there is sufficient evidence to conclude that both men and women are involved in constructing connections to the deceased. However, we need to know more about how gender might affect the nature of the connection, and if the relationship of the bereaved to the deceased makes a difference.

The model that sees grief as severing relationships was, as we noted in the first chapter, firmly established in empirical social science in the study of widows. All the chapters in this section challenge the concept that widows need to let go so they will have energy to reinvest in new relationships. Whatever the ultimate energy that drives human life, it is not titrated as in a test tube with a limited amount for a specific relationship. Rather, it appears that people have many relationships with different qualities, different commitments, and different inner representations of both living and deceased people. A new marriage does not replace the old as a new part replaces the worn part of a machine. "Letting go" is a poor metaphor. Even grief in conflicted or ambivalent relationships is a process of holding memories and interactions with the deceased in some new perspective. It is the new perspective that enables the bonds to be in the past, in the present, and in the future at the same time. Conant compares the activity of developing a new perspective to play. She sees internal role-playing as a way of building and consolidating new understandings of old attachments and of new attachments as well.

P. R. S.
S. N.

Chapter 9

Widowhood and Husband Sanctification

Helena Znaniecka Lopata

The ongoing life of a society and of its component social units must include methods for dealing with the loss of members through death or removal from active participation by other means. The social roles such members filled must be removed through disbanding of their social circles, or their replacements must be secured. On the macrosocial level and in the long run, replacement of members is ensured through birth, capture, incorporation of immigrants, or expansion of the political state, as well as through socialization and education of all into the major roles (Lopata, 1964, 1969; Znaniecki, 1965). Whatever system of replacement of a particular member goes into effect, the history of the social unit, such as a family or organization, usually requires an acknowledgment of his or her prior existence and the method of removal. His or her biography is recorded in announcements, folklore, as a statistic, or in the memory of others. The extent to which that biography is incorporated into the memory of the unit depends upon the importance assigned to that member, and/or even upon the events surrounding his or her removal.

The acknowledgment of the prior existence and termination of membership in a social group is particularly apt to be public and ritualized in the case of removal through death. Voluntary death through suicide and involuntary but violent death through wars, societal punishment, or intermember conflict bring with them variations of accounts and rituals of acknowledgment. Even involuntary death through "natural" causes such as depersonalized disasters or health problems is threatening to personal survivors and larger social units. Regardless of the social value of the member in the past or at the time of death, death reminds living members of their own mortality, as Freud (1917) observed in *Mourning and Melancholia*. Of course, some deaths go unnoticed by a society because of secrecy on the part of those who are involved or because the person had become so disengaged from social life that the final separation is not brought to societal attention (Cumming & Henry, 1961). Since human beings are self-conscious and usually fearful of their own death, they are likely to try to insure that their physical death is not accompanied by social death. Societies have insisted that the rituals of acknowledging the death be accompanied by rituals insuring continuation of social life (Bendann, 1930; Cowgill & Holmes, 1972; Vernon, 1970).

This chapter is adapted from "Widowhood and Husband Sanctification," by H. Z. Lopata, 1981, *Journal of Marriage and the Family, 43*, p. 439. Copyright © 1981 by the National Council on Family Relations. Reprinted with permission.

Whatever effects the death of a member has on the society at large, because of the need to replace the member, to weave the biography into social history, and to deal with the emotional reactions to death, the effects upon the social units personally involved with the deceased are also complicated. Members of those social circles in which she or he played social roles must adjust their own duties and rights or quickly find a replacement.[1] Social role interactions can involve deep human sentiments, and they are idiosyncratically developed so that replacements are difficult, if not impossible. This is particularly true in societies or subcultures idealizing individualistic involvement in social relations and the construction of the self as a unique being (Lofland, 1985). Thus, societies typical of Europe and America of recent times build expectations of person-focused relations into the culture and socialize its members into those expectations. In consequence, the circles of a deceased "significant other" expect personal grief following his or her death. The duties of the social person in the roles of wife or husband, son or daughter, father or mother, and friend include not only public acknowledgment of the death and organization of and participation in the funeral or other rituals, but also deeply felt grief and involvement in the mourning process.

There are many ways by which the obligations to the deceased by the survivors in American society are met. One is through his or her preservation as a positive social person in the memories of those to whom she or he supposedly "mattered" (Rosenberg & McCullough, 1979; Rubin, 1993). In fact, the funeral eulogy and rituals, such as the Jewish *shiva*, during which the bereaved are visited and given the opportunity to relive the past, including the death, tend to select not the total biography of the deceased, but only those aspects that are defined as positive (Vernon, 1970).

This duty to continue the social existence of the deceased and especially to redefine the biography along positive lines runs counter, however, to the companion task of grief work that requires the cutting of ties with that person. Basing their analysis on Freud's theories, Lindemann (1944) and succeeding psychiatrists have stressed the importance to the mental health of the bereaved of successful completion of the process of "grief work," by movement of the memory of the deceased away from the focal point of life. The survivors of death being discussed here are widows in metropolitan America. Their grief work is considered especially traumatic in marriage-oriented American society. Maddison and Walker (1967) stated,

A widow is faced with two concurrent tasks; she is required through the process of mourning, to detach herself sufficiently from the lost object to permit the continua-

[1]The Znaniecki/Lopata definition of social role as a set of interdependent social relations between a social person and a social circle, involving rights and duties is used here. Thus, the role of wife involves relations not only with the husband, but also with everyone to whom she has duties because she is his wife, and everyone who has duties to her that make possible her part of the role. The main beneficiary of the relations of a social person holding the role title and of the rest of her circle are usually understood by that title. Professors profess to students; the main beneficiary of the role of wife is the husband.

tion of other relationships and the development of new ones; at the same time, she has to establish for herself a new role conception as an adult woman without a partner. (p. 157)

It is the thesis of this chapter that the double-bind dilemma of a wife who survives her husband: the obligation to keep him socially alive while simultaneously establishing herself as a new adult woman, is accomplished by a process of sanctification.

HUSBAND SANCTIFICATION

The Random House Dictionary of the English Language (1966) defines "to sanctify" as "to purify or free from sin; to set apart as sacred" (p. 1165). Several studies of widows in America and related societies have reported a tendency toward idealization of the deceased. Vernon (1970) considers the idealization of the deceased as one type of adjustment to the death: "Through his symbolizing facility, through selective remembering, and through providing missing elements symbolically, a person may be able to create an idealized image of the deceased and of the person's relationships with the deceased" (p. 145).

Rees (1975) feels that this is a temporary phenomenon. "Early in bereavement these memories were marked by obvious idealization of the husband and the marriage" (p. 146). However, as we learned from the study of metropolitan Chicago widows, there does not appear to be a timeframe for sanctification.

The idealization of the deceased husband, even to the point of sanctification, can perform several functions for the widow. His social purification or reconstruction in memory can remove him from the role of critic and ever-present guide by raising him above mortal sentiments, such as jealousy, resentment over not being grieved deeply or long enough, irritation over her management of possessions with which he identified (Shuchter, 1986). It allows the widow to go about her daily living and to gradually reconstruct herself and other relations (Lopata, 1975a). Sanctification thus moves the late husband into an other-worldly position as an understanding and purified distant observer.

The idealization of the deceased can also help the widow's feelings about herself (diGuilio, 1989). If such an ideal man married and lived with her, then she must not be as bad a person as the moods of depression which often accompany grief make her seem to be (Shuchter & Zisook, 1993). Finally, it can wash out unpleasant memories of the past, forming a better foundation for dealing with the usually difficult readjustment process.

American society encourages this tendency to purify the deceased in the memory of the survivors with the help of the wake, the funeral eulogy, and the *shiva* or other postfuneral rituals (see also Berardo, 1967, 1968; Marris, 1958; Turnstall, 1966; Vernon, 1970). Friends and other associates tend to uphold this social obligation by speaking no ill of the deceased. The process is often assisted by the relative deprivation experienced by the widow in her life following the death of the husband. Many men die while "in the prime of life" or later, rather than early in marriage when they leave much "unfinished business" in their relationship with the wife (Blauner, 1966). Life for a couple who remained married over the years is apt to have been relatively satisfactory; at least the wife was adjusted to whatever unhappiness existed in the relationship. The children were grown and established in their lives and most of them "turned out all right" (Lopata, 1966, 1971). Conflict over them or other aspects of life was either an established routine or minimal.

The death of the husband is apt to create several specific situations bringing unhappiness. Income often drops, loneliness is experienced, housing and relational adjustments must be made (Lopata, 1969, 1973, 1979, 1980). Couple-companionate friendships become strained, and the absence of an escort and companion in activities tends to decrease social life space. It would not be surprising for a widow to evaluate the life she had with her late husband, and the man himself, as superior to her current situation and potential companions, and even to exaggerate the good qualities of the past considerably. Memory has a reality reconstructive effect, as evidenced by accounts of remembered childhood.

Of course, there is undoubtedly many a wife who is simply relieved by the death of her husband and who easily resists the culturally encouraged temptation to turn him and the marriage into perfection through memory reconstruction.

There are some distinct disadvantages to husband sanctification. Married friends who knew the deceased may become irritated over the reconstructed image of such a perfect man while they are living with imperfect husbands. Hunt (1966) found that divorced men do not want to date widows because they cannot compete with such perfection. Bernard (1956) states in *Remarriage* that the relation to a second spouse is different, depending on whether the prior marriage ended in divorce or widowhood, because of the tendency to idealize the dead, but not the divorced, spouse. Criticism of a deceased person constitutes a breach of taste. The first spouse may be so idealized, memories of him so selective, that the second spouse cannot compete.

CHICAGO-AREA WIDOWS

This tendency to idealize the late husband, even to the point of sanctification, was evident during the study of a modified area probability sample of 301 Chicago-area widows (Lopata, 1973, 1975a, 1975b).[2] It became even more apparent in the exploratory stages of a new study of widows of all ages who were or had been beneficiaries of Social Security Administration funds and who resided in metropolitan Chicago.[3] The initial plan of the second study had been to gain information on the economic, service, social, and emotional support systems of widows the year prior to the husband's fatal illness and at the time of the interview. How-

[2]The "role modification" study was funded by the Administration on Aging and Roosevelt University. Thanks go to A. Marvin Taves and the AOA staff. See Lopata, 1973.

ever, husband idealization by most of the widows interviewed in the pilot stage of research kept interfering with the picture of supports in the pre-illness period. It became apparent that the interview was not reaching life as it had been but life as it was reconstructed in the memory of the woman. We decided, therefore, that the idealization could become a subject of research of itself and constructed a "sanctification scale." The support systems study of metropolitan Chicago widows was funded by the Social Security Administration, whose statisticians insisted that the sample be weighted by the ratio in which subsamples were drawn. Thus, the sample of 1,169 women represented 82,085. The five subsamples included retirement widows who had reached the age of entitlement for benefits from the late husband's work record, mothers of dependent children, widows who received benefits in the past but whose children were past the entitlement age, or who remarried, and women who received only the "lump sum" payment to help defray funeral costs.

The interview focused upon the personal resources, such as education or income and relatives or friends of each widow, and on the economic, social, service, and emotional support systems in which she was involved. The sanctification scale formed part of a self-administered section and contained two segments. The first segment consisted of a set of seven semantic differential statements about the deceased, including good–bad, useful–useless, honest–dishonest, superior–inferior, kind–cruel, friendly–unfriendly, and warm–cold. These statements were found in several pretests to be the most differentiating, although they also tended to draw positive extremes.[4] The second segment of the scale consisted of seven statements, also extensively pretested, for which levels of agreement were obtained. These statements started with "My husband was an unusually good man," and ranged to the extreme of "My husband had no irritating habits." Each statement tended to be more emphatic than the preceding one, but they were not cumulative in effect.

The two questions to which this chapter addresses itself are: "How are American urban widows distributed in terms of scores on the scale?" and "Who are the widows who are located at the polar ends of the husband sanctification scale?"

[3]The study of the Support Systems Involving Widows in Non-Agricultural Areas was funded with a contract from the Social Security Administration (SSA-71-3411) and Loyola University of Chicago. The final wave of interviewing was carried out in the summer of 1974 through the Survey Research Laboratory of the University of Illinois. Many thanks go to its staff, to Dr. Henry P. Brehm, Chief of Research Grants and Contracts Staff, Social Security Administration; Dr. Adam Kurzynowski of the Szkola Glowna Planowania i Statystyki, Warsaw, Poland; and Dr. Nada Smolic-Krkovic of the Institute of Social Work in Zagreb, Yugoslavia, for all their help in construction of the schedule, and the staff of the Center for the Comparative Study of Social Roles, including Frank Steinhart, Carla Christiansen, Sister Gertrud Kim, and Monica Velasco, for all the help throughout the stages of the work.
[4]This segment of the scale was replicated in a study of divorcees by Kitson (see Kitson et al., 1980). The hypothesized differences between the widows and the divorcees in their memories of their spouses indicates that the scale measures differences in memory construction and experiences surrounding the dissolution of the marriage.

Frequency of Husband Sanctification

Semantic differential evaluations of late husbands by Chicago area widows showed that many widows did sanctify their late husbands, or that they had been married to very unusual men. Three-quarters of the Chicago area current and former beneficiaries of Social Security defined their late husbands as having been extremely good, honest, kind, friendly, and warm. The quality of "useful" drew the first place ranking, on a 7-grade scale, a little less frequently; and "superior" is the only quality at which the respondents balked, although even here only 6% of the women placed their late husbands below the median position of 4.

Interestingly enough, life together with the late husband was not idealized to the extent to which he was as a person. Such personal idealization of the husband may be difficult for a woman because of the reality pull of the connecting link to her and the children. The most extreme statement in that segment of the sanctification scale, "My husband had no irritating habits," drew disagreement from 36% of the widows, with an additional 8% disagreeing strongly. Even here, however, more than one fourth of the widows strongly agreed with the statement, one which few wives of living husbands (or husbands of living wives, for that matter) would be likely to accept. All but 5% of the respondents judged the deceased as having been a very good father, and almost as many defined him as having been an unusually good man. Thus, not only was he on the top of the good–bad continuum, but this location placed him above other men. This tendency toward favorable ranking of the husband did not force all the widows to agree that the marriage was above average, that they and the late husband spent all their nonwork hours together, that both of them felt the same way about everything, or that their home had been unusually happy. Still, about half of the respondents did go to such extremes in reconstructing their past.

There are different patterns in the items selected from the scale by the husband-sactifying widows. Interestingly, women who defined their late husbands as superior were not apt to rank them with equal fervor as friendly, warm, or even useful. The husband's warmth was frequently combined in the mind of the surviving wife with kindness and friendliness. Honesty, goodness, and kindness were also apt to be closely related to each other in the way the widow remembered her late husband.

Patterns were also discernible within the "life together" segment of the sanctification scale and the range of associations was similar to that of the other segment, 29 to 30 points, respectively. Widows who defined their late husbands as unusually good men also judged their marriages as above average to an overwhelming extent. On the other hand, evaluation as a good father did not translate itself in the widow's memory into a perception of the husband as a companion in all leisuretime activity or as a sharer of all feelings, or into absolution from all irritating habits. A picture emerges of a man remembered primarily for having been a good father, whose marriage was sex-segregated and traditional, and who was more apt to irritate his wife by his habits than was the man remembered as having shared an above-average marriage. There is a much stronger association between the widow's memory of the home as having been unusually happy, and of the marriage and the man as unusually good, than there is between the happiness of the home and the sharing of all activities judgments.

Widows who pushed themselves into defining their late husbands as "superior" were not as apt to have felt close to their husbands, to have shared activities and feelings with them, as were widows who defined the late husbands as extremely honest or kind. Good fathers were most apt to be portrayed as honest, least apt to be seen as superior or useful. A happy home was remembered as having contained an honest husband more often than a superior or friendly one. Kindness went with being unusually good as a man, as did honesty, though warmth and friendliness were not far behind. The greatest variation between the strength of association exists between the combination of honesty and good fatherhood on one side (gamma = .80) and good fatherhood and superiority (gamma = .59). Superior men, in the eyes of their widows, seemed to lack other human qualities. The least spread in gammas is between the agreement that the husband had no irritating habits and all the personal qualities—probably because of the note of realism which crept in here. All in all, although there are variations by item of the sanctification scale, the safe conclusion is that many, in fact most, of the Chicago area widows of this study tended to idealize their late husbands and even some aspects of life with them to the point of sanctification.

WHO SANCTIFIES?

The second question to which we want to address ourselves concerns the factors influencing the degree to which a widow sanctifies her late husband. Length of widowhood was hypothesized as an important variable (see Rees, 1975) but it proved insignificant, probably because all of our respondents had been widowed for more than a year and the process may have already crystallized by that time. Many other variables proved to be insignificant influences on husband sanctification, including current income, number of living children, number of friends, expressed feeling of loneliness or life satisfaction, and so forth. There was a relatively strong positive association between sanctification and the rank order assigned to the role of wife, which is not surprising. That is, women who tended toward extreme idealization of their late husbands also ranked the role of wife above all other roles a woman can perform. The main influence on the scores came from the following variables: age, education, income prior to the husband's fatal illness or accident, and race; all four were also mutually interdependent. The strongest association was between sanctification and race, the non-Whites being much less apt to idealize the late husbands to an extreme extent than were the Whites (gamma = .44 for the semantic differential and .30 for the life together segment).

Because of space limitations, we shall examine here only the effects of education and race upon husband sanctification. Table 1 contains three sets of data,

Table 1 Gamma Associations and Percentage of First-Place Ranks, Strongly Agree Judgments, and Mean Ranks of Items on the Santification Scale, by Years of Schooling Achieved by the Chicago-Area Widows

Scale Item	Gamma	Total	Mean Total	>8		8		9–11		12		13–15		16+	
				%	Mean	%	Mean	%	Mean	%	Mean	%	Mean	%	Mean
Good–bad	.27	75	1.62	58	2.32	77	1.63	78	1.55	81	1.35	80	1.32	78	1.30
Useful–useless	.18	72	1.68	56	2.43	80	1.49	73	1.63	76	1.46	74	1.46	72	1.41
Honest–dishonest	.20	82	1.47	71	1.78	84	1.43	80	1.54	84	1.35	86	1.34	92	1.15
Superior–inferior	.20	55	2.07	39	2.70	56	2.01	56	2.09	58	1.84	61	1.82	68	1.63
Kind–cruel	.22	78	1.56	64	2.07	80	1.57	82	1.53	83	1.33	80	1.36	84	1.31
Friendly–unfriendly	.13	79	1.53	66	1.88	85	1.53	84	1.44	80	1.44	78	1.45	81	1.34
Warm–cold	.22	76	1.61	60	2.13	79	1.52	77	1.63	82	1.41	80	1.40	80	1.40

the gamma associations between each scale item and years of schooling achieved by the Chicago area widows, the percentages of women within each schooling category who circled the extreme position on the semantic differential or the life together segments of the scale, and the mean rank for that category. (It must be remembered that the semantic differential offers a 7-point range, while the life together segment offers only a 4-point range.) The gammas are not very strong, the highest being .30 for the association between the statement "My husband was an unusually good man" and the widow's schooling. However, both the percentages and the means show significant differences between the very uneducated and the rest of the women. The lowest mean, that of 1.15, indicates almost perfect concentration on the first rank on the semantic differential by the most educated women ranking their late husbands on the honest–dishonest continuum. Ninety-two percent of them placed their husbands in the first rank, compared to 71% of the women with less than an 8th-grade education. The late husbands did not fare that well in any other personal or relational item so far as the most educated women were concerned. These women were particularly unlikely to rank their husbands as superior, useful, or good. They were the least apt to remember sharing activities with him or having an above-average marriage. The very educated women resembled the least educated in refusing to agree with the statement that the late husbands had no irritating habits, although probably for different reasons. The only credit many widows with less than eight grades of schooling gave their late husbands was that of being good fathers, and even for this item, they selected the first-place rank less frequently than did any other educational category.

Widows who finished 8th grade were very different from those with less schooling, on all items, coming close only in the infrequency with which they strongly agreed that the marriage had been above average (36 to 31%, respectively). They generally did not go below the second of the seven slots in the semantic differential statements scores. They and the high school dropouts were similar in many distributions, but the latter were much less apt to agree that they and their husbands felt the same way about things (means of 2.02 for the dropouts and 1.78 for those finishing 8th grade). Those who finished high school and college dropouts were also very similar to each other, both in percentages and in means, except that the latter did not claim as often to have always done things together with their late husbands or to have felt the same way. There was also a difference in their definition of the home as happy, and of the husband as a very good father, the college dropouts being less willing to strongly agree with these statements. The widows who had completed 16 years or more of schooling were least likely to judge their husbands as without irritating habits; they were also below the average in agreeing strongly that their homes had been unusually happy, that the husbands had been good fathers, or that the marriages had been above average. However, they were at least as extreme in the relational segment and much more frequently extreme on most of the semantic differential items than was the group as a whole.

Table 2   Extreme, High, Medium, and Low Scores of Chicago-Area Widows (by Race) on the Semantic Differential Segment of the Sanctification Scale (Percentages)

Race	Extreme	High	Medium	Low	Row total	N
White	48.7	21.3	20.1	9.9	85.9	69,049
Non-White	27.0	10.3	20.3	42.4	14.1	11,304
Total	45.7	19.8	20.1	14.4	100.0	
Total N	36,695	15,899	16,158	11,601		80,353

Note: Gamma = 0.50.

The most significant difference between categories of widows in their scores on the sanctification scale was between the White and non-White racial groups, the non-Whites being principally African Americans (see Tables 2 and 3). The difference was particularly strong in the semantic differential segment of the scale, both groups being more realistic in the relational or life together segment. Forty-nine percent of the Whites, but only 27% of the non-Whites, scored at the extremely high end of the semantic differential scale, while only 10% of the Whites and 42% of the non-White widows scored low. The two groups were distributed in the same proportion in the extremely high end of the life together segment, but the non-Whites were much more apt than the Whites to show a medium score, while the Whites scored high.

There are interesting variations in the scores on different items of the scale (see Table 4). The non-Whites were least apt to define their late husbands as superior, differing from the Whites most noticeably in this respect. Another strong difference between the two racial groups was in the frequency with which they assigned first rank on the good–bad semantic differential continuum and their mean rankings on this item. The third main difference was on judgments of hon-

Table 3   Extreme, High, Medium, and Low Scores by Chicago-Area Widows (by Race) on the Life Together Segment of the Sanctification Scale (Percentages)

Race	Extreme	High	Medium	Low	Row total	N
White	14.0	51.7	29.1	5.3	86.4	68,701
Non-White	14.2	35.5	37.2	13.0	13.6	10,776
Total	14.0	49.5	30.2	6.3	100.0	
Total N	11,126	39,341	23,991	5,019		79,477

Note: Gamma = 0.23.

esty. The two groups were alike in the means of ranks of the usefulness quality, but even here there were 23% more Whites than non-Whites who ranked their late husbands ideal on this trait.

The gaps between the two racial groups were not as large in the life together segment of the scale. The groups were most similar in refusing to agree with the statement "My husband had no irritating habits." The greatest variation in percentages of widows willing to agree strongly was on the statement that the husband was an unusually good man (a difference of 31%), and the greatest variation on the mean scores was on the statement that the husband and wife did everything together during nonworking hours.

Table 4   Gamma Association, Mean Scores, and Percentage in Extreme Rank of Whites and Non-Whites on Items of the Sanctification Scale

		White		Non-White		Gap between
Item	Gamma	%	Mean	%	Mean	mean scores
Semantic differential[a]						
Good–bad	.58	80	1.43	41	2.64	1.21
Useful–useless	.42	76	1.57	53	2.26	.69
Honest–dishonest	.67	86	1.31	52	2.38	1.07
Superior–inferior	.53	58	1.88	32	3.15	1.27
Kind–cruel	.59	83	1.40	53	2.39	.99
Friendly–unfriendly	.59	83	1.39	54	2.34	.95
Warm–cold	.57	81	1.47	49	2.38	.91
Life together[b]						
Husband unusually good	.54	69	1.41	38	1.93	.52
Marriage above average	.44	48	1.69	25	2.16	.47
Did things together	.46	53	1.70	29	2.34	.63
Felt same way	.45	58	1.93	33	2.35	.42
Good father	.32	37	1.32	23	1.77	.45
Happy home	.53	73	1.59	44	2.13	.54
No irritating habits	.28	29	2.19	21	2.54	.35

Note: Usual *N* = White around 69,000; Non-Whites 11,360.
[a]Possible range 1–7.
[b]Possible range 1–4.

There are many variables contributing to these differences between widows of the two racial groups, in addition to a possible variation between the subcultures in the obligation to sanctify the deceased husband. The differences show interesting patterns when significant variables, such as age and education, are tested while controlling for race. The non-White widows were less likely to have achieved much schooling, an expected finding. However, schooling had much stronger effects on the non-White than on the White widows. That is, the higher the schooling for the non-Whites, the more apt was the widow to have sanctified the late husband (gamma = .26), while the differences for the Whites were not that strong (gamma = .09). The main differences among Whites were between the women with less than a 9th-grade education and the others, the relation not being linear after that. Not only was the number of years of schooling more important for the non-Whites in their scores on the husband sanctification scale, but also the possession of a degree was more important (gamma = .38 and .11, respectively). Non-White widows without a grade school diploma were especially less apt to sanctify the deceased husband than were the White widows without a diploma. On the other hand, age was more important for the Whites than for the non-Whites in influencing the semantic differential segment of the scale (gamma = .25 and .10), while it had the opposite effect on the life together segment (gamma = .14 for Whites, .23 for non-Whites). The older White women tended to sanctify the late husbands, but not the relationships, in spite of educational differences, while the more educated non-Whites tended to sanctify the husbands regardless of age. Age had less effect on the Whites than on the non-Whites in the extent to which life before the husband's fatal illness or accident was positively defined. Another variable which indicates a difference between the Whites and the non-Whites was place of birth (gamma = .38 for non-Whites, .06 for Whites). Eighty-eight percent of the non-White widows were born outside of Illinois, and these women tended not to be the sanctifying respondents, unless they were relatively educated. The differences in the influence of education, age, and place of birth of the White and the non-White widows did not seem, however, to account for all the differences between the two racial groups in the extent to which they sanctified their late husbands and relationships with them.

SUMMARY AND CONCLUSIONS

The evidence presented in this chapter points to a tendency of many Chicago area widows to idealize their late husbands even to the point of sanctification. Although less likely to idealize the home situation before the husband's fatal illness or accident, the average woman from this group was apt to consider him to have been an unusually good father, husband, and man in general. Some went so far as to agree with the statement that the husband had been free from any irritating habits—an agreement which undoubtedly few wives of living husbands would venture.

The tendency to idealize the late husband was not, however, uniform. Older women, particularly older White widows, were more apt to sanctify their husbands than are the younger or the non-White women. Education positively influenced the willingness to idealize the husband, although the most educated did not go so far as to purify the spouse of any irritating habits. The least educated expressed hostility to the husband and dissatisfaction with the marriage. Blauner's (1966) conclusion concerning the problems facing survivors left with "unfinished business" with the deceased appears to be validated by the failure of younger widows to identify with the extreme of husband sanctification.

The differences in the degree to which White and non-Whites were able, or needed, to sanctify their late husbands may arise from the younger age and lower education of so many non-Whites, or from life experiences or subcultural norms. Further research on the subcultures is necessary before these variables can be separated. Of course, it is quite possible that all of the variables, younger age at widowhood, lower educational achievement, difficulty of life, and lower-class Black or other non-White subculture may merge in the construction of reality in memory to create a lower tendency toward sanctification of the deceased husband. The sanctifying norms of the European and American White cultures may soften the memory of harshness of life of older immigrants or ethnics, or the passing of years may have settled or removed former conflicts, facilitating husband sanctification among the White widows. The question arises, of course, as to the direction taken by widows for blaming, or praising, the quality of past life, the spouse, or fatalistically defined forces. The study of husband sanctification among Chicago area widows thus raises several questions as to the dynamics of memory construction that, it is hoped, other research will address. Such research can also teach us more about the contribution of husband sanctification to the life satisfaction of the surviving widow.

REFERENCES

Bendann, E. (1930). *Death customs: An analytical study of burial rites.* New York: Alfred A. Knopf.

Berardo, F. (1967). *Social adaptation to widowhood among a rural-urban aged population.* Agricultural Experiment Station Bulletin 689 (December). Pullman, WA: Washington State University.

Berardo, F. (1968). Widowhood status in the United States: Perspective on a neglected aspect of the family life-cycle. *The Family Coordinator, 17,* 191–203.

Bernard, J. (1956). *Remarriage.* New York: Dryden Press.

Blauner, R. (1966). Death and social structure. *Psychiatry, 29,* 378-394.

Cowgill, D. O., & Holmes, L. D. (1972). *Aging and modernization.* New York: Appleton-Century-Crofts.

Cumming, E., & Henry, W. E. (1961). *Growing old: The process of disengagement.* New York: Basic Books.

diGuilio, R. C. (1989). *Beyond widowhood.* New York: Free Press.

Freud, S. (1917). Mourning and melancholia. In *Collected papers* (Vol. 4, pp. 152–170). London: Hogarth Press.

Hunt, M. (1966). *The world of the formerly married.* New York: McGraw-Hill.

Kitson, G. C., Lopata, H. Z., Holmes, W. M., & Meyering, S. M. (1980). Divorcees and widows: Similarities and differences. *American Journal of Orthopsychiatry, 50,* 291–301.

Lindemann, E. (1944). Symptomatology and management of acute grief. *American Journal of Psychiatry, 101*,141–148.

Lofland, L. H. (1985). The social shaping of emotion: The case of grief. *Symbolic Interaction, 8*, 171–190.

Lopata, H. Z. (1964). A restatement of the relation between role and status. *Sociology and Social Research, 49*, 58–68.

Lopata, H. Z. (1966). The life cycle of the social role of housewife. *Sociology and Social Research, 51*, 5–22.

Lopata, H. Z. (1969). Loneliness: Forms and components. *Social Problems, 17*, 248–262.

Lopata, H. Z. (1971). *Occupation: Housewife*. New York: Oxford University Press.

Lopata, H. Z. (1973). *Widowhood in an American city*. Cambridge, MA: Schenckman.

Lopata, H. Z. (1975a). On widowhood: Grief work and identity reconstruction. *Journal of Geriatric Psychiatry, 8* (1), 41–55.

Lopata, H. Z. (1975b). Widowhood: Societal factors in life-span disruptions and alternatives. In N. Datan & L. Ginsberg (Eds.), *Life-Span Developmental Psychology: Normative Life Crisis* (pp. 217–236). New York: Academic Press.

Lopata, H. Z. (1979). *Women as widows: Support systems*. New York: Elsevier.

Lopata, H. Z. (1980). Loneliness in widowhood. In J. Hartog & Y. Cohen (Eds.), *The anatomy of loneliness* (pp. 237–258). New York: International Universities Press.

Maddison, D. C., &. Walker, W. L. (1967). Factors affecting the outcome of conjugal bereavement. *British Journal of Psychiatry, 113*(2), 1057–1067.

Marris, P. (1958). *Widows and their families*. London: Routledge & Kegan Paul.

Random House Dictionary of the English Language. (1966). New York: Random House.

Rees, W. D. (1975). The bereaved and their hallucinations. In B. Schoenberg, I. Gerber, A. Wiener, A. H. Kutscher, D. Peretz, & A. C. Carr (Eds.), *Bereavement: Its psychosocial aspects* (pp. 66–71). New York: Columbia University Press.

Rosenberg, M., & McCullough, B. C. (1979, August). *Mattering: Inferred significance and mental health among adolescents*. Paper presented at the annual meeting of the American Sociological Association, Boston.

Rubin, S. A. (1993). The death of a child is forever: The life course impact of child loss. In M. S. Stroebe, W. Stroebe, & R. O. Hansson (Eds.), *Handbook of bereavement* (pp. 285–299). New York: Cambridge University Press.

Shuchter, S. R. (1986). *Dimensions of grief: Adjusting to the death of a spouse*. San Francisco: Jossey-Bass.

Shuchter, S. R., & Zisook, S. (1993). The course of normal grief. In M. S. Stroebe, W. Stroebe, & R. O. Hansson (Eds.), *Handbook of bereavement* (pp. 23–43). New York: Cambridge University Press.

Turnstall, J. (1966). *Old and alone*. London: Routledge & Kegan Paul.

Vernon, G. M. (1970). *Sociology of death*. New York: Ronald Press.

Znaniecki, F. (1965). *Social relations and social roles*. San Francisco: Chandler.

Chapter 10

Remarriage of Widowed Persons: A Triadic Relationship

Miriam S. Moss and Sidney Z. Moss

Elsewhere in this book, evidence has been presented of the survivor's tie with a significant deceased person. Here, the focus is on the ways in which that tie may play a role in new relationships. Specifically, we examine how the tie with the deceased spouse influences the remarriage of middle-aged and elderly persons.

We shift here from a primary concern with a dyad—the survivor and the deceased person—to focus on a triadic relationship that includes the remarried widowed person, the deceased spouse, and the new spouse. As Simmel (1950) suggested, the addition of a third person to a dyad completely changes the quality of the social ties. Overall we suggest that the tie between any two persons in this triad is affected by the third person (Simmel, 1950). We focus on the ways in which the experience of the first marriage impacts upon the social construction of the second marriage.

We suggest that the bonds of a long-term marriage involve strong primary attachments that serve as a base for mutual security and protectiveness (Ainsworth, 1985; Bowlby, 1988). Bowlby describes the stages that the survivor goes through after an attachment figure dies as a process of decathexis much like the Freudian model (Freud, 1957). In his view, this distancing eventually allows for the development of a new assumptive world without the deceased (Parkes, 1988) and hence facilitates the formation of new ties.

The overall thrust of this chapter is to emphasize that within the reality of loss and letting go of the dead spouse, there are many significant ways in which the remarried person's tie to the deceased spouse persists. After briefly outlining how the remarried person lets go of the psychosocial bond with the dead spouse, we will emphasize the ways in which the widowed person holds on to the tie.

We focus on remarriage in middle and late adulthood because we wish to examine the persistence of ties rooted in a long-term commitment. The emphasis here is on the experience of widowed persons who have been married for several decades—often where half or more of their lifetimes were spent in the marriage. In order to reduce the complexity of this topic, we have oversimplified our discussion of gender and of the marital dyad, and we have minimized the impact of children of the earlier marriage. These are clear limitations of this chapter.

We emphasize the commonalties of the experience of remarriage for widowed persons. The many dissimilarities are beyond the scope of this chapter.

There is little doubt that there is some difference between the way men and women experience widowhood (Gallagher-Thompson, Futterman, Farberow, Thompson, & Peterson, 1993; Silverman, 1986) as well as the way remarried widows and widowers perceive their ties with the deceased spouses. It may be that neither gender is more tied or less tied to the deceased than the other, but that the bonds have different emphases and meanings. We leave to subsequent explorations a delineation of gender differences. Thus, from this point on we will refer to "widowed persons" whenever gender is irrelevant.

Finally, although we strongly support a family focus in understanding dyadic, triadic, and broader kin ties, in this chapter we will only briefly discuss the ways in which other family members of the surviving spouses are involved in the maintenance of the ties with the deceased spouses. No doubt children and other kin play significant roles in remarriage of widowed persons.

BACKGROUND

In recent decades, there has been an increasing tendency for marriages to involve persons who have been married before. National Center for Health Statistics data have shown that in the 1980s more than 40% of marriages were remarriages for one or both spouses (Wilson & Clarke, 1992). The overwhelming segment of remarriages is composed of divorced persons. Our focus here is on remarriages of widowed persons, a total of 149,000 in 1988, which represents less than 10% of all remarriages in that year.

Overall, the remarriage rate is negatively associated with age. Bumpass, Sweet, and Martin (1990) estimate that 89% of women who are divorced before age 25 remarry, while only 31% of those who are divorced at age 40 or later remarry. The rate of remarriage for widowed persons has also been found to decrease with age (Cleveland & Gianturco, 1976; Smith, Zick, & Duncan, 1991; Wilson & Clarke, 1992). In 1988, the estimated remarriage rate per 1,000 widowed persons age 25 to 29 was 144 for men and 88 for women. For those age 45 to 54, the rates were 69 for men, 23 for women; and for those age 55 and over, the rates were men, 23, and women, 3 (Wilson & Clarke, 1992).

The pool of widowed persons includes five times as many women as men, and widowed women tend to be older than widowed men. Also, widowers tend to marry women who are younger than themselves. Thus, there are relatively few widowers who are available as potential marriage partners for widows. There is a high ratio of nonmarried widows to nonmarried widowers: 3.5 for persons age 65 to 74; 4.4 for those 75 and over (Spanier & Glick, 1980). Thus, overall, the remarriage rate after widowhood has been found to be considerably higher for men than for women (Cleveland & Gianturco, 1976; Smith et al., 1991; Wilson & Clarke, 1992).

Widowed persons frequently marry other widowed persons (in 1988, 45% of the grooms and 42% of the brides did so). On the other hand, those who had been divorced in their previous marriages rarely (4%) married widowed persons in subsequent marriages (Wilson & Clarke, 1992).

The rate of cohabiting widowed persons has increased substantially in recent years (Wilson & Clarke, 1992). This may reflect the impact of changing patterns of cohabitation for younger cohorts, as well as some economic constraints on remarriage due to reductions of insurance and other benefits to widowed persons after remarriage.

In spite of their low proportion, we focus here on middle-aged and older widowed persons who remarry because their collective experience in remarriage casts in high relief the continuing role of the deceased spouse. Most remarried widowed persons are in this age group; in 1988 the average age of widowed grooms was 61, and of widowed brides 53 (Wilson & Clarke, 1992).

TIES WITH DECEASED SPOUSES IN WIDOWHOOD

This conceptual discussion has grown out of the authors' earlier writing, the clinical experience of one author, and qualitative interviews with four widowed persons who had been remarried from 3 to 20 years. The focus is on contemporary American culture, with the recognition that ethnicity and religious identification may account for considerable variation.

First, we briefly describe some ways in which the pervasive kinship bond of marriage persists (S. Z. Moss & Moss, 1980) and the widowed person maintains a tie with the deceased spouse. After that, the main thrust of the chapter focuses on how the attachment continues in remarriage.

The widowed person's relationship with the deceased spouse includes strong themes of both letting go and holding on. These two themes are intertwined and are not polar opposites. Letting go may begin even before the death of a spouse. There is often a period of anticipation in which the possibility of the death is considered. If a terminal illness was particularly incapacitating with reduced cognitive, physical, or sexual functioning, some aspects of the spousal relationship may have drastically changed. Later, a diagnosis of terminal illness followed by the physical death may further distance the survivor from the deceased. The ceremony of the funeral and the burial or cremation further concretize the separation.

Within the context of letting go, there is holding on to the tie with the deceased. Memory provides the major link between the widowed person and the deceased spouse. Memory holds together past and present and gives continuity to human life. Nostalgia and sentimentality about the past heighten the impact of recollections. Waller (1951) suggested that by combining and reworking selective memories, we maintain an image of the deceased and of his or her life.

It is not uncommon that the widowed person is socially perceived as tied to the deceased spouse, as if in some ways the marriage has not ended. Both the widowed person and family and friends in the social network tend to make efforts to maintain the marital link. For women, this may be heightened if the widow is referred to as John Jones' widow. Widows often keep the name of their husbands and are daily confronted with reaffirmations of the tie. Very often the widow's financial support is directly linked to her dead husband's work career.

Elsewhere (M. S. Moss & Moss, 1984), we have outlined five themes of the marital tie that tend to allow for continuity of symbolic interaction between the spouses throughout widowhood: caring, intimacy, family feeling, commitment, and reciprocal identity support. Before we examine the ways in which the tie is integrated into a remarriage, we will briefly review these five themes.

Caring develops out of years of affection and mutual concern for the welfare of the other even after death. The survivor maintains a continuing affection and concern for the deceased. The widowed person does not want to give up the person or the meaning of their relationship. Widowed people may believe that the deceased would wish to live on in the memory of loved ones and thus achieve a sense of immortality (Lopata, 1979). Reciprocal altruism continues. It is not unusual for the survivor to say, "I'm glad that (deceased spouse) doesn't know about (a tragic or upsetting situation)," or "I wish (deceased person) could see (a positive family or other event)." Frequently, survivors will express the satisfaction that their spouse is no longer suffering or in pain, and is now at peace, sometimes in "a better place" (Shuchter, 1986). Widowed persons not infrequently try to carry on a legacy and complete the tasks of their deceased spouse. Conversely, many widowed persons feel that their spouse is watching over them with concern and caring.

Intimacy grows out of decades of habitual daily interaction. Each partner has tended to anticipate the perceptions and reactions of the other. As Simmel (1950) suggested, intimacy represents the ingredients of the dyadic tie that each contributed to the other alone and to no other person. Spouses tend to develop a unique pattern of discourse and interaction that sets them apart from others and solidifies their sense of bondedness. Each sees the world through their own eyes as well as the eyes of the intimate other. There is a range of ways in which the widowed person maintains intimacy with the deceased spouse, from talking with the deceased, to thinking about what the deceased would have thought or done, to internalizing the orientation of the deceased (Bowlby & Parkes, 1970).

Family feeling is intrinsic to the marital tie. Marriage is a kinship bond with quasibiological characteristics (Schneider, 1968). Children offer concrete evidence of the genetic tie. Each spouse had become part of the other's family system, and these ties strengthen the marital dyad. The original sense of family in which the deceased was a central figure persists with an elasticity that allows it to be restored again and again. The survivor shares with children and other family members the sense of loss over the death. Each family member has a unique relationship with the deceased that continues to carry significance. This reinforces the sense that the family continues to include the deceased. The space and objects that were shared in the marriage represent the dyad and symbolize family bonds.

Possessions and home often facilitate the maintenance of the family tie (M. S. Moss & Moss, 1984; Rubinstein & Parmelee, 1992).

Commitment involves an intention to maintain continuity in the tie. During the marriage, each spouse had repeatedly affirmed the significance of their bond. After the death of one spouse, the survivor tends to reaffirm the bond. There is a sense of loyalty to the spouse who has died. One of the few cultural proscriptions for the widowed person is not to speak ill of the deceased spouse. The marital tie continues not only "until death do us part," but well beyond the grave. Queen Victoria's devotion to her husband continued for over four decades after his death, as she memorialized him in concrete ways while she continued to raise her family and to rule England with a strong hand (Strachey, 1921).

Reciprocal identity support is a fifth element of the marital dyad. Affirming the bond is a way of affirming one's self and the meaning of a significant part of one's life. Each spouse had been defined in part by the other as the marriage developed over the years. Bolstering the widowed person's pervasive sense of self is the fact that the identity of the survivor has been strongly interwoven with the deceased's image of him or her. Their tie is internalized as part of the widowed person's present sense of self. If the widowed person continues to do things that the deceased spouse liked or valued, this may enhance the widowed person's self esteem. Norris (1980) reported that many years after the husband's death, widows who have never remarried continue to carry the role of spouse into old age, and Matthews (1991) suggested that for some widows, the maintenance of the spousal role and the salience of the tie with the deceased spouse may be a significant personal resources.

MAINTENANCE OF TIES WITH THE DECEASED IN REMARRIAGE

After we explore some reasons why so little attention has been given to the remarried widowed person's continuing tie with the deceased spouse, we turn briefly to some of the ways in which the tie is weakened. Then, we explore in some depth the maintenance of the tie.

Why Is So Little Attention Paid to Tie Maintenance in Remarriage?

Freudian theory, and much of contemporary clinical work with the bereaved, stresses the importance for the widowed person of letting go of the deceased spouse. Traditional psychodynamic theory suggests that decathexis from the deceased facilitates development of viable ties with new persons. Only in recent years has there been an increasing emphasis on the importance of maintaining the tie (Goin, Burgoyne, & Goin, 1979; Klass, 1988, 1992–93; M. S. Moss & Moss, 1984; Rubin, 1993; Silverman & Worden, 1993).

There is probably some ageism in the tendency to ignore the dynamics of re-marriage for middle-aged and older widowed persons. Socially and culturally, their spouse's death may be seen as more acceptable and timely (M. S. Moss & Moss, 1989), and their remarriage as less socially meaningful.

The relative infrequency of remarriage of widowed persons vis-à-vis the di-vorced may also limit interest in the topic. Research on remarriage has been pre-dominantly focused on divorced persons. There is a dearth of literature that ex-amines the maintenance of the tie in the context of the development of new attachments after spousal death (for exceptions see diGuilio, 1989; McKain, 1969; M. S. Moss & Moss, 1980; also Ryan's 1991 self-help book). Relatively infrequent marriages for widowed persons reflect the demographics in the United States as discussed above.

Another reason for the paucity of literature in this area may be that in ordi-nary social interchange, remarried widowed persons probably talk little about their deceased spouses. This avoidance is undoubtedly multidetermined. The re-married widowed person may feel that his or her reference to the deceased re-flects a lack of affirmation of the new marriage. Not mentioning the deceased may demonstrate to others that the widowed person is committed to the new spouse and able to live independently of the deceased.

Letting Go in Remarriage

Prior to the remarriage, the widowed person has engaged in a process of tie-breaking. There is some evidence in other societies that rates of remarriage for younger widows are associated with such customs as the removal of the de-ceased's possessions, a taboo on the use of the name of the deceased, fear of the image of the deceased, or moving to a new residence (Rosenblatt, Walsh, & Jack-son, 1976). Before remarriage the widowed person has developed a new close re-lationship and has begun to think about life with a new partner. At some point, the widowed person removes the wedding ring, the "ultimate symbol" of the pre-vious marriage (Shuchter, 1986, p. 132). Each of these steps has involved dis-tancing from the deceased.

When a widowed person remarries there is a continuing tendency to see the tie with the deceased spouse as weakened. This has roots in the sociocultural mi-lieu, in the new dyadic tie, and in the intrapsychic world of the widowed person. If a woman changes her name, it symbolizes the legal and social aspects of the new marriage. A modified network of family and friends may tend to be support-ive of the new tie, reaching out to the couple as a viable unit. The social network may emphasize the primacy of the new bond.

We interviewed Steven Kaplan, a Jewish remarried widower, who had been married for over two decades to each wife. When we asked him about how his friends felt about his tie with his deceased wife, he said that after he remarried he had planned to continue to mark the anniversary of his first wife's death with tra-ditional ritual prayers (*yahrzeit*). However, a friend questioned this, saying, "You don't say *yahrzeit* after you're remarried." Mr. Kaplan no longer participated in the ritual after that, saying, "It's inappropriate when you're remarried."

Each person in the new dyad has a strong stake in a commitment to the other. There may be a tendency to remove possessions that had been shared with the deceased and replace them with those of the new spouse. The process of removing things that were part of one's everyday life in the past symbolizes letting go. Remarried widowed persons see their behavior as having to fit in with their second spouse, rather than their deceased spouse. The widowed person may tend to monitor references to the deceased and to the past that they shared. This pattern of controlling communication tends to affirm the new tie and deemphasize the old. New patterns of communication and behavior between the spouses develop. Each shift in behavior may enhance the viability of the new tie. The new couple constructs their own reality of caring, intimacy, commitment, sense of family, and identity support.

On an intrapersonal level, when the widowed person remarries, he or she takes on a new sense of self as a *re*-married person. Whether or not there is a name change, the remarried widowed person's sense of identity is intertwined with a new person. Different parts of the widowed person's self are emphasized in the new marriage, and this may further distance the person from the deceased.

Holding on in Remarriage

The tie with the deceased spouse plays a role in the remarriage. The plan to remarry may itself be influenced by the deceased. The widowed person may be more comfortable in developing a new relationship if she or he feels a sense of permission from the deceased spouse. There is some evidence that widowed persons decide not to remarry in order to respect, to preserve, and not to betray their ties with the deceased spouses (Lopata, 1979). Mrs Johnson is a widow who has been remarried 3 years after having been married for over three decades. She felt more at ease in her second marriage to Fred because he and her first husband, Arnold, had known each other through their church.

Glick, Weiss, and Parkes (1974) reported that widows who moved toward remarriage generally waited a year to begin to date in response to a personal sense of loyalty to their relationship with their deceased spouse and also in response to social disapproval for remarriage too soon after the death. Wilson and Clarke (1992) report that unlike divorced persons, who frequently married within the first 12 months, there is a spurt of remarriages among widowed persons at the 13th month after the death.

Remarriage creates an interactional system in which a new marriage is formed while bonds of kinship persist from a previous marriage. The triadic structure of the remarriage remains over time and is integral to the new tie. Bernard (1969) has suggested that "there are a least three or four persons involved in every remarriage. One or two, the previous spouses, may not be living in the flesh, but their memory may be very much alive" (p. 464). The quasi-biosocial tie with the deceased spouse persists.

Comparisons between the current spouse and the first spouse tend to keep the old tie alive and evoke a recurrent evaluative stance toward each spouse. It is not unlikely that the widowed person will regard some characteristics of the deceased spouse as a standard by which to judge the current spouse. Without saying anything at all, the widowed person may compare the two partners. Mrs. Johnson exemplifies this:

> **Interviewer:** *You bring up that word "comparison." . . . What does it mean when you say you don't compare them?*
> **Mrs. Johnson:** *What I mean is that when I'm talking with Fred I don't say, "Well, Arnold did it this way and you're doing it this way." Or anything like that. I might make mental comparisons (laughter). It would be a mistake to voice them.*
> **Interviewer:** *Do you think there is any way in which a person doesn't make mental comparisons?*
> **Mrs. Johnson:** *I don't see how it's avoidable, really . . . A person who has had two good marriages . . . it's interesting. It helps you to understand yourself, and them, and what's going on.*

Just as we would argue that there is no ex-mother or ex-father or ex-child, we suggest that the ex-spouse is a legal figment, and that the relationship persists. If this is true, then in a sense the remarried widowed person—to modify Bernard's (1969) phrase—engages in psychosocial bigamy.

> **Mrs. Johnson:** *I can think of Arnold without thoughts of disloyalty to him for having been remarried. I don't have this problem of what's going to happen when we get to heaven and there's a triangle (laugh). My view of such things does not include that.*

The Widowed Person and the Deceased Spouse

Many widows and widowers maintain continuing relationships with their deceased spouses indefinitely (Zisook & Schuchter, 1985). "Human attachment bonds are established and maintained at emotional levels so deep that the mere fact of physical death cannot truly disrupt these bonds. Our biological and psychological apparatus will not permit it" (Shuchter, 1986, p. 116). The deceased spouse can take the form of a shadow or a ghost in the new relationship (diGuilio, 1989). In a sense there is a space that can never be filled. There is no replacement or substitution for a deceased spouse.

The previous spouse may affect the remarriage if the widowed spouse tends to idealize the deceased (Bernard, 1969). Sanctification (Lopata, 1978, 1981) may put the deceased on a pedestal and create an idol unmatchable by the new spouse. Very few remarried widows (1%) and widowers (2%) in Bernard's (1969) study reported unfriendly attitudes toward their deceased spouses. Overall, however, widowed persons may be quite capable of remembering both the good times and the bad times in the previous marriage. Thus, they may think about some of the negative aspects of the relationship such as the spouse's selfishness or readiness to criticize, and favorably compare the new spouse to the old. Mrs. Johnson, who married Fred who had been divorced after an unhappy marriage, shared her own conflicts in the earlier marriage with him in order to de-sanctify the deceased.

> **Interviewer:** *Your marriage to Arnold did not end through choice, but Fred's did end due to his choice.*
> **Mrs. Johnson:** *I was partly aware of that. I talked about ways in which Arnold and I probably were not compatible . . . perhaps to ease Fred's feelings. . . . I was quite frank with Fred (about early expectations in the marriage that were not met). I was careful to explain to Fred that I wasn't idealizing the first marriage, thinking that it would ease his feelings.*

Memories of a deceased spouse's prolonged debilitating illness may affect the widowed person's attitude toward illness in the second spouse. Mr. Kaplan, whose first wife died after several years fighting cancer, many years later still vividly recalled the difficulties in the last stages of her illness. Any threat of serious illness for the second spouse may evoke the widowed person's fear of repetition of the pain of terminal care and of loss.

We know little about subtle constraints on the way widowed persons talk about the deceased: where, with whom, at whose initiative, how frequently, and with what kind of emphasis (e.g., nostalgia, regret, pleasure, criticism, or sadness). There may be a strong theme of protective silence adhered to by each partner in the new marriage. There are multiple factors that tend to minimize talk about the dead spouse. Both the widowed person and the new spouse may wish to avoid explicit comparisons with the deceased spouse. Each may believe that references to the deceased may be subtle ways of undermining the new marriage. Protective silence then is a mechanism to reduce the salience of the tie with the deceased. Widowed persons, in their efforts to affirm the tie with each of the spouses, may tend to engage selectively in tie-keeping talk about the deceased with persons other than their new spouse. Thus, there may be a subtle agreement between the widowed person and others to avoid references to the deceased when the new spouse is present.

> **Mrs. Johnson:** *I was aware (through my mother's experience) that someone coming into a marriage where a partner had been widowed could be very sensitive and yet not really show it. I think that alerted me to be careful. I know I refer to Arnold especially in conversations with friends who knew him, and it seems an appropriate time to refer to him. I consider whether it's appropriate in Fred's presence. I'm more apt to*

> *talk about Arnold when he's not there. Mary, an old neighbor, came by*
> *yesterday. . . . She was very fond of Arnold. We didn't talk about him un-*
> *til she and I were wandering around the garden.*

Mrs. Johnson also described her handling of Arnold's possessions as a subtle means of protective silence:

> *(I think of him when I look at) the things that we purchased on our trips*
> *together. . . . When Fred and I became serious about each other, I*
> *thought that it was appropriate to put away the photographs of*
> *Arnold . . . but many other things that are around the house (are still*
> *out). Fred would not be aware of my tie to Arnold through them.*

Themes in the Widowed Person's Tie With the Deceased Spouse

The five themes described above that are integral to the marital tie with the first spouse may continue to have a strong effect on the remarriage. *Caring* with its continuing affection and concern often persists in subtle ways. Family occasions or other important events that occur in the life of the remarried widowed person may be viewed as having some significance to the deceased spouse.

> **Mrs. Johnson:** *I often think about him in relation to developments of*
> *the kids' families, my kids' families . . . to share with him what is hap-*
> *pening. I often think of him that way. And I often think of him in relation*
> *to the garden that we worked on together, wishing that he could see this*
> *or that. Wondering whether he would be enthusiastic about this change*
> *or that change.*

The date of death of the deceased spouse may be a poignant reminder of loss, as well as an occasion for the widowed person to reaffirm the meaning of the tie. In spite of Mr. Kaplan's discontinuing *yahrzeit*, he vividly remembers the date of death and the pain of the ending.

There is a sense of mutual caring that persists. Mrs Johnson sees her husband as continuing to care when she says, "I rather think that he would, in an unselfish way, be glad that I'm enjoying companionship at this stage of life. That's what I really think." The new marriage tie involves caring for the second spouse. We suggest that the affection and concern toward the new spouse does not diminish the caring for the first spouse.

Intimacy with the deceased spouse may play a role in the life of the remarried widowed person. Even when there is a conscious effort to talk little of the deceased, there are often unexpected pangs of memories of the past that intrude on everyday life. Objects that were shared with the deceased spouse maintain the tie. Even the use of the name of the deceased may inadvertently be substituted for the name of the new spouse. Reminders of the similarity of the first and second spouse may be evoked in areas as mundane as cooking a special dish or seeing an old movie. The minutiae of daily life in the first marriage form the ground upon which the new couple develop their own web of intimacy. For example, the multiple ways in which the couple in the prior marriage had developed patterns of communication may guide openness in the new relationship.

The widowed person may engage in protective silence, feeling that any explicit reference to intimacies of the past marriage may stand in the way of developing current intimacy. Developing a significant relationship is a long-term ongoing process that involves the reduction of uncertainty and the assessment of the model of the other as it fits our personality (Duck, 1992). During this process, the widowed person may subtly compare the spouses with each other. This comparison may resurface again and again as the widowed person develops a relationship with the new spouse and learns the ways in which their values are similar or different, what upsets the spouse, and how to comfort the spouse, as well as how to avoid invoking the other's deep fears about his or her self.

In contrast to the more subtle caring and intimacy aspects of the bond with the deceased, the *family feeling* that persists is often more explicit in the remarriage. The wedding ceremony often provides the initial framework for the two families to meet. Each of the new spouses enters the marriage with his or her own sense of family. In some ways they continue to be separate, with "his" family and "her" family maintaining their boundaries. In addition, there may be a new sense of melded or blended family.

Issues of loyalty and allegiance to children with the deceased spouse enter in no matter how the widowed person negotiates the introduction of the second spouse into his or her family.

> **Mrs. Johnson:** *Came the time when we were to be married and the wedding certificate to be created, and I was to indicate what maiden name I was to use on the wedding certificate. Well, I chose to be Mary Keller (first husband's surname). At one point Fred very calmly, equanimically inquired as to whether that was not unusual, whether it would not be customary for me to use (my maiden name). And I told him that I have been Keller more years of my life than I had been (maiden name), and that I felt this tie to my sons, and that I would feel uncomfortable with it that way. He expressed no discomfort.*

Although our primary emphasis here is on the spouse, the children of the widowed person and the deceased spouse are highly salient in maintaining the tie. Interactions between these children and the second spouse (whether they involve warmth, comfort, disagreements, or friction) are likely to evoke some thoughts of the deceased parent. Children are concrete representations of the old tie. Their physical appearance, mannerisms, and behaviors combined with their personal histories from birth, embody a lifelong connection with their dead parent. Children tend to relate to one parent within the context of their tie with the other parent. The authors' ongoing research on the impact of parental death on middle-aged daughters provides evidence that even after death, adult children tend to think of their surviving mother as part of a parental dyad. Thus, when a widowed person remarries, children from the previous marriage help to strengthen the family tie with the deceased.

Commitment persists as the widowed person is invested in maintaining some continuity of the tie with the deceased spouse. Having been married for decades, the widowed person seeks to hold on to the past. The widowed person views the new spouse through the prism of the first marriage. Differences and similarities are perceived in all aspects of the marriage. The widowed person sometimes may consider what the deceased spouse would think of the new relationship and the new spouse. To the extent that some elements of the second marriage are more satisfying than the first marriage, the remarried widowed person may feel guilty or disloyal. Although the new pattern of companionship in the second marriage may be seen as providing some of the similar rewards as in the first marriage, commitment to a new relationship generally does not replace commitment to the earlier one.

The widowed person may have planned to be buried with the deceased, perhaps having had the widowed person's name already inscribed on the gravestone. After remarriage, the thought of long-term commitment may shift to include the second spouse as well. A sensitive arrangement was reported by one widow who plans to be cremated with half of her ashes buried with the first spouse and half with the second spouse. Thus, the commitment goes well beyond the grave.

Reciprocal identity support also may persist. Volkan (1985) has said, "We can never purge those who have been close to us from our own history except by psychic acts damaging to our own identity" (p. 326). A widowed person may tend to see his or her identity as rooted deeply in the relationship with the first spouse. Regardless of the quality of the tie, the widowed person may continue to find meaning in the long-term relationship. Because no person relates to two spouses in the same way, a widowed person may gain new insights into his or her own personality in a new marriage.

The widowed person has a persistent tie with the family of origin where the roots of identity lie, thus there is a tie with the earlier marriage. There is a sense of self that was created in the first marriage, which in turn leads to an affirmation of that marriage with all of its strengths and weaknesses.

> **Interviewer:** *Do you think there's a way in which who you are is related to your relationship with Arnold?*
> **Mrs. Johnson:** *I think that's absolutely very much the case. When you get married at the age of 19, away from your roots, and in a new situation, you grow in relation to your partner. . . . I am the person I am largely because of almost 40 years.*

There is a process of holding on and letting go of the strong sense of personhood that developed in the first marriage. One widow demonstrated this when she occasionally found that she was doing something that her first husband did not like and felt guilty about it. Repeatedly, then she would realize with relief that she could now do as she wished. The old sense of expectations persist alongside the new sense of self. This takes place in the context of the remarriage, where the relationship with the new spouse may further enhance the widowed person's self-esteem, as being a person who is valued and affirmed by a new partner (diGuilio, 1989).

The New Spouse Views the Triad

Although the primary focus here is on the remarried widowed person's tie with the deceased spouse, we want briefly to discuss three ways in which new spouses perceive themselves: as part of the triad that includes the first spouse, as "second" to the first spouse, and as an outsider to the spouse's family.

The new spouse, rather than being in a simple dyadic relationship with the widowed person, feels part of a triad that includes the deceased spouse. The new spouse is generally at considerable disadvantage in the triad, as he or she "must always box with a phantom" (Bernard, 1969, p. 464). In spite of this, Bernard reports that only 5% of the new wives and 8% of the new husbands reported being jealous or resentful toward the first partners of their spouses (p. 464). There is some evidence that the new spouse's acceptance of the widowed person's tie with the deceased spouse facilitates the success of the remarriage (Campbell & Silverman, 1987; McKain, 1969).

The new spouse recognizes that the widowed person had expected to continue the previous marriage and that it was not ended voluntarily (Bernard, 1969). Thus, the new spouse may in some ways feel insecure perceiving himself or herself as a second choice. Society continues to see the deceased spouse as the first. "First" often has the connotation of better, chosen, or preferred. "Second" may suggest second best, and in most all situations is defined in relation to the first. The second spouse occupies a similar role, but does not take the place of the first spouse psychologically or socially. In wanting to be known as the second Mrs. Steven Kaplan, Rachel Kaplan seemed to be affirming the viability of his first marriage. At the same time she is linked to the first wife, Rachel dislikes the fact that the pictures of Steven's children and first wife are the only ones displayed on his desk at work. On the other hand, Rachel seems very comfortable with the blending of Steven's first wife's possessions with her own as they continue to live in the house that came from his first marriage. Just as widowed persons struggle with the past, their new spouses exhibit patterns of holding on and letting go.

The new spouse may feel like an intruder. The marriage represents a change for persons in the widow's family and social network. With few exceptions, the spouse is a new adult member of the family and enters an emotional field (Bowen, 1978) that has deep roots in the past including the deceased spouse. It is a family group with its own sense of definition and its own boundaries. In addition, the widowed person's web of daily life and social interactions must accommodate to the new spouse. When memories of the past are shared by kin or friends, they often represent a world foreign to the new spouse. Gradually, the widowed person's family boundaries may be modified, thus reducing the new spouse's sense of being an outsider.

DISCUSSION

In spite of Lopata's (1979) finding that remarriage of widows seems to have positive effects on the lives of former widows, and evidence from others that remarriage is a positive coping response to widowhood (Gentry & Shulman, 1990), there has been little attention given to remarriage of widows, and even less to the remarried widowed person's tie with the deceased spouse. Overall, we have been stressing the significance of the pervasive kinship bond of marriage, and we have suggested ways in which the tie with a deceased spouse maintains significance for a remarried widowed person. We emphasize that most all surviving spouses, while accepting the reality of the death, maintain meaningful ties with the deceased and with the parts of their lives that they shared with them. We suggest that a prolonged attachment to a deceased spouse, even after remarriage, is timeless. As such it is generally neither pathological nor maladaptive (Wortman & Silver, 1990). Rather, we argue that the significance of the persistence of the tie with a deceased person can play an important role in viable ties with a new person.

When a widowed person remarries there is once again a partner in life, and thus the loneliness of widowhood may no longer be a force that leads the person to fall back upon the deceased spouse for a sense of support and security. The new attachment in this way would reduce the dependency on the deceased spouse. It does not follow, however, that the old tie has been significantly weakened.

With the passage of time, the new marriage takes on new levels of caring, intimacy, commitment, family feeling, and identity support. It is for future research to explore the process over time by which the old tie impacts upon the development of the new tie.

Remarriages between two widowed persons involve four persons. Research is needed to examine the complexities of two interlocking triads and the ways in which ties to deceased spouses are maintained. DiGuilio (1989) describes a creative celebration by two remarried widowed persons, each of whom would have been married 50 years at the same time that the new couple celebrated their fourth anniversary. The anniversary cake celebrated all three occasions! Only future research will ascertain the degree to which past ties are openly affirmed in remarriages.

Further study of remarriage using a larger number of widowed persons should examine the degree to which the quality of the relationship with the deceased spouse has an impact upon the new tie. Just as the previous marital relationship was multidimensional, its impact on the remarriage is likely to be equally complex. In addition, research is needed on widowed persons who marry divorced partners. Here, a distinct constellation is formed with the partner's living ex-spouse having an impact upon the new marital tie. The triads that we have described for middle-aged and elderly remarried widowed persons have some generic features that may apply to younger remarried widowed persons as well as to divorced persons.

Rather than seeing a new marriage as surrogate or substitute for the tie with the deceased spouse, the new marriage builds upon the old and goes beyond it. Old family ties are rarely if ever severed; new ties do not displace them. It is as if there were an arithmetic unique to families, in which there is no subtraction, only addition.

REFERENCES

Ainsworth, M. D. S. (1985). Attachments across the life span. *Bulletin of New York Academy of Medicine, 61*, 792–812.

Bernard, J. (1969). Remarriage of the widowed and the divorced. In R. S. Cavan (Ed.), *Marriage & family in the modern world* (3rd ed.) (pp. 463–471). New York: Thomas Y. Crowell.

Bowen, M. (1978). *Family therapy and clinical practice*. New York: Jason Aronson.

Bowlby, J. (1988). *A secure base*. New York: Basic Books.

Bowlby, J., & Parkes, C. M. (1970). Separation and loss within the family. In E. J. Anthony & C. Koupernik (Eds.), *The child in his family* (pp. 197–216). New York: John Wiley & Sons.

Bumpass, L., Sweet, J., & Martin, T. (1990). Changing patterns of remarriage. *Journal of Marriage and the Family, 52*, 747–756.

Campbell, S., & Silverman, P. R. (1987). *Widower*. New York: Prentice-Hall.

Cleveland, W. P., & Gianturco, D. T. (1976). Remarriage probability after widowhood. A retrospective method. *Journal of Gerontology, 31*, 99–103.

diGuilio, R. C. (1989). *Beyond widowhood*. New York: Free Press.

Duck, S. (1992). *Human relationships* (2nd ed.). Newbury Park, CA: Sage.

Freud, S. (1957). Mourning and melancholia. In J. Strachey (Ed. and Trans.), *The standard edition of the complete psychological works of Sigmund Freud* (Vol. 14, pp. 243–258). London: Hogarth Press.

Gallagher-Thompson, D., Futterman, A., Farberow, N., Thompson, L. W., & Peterson, J. (1993). The impact of spousal bereavement on older widows and widowers. In M. S. Stroebe & R. O. Hansson (Eds.), *Handbook of bereavement* (pp. 227–239). New York: Cambridge University Press.

Gentry, M., & Schulman, A. D. (1990). Remarriage as a coping response for widowhood. *Psychology and Aging, 3,*191–196.

Glick, I., Weiss, R., & Parkes, C. M. (1974). *The first year of bereavement*. New York: John Wiley & Sons.

Goin, M. K., Burgoyne, R. W., & Goin, M. J. (1979). Timeless attachment to a dead relative. *American Journal of Psychiatry, 136*, 988–989.

Klass, D. (1988). *Parental grief: Solace and resolution*. New York: Springer.

Klass, D. (1992–93). The inner representation of the dead child and the world views of bereaved parents. *Omega, 26*, 255–272.

Lopata, H. Z. (1979). *Widowhood in later life*. Toronto: Butterworths.

Lopata, H. Z. (1981). Widowhood and husband sanctification. *Journal of Marriage and the Family, 43*, 439–450.

Matthews, A. M. (1991). *Widowhood in later life*. Toronto: Butterworths.

McKain, W. C. (1969). *Retirement marriage*. Storrs, CT: Storrs Agricultural Experiment Station, Monograph 3.

Moss, M. S., & Moss, S. Z. (1980). The image of the deceased spouse in remarriage of elderly widow(er)s. *Journal of Gerontological Social Work, 3*, 59–70.

Moss, M. S., & Moss, S. Z. (1984). Some aspects of the elderly widow(er)'s persistent tie with the deceased spouse. *Omega, 15,* 195–206.

Moss, M. S., & Moss, S. Z. (1989). Death of the very old. In K. Doka (Ed.), *Disenfranchised grief: Recognizing hidden sorrow* (pp. 213–227). Lexington, MA: Lexington Books.

Moss, S. Z., & Moss, M. S. (1980). Remarriage: A triadic relationship. *Conciliation Courts Review, 18,* 15–20.

Norris, J. E. (1980). The social adjustment of single and widowed older women. *Essence: Issues in the Study of Aging, Dying and Death, 4,* 135–144.

Parkes, C. M. (1986). *Bereavement: Studies of grief in adult life* (2nd ed.). Harmondsworth, England: Penguin Books.

Parkes, C. M. (1988). Bereavement as a psychosocial transition: Processes of adaptation to change. *Journal of Social Issues, 44,* 53–65.

Rosenblatt, P. C., Walsh, R. P., & Jackson, D. A. (1976). *Grief and mourning in cross-cultural perspective.* New Haven, CT: HRAF Press.

Rubin, S. S. (1993). The death of a child is forever: The life course impact of child loss. In M. S. Stroebe, W. Stroebe, & R. O. Hansson (Eds.), *Handbook of bereavement* (pp. 283–299). New York: Cambridge University Press.

Rubinstein, R. L., & Parmelee, P. A. (1992). Attachment to place and the representation of the life course by the elderly. In I. Altman and S. M. Low (Eds.), *Place attachment* (pp. 139–163). New York: Plenum Press.

Ryan, J. (1991). *Loving again.* Grand Rapids, MI: Zondervan.

Schneider, D. M. (1968). *American kingship.* Englewood Cliffs, NJ: Prentice-Hall.

Shuchter, S. R. (1986). Continuing ties to the deceased spouse. In S. R. Shuchter (Ed.), *Dimensions of grief* (pp. 116–164). San Francisco: Jossey-Bass.

Silverman, P. R. (1986). *Widow-to widow.* New York: Springer.

Silverman, P. R., & Worden. J. W. (1993). Children's reactions to the death of a parent. In M. S. Stroebe, W. Stroebe & R. O. Hansson (Eds.), *Handbook of bereavement* (pp. 300–316). New York: Cambridge University Press.

Simmel, G. (1950). The isolated individual and the dyad. In K. Wolff (Ed.), *The sociology of George Simmel* (pp. 118–144). New York: Free Press.

Smith, K. R., Zick, C. D., & Duncan, G. J. (1991). Remarriage patterns among recent widows and widowers. *Demography 28,* 361–374.

Spanier, G. B., & Glick, P. C. (1980). Paths to remarriage. *Journal of Divorce, 3,* 283–298.

Strachey, L. (1921). *Queen Victoria.* New York: Harcourt Brace.

Volkan, V. (1985). Complicated mourning. *Annual of Psychoanalysis, 12,* 323–348.

Waller, W. (1951). *The family.* New York: Dryden.

Wilson, B. F., & Clarke, S. C. (1992). Remarriage: A demographic profile. *Journal of Social Issues, 13,* 123–141.

Wortman, C. B., & Silver, R. C. (1990). Successful mastery of bereavement and widowhood: A life-course perspective. In P. B. Baltes & M. M. Baltes (Eds.), *Successful aging: Perspectives from the behavioral sciences* (pp. 225–264).
New York: Cambridge University Press.

Zisook, S., & Shuchter, S. R. (1985). Time course of spousal bereavement. *General Hospital Psychiatry, 7,* 95–100.

Chapter 11

Memories of the Death and Life of a Spouse: The Role of Images and *Sense of Presence* in Grief

Roberta Dew Conant

Where does the attachment go after a death? Close attachments to loved ones provide a mirroring of self that both defines and provides continuity to life. Does the grieving widow stay in touch with the self she had been in the marriage while adjusting to life without her husband? What role does memory of the deceased play in this process?

The research literature includes reports of vivid imagery in all sensory modalities as part of the bereavement process. Several studies have found this to be particularly evident following sudden or untimely death (Balk, 1983; Cook, 1983; Glick, Weiss, & Parkes, 1974; Kalish & Reynolds, 1983; Matchett, 1972; Olson, Suddeth, Peterson, & Egelhoff, 1985; Parkes, 1987; Parkes & Weiss, 1983; Rees, 1971; Yakamoto, Okonogi, Iwasaki, & Yoshimura, 1969). Neither research nor theories of grief address the role imagery may play in this process. This chapter is a report of a study investigating widows' ongoing attachments to their deceased husbands and a sense of their presence (Conant, 1992).

WIDOWS PARTICIPATING IN THE STUDY

A group was chosen comprising widows who were at risk for intense grief because their husbands' deaths were sudden and untimely. These widows were contacted through their membership in professionally led bereavement groups. They were quite homogeneous on certain characteristics, in being Caucasian, middle-class women in midlife and homeowners in the suburbs around Boston, Massachusetts. About a third of those in the bereavement groups who met criteria for sudden death of the spouse participated. Efforts to locate widows of color or of other classes or minorities were not successful.

The women who were interviewed were 39 to 51 years old. Deceased husbands, ages 39 to 59, had been an average of 5.3 years older than their wives. These had been lasting marriages: an average of 18.5 years long, with the range being 7 to 24 years. Seven of these families had children living at home; two more had children or stepchildren out of the home. These widows were employed (8 of 10), cared for young children (5), went to school (2), changed careers (2), and managed their deceased husband's professional records (1). Educational levels of both widows and husbands varied from high school to graduate degrees. The husbands' deaths had been an average of 13.65 months before the interviews, with a range of 3 to 24.5 months. Causes of death were cardiac-related for eight husbands and rapidly growing cancers for two. Six of the 10 men died suddenly. Two more were unconscious or incoherent on medication from the time of diagnosed illness. Two declined in health for 3 to 6 months and thus gave some warning. The two widows who had more warning of their husbands' deaths were among the widows with multiple severe stressors. These stressors included caring for other terminally ill family members (2), death of one or both parents within 2 years (4), miscarriage (1), business failure (1), and being operated on for her own cancer (1).

FORMAT OF THE INTERVIEWS

Widows were interviewed in their homes. Interviews varied from 2 to 4 hours in length with an average of 3 hours, 5 minutes. We audiotaped the interviews and transcribed them verbatim. The initial unguided narrative was followed by specific questions about type of imagery, content, and understanding of the experience. We asked some questions chosen from similar research on memory and sense-of-presence experiences during grief (Jacobs, 1987; Olson et al., 1985; Rees, 1972). However, our questions differed since we were exploring the context for these experiences as well as the widows' feelings, understanding, and religious beliefs (Conant, 1992).

We asked widows about their experiences of remembering. These women responded by talking about the intensity of their feelings and imagery, of their concern for their deceased husbands and of their husbands' for them. They did not believe the death could suddenly end the caring by either person, alive or dead. We took a close look at what widows said about their imagery and sense-of-presence experiences as evidence of continuing attachment to the deceased.

The interviews were quite intense and informative. These women had a lot to say. All laughed, some through their tears. All cried at some point. Three cried for their entire interviews. All thanked us extensively for listening. In spite of the sadness, they appreciated sharing and reviewing the memories. We were impressed by the level of turmoil these women were facing and the integrity with which they did so. We also laughed; we also cried. These stories are hard to tell and hard to hear. These deaths were sudden and not supposed to happen. This is the story of the role of imagery and memory in personal trauma: that is, the untimely sudden death of a long-term, intimate partner. We analyzed content for themes using the methods of qualitative analysis of narratives (Bruyn, 1966; Glaser & Strauss, 1968).

FINDINGS

The striking impression from these interviews is the depth of pain these women felt. These women were wrestling with basic existential questions. What is the meaning of life? Is there life after death? What is my identity without the person I love most? Where is the deceased person I love now that he is dead?

The context for understanding the imagery, memory experiences and sense of presence that these widows reported involves seven themes that were woven through their stories:

1 confirming the reality of the death;
2 cognitive, emotional, and somatic pain;
3 facing their own mortality;
4 loss of purpose in living;
5 valuing the individuality of the deceased;
6 changes in personal identity; and
7 continued caring about where the husband was after death.

These themes emphasize the aspects of resolving the trauma of the sudden deaths of their spouses.

All 10 widows reported at least one experience that they felt as presence of their deceased husbands. Such mental events that would seem surprising at other times were often barely commented on. In part, the events were experienced appropriately as a very vivid internal experience. The internal experience of grief was so intense that their ways of expressing it were equally as intense.

The role of imagery and sense-of-presence experiences suggested in these interviews appears to be one of providing a place of inner safety from which to acknowledge a disturbing reality. There was evidence of transformative experiences that altered self-esteem. Widows also relied on the representation of the past relationships to guide them and encourage them in their present lives. The consoling quality of these experiences supports the findings of the Harvard Bereavement Study, 1965–1969 (Glick, Weiss, & Parkes, 1974; Parkes & Weiss, 1983).

THE WIDOWS' STORIES

The data will be presented first as a composite vignette illustrating the course of grief reported over the period of 3 to 24.5 months since the death, and then as further stories that elaborate certain aspects of imagery and experience. In the vignette that follows, particular stories are woven into a composite story about a possible widow, Jane. Individual quotations from the research data illustrate the composite story. All names have been changed. The individual quotations set within the story demonstrate the range of differences that were reported.

Indeed, one aspect of the data is that the women's stories were so different in their form of memory or imagery and yet similar in their intensity of affect. There was a desperation, fear, and sense of personal threat in the grief following these deaths—an immanence of the threat to the widow's own mortality that is not seen after deaths involving more warning, less close relationship, or less concomitant stress.

The culture does not provide any accepted pattern for thinking about deceased husbands, whether death is sudden or anticipated. Dwelling on thoughts of the deceased seemed to be seen as a danger, an impediment to new attachments without recognition of adjustment in internal processes. Thus, each widow invented her own way, an individual expression that was as private as the relationship had been. In fact, this imagery acted as a substitute for the private relationship that was lost.

Composite Vignette

Jane began the interview by gasping and saying that talking was hard. She launched into a detailed account of her husband's fatal heart attack, where he was, how she learned of it, and of their last contacts that day.

> **Ginny:** *And when I came out, he was playing with the dog. And he, you know, it was a typical morning. He was in a good mood. He was whistling. He was always happy, anyway. He was a happy-go-lucky kind of guy. And, um (chokes up) he just kissed me good-by and I waved. And I said, "See you tonight!" And he said, "We'll have a really nice weekend." You know. He said, "I'll come home." He liked to plan ahead, so he was listing the things we were going to do. He said, "When I come home tonight, we'll watch the ball game. The Red Sox are on tonight. And I want to watch "Chronicle" on Channel 5. There's a thing about blueberry picking in Maine. I want to see that." He said, "Tape it if I don't get home. Tomorrow, I have to work in the morning. And then, we'll go (chokes up) tomorrow afternoon and maybe go to some bookstores." And I said, "O.K." and that was the last that I saw of him. (Cries).*
>
> **Fran:** *My sister had no tissues so we used "Irish tissues": we used toilet paper. I remember her going to get it and I said, "What do you need toilet paper for?" and she said, "I have something to tell you." She brought me into the room and I should have thought of my father because my mother died 15 to 18 months prior to that. And I said, "It's Paul, isn't it?" And she said, "Yeah."*

Jane thanked us for listening, saying she felt isolated from friends who did not want to hear her sadness. She also knew telling the story helped even if she did not need to tell it as much as before.

> **Rachel:** *And at work, I had to pretend that I was O.K. And I learned that very quickly. . . . "How are you doing?" "I am really doing shitty today." They don't want to hear it. You have to tell them you are O.K. to*

allay their anxieties. . . . Oh God! They were so uncomfortable around me that I was like poison! I really felt like a leper.

Jane reported that it took over a year to get access to her memories of her husband. On the other hand, she occasionally felt like her husband was present in the house: she woke to hear his footsteps and wondered how he could do that since he was dead.

Cathy: *And I feel his presence. I know that in some way he is still part of my life. But I also am cognizant of the fact that he is not here making the decisions. He is not here shoveling the snow or doing chores. I'm doing that.*

Sometimes she talked to him, in her thoughts or aloud.

Linda: *So it's like I'm talking to him the whole time I'm getting myself ready to go to work. It's like this constant conversation he and I have. And I just don't know how else to say it. And it's like even though physically he's not here, that mentally I have this continual conversation going on with him. It's as though my life has not stopped. It still goes on with him. From anything I do!*
And I really believe that it is the spirit that he had in his life that is still living on. And this is what I am communicating with, this inner spirit that he had that is bringing me to communicate with him. On a different level. That I am able to, to reach out and still have a communication going on.

Jane described her sense of presence as "kind of eerie when I am awake but when I am asleep, it's that feeling of safety" that ended when he died. Waking in the morning felt like being told of the death all over again. She had one vivid dream vision that she reported as a "wonderful visit." This dream included expressing the good-bye they had not had and ended with revulsion at his autopsy scar.

When awake, the awareness of the death had been pervasive for the first 11 months. Her sense of inner turmoil in this period was wrenching to hear as she felt her anxiety mimicked the heart attack her husband had.

Fran: *I felt sharp pains in my chest area and down into my stomach. And I'd be awake into the night with it. Wanting to know if it would be best to just die in my bed or whether to call an ambulance so my kids wouldn't find me. Or, if it's really not a heart attack, do I look like a hypochondriac and call the ambulance anyway?*
Celeste: *I've always been a person that if I got too wound up that I would get palpitations and stuff. And after this happened, I noticed that I was getting them a lot. And I thought, "Well, this is reasonable for what I am going through. And it will pass." And I noticed that it wasn't passing and when I went to bed at night, it was really bad. I'd better get*

to the doctor. Who's to say? I could be here today and gone tomorrow. It was a real reality. And I went (to the doctor).

At the time of the interview, Jane no longer thought about her husband continuously. For her, that transition came between 10 and 11 months and was difficult as she felt she was losing him by not holding him in her thoughts.

> **Ginny:** *I feel, as time goes on, I'm losing my connection with him because I don't think of him 24 hours a day. I don't think of him all the time. And I feel kind of sad about that because I know that (cries) it's all (sob) changing and there's, oh, this real pulling away.*
> **Fran:** *And I noticed at about 14 months, it had been about a month that I would go for periods of time and not be totally encompassed in thoughts of Paul. . . . And, and that was O.K. with me. I didn't feel guilty about it. I just—I—was a realization. . . . I didn't notice it.*

Jane told of signs that her husband was okay: roses the color of those at his funeral bloomed on the anniversary of his death. She then said this was more a sign from God than her husband.

> **Ginny:** *This whole grief business is a very self-centered process, that's for sure. . . . At one point, I said, "Jesus, poor Joe is dead! How do I know how he is doing up there?" I was looking at numbers everywhere and interpreting them as signs from my husband. But, you know, there is a part of me that sort of still believes that. I know it sounds wacko but I see them in extraordinary circumstances, these couple of sequences of numbers. And I always say, "Oh" to myself, you know. "Oh. It's Joe. He's letting me know he's O.K." (Sniff).*

By 20 months, Jane was working successfully, making new friends, considering dating, proud of her children. She was also still painfully missing her husband who cared for her and cared for their children in a way no one else could. Jane sobbed through much of the interview.

This gives a picture of the progression and variety of experience of widows in the study. At this point, we are leaving Jane and moving to findings that are suggestive of the role of images and sense of presence in resolution of grief.

WIDOWS' EXPERIENCES OF THE MEMORY OF THE DECEASED

Widows eloquently spoke of the pain that represented their intense emotional turmoil.

> **Ginny:** *Well, it's funny because the things that stand out, I guess, are just mainly the prevailing emotions, not the memories, you know. . . but it was just like—like so strong! So anguished! Like I could understand*

all those images or things you'd . . . see or read in history books or hear—about people rending their clothes! You'd see (quoting voice) "and the women threw themselves on the funeral pyre." "And they rent their clothes apart." Or biblical things, they, you know, they—I could understand that, all of a sudden. I didn't do it but I could feel it.

For some, images of the death came up intrusively as flashbacks.

Rachel (a nurse): *The first were the flashbacks. Of the month in the hospital. Totally involuntary. It would happen at work. People would get pissed off that I stared into space. But I would relive a thing, a sequence of the month. It was like everything happened from a Friday to a Friday. A sequence that happened. And it was very involuntary. The flashbacks just came and were painful. In the middle of doing patient care. Very painful. Very painful.*

The widows saw even the pain of remembering the death as purposeful. They said that telling the story helps.

Sylvia: *The most vivid memories were of the morning that he died. That, that um, can really tend to come back and haunt me and pray over. And finally what I did was—I mean, I would allow myself to do that for a certain length of time, because, my own attitude was that you really needed to do that. I—I thought it was—almost like a rite of passage. It was one of the things you have to do until you get it out of your system.*
Ginny: *People who are in this position and have been widowed suddenly, I'm sure they all want to talk about it. In, uh, the ones I've met in the various groups, it's the common thing. Everybody wants to kind of go over their story again and again and again and again and again and again. And you keep saying it and you cry and you say it and you cry and then, I don't know, it just kind of . . . it must leech it out of you somehow.*

In addition to the pain of remembering, each widow also talked of images or experiences that gave an experience of current connection with the deceased. All 10 widows included these references in the unguided narrative that began with "Tell me about your memories of your husband."

Have These Experiences Reassured or Worried You?

This was one question included in the interview immediately after specific questions about sense-of-presence experiences. Responses to it indicated that widows saw these experiences as part of an ongoing connection to their deceased husbands. They continued to want to care for their husbands and believed he continued to care for them. They were reality oriented, aware of the death while maintaining contradictory actions and thoughts.

Sylvia: *(describing the impact of dreams she experienced as a real visit) That—that, yes, that was reassuring to me. Because in those two dreams, he had progressed himself. And that's what I wanted him to do. And what I wanted him to be. Certainly I wanted him to be a part of our lives, but I wanted him to be the best he can be. Because that is his life. That is where he is.*

Judith: *(describing the family belief that the lights dimmed when Dad's/ husband's spirit was present) Understand it, you don't! Like I say, comforting? Not particularly. It really depends on the mood that I am in. If I'm real depressed, I get angry at him for putting me in this situation. If it's—if it's not a depressing moment and it's supposed to be like her graduation, a happy moment: more so I get hurt that he is not with me. And you talk to the—I talk to the light bulb! (laughs) It's stupid! It's a sense of his presence that you've just got to believe that he is there but I know that he is not.*

Celeste: *(describing her experience of consciously meditating to produce a visit) So I—I wonder if he—he's meeting me. If he really is. Um . . . but I don't put a lot of energy into whether he really is or if he really is there when he is. I just believe in my mind that if it's making me feel better, that's good. . . . I don't know.*

Establishing Sense of Presence

Most of the widows also reported dramatic times that had convinced them of the husband's presence as a spirit, at least for the moment: driving in a hurricane, driving in dense fog, watching a daughter receive an award memorializing the deceased, extreme frustration on a hot day in performing a husband's task, attending a wedding alone, a feeling of being led "to constructive activity in the garden just at my darkest hour." These were highly emotional experiences that were felt to be consoling.

After the initial emotional experience, other less dramatic events were experienced as sense of presence. For example, as noted above, Judith explained that several important family events "that he wouldn't have missed" were accompanied by flickering lights. She and her children "came to believe" that dimming lights meant the deceased husband was communicating his presence.

With the exception of one woman, here identified as Celeste, who meditated to produce visits, the widows reported they had no feeling of control over these events. The vividness of the experience amazed them. The comparison to hallucinations was voiced spontaneously five times and was always denied. These were *not* hallucinations.

Cathy: *. . . they just startle me. It's not like I'm lying there conjuring . . . they make me stop in my tracks . . . stop in my tracks and go, "What was that!?" . . . so different from anything I have felt before that I don't have words to explain it.*

Linda: *. . . weird . . . really startled . . . really kind of blew my mind . . . almost hallucinating.*
Rachel: *. . . No one could ever convince me that those things were (pause) um, hallucinations. . . . (Either) you are a truly psychotic person or these things really do happen.*
Ginny: *. . . had the strongest feeling . . . don't know if I was hallucinating or what, but it felt really real! . . . kept looking and blinking and wondering . . . real weird.*
Cindy: *. . . peculiar feeling . . . whether your mind can do these things or not, I don't know. . . . will never forget it . . . the strangest thing.*

Some experiences were very surprising by the standards of a rational culture. A few widows reported brief, clear images or illusions of seeing, hearing or being touched by their husband.

Cathy: *I was at a birthday party for a little 3-year-old friend of mine. Was not thinking of Tom. Was just socializing. Was just kind of doing normal—whatever that is—stuff. And, all of a sudden, from nowhere, he appeared! I mean, I just—a vision of him was right in front of me. I mean, it lasted a split second. But, it was there. And I went, "hhhhh!" (gasping breath in). I mean, like—and I thought (whisper) Oh, my God! (returns to usual voice level) I didn't say anything to anybody, but I will never forget that.*
Sylvia: *There was, I don't know if it was the day he died or the day after he died. I think it might—I don't know. It was one of those nights. I can remember sitting in his chair in the room. And all of a sudden, I just had an unbelievably (pause) warm feeling right down one whole—the right side of me. It was down the right: my shoulder, my arm, my side, right through the ear. And I looked around because I said, "The heat must have clicked on." That was how strong it was. Um. And it wasn't [the heat].*

Other widows described experiences where they were startled by a vague feeling or indistinct image or touch. They seemed to be amazed by the emotional power of the experience more than by its vividness because of the conviction they had been in contact with the spirit of the deceased.

Cindy: *About a week ago, I was out in the other room. And it was just a very peculiar feeling. And that was where Larry died. . . . And the first thing that came into my mind was something that my mother said as she was standing at the sink. She said, "Cindy, I swear to God, your father just put his hand on my shoulder and spoke to me." . . . Just an odd feeling of his presence in that room. Now whether it, where it comes from is desire? almost a feeling that . . . did you ever think you saw something out of the corner of your eye-type of feeling? That type of sensation. And I thought it was odd.*

While illusions of presence grabbed the widows' attention, they were not frightened by the experiences.

> **Cathy:** *It hasn't frightened me at all. I've felt like: Oh, gee! This is weird! and I've thought, well, if you're here, Tom, just make yourself known!*
> **Ginny:** *It didn't frighten me at all. Didn't frighten me. I—I felt strangely, um, comforted (cries). It was (cries) like my husband's spirit or something—as he was leaving. . . . That was real weird. And it wasn't spooky and it didn't scare me. And after that, I remember thinking: there's nothing about my husband that would scare me!*
> **Sylvia:** *And then I just smiled. I said, O.K. I'm not going to read into this. But I really felt that he was in the house. (She looked relaxed and happy in thinking of the incident.)*

Whether startling or practically subliminal, awake or asleep, the illusions or sense of the husband's presence were a mental collision, a bumping up against the outer world by an inner world in protest. For a brief instant, the widow might believe her husband was standing in front of her or hear him call her name. Then the perception disappeared and she became aware of both realities: the image of the living husband and the memory of the death. As seen in these examples, the widow was often left with emotional peace, a conviction of ongoing spiritual life for the deceased and of resolution of her internal conflict over the death.

There also is a cultural tension expressed here. Grief was to be hidden. Several widows described how uncomfortable others were with their grief. Ongoing contact with a spiritual presence had the connotation of craziness. Beliefs about what happened varied among the widows and for each woman at different times within the interviews. The report of the experience itself, without interpretation, was quite open.

Indeed, this is one finding of the study: These events were an experiencing that was acceptable and familiar to the widow. They were not disturbed by them. Even when there was an experience of externality or realness, the widows treated the experience as private.

Individual Differences in Sense of Presence

Each widow had an ongoing intense expression of grief that was characteristic for her. For most of these widows, sense of presence was in the background of their experiences. For a few widows, the repeated, dramatic experiences of presence were the dominant pattern.

These individual differences did not seem to be related to acceptance of the deaths. The two widows who experienced more astonishing and unbidden contacts throughout their grief also continued to have vivid images and sense-of-presence experiences through the second year. Both of these widows demonstrated successful adjustment to the death: increasing happiness in daily life, interest and attachment to new goals and activities, new friends, positive shifts in self-concept, altering the house, and a returning sense of purpose in living. Another difference for these two widows is that they were more involved than the others in performing music, practicing the visual arts, and in religious practice. This suggests a difference in style of processing that might predispose these individuals to nonverbal image experience.

Widows' Interpretation of Sense of Presence

Interpretation of these experiences changed over time and varied even within the interview. Women said that they did not analyze these experiences, that they just happened. These women felt they had learned they had to "go with the flow," to just accept the bereavement experience without trying to control it. These experiences seemed to fall into an area of experience that they did not scrutinize, but just accepted.

> **Cindy:** *You are not really sure of a lot of it. And you don't really sit down and analyze what you are doing. You know, when someone asks you a question, you have to say, "Well, gee, actually" and it makes you put it into a—in a perspective where you never thought of it before, of some of these things that you are saying, or pouring out of you. You never really stopped to think about. It just was. You didn't put a name on it. You just knew that you kept going. You know. Hm.*
> **Judith:** *I guess a little piece of me wants to believe that he is still there taking care of me. Yeah. Um. Psychologically, I think it is just helpful. To know that somehow he is looking over my shoulder and that I will be O.K. So, you know, he's not here but somehow I want to believe that he is still—his presence is part of my life. I haven't given him up completely. At all.*

These widows were aware that their culture did not accept spiritual contact interpretations of experience. In this cultural context, their beliefs differed about whether these experiences were actual spiritual contact with the deceased. Some women were definite in their beliefs. Some were hopeful and some clearly doubted this interpretation. Some women dismissed even vivid experiences as "something your mind can do." Widows held simultaneous, contradictory views and altered their statements through the course of the interview. Two women were consistently committed to the belief that this was communication with the husband's spirit.

> **Rachel:** *Intrinsically, I believe (5-second pause) Could I face that we just have this life and death is the end of it? It's kind of hard to believe when you have people running around in your life that are between worlds!*

Changes Over Time: Role of Sense of Presence

Most widows described sense-of-presence experiences as a *type of caring by the deceased husband* as well as a way they could reassure their need to care for their husbands. They saw it as evidence of a period of transition for both the widow and the deceased. Four women reported they were no longer preoccupied with thoughts of the deceased starting in the period of 11 to 17 months. Three others felt that the spirit of the deceased had moved on: at 13, 18, and 21 months. It was inconceivable that the husband would leave without saying good-bye as well as making sure she would be okay. There was a *recognition of her importance in his life, of the permanence of his caring.*

Some changes in the second year led to *decreases in self-esteem*. Rachel and Sylvia saw their husbands in a more idealized way as memories of their daily foibles became fuzzy. Neither of them made the conscious connection, but they both juxtaposed statements of increasingly "putting him on a pedestal" with statements about their own feelings of low self-worth. Their own daily shortcomings were sharp and clear while those of their husbands faded.

Taking the husband's point of view as her own seemed to be important in repairing the loss of self-esteem some widows reported as accompanying grief.

> **Cathy:** *Even though I feel like I died when Tom died, what's left of me to go on deserved to be O.K. And the reason that I feel that way maybe sounds bizarre but I respected my husband so much. My husband was a very special person. And I feel if someone like him could love me, then I must be all right. Even if I don't always feel all right. He was no dummy and he couldn't possibly love somebody that was a slouch. . . . He was pretty particular. And he was very bright. I mean, if somebody like him could love me, then I must be all right. So. And I feel that I owe it to him to move on with my life.*

For Cathy, the central issue was *re-awakening parts of herself that were not tied to her grief*. She took a new job at 14 months into her bereavement "to escape the realities of my life." Three months later, she found that the escape was "becoming my new reality," an identity she described as "not being Tom's widow." She began to think about dating.

Important self-growth also came from *incorporating qualities valued in the husband as her own*. This process of allowing characteristics of the husband to live on in the widow's new identity had a positive effect on Cathy's personal crisis of who she was without her husband. Her sense-of-presence experiences actually intensified at the time she was identifying more with her "not Tom's widow" self.

Widows described *resolving what they could or could not control in life*, relating this directly and indirectly to their *lack of control over death*. Sylvia talked of learning to fix what could be fixed and to not "spend too much mind time" on the rest. For instance, Sylvia said she met the challenge of her son's broken arm with a new composure and confidence. She described this as *taking on a way of doing things that would have been characteristic of her husband.*

Rachel had allowed herself to reexamine her involvement in work that was always in crisis and oriented toward high-prestige achievement in a medical field. She wondered if the activity was a way of proving her self-worth and superhuman status, even by controlling death. By the time of the interview, she was proud of herself for taking a small, low-prestige evening job that offered social contact with elderly people. This filled her loneliest hours with activity she enjoyed. She was *able to please herself*, no longer preoccupied with preventing death or proving herself.

HEURISTIC MODELS FOR THE ROLE OF SENSE OF PRESENCE IN GRIEF: TRANCE, COMMUNICATION, PLAY, AND PERSONAL RELIGION

A qualitative study is designed to seek out patterns for further exploration. Several comparisons to similar phenomena suggest themselves based on the stories of sense of presence told by these widows. The following are hypotheses about the role of sense of presence in grief based on the stories from the study.

Trance

Rachel's description of her sense of presence of being led in her thoughts by her husband's spirit has *the form of a natural trance.* Rachel's sense of presence included a feeling of her husband "touching my thoughts" with the purpose of guiding her and giving her permission to be active in pleasing herself.

> **Rachel:** *And sometimes when I'd be sitting in the house . . . I would be just so desolate that he wasn't here. I swear! I swear! I felt this for a long time. It was like somebody—interfering with my thoughts—somehow. Or gently touching my mind. His daughter says this, too. It would be almost like he'd be saying, "Go out in the garden and work it off. And get out there."*

Thus, sense of presence may play a role in *resolution of helplessness and feeling unsafe after the death.* Intuitively, it makes sense that in order to regain feelings of safety in the present, one would go back to memories of calmer times. One can then approach the painful event and the ongoing difficulties in the present with the resources of the past. Techniques in hypnosis include finding safe memories as anchors (Gilligan, 1987), that is, an internal thought one can return to when overwhelmed. One can then proceed to explore the painful memories and current realities, balancing the positive and negative experiences. Another technique in hypnosis involves placing the two sides of an ambivalence together to allow embracing them both. Mentally one can be both a widow and not a widow. Resolving grief may require recognizing that one is attached to both the past and the present. Ongoing attachment to the deceased spouse gave meaningful continuity to the widow's current life by honoring the past.

Communication Alleviates Isolation

Sense of presence offered *hopeful resolution to feelings of helplessness by substituting isolation with communication.* Other situations with a threat of death combined with social isolation lead to reports of private appearances: being taken hostage, being entrapped in mines, and being a pulmonary patient in intensive care are known to lead to experiencing private appearances (Bryden, 1983; Comer, Madow, & Dixon, 1967; Siegel, 1984). Comer et al. (1967) found that the content of the images invariably reflected an intense wish for a change in the reality of the situation in which the distressed persons found themselves. The visions also tended to be consoling and hopeful, offering release. Persons in intensive care units who are unable to speak experience hallucinations until they are given some method of communicating (Bryden, 1983). The experiencing of a visit by the deceased during grief is the comparable wish for a bereaved individual. The widows intensely missed communication with their husbands. They also lived in a particular culture and social group that fostered keeping their grief private.

Play as Effective Coping

One measure of child mental health is the capacity to play. Play involves *exploring the edge of self: what one can understand about changes in life and what is confusing.* Sense-of-presence experiences have a number of qualities similar to a child's play. Both are forms of internal role-playing that build and consolidate understanding. Keeping sense-of-presence experiences private is similar to the child who tells adults who intrude on play to go away. Most widows in this study said that the experiences of sense of presence were so personal that they did not tell anyone.

Personal Religion

Experience of presence, even if the spiritual interpretation was doubted or believed inconsistently, allowed reassurance that life after death was possible for the deceased. This continued to be important because the attachment to the deceased continued: the widows wanted an afterlife for their husbands as well as for themselves when they would eventually die.

DISTRESS IN THE INTERVIEW/ COPING IN LIFE

There was an intensity of the pain of grief in all 10 interviews that was impressive. What was equally impressive was the high level of coping evident at the time of the interviews: widows were working or productive at home; several were in school. Some of the widows who were into the second year since the death were dating, moving into a new house, buying new furniture, changing careers.

Several clues as to how to interpret this were present. The content of an interview asking about memories of the deceased put the widows into a frame of reference that accessed their pain. They communicated the memory of their intense sadness. This was only a partial picture of who they had become. The interview itself shaped which part of their experience the widows reported. For instance, one of the most despondent interviews changed abruptly when the questions about memory ended. This widow then talked for another hour about her plans for returning to school. Her expression and posture shifted markedly to a happier demeanor; she looked like a different person.

A second important contextual factor was the sampling of widows from bereavement support groups. These women had felt extremely isolated. They found the culture lacking in rituals and acceptance of sharing grief. Their particular Caucasian, middle-class culture essentially condoned only private processing of their grief. They had acted to do something to change that: they sought professional help, many of them individually as well as in the groups.

IMPACT OF BEREAVEMENT GROUPS

After 4 to 6 months of therapeutic intervention, widows in the second year in this study were doing better on measures of coping than the widows not in treatment who were described in longitudinal research on grief after sudden death (Parkes, 1987; Parkes & Weiss, 1983). Widows in this study were currently in bereavement groups. Some were in individual psychotherapy as well. They were in the process of regaining purpose and trust in life. They still felt the need of support. However, they had made significant progress toward regaining their personal balance and feeling of safety in the world.

CONCLUSIONS

Coping well in this group of widows did not mean they were beyond the pain of the deaths or the attachment to the deceased husbands. It is more accurate to say they were in the process of incorporating the past relationships in their current personalities.

These widows continued to be sad in recalling their husbands. They continued to love these husbands even as their own identities broadened to go beyond being widows. They brought their husbands into the present, sometimes without realizing it, by taking on tasks, roles, and personal qualities of their husbands. These women became fathers as well as mothers to their children—calmly dealing with a child's broken bone, resourcefully coping with repairing an apartment. They took their husbands' point of view more consciously in knowing the departed men would care that they recovered and were okay. They felt the deceased's permission to go on with their lives. They continued to have relationships to the husbands in the past just as they had relationships to their own pasts and who they had been. They internalized the positive valuing and concern that had made them feel safe in the past in order to deal with issues of mortality in the present.

The widows who continued to have vivid illusions of perceiving the deceased did not differ from other widows in the study in their acceptance of death, apparent self-esteem, or movement to building a new life. They also did not seem to be more isolated socially or to perceive themselves as more abandoned. They seemed rather to be better at this style of expressing grief, more accepting of it and more convinced of its meaning. The pain of loss continued for all of them as these widows moved on to new work and new relationships and felt increased purpose in living.

It seems appropriate to put sense of presence in the category of one of several types of experience that are possible during grief. Sense of presence may be more likely when mortal threats are present, when communication of feelings of grief is discouraged, or when the widow feels helpless. However, sense of presence also represents positive coping with the existential issues and transformation of the internal relationship, and as such need not be seen as a symptom of anything.

Widows experienced the deaths of their partners as if a death of self, both because the men were extensions of the women's selves and because, through their deaths, the women were reminded that they were also mortal. These sudden, untimely deaths undermined trust that life is continuous in an expectable fashion.

Memories of the deaths and images of living persons were important complementary sides of this process of shifting relationship to incorporate loss and maintain meaning in life. Together, they served consolidation of new self-identities that included valued aspects of the marriages. Memories served to ground the widows in reality. Sense of presence served to make that reality bearable by continuing to draw on internalized relationships. Sometimes these were interpreted as spiritual, sometimes as existing in memory. Some sense-of-presence experiences were described as transformative experiences allowing the widows to recognize they were alone in life and could only visit their deceased husbands in spirit. Sense of presence seemed to facilitate resolution of the central issue of loss of trust in the continuity of life as well as the social and emotional isolation in which widows found themselves.

> **Cindy:** *Is it real or is it something that your mind plays tricks on you? Who knows these kinds of things? It just was. It feels real. I don't have*

explanations for it. My own feelings—are, as I say, [that] in a dream I call it a visit. Like I said, you call it so you can enjoy it. Rather that, turn it into something positive. Otherwise, it would be horribly painful. And we have to let some things be painful. But I don't think you have to let all things be painful. It's maybe a fine line that it will bowl you over and it doesn't have to if you can do something with it.

Linda: *It's like we lived and we loved and we laughed together. And even if I can't laugh now, I still can live with that love that I had. And I—I believe that it is still there and it will always be there and that is what is going to get me through until, you know, my life ends.*

Where does the attachment go after a death? The relationship grows and shifts and gets reorganized into a new form with a familiar face. The attachment can enhance attachment to the future when it functions in a positive manner. In this study, memories of the deceased spouse served as a safe haven to help mend the trauma of loss, as an inner voice to lessen current social isolation, as an internal reworking of self to meet new realities and as reassurance of the possibility of immortality. The memory and images of the deceased were a source of current strength when affirming permission to move on in life while maintaining meaning in the past. The intense pain of grief was an acknowledgment of the present reality, not an end to the caring.

REFERENCES

Balk, D. (1983). Adolescents' grief reactions and self-concept perceptions following sibling death: A study of 33 teenagers. *Journal of Youth and Adolescence, 12*(2), 137–161.

Bruyn, S. T. (1966). *The human perspective in sociology: The methodology of participant observation.* Englewood Cliffs, NJ: Prentice-Hall.

Bryden, D. S. (1983). *Development of a computerized man/ machine/ staff interface system to psychologically support patients in an I.C.U. environment.* Unpublished doctoral dissertation, Massachusetts School of Professional Psychology, Boston.

Comer, N. L., Madow, L., & Dixon, J. J. (1967). Observations of sensory deprivation in life threatening situations. *American Journal of Psychiatry, 124*(2), 68–73.

Conant, R. D. (1992). *Widow's experiences of intrusive memory and "sense of presence" of the deceased after sudden and untimely death of a spouse during mid-life.* Unpublished doctoral dissertation, Massachusetts School of Professional Psychology, Boston.

Cook, J. A. (1983). A death in the family: Parental bereavement in the first year. *Suicide and Life-Threatening Behavior, 13*(1), 42–61.

Gilligan, S. G. (1987). *Therapeutic trances: The cooperation principle in Ericksonian hypnotherapy.* New York: Brunner/Mazel.

Glaser, B. G., & Strauss, A. L. (1968). *The discovery of grounded theory: Strategies for qualitative research.* Chicago: Aldine.

Glick, I. O., Weiss, R. S., & Parkes, C. M. (1974). *The first year of bereavement.* New York: John Wiley & Sons.

Harriman, P. L. (1937). Some imaginary companions of older subjects. *American Journal of Orthopsychiatry, 7,* 368–370.

Jacobs, S. C. (1987). Measures of the psychological distress of bereavement. In S. Zisook (Ed.), *Biopsychosocial Aspects of Bereavement* (pp. 125–138). Washington, DC: American Psychiatric Press.

Kalish, R. A., & Reynolds, D. K. (1983). Phenomenological reality and post-death contact. *Journal for the Scientific Study of Religion, 16*, 209–221.

Matchett, W. F. (1972). Repeated hallucinatory experiences as part of the mourning process among Hopi Indian women. *Psychiatry, 35*, 185–194.

Olson, P. R., Suddeth, J. A., Peterson, P. J., & Egelhoff, C. (1985). Hallucinations of widowhood. *Journal of the American Geriatric Society, 33*, 543–547.

Parkes, C. M. (1987). *Bereavement: Studies of grief in adult life* (2nd Am. ed.). Madison, CT: International Universities Press. (1st ed., 1972: Tavistock)

Parkes, C. M., & Weiss, R. S. (1983). *Recovery from bereavement.* New York: Basic Books.

Rees, W. D. (1971). The hallucinations of widowhood. *British Medical Journal, 4*, 37–41.

Rosenblatt, P. C., Walsh, P., & Jackson, D. A. (1976). *Grief in cross-cultural perspective.* New Haven, CT: Human Relations Area Files.

Siegel, R. K. (1984). Hostage hallucinations: Visual imagery induced by isolation and life-threatening stress. *Journal of Nervous and Mental Disease, 172*(5), 264–272.

White, M. (1989). Saying 'Hullo' again: The incorporation of the lost relationship in the resolution of grief. In *Selected papers.* Adelaide, Australia: Dulwich Centre Publications.

Yakamoto, J., Okonogi, K., Iwasaki, T., & Yoshimura, S. (1969). Mourning in Japan. *American Journal of Psychiatry, 125*, 74–79.

Part Five

Parental Bereavement

When does a parent stop being a parent? Death does not seem able to sever this bond. Yet, bereaved parents are often misunderstood when they continue to include their dead child as one of their offspring and include the child in their lives. Society does not legitimize the long-term grief of a parent whose child has died. In the chapters in this section, we see many examples of "old grief" that is stirred over time. The content of this long-term grief is the relationship with the dead child. Emotional and social development continues in adulthood. Simon Rubin, in Chapter 13, reminds us that memory does not remain either cognitively or affectively frozen. In healthy resolution of grief, the relationship to the deceased remains fluid and coexists as an adjunct to ongoing interactions in the parents' daily life.

If we allow parents to educate us from their own experience, we find a good example of Bruner's folk psychology in operation. Parents are often aware of the theory of grief that would delegitimate their experiences. Parents are keenly aware of the social isolation they experience as they find a place for their dead child in their lives. If we will listen, bereaved parents will tell about their inner and social worlds and what works for them.

In Chapter 12, Dennis Klass describes the experiences of parents who have joined a self-help group. We see how the organization serves to legitimize the parents' experience, helps them feel less alone in their pain, and offers guidance in coping with the pain. We also see the special value of help offered by someone who has "been there," and the important shift from the role of one who is helped to the role of helper. In the setting of the support group, it is possible to transform the bond with the dead child so there is a place for the child in both the inner and social worlds of the parents.

Rubin, meanwhile, is particularly concerned with the professional evaluation that measures how well the person is functioning. He provides a diagnostic guide for integrating all aspects of bereavement, including the continuing bond with the deceased.

As we first saw in Chapter 8, by Kirsten Tyson-Rawson, one of the dangers in seeing the positive role of the inner representation of the deceased in the survivor's life is that we can easily overlook interaction with the deceased that has negative consequences for the bereaved. The case example Rubin presents focuses the clinical issues in negative interaction. In such cases the clinician typically would encourage the family to disconnect or to let go of their attachment. A more appropriate treatment strategy might be to help the family develop a more realistic assessment of the deceased and to find a way in which the deceased can continue to be part of the family without displacing other family members.

P. R. S.
S. N.

Chapter 12

The Deceased Child in the Psychic and Social Worlds of Bereaved Parents During the Resolution of Grief

Dennis Klass

The dynamics through which grief is resolved by bereaved parents in the self-help group Compassionate Friends involve transformations of the inner representations of their dead children in the parents' inner (psychic) and social worlds. When the reality of a child's death and the reality of a parent's continuing bond with the child are made part of the socially shared reality, the inner representation of the child is transformed in the parent's psychic life. The end of grief is not severing the bond with the dead child, but integrating the child into the parent's life and into the parent's social networks in a different way than when the child was alive. This chapter traces such transformations of inner representations as they progress with the help of Compassionate Friends.

INTRODUCTION

The beginning, middle, and end of our story is the answer to the question, "Who is this child to you?" We will trace the transformations of the parent's inner representation of their child after the child has died. The end of our story will be how the inner representation of the child functions in the ongoing life of the parent after grief is resolved. The prologue of the story is the representation of the living child in the parent's world. The middle is how interaction with the inner representation helps bring a resolution of grief. One of the central themes we trace is the relationship between the inner representations in the parent's psychic and social worlds.

Data for this chapter are drawn from a long-term ethnographic study of a local chapter of the Compassionate Friends, a self-help group of parents whose children have died (Geertz, 1973; Glaser & Strauss, 1965; Hammersley & Atkinson, 1983; Klass, 1988; Powdermaker, 1966; Wax, 1971; Whyte, 1973). The study began when the author was asked to be the professional advisor to the chapter. There have been many opportunities to gather material in ongoing conversations and open-ended interviews with members, in attending meetings in which members shared their grief and meetings at which they did business and planning. An especially valuable source of understandings was the group's newsletter in which members wrote for themselves and for each other, to share their pain, their progress, and their insights. The study began as the chapter was formed. During the study, the chapter spawned two other groups: the infant/ toddler group and a local chapter of Parents of Murdered Children. Monthly attendance for all the meetings has averaged about 130 for several years. Somewhat apart from the author's role within the group, the data include 5 years of summary observations in his clinical psychological practice with bereaved parents. As they reached resolution, some of those therapy clients, at his request, have written extended reflections on their journeys.[1]

We can define grief as the processes by which the bereaved move from the equilibria in their inner and social worlds before a death to new equilibria after a death. Equilibrium is difficult to measure, but easy to subjectively sense. The parents in our study say that typically it takes 3 to 4 years before the new equilibria seem steady enough to trust.

We can define inner representation, following Fairbairn (1952) and Kernberg (1976), as the part of the self actualized in the bond with the person, characterizations, and thematic memories of the person, and the emotional states connected with the characterizations and memories. The word "inner" in inner representation may be somewhat misleading, for our psychic life is structured to a great extent by social bonds. A child, living or dead, plays roles within the family and psychic system. The role can be as simple as the child being the one who will live out the parent's ideal self or as complex as the child being the parent's surrogate parent (Benedek, 1959, 1970, 1975). Phenomena that indicate interaction with the inner representation of the dead child are a sense of presence, hallucinations in any of the senses, belief in the child's continuing active influence on thoughts or events, or a conscious incorporation of the characteristics or virtues of the dead child into the self. These phenomena can be private or shared within the family and community.

The key dynamic we will trace in this chapter is the way parents integrate the inner representation of the dead child into their family and community systems. To a great extent, the degree to which parents in our study feel integrated in the social system, and the degree to which they can find social support in their grief, and therefore the ease with which they can resolve their grief, is the degree to which the inner representation of the child is integrated into their social world.

---

[1]In the contemporary developed world, as civic discourse has transformed into opinion polls and as work has moved into bureaucracies, home and children have become the basis of personal identity and the constellation of meanings by which important decisions can be made (see Baumeister, 1991; Coontz, 1992). It may be, therefore, that contemporary parental grief has unique features. Yet clearly, many of the dynamics we will discuss are true across cultures. Smart's (1994) history of parental grief in Anglo American culture shows that during the time for which her sources have good records, the thoughts and feelings are much the same, though there are swings in the culture's willingness to accept expressions of those thoughts and feelings. LaFleur's (1992) study of Mizuko-jizo in Japan shows many similarities to what the author has observed in the Compassionate Friends.

INTERACTIONS THROUGH THE COURSE OF GRIEF

It seems reasonably well accepted today that there are no easily defined stages in grief. Over the years, however, members of the Compassionate Friends have devised a language by which they locate themselves and others in their journey. They define members of the group as "Newly Bereaved," "Into Their Grief," "Well Along in Their Grief," and "Resolved as Much as It Will Be." It is not a formal system, and other terms may be used; for example, "Into Their Grief," can also be called "That First Year," and at the end they may be called "Pretty Much Resolved." Because the system was developed by the subjects of our study to explain their own experience, we are appropriating it as a way of organizing this chapter, but the scheme may not describe experiences other than those within the Compassionate Friends. In each of these phases we will discuss the representation of the child in the parent's inner world and in the communities of which the parent is a member.

Newly Bereaved

The Parent's Inner World   For parents, their child's death is an awful truth that seems unreal. Kauffman (1994) has recently pointed out that the initial response to traumatic death is not denial but dissociation, and that the mourning process is best conceived as an interplay between integration and dissociation. In the newly bereaved parents we see the realization of the loss of the child, and a recognition that a part of the self has been cut off. A newsletter article reads:

> We awaken to the sun shining in our windows—a beautiful day. But wait, was I dreaming, or is something wrong? Why do I hesitate to become fully awake? No, it isn't a bad dream, it's reality. The room is empty.
>
> He wasn't there when we went to bed, he isn't in his bed this morning. It can't be. . . . Our hearts are left with an empty room that will never be filled again. . . . His presence fills the room, although we know he is gone. . . . Today is a bad day. The door is closed. Someone is pretending it never happened. Will it be open again tomorrow? It's hard to say as we are just trying to make it through today. So we turn our heads when we go by. The urge to beat on the door and cry out, "Please come back," is almost too much to bear.

As the shock of the reality is hitting them, parents often have intimations of the future bond they will have with the child. In a newsletter poem, a mother describes a recurrent dream that she feels "as though you were still there." When she reaches out to touch the child, he disappears. The mother's interpretation of the dream is that the child is sending a message that the child has not yet gone and is still with her. We can see that the child and the parent are not separated, for the poem shifts from the parent's dream to the child's dream and she feels herself in the child's dream just as the child is in hers.

> For in your dreams each night, God lets my love shine through.
> God sends you all the pictures, for in your mind to view,
> of all the precious times we had, and all the love we knew.

In the poem, the mother knows that death is real and that she will not see her child again in her lifetime. Though at this time the parent does not experience the presence of the child, that presence is projected into the future. She looks forward to heaven when they will be reunited.

During this early grief, parents often establish a connection with the dead child through a linking object (Volkan, 1981) that will transmute over time, but will be long lasting. Three years after her 21-year-old daughter died, a mother reported:

> Raggedy Ann and Andy still sit there, perched on top of a bookshelf in what used to be Ellen's room. . . . Years ago I tried to throw the forgotten dolls away, and my then-teen-aged daughter indignantly rescued them from the trash. "Not Ann and Andy!" she cried, settling them in her room. . . . Ellen is gone now . . . her beautiful promising young life snuffed out by a drunk driver. . . . Our lives have been changed, and so has Ellen's room. We use it primarily as a computer/word processor room now, but many of the reminders are still there—including Raggedy Ann and Andy.

The Parent's Social World   The disequilibrium and dissociation parents feel in their inner life extends into their experience of their social world. Newly bereaved parents care whether other people share the loss. Parents report if people came to the funeral, if there was a memorial planned at the school, if they see other people deeply affected by their child's death. But for a significant number of parents, the pain they experience is not felt within their communities. It often seems to them that neither the child nor the child's death has any social reality. They find people will not mention the child's name in their presence, that inquiries about how they are doing imply that it doesn't hurt as bad as it does, that the child can be replaced by a new baby, or that God loves the child in heaven better than the parent could have loved the child here. When a child dies, it seems to the parent that their lives have stopped while other people's lives go on. The sense of isolation can be bitter.

> Thick layers of gauze,
> Its contents, my heart.
> A clinical perspective for friends,
> Enough so the blood does not drip.
> Only at the solitary presence of his tiny grave,
> Do I sit and unwind all the layers
> and view the deep gash.
> It will never heal . . . I will only wrap it differently with time. (Serpliss, 1993).

One of the reasons for the Compassionate Friends' existence is that the symbols of the mainline culture or of the parents' community affiliations are inadequate to help make sense of their experience. Their symbols do not meld with the reality that the child is dead and with the reality that the parent is still bonded to the child. A continual theme in the newsletter is an appeal to friends and family to understand and to accept the parents' feelings and behaviors. One of the early discoveries is that other bereaved parents are treated in a similar way.

> Please don't tell us to turn off our memories, to snap out of it, that he/she is dead and life has to go on. But our love for them doesn't end with death. . . . Yes, we fully realize that he/she is dead, gone forever, and that's what hurts.
> Please have patience with us. Try to understand why we are acting or feeling the way we are today. In a small word or gesture let us know it's allright with you for us to love, to cry, to remember. We aren't doing it to make you uncomfortable or to gain sympathy. We are just trying to cope.

A mother whose child was born with a defective heart and died a few weeks later wrote in a newsletter about how differently her community responded to the news of her pregnancy than to the news of her child's death. When she was expecting, everyone told her that this was the most blessed of life's events and that her baby was a new person, a unique individual, different from anyone else. She was told that this new person would change her life forever.

> And yet when this most blessed and unique person dies, everybody acts like it's nothing: "Oh well, better luck next time"; "It's better he died before you got to know him"; "You'll have more babies." . . . So parents who lose a baby will generally try to hide their feelings of grief from others for fear of ridicule, disapproval, or stern lectures about how lucky they are—to have other children or the ability to have new (and obviously improved) babies.

Into Their Grief

The Parent's Inner World   As parents "move into their grief," the complexity of their bond with the child becomes expressed in the complexity of their grief. The more the parent's daily psychic and social worlds involve the inner representation of the child, the more difficult it will be for the parent to separate out the inner representation of the child. We see differences in the way the child is integrated into various parts of the parent's self, and thus into the different social systems in which the parent participates. A crucial issue is how the child's death affects the work life. For some parents, work is an island in a stormy sea, for tasks and relationships on the job seem "normal." Other parents find work difficult and their performance diminishes. The difference seems to be the degree to which their selfhood at work involves the child. For those who can work, the transition from work to home is marked by a surge of emotion. A mid-level executive said she functioned well at work, though she was occasionally teary. During the drive home, however, she became overwhelmed by the thought that her son was gone forever. She had the same surge of thoughts and feelings returning to the hotel room when she is out of town.

Some difficulty in marriages grows out of this experience (see Gilbert, 1989). One salesman felt he had to control his grief severely, because he was expected to be his old self with clients. He was fired from one job because his grief impaired his production and had a hard time finding another. His wife kept her job, but was moved to a position where little was expected of her. On his new job, the husband was afraid of the financial consequences of his grief. This brought prolonged conflict in the marriage, for his wife could not understand how he could turn off feelings that were for her so uncontrollable. It seemed to her that he could not have loved the child as she did.

Before an inner representation can be established, many parents must spend time separating from their inner sense of the living child and separating conflicting representations of the child from each other. In our study, there were some parents whose ability to function was highly dependent on the availability of the child (see Horowitz, Wilner, Marmor, & Krupnick, 1980; Rynearson, 1987). In a few of those cases, the inner representation of the child was integrated directly rather early in the grieving process in such a way that the child was maintained in the self system as before the death. For example, one recently reformed alcoholic whose 15-year-old daughter, Kim, was shot as a bystander in a holdup was having trouble maintaining sobriety in the painful months after her death. From her childhood, Kim had been the one in the family who "could tell me off when I was being stupid. She would just say, 'Dad, cut the crap.' She loved me and didn't back off like the boys did. When she told me to stop it, I did."

About 6 months after the death, he was standing at the grave when he heard a voice, "Dad, why are you acting this way? This is what you were like when you were drinking." Within a week Kim was his constant inner companion helping him control his rage and maintain his hard-won sobriety. A strong bond with other members of the Compassionate Friends later allowed him to separate himself from the direct dependence on Kim. As he became active in the group, Kim became more than just the voice telling him to control. She became part of his good self that was expressing itself by helping other bereaved parents.

As parents begin to separate from the inner representation of the living child, many find that the first point of connection between them and their dead child is the pain of their grief and the pain the child knew. We interviewed a woman whose 2-year-old daughter died after several months in the hospital. The child had blood drawn many times and feared the procedure, for it always hurt her. A few months after the death, the mother went to the clinic to have blood drawn.

> As I went in, I found myself saying over and over, maybe even out loud, "Look at Mommy, she can have them take blood, and she will be a big girl so it will not hurt. See, Julie, Mommy is going to be a big girl." When they stuck me it really hurt. I have given blood a lot and it never hurt like that—I mean, it never hurt before, but this time it really did. When I told my mother about it she said, "This may seem

strange, but I think that was Julie who was hurt." I think she is right. I cried all the way back to work and I knew what she had suffered. The next time I had blood drawn it was like always, just a little prick.

The child's pain can come in many forms. A woman whose daughter had an incurable degenerative disease said, "I never let myself experience her pain," because the medical staff urged the mother to be the voice of hope and determination. When her daughter cried and wanted to give up, it was the mother who insisted she get up and try again. "Well," the mother said in an interview, "I know the pain now." Several parents whose children committed suicide used the phrase, "Suicide is a way to pass the pain."

As parents come to terms with the inner representation of the living child, they often must come to terms with the ambivalences in the attachment between parent and child. Inner representations that are of the less-than-good self or that are extensions of attachments to negative figures in the parents' history produce more difficult griefs. Separating these inner representations from each other can be simply a matter of purging the representation of stressful memories and holding the child in an idealized way. Most parents do this to some extent, for we typically find them describing the dead child in glowing terms. Purging inner representations can also take the form of coming to terms with guilt stemming from what the parent now sees as less than adequate parenting.

It is not unusual for serious marital conflict to develop from the ambivalence and guilt in the negative inner representations of the child. For example, the son of a strict Pentecostal couple in the group died on drugs. His mother attributed his behavior to the father's strict discipline and distant emotional relationship to the boy. She blamed herself only for acquiescing to her husband's child-rearing ideas. She felt the fault was the husband's, not the son's. The difficulty was resolved only after the mother, as part of her anger at her husband, acted out a part of her own "bad" self. In coming to terms with the resultant guilt, she was able to reconcile herself to her negative inner representation of her son.

In the most difficult cases, the inner representation may be purged almost completely. A sociopathic young man, whose parents came for psychotherapy, had died in a hold-up attempt. His mother had supported him, but to do so, she repressed memories of violent episodes toward her. In the therapy, those memories returned. In the third year after he died, she went through 4 months of seeing him. She thought he was coming back to hurt her. She did not believe the body in "that box in the ground" was her son. She missed a therapy session and reported that she had found herself at the cemetery. As she lay on the grave for a long time she sensed that the bad side of her son was in the box. Gradually over the next few weeks, she found she no longer saw him lurking around, and she learned to feel safer.

The Parent's Social World   As parents separate the living child from the sense of self and come to terms with their ambivalent bonds with their children, they are aided by integrating the inner representation into their social world. Many of the unique aspects of the Compassionate Friends are expressions of the shared bond they have with each other's children. Thus membership in the community means membership as a bereaved parent, a person whose life is not as it was before, and a person who is to be related to differently than before. And membership in a community means that the dead child is also a member of the community, that the child is valued, remembered, celebrated, and loved.

Sharing a bond with the child begins with sharing the pain that the death of the child has brought. This sense of sharing pain is summed up by a phrase that continually reoccurs in members accounts of what they need from people: "just being there." Being there means being with the parent in such a way that the reality of the child now dead and the reality of the pain are not the parent's alone. The phrase is turned somewhat differently when members describe how the group is helpful to them. They say the people who can really understand are other bereaved parents, for they have "been there."

Sharing the pain also means sharing ways to relieve some forms of the pain, especially in the parent's social world. Often meeting time is devoted to practical issues—for example, how to include the child in the holidays. There are several ways these issues may be solved, but each answer is really a stance, a way of being-in-the-world. One mother made a holiday wreath for the front door with many colored ribbons, including a black one. "It is there," she said. "If they want to see it and mention it, they can. It is not me that didn't bring it up." Using the solution someone else suggests proves that the pain is shared.

These answers to practical problems lead to parents finding new stances in their family and community. It is common for parents to report that they are the ones who have to teach family and friends how to relate to them. Often what they teach is what they have learned at Compassionate Friends. A member wrote a poem addressed to those who would help her:

> Please listen to me, Hear what I'm saying.
> Not just the words that come from my mouth.
> For I can talk and not really say what I mean. . . .

She says not to give her advice and not to tell her how to feel because she will just turn us off, knowing we do not understand. But, she says if we can

> Be here with me and cry with me
> And then I'll know you've truly listened and heard, and understood.
> Then—I'll be comforted.

As the dead child is integrated into the social network, the experiences by which parents maintain contact with their children can be socially validated. Seeing, hearing, and sensing the presence of dead children is not easily integrated into the social reality of most communities, yet for many bereaved parents, such experiences are part of their daily reality. Most of the members have kept something of the child as a linking object. To validate keeping these linking objects, members may tell each other about them. Parents often report holding an item of clothing and smelling the child's odor. It is common at meetings for parents to tell about the solace they feel from these objects and to have that experience mirrored as they hear about other parents doing the same thing.

There has been a development within the group over the 10 years of our study in the way experiences that fall outside socially sanctioned reality are brought into the group. Early in the study, the group did not have a language to talk about these phenomena, and the attempts to share them were often very tentative. As the study progressed, such experiences were integrated into the shared beliefs of the group. At the same time, there was a steady stream of discussion in the popular culture about near-death experiences (see Zaleski, 1987) and to a lesser extent, postdeath contact. Now, the experiences are routinely reported and integrated into the group's fund of knowledge about grief. The group maintains the Compassionate Friends principle of not holding to any doctrinal position; yet at the same time it validates the experience by saying that the experiences are real, but are different for different people and that what is learned in the experience is for the parent, not for everyone. Nearly every year, one meeting is devoted to these experiences and several members have become well read on the topic. At national and regional meetings, sessions on nonordinary experiences are well attended.

Well Along in Their Grief

The Parent's Inner World   As Compassionate Friends members begin to find a new equilibrium in their lives, they hold their child differently. The movement is often cast in terms of letting go and holding on. The group's logo has a circle with a child figure distant from a pair of hands. One mother reported that her 4-year-old asked why the kid was so far from the hands. She replied that "because the kid has died and the hands are Mommy's or Daddy's reaching for the child." The 4-year-old disagreed: "I think you're wrong, Mom. I think the hands are letting him go." For the mother, the child's interpretation was right.

> She made me see that I was still reaching. It has been 2 years since B. was stillborn, but I continue to reach for something. Just what that something is, I don't know, but I'll know what it is when I find it. Perhaps then a part of me can let go.

The "something" she is reaching for is a positive bond with the child. The idea of letting go of the pain in exchange for a clearer, comforting inner representation of the child is one of the central insights in Compassionate Friends. Rather than identifying with the child's pain, the parent identifies with the energy and love that was in the living child. In a speech at a holiday candlelight service 5 years after her son's death, a mother reflected on her progress:

I was afraid to let go. Afraid that I would forget the details of him, the peculiar color of his eyes, the shape of his nose, the sound of his voice. . . . In a strange way my pain was comforting, a way of loving him, familiar. . . . Finally I had to admit that his life meant more than pain, it also meant joy and happiness and fun—and living. The little voice in my heart was telling me that it was time for me to let go of him. When we release pain we make room for happiness in our lives. My memories of Scott became lighter and more spontaneous. Instead of hurtful, my memories brought comfort, even a chuckle. . . . I had sudden insights into what was happening to me, the pieces began to fit again, and I realized Scott was still teaching me things.

One of the clichés of bereavement work is that grief is the price we pay for love. In a newsletter article, a father worked through the balance: "If the price I pay for loving Douglas is the pain and sorrow I now have, I still think I got a bargain to have had him for 13 years."

The developing bond with the dead child is often quite explicitly linked with the parents' thoughts about their own healing. A father reported that when he began running, his 17-year-old daughter encouraged him to keep it up by registering both of them to run a 5-kilometer race. She was killed in an accident 2 weeks before the race. He thought about quitting running but did not because he thought she would have been disappointed to think she had caused him to abandon running in general and the race in particular. He ran wearing her number. After that, she became part of his running.

Every time I ran, I took a few minutes to think about Maria and how I was dealing with her death. I was alone with no distractions but the pounding of my feet, and I could focus on her and my feelings. I tried to coach myself a bit, inch myself toward the light. That done, I often moved on to report silently to her about what I'd been doing lately, about what I thought of the weather, how my conditioning was going, what her younger brothers were up to. Frequently, I sensed she was nearby, cruising at my elbow, listening.

The Parent's Social World The socially shared inner representation stabilizes the inner representation in the parent's life. One mother whose living children have moved away reflected in the newsletter on how she keeps the bond with all her absent children, including the one who is dead. She finds she does it in similar ways, but that while she can hold her living children on her own, she needs the Compassionate Friends so as to hold the bond with the dead child.

The one thing about The Compassionate Friends is that mention of your child's name won't cause an awkward gap. You know, the kind that makes you feel somehow you shouldn't have said anything. How can anyone else know that your child is still real? That they were real and are real? I want to scream sometimes that my boys are real! See, he's here in my heart. Oh, and when I stopped at a traffic light today, there was a boy in the car next to me who put his hand to chin just like my son did. It was amazing—that gesture, that hand—just like my son's.

The little one is not so clear in my mind anymore, but he's real. How many children do I have? Three. My daughter is married and living in New York. And the boys? Well, one will always be four and a half. I heard him laughing the other day in the giggles of some preschoolers. And my oldest son? I told you . . . he made sergeant? And that I saw him in the gesture of a boy waiting at the traffic light?

As the bond with the child is made part of the parent's membership in Compassionate Friends, the inner representation can be more fluid and thus can be transformed within the parent's inner world. We can see many of the dynamics of Compassionate Friends in the publicity written by the coordinator of the annual picnic. She says there will be good food and games, but

these are the sidekicks of our picnic. The center, the best, the reason we come back year after year is simply to be together. Whether meeting new people, talking to old friends, playing or just being there, it is the gathering that makes this event so special for so many of us.

If our gathering is the center, our children lost are the heart and soul of our picnic. It is for and because of them that we have come, and it is for them that we have our cherished balloon released, a time set aside in our day to remember and include our special children.

Helium-filled balloons are passed out, along with markers, giving us all one more chance to tell our children the things we most long to say—mostly, "I love you." And then, oblivious to the world around us, we stand as one, but each involved in his own thoughts, prayers, and emotions as we released hundreds of balloons to the sky and they disappear; to a destiny we are certain they will reach.

The children are the heart and soul of the group, for it is the shared inner representations of the dead children that bond the members to each other. The children are in the midst of the group, not simply within each of the individual parents. Yet the inner representations of the children are also wherever balloon messages are carried. The ritual provides a means by which the parent can both reach out to the dead child and feel the presence of the child within. They "stand as one, but each involved in his own thoughts, prayers, and emotions." Because the bond with the child is shared within the group, the parents can be in touch privately with the individual inner representation of their child. Because the group shares in the strong bond with the child, there is tremendous strength within the group. Because there is such strength within the group, the bond with the child feels surer. One balloon sent into the sky would seem a lonely and fragile message. Hundreds of balloons, each addressed to an individual child, are sure to get through.

In meetings the pain is shared and in that sharing, the bond with the child is shared. In the ritual with which each meeting begins, everyone around the circle introduces themselves, giving their name and then their child's name and something about their child's death. Often parents add a sentence or two about how good or bad a month it has been or if there is a significant date such as a birthday or death anniversary near. If both parents attend, usually one of them tells about the child while the other just says, "I'm Mary, James's mother." At the end of the introductions, the cumulative effect of all those names and all that pain is a deep quiet punctuated by the soft sobs of some newly bereaved.

Just to be able to say and hear the name is important; a father's poem concludes:

> He is real and shadow, was and is.
> Say Orin to me and say Orin again.
> He is my son and I love him as I always did. Say Orin

A mother said that her child's name may bring tears to her eyes, but music to her ears. Nearly every year for a meeting program, everyone brings and passes around pictures of their children and tells stories about them. At national and regional meetings, there are long lines of picture boards. Parents from around the country often begin talking as they stand looking at the pictures of the children. Cards and phone calls come on the children's birthdays. The sense of oneness with other bereaved parents and the sense of oneness with the inner representation of the dead child can be seen in the national group's credo:

> We reach out to each other with love, with understanding and with hope. Our children have died at all ages and from many different causes, but our love for our children unites us. . . . Whatever pain we bring to this gathering of The Compassionate Friends, it is pain we will share just as we share with each other our love for our children.

As they learn to share the child in Compassionate Friends, members find ways to include the child in their other communities. One woman reported that 6 years after her daughter's death, she decided she wanted the child included in the family Christmas gift exchange.

> Last year I shocked my sister who usually organizes the name exchange. I called her ahead of that day and said, "I want Jane's name in the exchange, too." Well, there was silence on the phone. So I began to explain—whoever gets Jane's name can make a donation to a charity in her name. Yes, her name was included and for the first time since 1985, I felt she was part of things.

Resolved as Much as It Will Be

The Parent's Inner World   Members of the Compassionate Friends are adamant in their conclusion that "you don't get over your grief." They often add, "but it doesn't stay the same." The message to newly bereaved parents at their first meeting is unequivocal, "It will always hurt, but it will not hurt they way it does now." What, then, can resolution mean?

At an "alumni gathering," the group went around the room doing the ritual of introduction. There was a lot of humor. The fourth person, who had been a group facilitator a few years earlier, paused for a moment after she introduced her child and said, "Gosh, it feels so good to say that and not cry. Look, we are doing this and we are sitting around laughing. Isn't that really nice to do." There was a lot of agreement. Several said there were moving on with their lives, noting with a laugh, "We are not even on the mailing list any more." A man said, "The first time I went to candlelight I didn't think I could stand to be there. I went because I needed to. After 5 years, I was one of the people who read the names. And do you know what, this year it skipped my mind. We forgot about it. I guess that shows how far we've come." Several said they remember their child regularly and that it is a good feeling. Occasionally they still cry, but that's okay, too. Their sadness is part of them and they can recognize it and not be afraid of it.

In a newsletter, a mother wrote about gentler "older grief."

> It's about sudden tears swept in by a strand of music . . . .
> It's about feeling his presence for an instant one day while I'm dusting his room.
> It's about early pictures that invite me to fold him in my arms again.

She concludes:

> Older grief is about aching in gentler ways, rarer longing, less engulfing fire.
> Older grief is about searing pain wrought into tenderness.

The bonds we have with our children are complex, so transforming the bond can be a long and exhausting task. But eventually the parents in our study are able to reestablish the inner representation of their dead child as part of their ongoing life. One of the paradoxical feelings often mentioned in meetings is that finally completing the grief process is itself a kind of loss. Moving on with life has its own ambivalence for bereaved parents, but the ambivalence is somewhat mollified by the reestablished inner representation of the child. Betty Johnson writes in the newsletter:

> Time roars on, but I rear back,
> Resisting, afraid to move on and leave you behind.
> I was safe with you, unafraid in my own realm.
> If I heal, will you be gone forever?
> Your leaving opened new worlds.
> I have time now and my days and energies no longer revolve around your needs.
> I want you to come with me into the future.
> Your youth protected my youth, but now new beginnings eclipse the past.
> My eyes strain as they search my heart for distant memories.
> But your face fades as I reach out to you.
> All that remains are warm feelings, smiles, tears, and
> Glimpses of your love, left in the wake of your parting.
> Will you forgive me if I go on?
> If you can't make this earthly journey through time with me,
> Will you then come along in my heart and wish me well?

The parents in our study often tie the resolution of their grief to their bond with the inner representation of their child. The parents' newfound interest in life is often described in terms of the active inner representation. As the child comes along in their heart to wish them well, many report that the peace they have found in their resolution is what their child wishes or would have wished for them:

> It was an unmistakable thrill that moment I first noticed
> I think more about his life now than about his death!
> It's just what he would have wanted!

The Parent's Social World   Part of the resolution of grief is making the pain count for something, or, put another way, of making the parent's life, especially the experience of the child's death, count for something. In making their own life meaningful, the inner representation of the child is made real. One of the ways parents' lives can count, and the child be real, is to help others. The organizational life of Compassionate Friends depends on some people staying and leading the group as a way of expressing the change in their lives, made by their children and their grief. A man who led the committee planning the candlelight ceremony wrote, "I wanted most to do it for Jason. All that I do now I do to honor his memory and his life." He continued,

> We do need to find a positive outlet for all the anger and pain. Find a charity, or a cause that has personal meaning; get involved with The Compassionate Friends; plant a garden; get into shape; do something that illustrates the positive effect that your child had on you—even if you are the only one to see it.

Early in their membership in Compassionate Friends, parents found they could be bonded with their child in their affiliation with the group. Over time that bond changes, for as the bond with the child becomes more secure in their life, the bond with the group becomes less focused. In a meeting of a committee rethinking the organizational structure, a discussion centered around the idea that the group works best when there is a steady turnover of meeting facilitators. Two former facilitators said that they just knew when the time in their grief process had come for them to move on from that job. A woman whose daughter had been dead 2 ½ years and who had just taken on the task of facilitating a meeting said, "I don't understand. The time I give to Compassionate Friends is my Angela time." She thought of the energy and care she gives the group as care and energy she would be giving to the child. She worried, "So, what does it mean to move on? Do I lose my child? Does that mean I won't have that any more?" A veteran who no longer attends meetings replied,

> No, you don't lose that. It has been 13 years for me. I was like you when I was facilitating the meeting. That was my connection with Bruce. It was real direct; when I was doing The Compassionate Friends work that was for Bruce. I can't say exactly when it changed or how, but now he is there all the time. He is just there; he is part of

me. It isn't my connection with The Compassionate Friends that connects him to me. But The Compassionate Friends gave me something important when I needed it and I want to give something back. Sometimes it is good for me to be very involved and other times it seems like I should pull back more. Right now I feel like getting more involved again. But that is because it feels right to be part of something good. Bruce is part of that, but Bruce is part of many things in my life.

This dynamic creates some moments of irony, such as when a person was honored for extraordinary service to the national organization. After he got a long standing ovation at the convention, he said, "I just had a funny thought. I thought if Tim were here, wouldn't he be proud. But if he were here, this wouldn't be happening." But the irony is not expressed too often, for the interactions in the life of the group have an authentic feel. The tasks are important and difficult. Members take long calls from newly bereaved, spend 2 days a month with a small group folding and labeling newsletters for mailing, or make calls all over the city to get donations for the picnic that will include the balloon release. Meeting facilitators prepare for several days and then spend hours debriefing each other as they try to keep abreast of members' progress and the complex interactions in the meetings. The organization has proved itself to these parents, for it was affiliation with other bereaved parents that allowed them to find resolution to their grief. In giving back to others, their experience becomes a part of their better selves.

Dead children are often melded into the parents' better selves in a way that makes the children seem like teachers of life's important lessons. The father of a child born with multiple congenital heart defects, but who lived "2,681 days," ties his present activity in Compassionate Friends to those lessons:

> He not only taught me the importance of what really matters in life, but through his death, also how we can make even more use of his life.
>
> Because of Jerrold we make ourselves available to other bereaved parents who are at some point on death's desolation road. . . . So whenever people ask if I'm done grieving for my precious son, I answer with much conviction: "Most assuredly so. But I will never be done showing my appreciation for having been blessed with such a gift."

Early in their grief, parents searched for community through which they could keep their bonds with the deceased children. They were angry when those children were not included in their interactions with family. An important element in transforming the bonds was sharing them with others. For those who stay with Compassionate Friends as leaders, the bond with the child remains part of their work in the group. As their grief resolves, parents find that this bond is a natural part of many of their social affiliations. At a meeting a father whose son had been dead over 10 years reported that early in his grief, people seemed afraid to talk to him about his son. But as he is more resolved, the boy becomes part of many spontaneous conversations. At work he keeps a piece of metal from his son's welding class on his desk as a paperweight. He reported that even people who could not have known what the object was used to avoid asking about it.

> For a couple years there, you could just see them trying not to look at it, let alone mention it. Now someone will see it and ask and when I tell them what it is and why I keep it there and what it means to me, they just accept it and seem comfortable with how I feel about my son.

And then the conversation moves on to business. Thus, the inner representation of the child is integrated into the parent's social world in ways similar to how the inner representation of a living child would be.

The phenomena that indicate active interaction with the inner representation of the dead child—a sense of presence, hallucinations (though the parents might argue that "hallucinations" is an inappropriate word here), belief in the child's continuing active influence on thoughts or events, or a conscious incorporation of the characteristics or virtues of the child into the self—are no longer occasions for the parents' concern about their own sanity. The phenomena are accepted as a positive part of everyday living. On the 20th anniversary of her son's death, Margaret Gerner, the founder of the St. Louis Compassionate Friends, reflected in the newsletter on his place in her life and sent him a message of love and care.

> Arthur is still a big part of my life even today. As a family . . . we don't hesitate to mention him, even to strangers, if he fits into the conversation. . . . We tease about him. Pictures get crooked on the wall and we say "Arthur's been at it again. . . . We ask his help. Something big is in the wind for one of us and we tell Arthur "get working on it."
>
> Arthur's death has had a tremendous impact on my life. His death has been an impetus for positive change and growth for me. . . . I had Arthur for only a few short years, but he has given a special love to my life. He can't receive my love, but, nonetheless, I can send it to him by giving it to others.
>
> Arthur, years ago in my heart, I let you go—to run and play in Heaven and not to have to worry about how I'm doing.
>
> Now, on the twentieth anniversary of your death, again my heart is stopping by Heaven's playground to just say Hi! and to tell you how much I love and miss you.

CONCLUSION

The dynamics by which grief is resolved by parents in the Compassionate Friends are transformations of the inner representations of the dead children in the parents' inner and social worlds. As the reality of the children's deaths, as well as the reality of the parents' continuing bonds with the children, are made part of the socially shared reality, the inner representations of the children can be transformed in the parents' psychic lives. The end of grief is not severing the bond with a dead child, but integrating the child into the parent's life in a different way than when the child was alive. Phenomena that indicate interactions with the dead child change from being mysterious to being an everyday part of life. The Compassionate Friends seems a temporary affiliation in members' lives in that the group is the social bond in which the pain can be shared and the bond with the child acknowledged and honored. When parents stop active participation in the group, however, it is not because they have moved away from their dead children. At the end of their time in the Compassionate Friends, the children are part of their ongoing inner lives and part of the social bonds in which they feel at home.

REFERENCES

Baumeister, R. F. (1991). *Meanings of life.* New York: Guilford.

Benedek, T. (1959). Parenthood as a developmental phase. *American Psychoanalytic Association Journal, 7,* 389–417.

Benedek, T. (1970). The family as a psychologic field. In E. J. Anthony & T. Benedek (Eds.), *Parenthood: Its psychology and psychopathology.* Boston: Little, Brown.

Benedek, T. (1975). Discussion of parenthood as a developmental phase. *Journal of the American Psychoanalytic Association, 23,* 154–165.

Coontz, S. (1992). *The way we never were: American families and the nostalgia trap.* New York: Basic Books.

Fairbairn, W. D. (1952). *An object-relations theory of the personality.* New York: Basic Books.

Gilbert, K. R. (1989). Interactive grief and coping in the marital dyad. *Death Studies, 13,* 605–626.

Geertz, C. (1973). *The interpretation of cultures.* New York: Basic Books.

Glaser, B. G., & Strauss, A. L. (1965). *Awareness of dying.* Chicago: Aldine.

Hammersley, M., & Atkinson, P. (1983). *Ethnography: principles in practice.* New York: Tavistock.

Horowitz, M., Wilner, N., Marmor, C., & Krupnick, J. (1980). Pathological grief and the activation of latent self-images. *American Journal of Psychiatry, 137*(10), 1157–1162.

Kauffman, J. (1994). Dissociative functions in the normal mourning process. *Omega, Journal of Death and Dying, 28*(1), 31–38.

Kernberg, O. F. (1976). *Object-relations theory and clinical psychoanalysis.* New York: Aronson.

Klass, D. (1988). *Parental grief: Resolution and solace.* New York: Springer.

LaFleur, W. R. (1992). *Liquid life: Abortion and Buddhism in Japan.* Princeton, NJ: Princeton University Press.

Powdermaker, H. (1966). *Stranger and friend: The way of an anthropologist.* New York: Norton.

Rynearson, E. K. (1987). Psychotherapy of pathologic grief: Revisions and limitations. *Psychiatric Clinics of North America, 10*(3), 487–499.

Serpliss, C. R. (1993). Exposing my wound (poem). *SHARE Newsletter 2,* 33.

Smart, L. S. (1994). Parental bereavement in Anglo American history. *Omega, Journal of Death and Dying, 28*(1), 49–61.

Volkan, V. (1981). *Linking objects and linking phenomena: A study of the forms, symptoms, metapsychology, and therapy of complicated mourning.* New York: International Universities Press.

Wax, R. (1971). *Doing fieldwork: Warnings and advice.* Chicago: University of Chicago Press.

Whyte, W. F. (1973). *Street corner society: The structure of an Italian slum.* Chicago: University of Chicago Press.

Zaleski, C. (1987). *Otherworld journeys: Accounts of near-death experiences in medieval and modern times.* New York: Oxford University Press.

Chapter 13

The Wounded Family: Bereaved Parents and the Impact of Adult Child Loss

Simon Shimshon Rubin

INTRODUCTION AND THEORY

The loss of a son or daughter is often considered more painful, more engrossing, and more likely to require psychological intervention than the loss of a spouse (Gorer, 1965; Schechter, 1994). We may presume that the psychological meaning of the relationship and the significance of the parent–child bond contribute to the wrenching life readjustment that is required following adult child loss. It is with some bafflement, however, that we confront the fact that the depth and richness of the parent–child attachment bond and its transformation following loss is not adequately reflected in the conceptual frameworks of those who have been spared the experience. In one recent study, we showed that lay observers evaluated bereavement outcome with little attention to the fluctuations in the memories or thoughts of the deceased. When presented with specific indications of difficulty and dysfunction following loss, the observers tend to place the greatest stress on indications of gross dysfunction at work and to downplay the significance of how the deceased is remembered and recollected (Schechter & Rubin, 1994). To put it another way, while there is some intuitive understanding that something about relationships is critical to how people respond to loss, that knowledge does not extent to a consideration of how the quality of the recollected and internalized relationship to the deceased continues to affect individuals.

Since the time of Breuer and Freud (1893/1957), the psychological and psychiatric literatures addressing loss have lurched back and forth between two poles of thought. On the one hand, the relationship to the deceased has been considered the cornerstone of the mourning process, and yet on the other, it is the ability to return to robust functioning, unencumbered by indices of difficulty or psychiatric symptoms, that has served as a definable benchmark for professional and nonprofessionals alike in assessing the impact of the response to loss.

The author wishes to thank Professor Phyllis Silverman, Dvorah Katz, and Liat Ariel for their helpful comments on earlier drafts of this chapter. The final version was completed while the author served as Visiting Associate Professor of Psychology in the Department of Psychiatry at the Harvard University Medical School, Boston, Massachusetts.

Thus, for many people, it is the absence of symptomatology years after loss that is taken as an indication that the bereavement has been overcome. When a survivor has been able to return and fill a productive role in society, this is taken as an indication that loss has been resolved. When the stages of mourning— protest, searching, disorganization, and reorganization (Bowlby, 1980)—have been traversed, it is often thought that mourning has been completed success- fully. The prevalent premise that mourning is incomplete only in the presence of difficulties in one or more areas of functioning is characteristic of the great weight given to overt behavior and dysfunctional affect in the assessment of reac- tion to loss. For years, attention to the overt behavioral and psychiatric indica- tions of postloss difficulties has been a major theme of papers published on out- come to loss (Kleber & Brom, 1992; Rando, 1983; Videka-Sherman, 1982). Until the last decade, this emphasis on function tended to overshadow the quality of the recollected and remembered relationship to the deceased as a significant and in- dependent feature of the outcome to mourning and loss (Rubin, 1984a). Reflect- ing this bias, the bulk of the research literature dealt with the theme of relation- ship sparingly (Guisinger & Blatt, 1994; Rubin & Katz-Dichterman, 1993).

In earlier papers, this author has attempted to bridge and organize the two themes described above by proposing a Two-Track Model of Bereavement. Rather than emphasize either functioning or relationship to the deceased, the Two-Track Model of Bereavement reflects a multidimensional viewpoint (Rubin, 1981, 1982, 1984a, 1984b, 1985, 1990a, 1992, 1993b). Whether to understand loss, to assess its impact, or to plan for psychotherapeutic intervention, we rec- ommend a focus on the dimensions of function and relationship to the deceased. Early in the course of the response to uncomplicated loss (and more generally in maladaptive response to loss), these dimensions may seem hopelessly inter- twined. They are, however, sufficiently distinct at both the conceptual and experi- ential levels as to warrant separate consideration. Further elaboration of the re- search and clinical applications of this approach are contained in other sources (Rubin, 1986, 1990b, 1994; Rubin & Nassar, 1993). A visual representation of the model is contained in Figure 1. The assessment of functioning following loss is represented on Track I by 9 areas that allow for a comprehensive evaluation of somatic, interpersonal, affective, and cognitive indices. The evaluation of the on- going relationship to the deceased is represented by Track II along 9 areas that fa- cilitate our understanding of the relationship to the representation of the deceased and their impact on the bereaved (Rubin, 1990b, 1993a, 1994; Sadeh, Rubin & Berman, 1993; Schafer, 1992).

The trajectory of the bereavement process reflects the human need to assimi- late and accommodate to the painful reality of loss. The affective, behavioral, cognitive, interpersonal, and psychophysiological changes that accompany the bereaved's response to loss are generally indications that the grief and mourning processes have begun, but these manifestations of disequilibrium are not identi- cal with the mourning process itself. The bereaved can remain consciously and unconsciously involved with processing the loss without necessarily manifesting

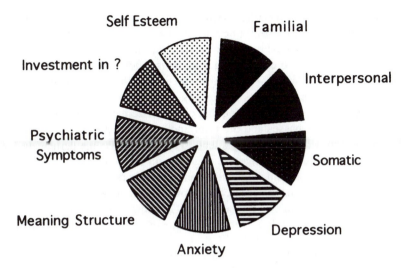

Figure 1a   Track one: functioning multidimensional assessment.

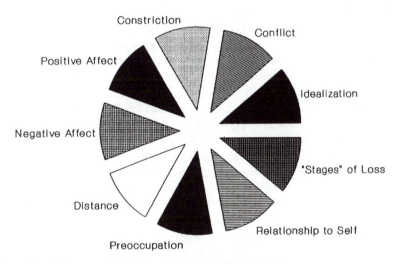

Figure 1b   Track two: relationship multidimensional assessment.

functional and symptomatic indicators associated with grieving. The mourning process of reorganizing one's internal world view with the need to adapt to a changed external reality is something more than mere adaptation to change (Parkes, 1988; Silverman, 1988). It is also a process of reorganizing much of the covert internalized relationship with the deceased as a result of the shocking and painful unavailability of the deceased (Freud, 1917/1957; Horowitz, Bonanno, & Holen, 1993; Silverman, Nickman, & Worden, 1992).

The response to loss has often been viewed as a process that one enters and exits over time (Parkes, 1986). While it is relatively easy to agree on how one enters and progresses along the bereavement process, agreement on how, or even if, one really "completes" the mourning process is much more difficult (Rando, 1993; Rubin, 1984a; Weiss, 1993). At its inception, the reorganization of the memories, associations, thoughts and feelings associated with the deceased proceeds alongside shifts in functioning that characterize the bereaved overtly and covertly. Yet as time passes and the grief and mourning processes unfold, the symptomatic and behavioral changes tend to subside or become permanent features of personality. The cognitive and affective links with the deceased continue on in varying degrees in both overt and covert ways. Years and decades after loss, some preoccupation with the deceased is common and may well be normative although symptoms as such may not be present (Breznitz, 1993; Friedlander, 1979; Rando, 1983; Rubin, 1992; Silverman, Nickman, & Worden, 1992; Stroebe, Gergen, Gergen, & Stroebe, 1992).

For many people, the initial stages of grief and mourning are periods of acutely painful affects and numerous changes in routine function. With the passage of time, however, the preoccupation with the deceased and the affects associated with loss gradually lose some of their poignancy. During the grief and mourning periods, the bereaved reviews his or her relationship to the deceased and learns to cope anew with a world that no longer contains the loved one. The adaptive task of the bereavement response, fully accepting the reality of loss (Freud, 1917/1957), is considered relatively complete when the psychologically intense relationship to the deceased is defused and the irreversibility of the loss is accepted at conscious and unconscious levels. When the bereaved's level of functioning has reached homeostasis, the loss has been accepted as permanent, and the covert internal relationship to the deceased has stabilized, we may then assume that the manifest mourning process has concluded. The internal process of relating to the memory of the deceased will continue. In what we call the epilogue to mourning, less intense but emotionally charged memories, associations, and representations of the deceased will continue to accompany the bereaved at some level for the rest of his or her lifetime. With the conclusion of the mourning process, it is possible to consider the nature and quality of the representation of the deceased and the ongoing relationship to him or her as a permanent, albeit evolving, feature of outcome to loss and the subsequent mourning process.

Resolution of loss (Rubin, 1984a) is the process that supplements and continues beyond adaptation and/or coping with loss. The connections to the representations of the deceased and to the memories of the relationship to the deceased continue on across the life cycle. The ongoing relationship to the representations of the deceased are similar to the way in which the mental representations or internal working models of the living are organized (Blatt, Chevron, Quinlan, Schaffer, & Weins, 1988; Bowlby, 1977; Lavon, 1993; Levi, 1989; Sadeh et al., 1993). In the case of bereavement, however, another element is present as well. In bereavement, the cessation of present and future interactions with the other in the real world leave the internal psychological elements to bear the full burden of the recollected relationship. The greater the comfort and fluidity with which the bereaved recollects and remembers the deceased, the more appropriate it is to use the term "resolution" in the context of loss. In all too many cases, however, the intensity, conflict, depression, or anxiety engendered by thinking of the deceased suggest that the term resolution is not apt (Horowitz et al., 1993; Weiss, 1987).

Approaching bereavement on the basis of the relation to the internal representations and memories of the deceased, and to the relationship with him or her, helps structure and focus our thinking on resolution of loss. Although the nature of the representations of the deceased and the relationship can be considered at any time following loss (and in the Two-Track Model of Bereavement they are considered all the time), there is an expectation that some closure and peace of mind are associated with the resolution of loss.

The relationship to the representations of the deceased move in two directions. In the first direction, what is of interest is the relationship of the bereaved to the deceased (Lopata, 1981). Here the expectation is that the perceptions and memories of the deceased and the relationship are open to change. As the bereaved individual changes and develops over the course of a lifetime, the complex of memory and reverie associated with the deceased cannot remain frozen either cognitively or affectively without extracting a price in emotional hibernation/stagnation. Similarly, the psychological attention and emotional investment in the deceased cannot function as a substitute for relationship with other living individuals without the dysfunctional aspect overshadowing the other elements of internal psychological equilibrium. Rather, the relationship to the deceased should be both fluid and manage to coexist as an adjunct to the ongoing relationships with the living.

In the second direction, it is the impact of the deceased upon the bereaved that concerns us. Here resolution assesses the impact of the recollected relationship as it relates to the bereaved's sense of self. If memories of the deceased evoke a sense of well-being, the impact can be seen as positive. If recalling the deceased, either consciously or unconsciously, consistently evokes significant guilt, fear, depression, or relief at the death, then resolution would be an inappropriate term. At some point beyond coping, we look to define resolution. When the memories and representations of the deceased and the relationship are available casually, when the recollections are experienced as affirming rather than threatening, and when the thoughts and memories provide comfort and warmth, then resolution is indeed suggested. When the thoughts and feelings associated with the deceased lean with rather than against the core experience of self, then the representations of the deceased and the relationship with him or her can continue to be woven into the fabric of life. A satisfactory dynamic resolution of the external and internal realities of loss and yet of continued connection with the deceased (Freud, 1961, p. 386) are then implied.

RESEARCH ON BEREAVED PARENTS IN ISRAEL

At the University of Haifa, a number of research studies have been conducted utilizing the Two-Track Model of Bereavement in examining the outcome of loss over time (Caspi-Yavin, 1987; Dichterman, 1989; Frydman-Helfant, 1995; Rubin, 1982, 1987, 1990, 1992; Schechter, 1995; Tamir, 1987). The study of parental response to child loss has been a particular focus of a number of these studies. Findings have consistently indicated that when bereaved and nonbereaved were compared on a range of measures, there were demonstrable effects of bereavement more than a decade later. On the basis of these studies, we concluded that there are measurable effects of bereavement across the life cycle for the bereaved as a whole, despite major variations that are related to gender, personality style, and numerous risk and mitigating/ameliorating factors such as poverty, social support, etc. (Brown & Harris, 1978; Sanders, 1989; Vachon et al., 1982).

In the present section, we wish to consider the effects of adult child loss on areas of cognitive, affective, and somatic functioning as they parallel and interact with the continuing attachment to the deceased. As theoreticians and clinicians, we believe that the relational features of parents' continuing attachment to their deceased children ultimately impact the self-system, interpersonal relationships, and the parents' ability to invest interest and energy into their surroundings. These, in turn, function in a feedback loop to influence the nature of the relationship to the deceased and how it is maintained as well. In order to maintain a proper balance between the ability of parents to manage life tasks on the one hand (including relationship to the self and to significant others), and to manage their relationship to the deceased on the other, we submit that the Two-Track Model of Bereavement can assist us in keeping this in focus.

In a major study of Israeli parents bereaved due to the loss of adult sons in war, 102 bereaved and 73 nonbereaved parents participated. The responses to loss for a cohort bereaved 4 years earlier in the Lebanon war of 1982, and a cohort bereaved 13 years before, in the Yom Kippur war of 1973, were examined. The results of the study have been published elsewhere (Rubin, 1992).

On measures of general functioning drawn from the Partial Grief Experience Inventory (PGEI) (Rubin, 1990a; Sanders, Mauger, & Strong, 1979), and on the State/Trait Anxiety Inventory (Spielberger, Gorsuch, & Lushene, 1970), the results pointed to a sharp distinction between the bereaved and nonbereaved in different ways. The bereaved were more anxious than the nonbereaved and the passage of time did not affect the outcome. The results suggested that bereavement had affected a permanent shift in the regulation of anxiety. On the more multivariate aspects of functioning as assessed by the PGEI, however, the passage of time did serve to soften some of the continuing effects of loss. While those bereaved more recently differed significantly from the nonbereaved, the 13-year bereaved group tended to a middle position—sharply distinguished from neither the nonbereaved or those bereaved 4 years earlier. Along Track I, functioning, the results had demonstrated permanent change following loss.

Next, the complete range of grief-related behaviors and experiences contained in the Grief Experience Inventory (GEI) was examined to provide information on the parental response in the first year of loss and in the present (Rubin, 1992). The passage of years did not differentiate between the bereaved groups. The additional 9 years that separated the bereaved groups did not show differences on anxiety, preoccupation with loss, somatic symptoms, or social behavior. Gender variables were present, however, with women reporting significantly more difficulties in the first year of loss but not later. Although the overall tendency for women to report more symptoms than men was a consistent feature of the data, these differences did not always reach statistical significance. We do understand these as related to gender differences in both the subjective experience and willingness to report distress.

An important finding was how initial distress and coping patterns of the first year of loss predicted later outcome. Utilizing Moos' (1984) measure of coping behaviors, we found that the coping style that was of particular risk to the bereaved was avoidance. Those people who in the first year after the loss tended to avoid others; refused to believe the loss was real; kept their feelings to themselves; and used smoking, drinking, or drugs to reduce tension did not differ from the other bereaved parents in the first year after loss. However, 4 or 13 years later, the avoiders tended to suffer emotional, social, cognitive, and somatic difficulties that were significantly more severe than those of the bereaved who did not avoid the loss. While we cannot be sure of the extent to which these outcomes are due to avoidance of the loss, and the extent to which the general personality style may be a risk factor as well, the results are suggestive. The conventional clinical wisdom that avoiding the pain of loss has deleterious consequences certainly does fit with the data (Bowlby, 1980).

Moving away from the attention to symptoms and function characteristic of Track I, we turn to indices of relationship. In the research, we also sought to examine the nature of the continuing internal relationship to the deceased and how it compares with the internal relationship to children who are alive. The data on continuing relationship, termed Track II in our model, provided important insight into both loss and attachment. Repeated indications that bereaved parents view and relate to the deceased differently than do parents of living children were present. On semantic differential measures of self and child, not only did parents evaluate deceased sons more favorably than did parents of living children, they also viewed them as less distant and less unavailable than the living. In other words, the living were seen as less accessible and less present than the dead! In contrast to symptoms of dysfunction that tend to decrease over time, here the pattern was reversed. The parents bereaved 13 years earlier were the most different from the nonbereaved, suggesting that the passage of time involved the bereaved more and not less with the image of the deceased. Interestingly, all the groups of parents tended to view their adult children more favorably than they viewed themselves. This tendency underscores the continuing significance of the parent–child bond for parents in middle adulthood and beyond.

The second method of considering the group differences utilized open-ended descriptions of the adult children. Parents' written descriptions of their children were analyzed and compared (Blatt et al., 1988; Sadeh et al., 1993). Once again, the bereaved described their offspring in a manner consistent with greater involvement and enmeshment than the living. Whereas the parents of living sons tended to mark greater separation from the recollection and description of their sons, the bereaved suggested more enmeshment and more involvement with their deceased sons. The implications may well have to do with the vitality and tension that characterize relationships between living individuals and that encourage a greater degree of separateness between individuals. The degree of separateness is an important element in interpersonal relationships in general, and between family members in particular. It is maintained, in part, by the boundary regulation that occur in the give and take of relationships between living people.

The written descriptions of the bereaved parents were analyzed for one additional feature. Most of us are used to thinking of mourning as progressing roughly along a pathway that lends itself to conceptualization along a stage theory. Bowlby and Parkes' four-stage theory spanning numbness, searching and yearning, disorganization, and reorganization is an excellent example (Bowlby, 1980). Our approach was somewhat different. We adopted Bowlby and Parkes' paradigm, but rather than examining only progress in mourning, we examined the extent to which elements of each stage could be measured as currently present. We found that parents bereaved both 4 and 13 years earlier were very much alike. They continued to experience a sense of shock and numbness, yearned and maintained a continuing search for the deceased, and also suffered from elements of disorganization and depression following loss. There were no differences between the bereaved in either time elapsed or gender on any of these variables. On the indices of reorganization, however, we found a difference. The 9 years that separated the two bereaved groups did not differentiate them on most of the features associated with response to loss. The more dramatic reductions in shock, yearning, and disorganization tend to occur in the initial years following loss. Nonetheless, there is a residue of parental pain and involvement with the loss that remains intertwined with their descriptions of their dead sons. The passage of additional time, however, tends to soften the loss by adding perspective, rather than diminishing the continuing involvement with the deceased. In line with how resolution of bereavement was described above, continuing involvement with the deceased is to be expected. It is how the involvement is maintained, and at what or whose cost, that becomes the important question.

Behavioral and cognitive indices of involvement with the deceased are significant elements that add a welcome concreteness to consideration of continuing involvement and attachment to the deceased. For example, the frequency with which our bereaved parent sample went to the cemetery was one index of the extent of preoccupation with the deceased. One third of the bereaved parent sample visited their son's grave between 1 and 3 times a week for as long as 13 years. The frequency of cemetery visits per se was not related to measures of dysfunction or difficulty for our sample. Rather, it is indicative of cultural and anthropological features of how war dead are memorialized in Israel (Malkinson & Witztum, 1993). Other indications of the strength of continuing involvement with the deceased as normative were parental reports of constant recollections of the fallen son and high levels of affect surrounding the recollections independent of the passage of years. The physical presence of the deceased sons in the home by way of a memorial corner or room and similar memorials also indicated the extent to which the presence of continuing involvement with the deceased is central to this type of loss.

Ultimately, the idea that there is a continuing involvement with the deceased is both a simple and a complex concept to grasp. It is a simple concept in that we all are intuitively aware that we remember and recall relationships with significant others from time to time, and that the fact that they are living or dead is not a deterrent to their recollection. It is a complex concept, however, because it relates to the question of unconscious or unmonitored thinking and the extent to which we may be preoccupied or troubled by a relationship that we may not even be aware of as preoccupying us! Given that relationships are unfolding processes that contain numerous interactions and emotions of varying importance and intensity along both positive and negative poles, constructing a mental map of such things can be accomplished for some of the most significant features (Horowitz, 1989; Main, Kaplan, & Cassidy, 1985). There are other aspects to the continuing relationship with the deceased that are more difficult to specify.

In the next section, we examine in greater detail a family from our research sample that embodies many of the features we have been discussing.

THE WOUNDED FAMILY: A STUDY IN FUNCTION, RELATIONSHIP, AND THE CHALLENGE OF RECOVERY AND RESOLUTION OF BEREAVEMENT

Walking into the living room for an interview with the Hasers was like walking into a memorial hall. On one wall were maps and pictures of the 4-year-old Lebanon campaign, documenting the progress of the battles there. A glass display case off to the side illuminated the battle ribbons and memorabilia of Ami. On the walls behind and opposite the sofa were large photographs either of Ami or taken by him. There was no chance of making a mistake. Here was the family of a young soldier who had been killed in battle.

Mr. and Mrs. Haser had volunteered to participate in the research to help other bereaved families. It seemed that their somewhat more covert reasons had to do with an interest in talking about their son and in having others know more about him. The parents were warm, sensitive, and engaging people who were keen to review their experiences over the last 4 years. From the outset of the interview to its conclusion, however, there was one theme they could not make sense of. From time to time, they wondered aloud what was going on with their other son? Why, for example, did their surviving son Joshua refuse to bring his friends to the house? Why did he tell them, "You live with the dead, not the living"? As we examine the responses of these parents in some detail, we may be able to shed some additional light on their difficulty.

Mr. and Mrs. Haser, an attractive couple in their early 50s, were a secular family of Sephardic origin. They lived in Tel Aviv and had two sons separated by 6 years. Mr. Haser was a teacher and Mrs. Haser was an office worker. Both parents found their jobs enjoyable and were successful in their work. Their oldest son Ami, age 24, had been killed in the Lebanon war 4 years earlier. He had been engaged for a year and had not yet fathered any children. His former fiancee had recently married. The surviving son, Josh, was currently serving in the military and they were not aware of any difficulties in his functioning that interfered with his service.

On the written portions of the research protocol, Mr. Haser came across as a hard-working man who is satisfied with his family relationships and his work, and who described himself as "generally" satisfied with his life. He had no interest in psychological assistance following the loss of his son, nor was he interested in attending the meetings of bereaved parents that were organized by the Rehabilitation branch of the Ministry of Defense.

In the first year following the death of his son, Mr. Haser's coping involved being open about the loss to his wife and other people, expressing his emotions, and keeping himself active—along with a marked increase in his smoking. On the GEI, Mr. Haser's scores for the first year of loss were at the midpoint for bereaved fathers. Four years later, he was doing a bit better than most of the bereaved fathers. His anxiety scores were indicative of some difficulty. While he had significantly lower anxiety at the time of participation in the research (state anxiety), his general tendency to anxiety (trait anxiety) was moderately above that of the other fathers. (In no case, however, did his functioning differ by more than a single *SD* from the other bereaved fathers.)

The course of the years had led to much change in how Mr. Haser was functioning. He reported that in the first year of loss, but not now, the following were true for him: experiencing feelings of anger and guilt around the loss, feeling the need to complete projects of his sons, feeling pain when viewing photos of the deceased, feeling that life was empty, experiencing the presence of his son, wishing to die, searching for his son in crowds, and feeling guilty when experiencing pleasure. While the improvement in the quality of Mr. Haser's life was quite significant, the picture of change was not linear. In some areas, there were indications of increased difficulty in functioning (such as increased complaints of headaches), and in others, indications of relative imperviousness to dysfunction (such as interest in sex). Nonetheless, Mr. Haser embodied the picture of someone who had been able to cope and adapt in many areas of functioning following loss.

Although Mr. Haser had been able to detach himself in many ways from the involvement with bereavement's characteristic sequellae (for example, depression or the searching for his son in crowds), still there were clear indications of continuing involvement with the deceased evident on the GEI. He reported that both in the first year of loss and now 4 years later, his longing for his son was pronounced, he had difficulty parting with Ami's personal effects, and that he dreamt about his son as alive and not as dead.

Examining the relationship to the son further across his entire protocol, we find that on the item of relationship, he rated the relationship to Ami as "the closest relationship I ever had" (Zisook, 1987). On the semantic differential measure, where he had to choose how to rate his son on numerous qualities, Mr. Haser saw Ami as possessing the highest degree of the many positive qualities listed. Similarly, his open-ended description of Ami (Blatt et. al., 1988) portrayed him as possessing the highest degree of desirable personal and social qualities. Yet it is the conclusion to this brief description that conveys the relationship to Ami in its beauty and its tragedy: "In addition to loving him as my son, he was my best friend. I lost a son and a good friend. His loss is so great that nothing can fill the hole that has been created."

Mrs. Haser is a hard-working, handsome woman who is satisfied with her economic situation, happy in her work, and satisfied with family relationships. Dressed in black, she indicates that she prefers black since her son's death, but now permits herself a touch of color as well.

Mrs. Haser described her coping in the first year of loss as difficult. She talked with her spouse and friends about her loss, expressed feelings including her anger and depression, and constantly thought about Ami's death. On the GEI, she was somewhat above average for bereaved women but not significantly so. In contrast to her husband, her anxiety level was typical for bereaved women in the sample.

In general, item analysis on the GEI showed that Mrs. Haser indicated less change over the course of the years than had her husband. She reported anger and tension, depression, a sense of depersonalization at times, experiencing life as empty, a wish to be alone, and problems of sleeping and digestion. While these features of her response to loss continue to trouble her 4 years after the death of her son, her responses did not differ greatly from those of the other bereaved women in our sample. There were, of course, indications of improvement over time. For example, the nightmares she had suffered from had disappeared. Asked how the loss had changed her for the better, she said she was more self-assured and independent.

Again, however, it is the relationship to the deceased Ami, both in the first year of loss and at present, that resonates as the major theme of her life. Mrs. Haser reported doing things her son had done, dreaming about him as alive, missing him, feeling his presence near her, feeling guilty about enjoying herself, wishing to switch places with her son frequently, looking for him in crowds, and frequently talking to his pictures.

On the semantic differential, she too portrayed her son as possessing the best and most positive of qualities. Like her husband, she indicated that the relationship with Ami was "the closest relationship" she had ever had in her life. The theme of Ami's connectedness to his parents and others was a major theme in her open-ended description of Ami:

> All his life he gave his parents, brother and community great happiness. . . . He never refused to do something for the other person. He dedicated himself to family and friends. He knew only how to love . . . shared his problems with us and was always willing to take advice. . . . He would take counsel with his parents before buying clothes . . . wrote a lot to parents and many friends, and was attached to his family.

The Haser family are not atypical for our sample of war-bereaved parents of adult sons in Israel. Neither their scores nor their behaviors set them apart from the other parents we met and interviewed. Indeed, the generally positive course of reduction in symptoms of functioning place them in the portion of our sample that tended to "recover" function with the passage of time. If we return to the terminology and focus of the Two-Track Model of Bereavement, we note that the track of functioning is not symptom-free. Nevertheless, the major areas of functioning such as ability to invest in work and interpersonal relationships are not significantly harmed. The spousal relationship was perceived by both parents as warm and close. The interviewer's visit with them was rated subjectively as genuine, moving, and not overlaid with a sense of individual psychopathology. Utilizing the perspective of the Two-Track Model of Bereavement, we are able to document much more carefully the extent of impact that loss has had on both functioning and the continuing relationship to the internal introject, or complex of memories, thoughts, and feelings, associated with the deceased.

The relationship with the deceased, Track II, was the main area in which difficulties in the response to loss were apparent. Yet in one specific area of functioning, there were indications of difficulty. Returning to the relationship to the surviving son, Joshua, we begin with the parents' question: what is "his" problem? If we contrast how Ami and Joshua are described in the interview, we are soon struck by what appears to be a shallowness of empathy, emotional closeness, and investment in the surviving son. It is only in response to direct questions about Joshua that we find out that he is a gifted student, poet, writer, and athlete who has many friends. Prior to that point in the interview, Josh was mentioned only in the context of their lack of understanding his distancing from Ami. Further probing elicited the information that Joshua had volunteered to serve in his brother's army unit as a way of identifying and that paradoxically for them, his being stationed some distance from home, had yielded a less conflictive relationship with him. Finally, it emerged that each of the parents feel that Joshua is relatively carefree when he is alone with either of them. It is only when they are together with him, and we may add without Ami, that the tension and withdrawal they complain about emerge with full force.

To what extent is the parental response to Joshua a continuation or exacerbation of a family dynamic present before Ami's death? The family probably gave a great weight to Ami's role as older son and brother prior to his death. Yet we suspect that the sudden death of Ami robbed the Haser family of their flexibility and ability to embrace the coming of age of Joshua, a talented and special young man. When the parents are together, the space available for Joshua seems to shrink. When either of them are alone with him, the interaction is richer— although still in the shadow of the loss of the "wonderful" older son.

The Haser family is a wounded family. It is wounded not only by the death of the older son Ami, but also by the pain and estrangement experienced by the surviving son Joshua. It is a sad irony that these grieving parents, bereaved of one son, unintentionally are "losing" so much of the other. The ongoing relationship to the deceased we see here is not the open and evolving relationship characteristic of resolution of bereavement. In many areas, the Hasers seem to be negotiating a range of life's tasks adequately. The parents are working and successful, as is the surviving son. Yet it is hard to deny that the relationship to Ami, the deceased son, is the core of these parents experience. The relationship to Ami is so overpowering that they lose sight of their second son. They are genuinely unable to make sense of Josh's statements that they live with the dead, and they "wonder" what is going on with him.

Based on extensive research with bereaved parents, we believe that the intense focus on the deceased child and his or her memory occurs frequently and should be thought of as significant risk factors following child loss. This involvement can occur either in the absence or presence of parental depression or other marked symptomatic difficulty (Klass, 1988). It is an aspect of continuing attachment to the deceased that can exist in more or less adaptive measure.

CONCLUSIONS

Ultimately, the conundrum of loss and remembrance is central to appreciating the complexity of the human condition. In depicting two different modes of responding to loss, Wikkan (1988) touched upon a dilemma that is central to individuals as well as to cultures: What is the adaptive response to the loss of a loved one? On the one hand, if we remain rooted to the past and totally preoccupied with the loss, we risk losing the opportunities and relationships of the present. On the other hand, if we distance ourselves too much from what was but is no longer available, we remove ourselves from our origins and root relationships. To deny the importance of our core relationships either at conscious or unconscious levels is to risk losing the ability to feel secure in the very inner fiber of our being. For if we cannot depend on the ongoing experience of having been loved and cared for in the past, via our memories and experiences with significant figures, the basic security that is provided by our early attachments is compromised.

The continuing attachment to the deceased and the past is not without risks. In keeping with the Two-Track Model of Bereavement, we recognize that assessing the bereaved's functioning following loss is but one domain of understanding response to loss. The ability to interact with and manage the ongoing relationship to the representation of the deceased is equally a feature of assessing adaptive and maladaptive response to loss. In the study of relationship (Track II), it is not whether there is an ongoing relationship to the deceased following loss that is of interest. To this author's way of thinking, that is a given. Rather, it is the nature and place of that relationship in the inner and outer worlds of the survivors that deserve our attention.

The psychological literature on loss is currently renewing its understanding that ongoing relationship to the deceased is normative, evolving, and with great capacity to be adaptive (Stroebe et al., 1992). The earlier absence of this awareness encouraged the neglect of the importance of continuing relationships across the life cycle (Bowlby, 1977) or encouraged a viewpoint that the ongoing relationship to the deceased was itself an indication of pathology. Mercifully, these strict and uncompromising views are much less in evidence today, and their impact on the field of loss is smaller than it was in the past. Relationship and attachment, of course, have extraordinarily basic functions in the maintenance of personality and functioning. It is only by accommodating to our relationships, despite the occurrence of the deaths of significant attachment figures, that we can speak of bereavement as a process with outcomes allowing for adjustment, adaptation, and resolution. How else can life be fully lived?

REFERENCES

Blatt, S. J., Chevron, E. S., Quinlan, D. M., Schaffer, C. E., & Weins, S. (1988). *The assessment of qualitative and structural dimensions of object representations.* Unpublished manual, Yale University, New Haven, CT.

Bowlby, J. (1977). The making and breaking of affectional bonds. *British Journal of Psychiatry, 130 ,* 201–210/421–431.

Bowlby, J. (1980). *Attachment and loss: Vol. 3. Loss.* London: Hogarth.

Breuer, J., & Freud, S. (1955). On the psychical mechanisms of hysterical phenomena: A preliminary communication. In J. Strachey (Ed. and Trans.), *The standard edition of the complete psychological works of Sigmund Freud* (Vol. 2, pp. 1–17). London: Hogarth Press. (Original work published 1893)

Breznitz, S. (1993). *Memory fields.* New York: Knopf.

Brown, G. W., & Harris, T. (1978). *Social origins of depression.* London: Tavistock.

Caspi-Yavin, Y. (1988). *Coping and outcome in war bereaved Israeli parents.* Unpublished master's thesis (Hebrew), University of Haifa, Haifa, Israel.

Dichterman, D. (1989). *Personality and interpersonal history and their relationship to long-term outcome to child loss in Israel.* Unpublished master's thesis (Hebrew), University of Haifa, Haifa, Israel.

Frydman-Helfant, S. (1995). *Sibling loss and the Two-Track Model of Bereavement.* Unpublished master's thesis (Hebrew), University of Haifa, Haifa, Israel.

Friedlander, S. (1979). *When memory comes.* New York: Farrar, Straus, & Giroux.

Freud, E. L. (Ed.) (1961). *Letters of Sigmund Freud.* New York: Basic Books.

Freud, S. (1917). Mourning and melancholia. In J. Strachey (Ed. and Trans.), *The standard edition of the complete psychological works of Sigmund Freud* (Vol. 14, pp. 243–258). London: Hogarth Press.

Gorer, G. (1965). *Death, grief and mourning in contemporary Britain.* London: Tavistock.

Guisinger, S., & Blatt, S. J. (1994). Individuality and relatedness: Evolution of a fundamental dialectic. *American Psychologist, 49*(2), 104–111.

Horowitz, M. J. (1989). Cognitive structure and change in histrionic personality. In *Nuances of technique in dynamic psychotherapy: Selected clinical papers* (pp. 195–268). N.J.: Jason Aronson.

Horowitz, M. J., Bonanno, G., & Holen, A. (1993). Pathological grief: Diagnoses and explanations. *Psychosomatic Medicine, 55,* 260–273.

Klass, D. (1988). *Parental grief: Solace and resolution.* New York: Springer.

Kleber, R. J., & Brom, D. In collaboration with Defares, P. B. (1992). *Coping with trauma: Theory, prevention and treatment.* Amsterdam: Swets & Zeitlin.

Lavon, O. (1993). *Adult attachment, representations of relationship with parent, and the experiences of depression.* Unpublished master's thesis (Hebrew), University of Haifa, Haifa, Israel.

Levi, P. (1989). Title story in *The mirror maker: Stories and essays* (pp. 47–51). New York: Shocken.

Lopata, H. Z. (1981). Widowhood and husband sanctification. *Journal of Marriage and the Family, 43,* 439–450.

Main, M., Kaplan, N., & Cassidy, J. (1985). Security in infancy, childhood and adulthood: A move to the level of representation. In I. Bretherton & E. Waters (Eds.), *Society for Research in Child Development Monographs: Vol. 50. Growing points in attachment theory and research.* Chicago: University of Chicago Press.

Malkinson, R., & Witztum, E. (1993). Bereavement and commemoration in Israel: The dual face of the national myth (Hebrew). In R. Malkinson, S. Rubin, & E. Witztum (Eds.), *Loss and bereavement in Jewish society in Israel* (pp. 231–258). Israel: Canah/Ministry of Defense.

Moos, R. H. (1984). The coping scale. *American Journal of Community Psychology, 112*(1), 5–25.

Parkes, C. M. (1965). Bereavement and mental illness. *British Journal of Medical Psychology, 38,* 388–397.

Parkes, C. M. (1986). *Bereavement: Studies of grief in adult life.* Hammondsworth, England: Penguin.

Parkes, C. M. (1988). Bereavement as a psychosocial transition: Process of adaptation to change, *Journal of Social Issues, 44,* 53–66.

Parkes, C. M., & Weiss, R. (1983). *Recovery from bereavement.* New York: Basic Books.

Rando, T. (1983). An investigation of grief and adaptation in parents whose children have died from cancer. *Journal of Pediatric Psychology, 8*(1), 3–20.

Rubin, S. (1981). A two-track model of bereavement: Theory and application in research. *American Journal of Orthopsychiatry, 51,* 101–109.

Rubin, S. (1982). Persisting effects of loss: A model of mourning. In C. Spielberger and I. Sarason (Eds.), N. Milgram (Guest Ed.), *Stress and anxiety* (Vol. 8). Washington, DC: Hemisphere.

Rubin, S. (1984a). Mourning distinct from melancholia. *British Journal of Medical Psychology, 57,* 339–345.

Rubin, S. (1984b). Maternal attachment and child death: On adjustment, relationship and resolution. *Omega, 15*(4), 347–352.

Rubin, S. (1985). The resolution of bereavement: A clinical focus on the relationship to the deceased. *Psychotherapy: Theory, Research, Training and Practice, 22*(2), 231–235.

Rubin, S. (1986). Child death and the family: Parents and children confronting loss. *International Journal of Family Therapy,7,* 377–388.

Rubin, S. (1987). *The long-term adaptation of parents bereaved of adult sons to war.* Final research report to the Office of Rehabilitation, Ministry of Defense, Israel.

Rubin, S. (1990a). Death of the future: An outcome study of bereaved parents in Israel. *Omega, 20*(4), 323–339.

Rubin, S. (1990b). Treating the bereaved spouse: A focus on the loss process, the self and the other. *The Psychotherapy Patient, 6*(3/4) , 189–205.

Rubin, S. (1992). Adult child loss and the Two-Track Model of Bereavement. *Omega, 24*(3) , 183–202.

Rubin, S. (1993a). The death of a child is forever: The life course impact of child loss. In M. S. Stroebe, W. Stroebe, & R. O. Hansson (Eds.), *Handbook of bereavement* (pp. 285–299). Cambridge: Cambridge University Press.

Rubin, S. (1993b). Loss and bereavement: An overview of the field. (Hebrew). In R. Malkinson, S. Rubin, & E. Witztum (Eds.), *Loss and bereavement in Jewish society in Israel* (pp. 21–38). Israel: Canah/Ministry of Defense.

Rubin, S. (1994). Psychotherapeutic intervention with chronic grief: Clinical use of the Two-Track Model of Bereavement. Paper presented at the 4th International Conference on Grief and Bereavement in Contemporary Society, Stockholm.

Rubin, S., & Katz-Dichterman, D. (1993). The contribution of attachment history and object relationship to bereavement outcome (Hebrew). In R. Malkinson, S. Rubin, & E. Witztum (Eds.), *Loss and bereavement in Jewish society in Israel* (pp. 51–67). Israel: Canah/Ministry of Defense.

Rubin, S., & Nassar, H. Z. (1993). Psychotherapy and supervision with a bereaved Moslem family: An intervention that almost failed. *Psychiatry, 56*, 338–348.

Sanders, C. (1989). *Grief: The mourning after*. New York: John Wiley & Sons.

Sanders, C. M., Mauger, P. A., & Strong, P. N. (1979). *A manual for the Grief Experience Inventory*. Palo Alto, CA: Consulting Psychologists Press.

Sadeh, A., Rubin, S., & Berman, E. (1993). Parental and relationship representations and experiences of depression in college students. *Journal of Personality Assessment, 60*(1), 192–204.

Schafer, R. (1992). *Retelling a life*. New York: Basic Books.

Schechter, N. (1995). Perception of reactions to child and spousal bereavement: The Two-Track Model of Bereavement, empathy, social support and the passage of time. Unpublished master's thesis (Hebrew), University of Haifa, Haifa, Israel.

Schechter, N., & Rubin, S. (1994, June). *How do people think about bereavement?* Paper presented at the 3rd National Conference on Bereavement and Israeli Society, Tel Aviv.

Spielberger, C., Gorsuch, R., & Lushene, R. (1970). State-Trait Anxiety manual. Palo Alto, CA: Consulting Psychologists Press.

Shuchter, S. R., & Zisook, S. (1993). The course of normal grief. In M. S. Stroebe, W. Stroebe, & R. O. Hansson (Eds.), *Handbook of bereavement* (pp. 23–43). Cambridge: Cambridge University Press.

Stroebe, M., Gergen, M. M., Gergen, K. J., & Stroebe, W. (1992). Broken hearts or broken bonds. *American Psychologist, 47*(10), 1205–1212.

Silverman, P. R., Nickman, S., & Worden, J. W. (1992). Detachment revisited: The child's reconstruction of a dead parent. *American Journal of Orthopsychiatry, 62*(4), 494–503.

Tamir, G. (1987). *Functioning and attachment in war bereaved Israeli parents*. Unpublished master's thesis (Hebrew), University of Haifa, Haifa, Israel.

Vachon, M. L. S., Sheldon, A. R., Lancee, W. J., et al. (1982). Correlates of enduring distress patterns following bereavement: Social network, life situation, and personality. *Psychological Medicine, 12*, 783–788.

Videka-Sherman, L. (1982). Coping with the death of a child: A study over time. *American Journal of Orthopsychiatry, 52*(4), 688–699.

Volkan, V. D. (1981). *Linking objects and linking phenomena*. New York: International Universities Press.

Weiss, R. S. (1987). Principles underlying a manual for parents whose children were killed by drunk drivers. *American Journal of Orthopsychiatry, 57*, 432–440.

Weiss, R. S. (1993). Loss and recovery. In M. S. Stroebe, W. Stroebe, & R. O. Hansson (Eds.), *Handbook of bereavement* (pp. 271–284). Cambridge: Cambridge University Press.

Wikkan, U. (1988). Bereavement and loss in two Muslim communities: Egypt and Bali compared. *Social Science and Medicine, 27*, 451–461.

Zisook, S. (Ed.) (1987). *Biopsychosocial aspects of bereavement*. Washington, DC: American Psychiatric Press.

Part Six

Bereaved Siblings

When a child dies, unless he or she is an only child, there are almost always bereaved siblings. As Nancy Hogan and Lydia DeSantis point out in Chapter 14, these children constitute a sizable group. Often they are overlooked, for the primary mourner is the parent, as we see from the case Rubin presented in Chapter 13 of the previous section.

In his poem "We Are Seven," William Wordsworth described the tenacious tie between siblings:

> "How many are you," then said I,
> "If they two are in heaven?"
> Quick was the little maid's reply,
> "O Master, we are seven."
> "But they are dead; those two are dead!
> Their spirits are in heaven!"
> 'Twas throwing words away; for still
> The little maid would have her will,
> And said, "Nay, we are seven!"

The grave does not obliterate the place of the sibling in the family. Hogan and DeSantis introduce several new dimensions to the discussion of the connection siblings maintain with their brothers or sisters. These dimensions clearly apply to all bereaved siblings. They see the ongoing attachment providing energy that assists in the transformation of bereaved siblings into resilient survivors. They also see it as the silent variable that mediates between the construct of grief and the construct of personal growth. The ongoing attachment facilitates, enables, and transforms. The association of the continuing bond with resilience is important because clinicians and researchers have often seen the bond as an impediment to the bereaved making accommodation to the loss.

After reading the Hogan and DeSantis chapter, we can revisit the Hasar family in Rubin's chapter from the point of view of the brother, Joshua. We know little about his grief, except that he volunteered to serve in his brother's army unit. By doing so, Joshua not only identified with his brother, but brought himself closer to his dead sibling.

This chapter raises an interesting question about the association of the continuing bond to the sibling's belief in an afterlife. Hogan and DeSantis think this is an important dimension in the ability to sustain a relationship. We have seen in other chapters that the ability to construct and to hold an inner representation of the deceased seems unrelated to a belief in life after death. It seems, instead, more related to the processes by which we internalize others and the meanings we make as we connect with that internalized other. As the new model of grief is developed, the interface between belief and interaction with the inner representation will need to be fully explored. Self reports of belief are easy to quantify. Research that uses only the manifest content of belief will be of little use if the research does not also examine the way belief and interaction with the dead fit into the psychic and social worlds of survivors.

P. R. S.
S. N.

Chapter 14

Basic Constructs of a Theory of Adolescent Sibling Bereavement

Nancy Hogan and Lydia DeSantis

The future is the continual possibilization of possibilities.
—Sartre, 1956, p.105

Each year in the United States approximately 1.8 million children from birth through 18 years of age become bereaved siblings.[1] Despite the large number of children and adolescents experiencing this catastrophic personal and family crisis, there is a lack of theoretical constructs from which to generate a theory of adolescent sibling bereavement. Such a theory is essential for two major reasons. If the needs and concerns of bereaved adolescents in the United States and elsewhere are to be understood and ministered to, a theory of adolescent sibling bereavement is vital to guide health care providers, specialists in child development, teachers, and persons working with displaced and refugee children and their families.

A second reason for a theory of adolescent sibling bereavement is the effect the loss of a brother or sister has on the overall development of the surviving adolescent. The role and function sibling relationships play in identity formation is becoming recognized as a potent force in personality development (Provence & Solnit, 1983).

Adolescence is a time of change, a time of upheaval, and a time of attempting to define and redefine a theory of oneself. The work required to accomplish these developmental tasks takes place in the social environment of parents, siblings, friends, and peers (Erikson, 1963, 1964). During this period, the adolescent asks the critical questions: "Who am I?" and "Who will I become?" Bank and Kahn (1982) have emphasized the critical nature of the sibling bond in human development. They state:

> The research for a personal identity emerges as the vital ground where brothers and sisters become significant to one another (p. 49). . . . Siblings, early in life, can acquire meaning for one another and become locked into a complementarity in which a vital part of one's sibling's core identity becomes fitted to deep parts of the other's

---

[1]The figure of 1.8 million was extrapolated from child and adolescent mortality statistics compiled by the U. S. Department of Commerce (1991). We are grateful to Eric Soldau for his assistance in calculating this datum.

core identity (p. 30). . . . [Sibling relationships evolve to become a] fitting together of two people's identity. (p. 15)

Nadelman (as cited in Lamb & Sutton-Smith, 1982) described how sibling relationships provide an environment for acquiring life skills such as "learning cooperation, practicing negotiating skills, competing and establishing territoriality, and learning that others have rights and needs at different times" (p. 15). Dunn and Kendrick (1982) noted that the sibling relationship includes the frequent and free expression of qualities such as pleasure, play, affection, aid, attention, and amusement, as well as hostility, aggression, jealousy, rivalry, frustration, and combat.

The death of a sibling alters the constant, interactive, dyadic, comparison through which personal identity is learned reciprocally by siblings during adolescence. In addition, bereaved siblings coping with the developmental crisis of adolescence must now cope with the accumulated stresses of the situational crisis of sibling death and its aftermath.

> The death of a child leaves a legacy that influences all future transactions among the surviving family members. It compounds the experience of bereavement with the status of survivorship, the latter fraught with its own special psychological stresses. (Krell & Rabkin, 1979, p. 471)

The death of a sibling is especially significant in the United States, where the average family size is 3.17 persons (U.S. Bureau of the Census, 1993, p. 55). With the death of a brother or sister, the surviving sibling in the majority of U.S. families becomes an only child. (3.17 represents the average size of all families in the United States in 1992. Two-parent families with two children represent 65% of all families in the United States and 66% of all white families [U.S. Bureau of the Census, 1993, p. 60]). Two-parent white families are representatitve of the sample from which the data in this discussion are drawn. Losing the role and status of being and having a brother or sister is a "deeply lonely experience" (Hogan & DeSantis, 1994). As one bereaved sibling stated, "I can't even express how much I hate being an only child . . . it was like my mom and dad had each other, and I had no one" (Hogan & DeSantis, 1994, p. 140).

The remainder of this chapter will discuss three foundational constructs from which an initial conceptualization of a substantive theory of adolescent sibling bereavement is hypothesized. The constructs are grief, personal growth, and ongoing attachment. The discussion and theory will relate to normative grief, bereavement, and the bereavement process.

REVIEW OF LITERATURE

The review of literature will focus on the major themes that have emerged from child and adolescent bereavement research in the decades of the 1980s and

1990s. The literature dealing with adolescent sibling bereavement in nonpsychiatric populations is rather recent, covering a span of approximately 13 years.

Research in the 1980s

The first research conducted with a nonpsychiatric population of bereaved siblings was the seminal study by Balk (1981) that described the impact of adolescent sibling bereavement on self-concept. Since that time, attention has been primarily devoted to describing the way children and adolescents grieve and the meaning of their loss. The focus of those studies has been on the variables and conditions believed to be associated with the bereavement process rather than on studying grief directly. While variables studied included self-concept (Balk, 1981, 1983a, 1990; Guerriero & Fleming, 1985; Martinson, Davies, & McClowry, 1987; Micheal & Lansdown, 1986) and issues related to physical health (Guerriero, 1983; Guerriero & Fleming, 1985), the majority of the research has investigated issues related to psychological health, such as behavior problems (Demi & Gilbert, 1987; McCown & Pratt, 1985), anxiety (Birenbaum, Robinson, Phillips, Stewart, & McCown, 1989–1990; Brent, 1983), post traumatic stress disorder (Brent, 1983), and depression (Balk, 1983b, 1991a; Bierenbaum et al., 1989–1990; Brent, 1983).

A sufficient number of studies were completed in the 1980s to fill an issue of the *Journal of Adolescent Research* dedicated to childhood and adolescent bereavement (Balk, 1991a). Included in the journal was a review of the bereavement of children and adolescents who had lost a parent, sibling, or friend (Balk, 1991a). The first literature review focusing exclusively on child and adolescent sibling bereavement was published in 1993 (Walker, 1993).

Research in the 1990s

During the 1990s, the trajectory of the childhood and adolescent bereavement process emerged as a target area of investigation. The major questions addressed are: "When does grief end?" and "Is it 'normal' to continue to grieve after a prescribed length of time has passed?"

The commonly held belief posits that "normal" bereavement can be resolved and that grieving beyond a certain endpoint in time portends a dysfunctional outcome. Prevailing criteria for identifying normative and nonnormative bereavement are based on the notion that an endpoint is a necessary condition of living fully and successfully following a significant death. However, a number of bereavement researchers noted that children continue to grieve for indeterminate periods of time (Balk, 1991a, 1991b; Balk & Hogan, 1995; Davies, 1991; Martinson & Compos, 1991; Martinson et al., 1987).

The validity of the prevailing notion of an endpoint to grief was recently challenged by empirical data from a community-based study of 157 bereaved adolescent siblings (Hogan & DeSantis, 1992). Data revealed that surviving adolescent siblings maintained a continuing, ongoing attachment to their dead brother or sister. The bereaved adolescent siblings continued to miss and to love their deceased siblings and to anticipate their eventual reunion in heaven/afterlife. Hogan and DeSantis (1992) conceptualized this phenomenon as "Ongoing Attachment." They state,

> It is this continuous emotional attachment that maintains the ongoing presence of the deceased sibling in the life of the bereaved sibling. This notion of "ongoing presence" . . . challenges the current conceptualization of the bereavement process as having a discrete resolution, that is, that there is a defined endpoint of the psychoemotional, cognitive, and physiological manifestations of grief symptomatology.
>
> In the adolescent sibling bereavement process . . . the bereaved siblings learn to live with the physical absence and the simultaneous emotional presence of their deceased brother or sister. At the same time, the surviving siblings are anticipating a physical and social reunion in heaven with their deceased sibling. The simultaneous interaction of the phenomena of timelessness and ongoing attachment results in a sense of "everywhen" (Stanner, 1965, p. 271), a sense in which the past, present, and future are blended into a oneness. They are at one together (Stanner, 1965, p. 271). In the timeless gestalt of "everywhen," the bereaved adolescents experience a sense of conceptual, emotional, and social eternity with their deceased siblings in the face of their physical absence. (p. 174)

The possibility that siblings experience personal growth following the death of a person with whom they were meaningfully attached also began to receive attention from bereavement researchers in the 1990s (Balk, 1990; Hogan, 1987; Klass, 1993; Lehman et al., 1993; Oltjenbruns, 1991; Yalom & Lieberman, 1991). For many years, theorists have posited the notion that personal growth can occur for adults (Collins, Taylor, & Skokan, 1990; Lopata, 1973, 1975; Taylor, Lichtman, & Wood, 1984) and adolescents (Offer, 1969) following a life crisis. Research with bereaved siblings suggests that an increased personal sense of maturity, resilience, and psychological growth occurs as they cope with the trauma of becoming survivors of sibling death (Hogan, 1983; Hogan & DeSantis, 1994). Growth-producing aspects include the bereaved siblings' appraisal that they have (a) become more mature than friends; (b) been able to cope more successfully with stress; (c) become closer to other family members; (d) refocused their priorities; and (e) experienced an increased empathy, compassion, and tolerance toward themselves and others (Balk, 1981, 1983b; Bank & Kahn, 1982; Hogan, 1987; Martinson et al., 1987; Offer, 1969; Oltjenbruns, 1991).

ASSUMPTIONS ABOUT BEREAVEMENT

The following are assumptions made about the bereavement process.

1   Bereavement is a process that follows the death of a person to whom the survivor has been and continues to be meaningfully attached. Such a person is one to whom the survivor has attained and continues to retain spiritual proximity.

Bowlby (1980) talks about physical proximity. In adolescent sibling bereavement, physical proximity is lost, but emotional proximity is maintained (Hogan & DeSantis, 1992).

2   Grief symptoms occur in response to the realization that death is permanent and irrevocable. Death ends sharing life together on earth now or in the future. This realization shatters all expectations and anticipations the bereaved adolescents had for a shared future in life on earth with their deceased brother or sister.

3   The phenomenon of "Ongoing Attachment" (Hogan & DeSantis, 1992) occurs as a response to the vital need to construct a new meaning of life and sense of self through maintaining spiritual proximity with the deceased (Balk & Hogan, 1995).

CONSTRUCTS

The constructs of grief and personal growth were derived from a community-based, national sample of 157 bereaved adolescents. The items in Table 1 and Table 2 are from the Hogan Sibling Inventory of Bereavement (HSIB) instrument (Hogan, 1990). The items are the actual statements made by the bereaved adolescents who participated in the sibling bereavement groups that yielded the data for the HSIB. For more detail on the construction, factor analysis, and parametrics see Hogan (1987), Hogan and Balk (1990), Hogan and Greenfield (1991), and Blankemeyer (1994).

The construct of ongoing attachment was derived from the same community-based sample. Participants were asked to respond to the semistructured question, "If you could ask or tell your dead sibling something, what would it be?" For further detail on analysis of the responses, see Hogan and DeSantis (1992).

The Construct of Grief

The categories and properties (items) of grief are derived from the 24 items that comprise the grief factor on the HSIB. They are detailed in Table 1. Each category was conceptualized from one or more of the properties. The meaning derived from the properties and categories are also shown Table 1. Each category will be described briefly.

Category 1: Permanently Changed Reality of Self and Family   Items contained in this category show that the bereaved adolescents believe the event of having a sibling die has irrevocably changed their lives and the lives of family members. The death of a sibling resulted in a quantitative and qualitative shrinking of the family. A family of three children becomes a family of two children. Although the particular contributions that the deceased child made to their lives will persist in their memories, the family's hopes, wishes, and dreams of an anticipated shared life with the child/sibling are shattered and cease due to the death. This sense of the incomplete family resembles the changed perception of family

Table 1 Categories, Properties, and Meanings of Grief Items from the Hogan Sibling Inventory of Bereavement Instrument

Categories	Properties (items)	Meanings
1. Permanently changed reality–self/family	My family will always be incomplete.	Family dismemberment
	I know I will never get over his/her death.	Self dismemberment
2. Physical effects	I am often sick.	Lack of sense of well-being
3. Increased vulnerability	I worry about everything.	General anxiety
A. Fear	I am afraid that more people I love will die.	Anticipatory anxiety
	I believe I have little control in life.	Helplessness
	I believe I will lose control when I start thinking about him or her.	Anticipatory anxiety
	I have panic attacks over nothing.	Panic anxiety
	I believe I am going crazy.	Insanity anxiety
B. Guilt	I am uncomfortable when I am feeling happy.	Survivor guilt
	I am uncomfortable when I am having fun.	Survivor guilt
	I should have died and he/she should have lived.	Survivor guilt
C. Depression	I feel depressed when I think about him/her.	Despair
	I have no control over my sadness.	Despair
	I don't think I will ever be happy again.	Despair
	Family holidays such as Christmas are sad times for us.	Situational sadness/anniversary reaction
	I have difficulty sleeping at night.	Sleep disturbance
	I have nightmares about his/her death.	Sleep disturbance
	I don't care what happens to me.	Apathy
D. Isolation	People don't know what I am going through.	Sense of loneliness
4. Cognitive interference	I have difficulty concentrating.	Difficulty staying "on task"
5. Desire for reunion with sibling	I want to die to be with him/her.	Reunion wish
6. Coping behavior	I take risks to help me forget he/she is dead.	Risk taking

that McClowry, Davies, Kulenkamp, and Martinson (1987) defined as "empty space."

The item, "I know I will never get over his/her death," is frequently used by bereaved adolescents to mean "life will never be the same again" (Hogan & De-Santis, 1992, 1994). At the beginning of grief, the surviving siblings experience a sense of a lack of wholeness about themselves and their families. In effect, the family has been dismembered by the sibling's death. Consequently, they believe their personal and family grief will never end. Their ultimate appraisal at this point is that life will never be "normal" again.

Category 2: Physical Effects   Bereaved siblings believe their physical well-being is altered and they are more vulnerable to illness following the death. They have a sense of not feeling as well physically since the death of their brothers or sisters.

Category 3: Increased Vulnerability   This category contains four subcategories: (a) fears, (b) guilt, (c) depression, and (d) isolation. The subcategory of fear is defined by seven properties that convey a generalized worry or anxiety that death may happen to other loved ones. The bereaved adolescents experience a sense of overall helplessness and come to believe they will not regain their psychological equilibrium.

The subcategory of guilt has been described well in the literature on sibling (Balk, 1983b, 1990) and adult survivors (Demi & Miles, 1988). The first items, relating to discomfort when feeling happy or having fun, indicate bereaved adolescents experience guilt when engaging in activities other adolescents take for granted and regard as fun. They question the appropriateness of enjoying life when the lives of their dead brothers or sisters have ceased. The sobering event of sibling death and its aftermath changes the bereaved adolescent's emotional life and sense of a right to happiness. The third item indicates that the surviving siblings believe they should have died and that their dead siblings should have lived. The questions that survivors ask are: "Why did he/she die?" and "Why was I spared?" Survivor guilt is described well in the literature on child survivors (Osterweis, Solomon, & Green, 1984).

In the third subcategory of depression, bereaved siblings feel depressed when they think about the death and aftermath of missing their brothers or sisters. Depressive reactions include sleeplessness, nightmares, and having little control over sadness.

Bereaved adolescents also experience continued, profound sadness when they think about their dead siblings and during holidays and other times when families traditionally share and celebrate together. Grief associated with particular times and dates is commonly referred to as "anniversary reactions" (Balk, 1983b).

The item of not caring what happens to them indicates the bereaved adolescents experience apathy and indifference toward life. They see their lives as hopeless and meaningless, and hold few expectations that they will ever be happy again. Life is bleak.

In the fourth subcategory of isolation, the bereaved adolescents feel exceptionally alone. They appraise that no one can understand their grieving. They see their relationships with their dead brothers and sisters as unique and their grief as unique. Their losses are beyond the capacity of others to comprehend.

Category 4: Cognitive Interference   The ability of bereaved siblings to selectively concentrate is sacrificed for the task of maintaining control over uninvited, intrusive thoughts and feelings associated with fear, guilt, and depression. They are concentrating on preserving their tenuous cognitive equilibrium. Due to the highly charged cognitive demands of their intrusive thoughts, the bereaved siblings are unable to concentrate on the everyday mundane such as schoolwork.

Category 5: Desire for Reunion with Sibling   Bereaved siblings sometimes feel such separation pain and a need for proximity to their deceased brothers or sisters that they express wanting to die in order to reunite with their siblings. This desire is most common early in the bereavement process.

Category 6: Coping Behavior   Bereaved siblings attempt to cope with grief by doing things that place them in danger such as driving too fast and using alcohol and mind-changing drugs. Engaging in high-risk behavior helps distract them from the pain of their grief. Escape through risk behavior, while relieving the stressor of remembering, increases the possibility of their injury or death.

The Construct of Personal Growth

The categories and properties of personal growth are derived from the 22 items that constitute the growth factor on the HSIB. The categories, properties, and their meanings are detailed in Table 2. Each category will be discussed separately.

Category 1: Permanently Changed Reality   The first three items indicate that experiencing the death of a sibling and its aftermath brings the bereaved sibling a new sense of awareness about the impermanence of life; that is, life is fragile and relationships are precious. They learn to take nothing for granted. The shared life that exists today can be gone today. The last property shows a recognition of the need to reprioritize what gives value and meaning to life.

Category 2: Increased Sense of Others   There are two subcategories that relate to others: (a) attachment, and (b) sensitivity. Bereaved siblings have feelings of a greater sense of love for others and family. They have a higher level of prosocial behavior such as more compassion, tolerance, kindness, understanding,

Table 2 Categories, Properties, and Meanings of Personal Growth Items from the Hogan Sibling Inventory of Bereavement Instrument

Categories	Properties (items)	Meanings
1. Permanently changed reality	I know how fragile life is.	Impermanence of life
	I have learned that all people die.	Sense of mortality
	I don't take others for granted.	Valuing others
	I have changed my priorities.	Reevaluate priorities
2. Increased sense of others		
A. Attachment to others	I am a more caring person.	Love for others
	I care more deeply for my family.	Love for family
B. Sensitivity to others	I am more tolerant of others.	Accepting others
	I am more understanding of others.	Empathy
	I am more aware of others' feelings.	Empathy
	I have more compassion for others.	Empathy
	I try to be kinder to other people.	Empathy
3. Increased resilience		
A. Optimism	I have a better outlook on life.	Sense of hopefulness
B. Maturity	I have grown up faster than my friends.	Increased maturity
	I have learned to cope better with my problems.	Deal with problems
	I have learned to cope better with life.	Deal with life
	I am stronger because of the grief I have had to cope with.	Sense of increased competence
C. Self-worth	I am tolerant of myself.	Increased self-esteem
	I am a better person.	Increased self-esteem
	I am more creative.	Increased openness to new possibilities
4. Sense of faith	My faith has become more important to me.	Increased awareness of faith
5. Ability to give and receive help	I can give help to others who are grieving.	Support to/for others
	I can get help for my grieving when I need it.	Support from others

243

and empathy. They also recognize an increased sense of responsibility for the well-being of others. They have a greater consciousness for the rights and needs of others. While egocentrism is more commonly associated with adolescence, it appears that ultracentrism is an outcome of experiencing the existential crisis of the death of a brother or sister. The ultracentrism is reflective of a higher sense of morality. This sense of morality is supported by recent empirical research using standardized instruments. Bereaved siblings scored significantly above the mean when compared to nonbereaved adolescents on the morals subscale of the Offer Self-Image Questionnaire for Adolescents (Balk, 1981; Hogan & Greenfield, 1991). Davies (1988) also found bereaved siblings scored significantly higher than the standardized norm on the morals and religion subscales of the Moos Family Environment Scale.

Category 3: Increased Resiliency   There are three subcategories: (a) optimism, (b) maturity, and (c) sense of self. The bereaved siblings come to believe they are stronger because of the grief they have endured and survived, their increased ability to cope with problems and life in general, and their greater sense of self-awareness and self-worth. The greater strength that ensues provides them with an optimistic view of life and better prospects for the future.

Category 4: Increased Faith   The bereaved adolescents also experience an increase in "faith consciousness" (Fowler, 1976, 1991). They begin to reexamine and reevaluate their values and beliefs. They view themselves and life in relation to their siblings' deaths. They emerge with a new personal belief system or faith in their inner strength to cope with those deaths and with future life events (Hogan & DeSantis, 1994). Their new "faith consciousness" also embodies and stimulates their increased sense of "other consciousness." For some of the bereaved adolescents, their increased "faith consciousness" or sense of spirituality also includes a reawakening or strengthening of their religiosity (Balk, 1983a; Balk & Hogan, in press; Hogan & DeSantis, 1994). For others, it initiates an exploration into religious support.

Category 5: Ability to Receive and Give Help   The bereaved adolescents have gained the ability to ask for and receive help when they need it. Family members and peers are seen as "being there" for them, caring and comforting them, sharing memories of the deceased sibling/child, and just letting them grieve on their own terms (Hogan & DeSantis, 1994). At the same time, the bereaved adolescents are able to be there for others who are grieving. The bereaved adolescents, in turn, help their surviving siblings, family members, and peers with the grieving process. They feel they are there for them (Hogan & DeSantis, 1994).

At this point, it is important to note that analysis of the constructs of grief and personal growth through triangulation of quantitative data (factor-analyzed items) and qualitative data (semistructured questions) reveals that they are orthogonal and independent in nature (Hogan & DeSantis, 1992, 1994). The inter-correlation between the grief factor and the personal growth factor on the HSIB used with this population is .19. The independence of the constructs of grief and personal growth has also been empirically identified by Lehman et al. (1993) for parental and spousal bereavement.

The Construct of Ongoing Attachment

Table 3 summarizes the categories and subcategories of the construct of Ongoing Attachment. Each category will be described briefly.

Category 1: Regretting The bereaved adolescents were sorry for the way they had treated their deceased brothers or sisters in life and wished they had had closer, more loving relationships. They missed sharing their lives with their dead siblings—telling secrets to each other, teasing one another, hugging and kissing, and doing "stuff" together.

> Even when we got into fights and said cruel things to each other like "drop dead!" . . . I didn't mean it.

> Sorry I wasn't a better sister. I will never forgive myself for the way I treated you. I miss you so much. I should of listened to you and been there for you when I had the chance.

> I am sorry for fighting with him. I would also thank him for all of the fun times we had together.

> I am sorry for all the mean things I did and said to him.

Category 2: Endeavoring to Understand The bereaved adolescents raised critical questions about the circumstances surrounding the deaths of their siblings. They tried to puzzle through the "how" and "why" of the deaths. If their siblings died by homicide or suicide, they searched for conditions that may have contributed to the deaths. They agonized over the "why" of the deaths.

> Why did you do this to yourself?

> I would ask her what really happened that night of the death, and why she wouldn't let me know if she was going to do something.

> I'd ask him if he meant to do what he did (suicide) or if it was an accident?

> How did you get in the center divider? Were you sleeping or did someone run you off the road? When you came out, did you over-correct and then flip? Did you feel anything?

Category 3: Catching Up The bereaved adolescents kept spiritually in touch with their dead brothers or sisters by updating them on current events, by reassuring them that everything and everyone in this world were fine, and by of-

Table 3 Categories, Properties and Meanings of Ongoing Attachment

Categories	Properties (items)	Meanings
1. Regretting	Desiring to have a better relationship	Sorrow for the way they had related/Wish for a closer, more loving relationship
	Longing to share activities	Miss doing things together/Wanting to share things
2. Endeavoring to understand	Wanting to know the circumstances surrounding the death	Need to make sense of the death
	Searching for reasons why the sibling chose to die	Need to understand the decision to suicide
3. Catching up	Bringing the sibling up to date on current events	Convey assurance that family and things in general are alright
	Asking how things are	Need to know if things are better or all right/want to know how they can be of help to make things better or to relay messages
4. Reaffirming	Continuing emotional bond with the deceased	Expression of ongoing loneliness and love for the sibling/Vow to forever remember the sibling
5. Influencing	Seeking guidance	Need for continued mentoring and role modeling by the deceased/desire to live up to the expectations of the deceased
	Keeping the memory of the sibling alive	Desire to carry on their work/deliberate intent to symbolically keep the sibling "in my heart"
6. Reuniting	Anticipating reunion in heaven/afterlife	Anticipate joining the dead sibling

Note: Table adapted from Hogan and DeSantis (1992). Subcategories and meanings relate to the deceased sibling unless otherwise specified.

246

fering to deliver messages and greetings to other survivors. They sought reassurance from their deceased siblings that they were well and happy in heaven/afterlife. They also asked their deceased sibling what heaven/afterlife was like.

> I just can't help but think about all the things that she wanted to do but never was able to do on this earth. . . . Does she get to do those things now? Is she having fun? Is she happy?

> Are you having fun?

> Mom's doing great. Everything's allright. How's everything up there?

> I spend one afternoon a week at the cemetery. I talk to Ben. I pray for him. It's like having your own special saint watching over you.

> I would ask what it was like to die, and what it is like where she is at.

Category 4: Reaffirming   The bereaved adolescents continually reaffirmed their ongoing relationships with their deceased siblings. They declared their love for them. They expressed how much they missed their dead brothers or sisters. They vowed to remember their dead siblings "forever."

> I'd tell him I love him very much, and I'd never forget him.

> I would tell my brother . . . that we miss him very much. . . . I would tell him that I missed him very much and wished he was here, because I miss him greatly.

> I would tell Steve how much I love him. Even though we had our fights, I would give anything in this whole world to have another one. I miss him so much.

Category 5: Influencing   The bereaved adolescents continually sought assistance from their deceased siblings. They sought guidance from them about boyfriend/girlfriend relationships and other problems of life. They also wanted some assurance that they were living up to the expectations of their dead siblings.

The bereaved siblings declared their intent to keep the memory of their deceased brothers or sisters alive by carrying on their "work" and not letting their dreams die. By keeping the memory of their deceased siblings alive, the bereaved adolescents reaffirmed their commitment to spiritual relationships with their siblings.

> I'll never, ever forget him.

> [I'd] ask him for his advice on a lot of problems and situations I have.

> Will you promise to be with me and help me? Will you help me to never, ever forget . . . [you]?

> I would ask her if I was doing the right thing with my life.

Category 6: Reuniting   By anticipating reunion with their deceased siblings, the bereaved adolescents were confirming their sibling relationship for eternity—that is, the relationship continues beyond death. In effect, the bereaved adolescents were stating that the sibling relationship supersedes and transcends death.

I'll see you later!

I'm looking forward to when I can be with her again.

I . . . would tell him to look for me.

I'll see him later on!

The strength of the concept of reuniting is further validated in the quantitative portion of the study. Reuniting had the highest mean score of all items on the HSIB. The reuniting item was phrased as: "I believe I will see my dead brother or sister in heaven." This triangulation of qualitative and quantitative responses relating to reunion confirms the significance of the bereaved adolescents' belief that they will see their dead siblings in heaven/afterlife and that their relationships have not been ended by death. The reunion item also had the highest mean score when the HSIB was administered to another community-based population of 40 bereaved adolescents (Hogan, 1987).

DISCUSSION

The constructs of grief, personal growth, and ongoing attachment constitute a complex phenomenon and process. There are multiple pathways through grief and toward personal growth. Additional variation occurs due to factors such as cultural orientation, cause and circumstances surrounding the death, nature of the affectional bond, and characteristics of the survivors and the deceased.

The constructs show that surviving the death of a person to whom one is meaningfully attached is an existential experience, if not *the* existential experience. In adolescent sibling bereavement, the bereaved adolescents who become resilient survivors find meaning in life through the process of suffering (Frankl, 1984) over the death of their brothers or sisters. Those who become vulnerable survivors struggle unsuccessfully to find meaning in life after the deaths of their siblings. They remain mired in despair and misery. The ensuing discussion will focus on the process of becoming a resilient survivor after the death of a brother or sister.

The Trajectory of Grief

Prior to the death event, life is "normal." The world works—it is understandable and familiar. The adolescents are going through life with the naive assumption that what they may desire is possible and conceivable. Their families have all their members. They are experiencing shared lives with their brothers or sisters that includes both the positive and negative aspects of normal sibling relationships. They are sharing physical, social, and psychological proximity with their siblings.

With the deaths of their brothers or sisters, the lives of the surviving siblings and their families cease to be "normal." The previous naive assumptions and "working models" (Bowlby, 1969) of their lives are no longer valid.

Notification about the death of a brother or sister combined with the social mourning rituals associated with wakes, memorial services, and burial serve as external validation that the sibling is, indeed, dead. After the initial shock and numbness of knowing the sibling is dead and going through the public rituals surrounding death, bereaved adolescents begin to learn the existential meaning of the physical absence (lack of proximity) of the dead brother or sister. There is a realization that their world is broken—nothing is as it was before.

Life becomes hapless for the bereaved adolescents. The world no longer has a plan, order, or direction. They are encompassed by hopelessness (*Webster's dictionary*, 1989) and despair and are powerless to help themselves. Their helplessness is combined with a profound state of loneliness in that they feel no one can help or understand them. They essentially become consumed by their irrevocably changed reality. Their grief also has physical, social, psychological, and cognitive dimensions (see Table 1).

At their lowest point of grief (when grief is the most intense), the bereaved adolescents who become resilient survivors experience a turning point. They come to two simultaneous realizations. One is that their deceased brothers or sisters will never, ever return. The other realization is that they must somehow actively "take hold" of their lives in spite of the permanent lack of proximity to their deceased siblings. This dual, simultaneous realization is associated with the bereaved adolescents beginning to learn to let go of the pain of grief and beginning to regain a sense of hope for the future (*Webster's dictionary*, 1989). Their grief symptomatology begins to diminish as they engage in the process of rebuilding their lives and creating a revised model of the world based on a new reality and normality. However, their grief will continue to reemerge during significant life events in which their deceased siblings would have been expected to participate, such as family graduations, marriages, births, and deaths.

The Trajectory of Personal Growth

Prior to the death event, the world and people are taken for granted. Priorities are egocentric and driven by developing a sense of personal identity based upon seeking answers to the basic questions, "Who am I?", "Where am I going?", and "How will I get there?" (Erikson, 1964). Answering those questions is dependent upon their relationships and shared life with members of their interpersonal network.

With the death of their brothers or sisters, the bereaved siblings become aware of just how fragile life is, and they cease to take others for granted. They also come to realize how vital their deceased siblings were to their very being. To the point of the death of their siblings, the bereaved adolescents have partially foraged the answers to the identity questions through sibling relationships. With the death of a brother or sister, the roles and relationships of the bereaved adolescents, their families, and others in their interpersonal network must now be redefined. The identity questions the bereaved adolescents need to answer have become, "Who am I *now*?", "Where am I going *now*?", and "How will I get there *now*?"

The answers to the revised identity questions must now be foraged in the absence of their primary referent. The quest for answers results in a reprioritization in the search for meaning in their lives and a shifting of focus from egocentrism to ultracentrism. Their transcendence of self and others is characterized by an increase in the bereaved adolescents' sense of and love for others, resiliency, faith, and ability to receive and give help (see Table 2, Categories 2 through 5).

It is the transcendence of self and others that leads to personal growth in bereaved adolescents. The personal growth experience continues as they go on to construct a new model and meaning of life in the proximal absence of their dead siblings.

Ongoing Attachment

Death tolls the end of the "continual possibilization of possibilities" (Sartre, 1956). Death of a sibling is permanent and irrevocable and shatters all expectations and anticipations of the surviving siblings for a shared future that is not to be. Creating a fulfilling life after the death of a brother or sister requires bereaved adolescents to replace a sense of helplessness with helpfulness, a sense of hopelessness with hopefulness, and a sense of meaninglessness with meaningfulness. The phenomenon of ongoing attachment occurs in response to the vital need of bereaved adolescents to find help, hope, and meaning by anticipating proximity (possible reunion) with their deceased sibling again. This anticipated reunion/proximity is accomplished by reconceptualizing the "future" to include the expectation of reunion with the deceased brother or sister in heaven/afterlife (the possibilization of possibilities).

While grief and personal growth can be conceptualized as spiraling trajectories, ongoing attachment can be seen as a type of motivational energy that assists in transforming bereaved siblings into resilient survivors. When grief is the most intense and bereaved adolescents are mired in hopelessness and feel life has lost its meaning, ongoing attachment becomes manifest. The bereaved siblings undertake an introspective scrutiny that brings about a gradual realization that shared relationships with their dead brothers or sisters is irrevocably lost. This gradual realization results in accepting the impossibility of recovering the life that was. The acceptance of the impossibility of life as it was frees the energy of the bereaved siblings to reformulate a reality that includes the spiritual presence of their deceased siblings. It is the possibility of reunion in heaven/afterlife that begins the process of lessening the intensity of grief and that revitalizes the bereaved adolescents' sense of hope.

Ongoing attachment also leads to an expanding and transcending sense of self, sense of others, and sense of responsibility for others. This transcendence leads to a perpetually expanding phenomenon that becomes all-pervasive and encompassing as the process of personal growth evolves. It is this evolving nature of personal growth that facilitates the bereaved adolescents in redefining their identity and world within their altered interpersonal network.

Ongoing attachment, then, is the silent variable that mediates the construct of grief and the construct of personal growth. While ongoing attachment becomes manifest when grief is at its most intense, it begins to emerge at the death of a brother or sister in the construct of personal growth. This emergence of ongoing attachment accelerates and expands the process of personal growth across time. The interactions between ongoing attachment and the constructs of grief and personal growth are bidirectional. However, in adolescent sibling bereavement, grief and personal growth remain independent despite the fact that they both occur during the phenomenon of sibling death.

CONCLUSIONS AND RECOMMENDATIONS

The three formative empirical constructs of grief, personal growth, and ongoing attachment have been derived from a triangulation and synthesis of qualitative and quantitative research. They identify characteristics and the complex nature of the adolescent sibling bereavement process. The theory that has emerged from the data provides a paradigm for future empirical testing that will allow a differentiation of normative and nonnormative adolescent sibling bereavement. The following are recommendations for future research:

1   Longitudinal studies across cultural groups, religious denominations, and believers or nonbelievers in the concept of an afterlife.

2   Comparative research with other age groups and affectional bonds—for example, death of a spouse, parent, or child.

3   Identification and exploration of other antecedent characteristics such as: (a) gender of the survivor and deceased, (b) life experiences of the survivor, and (c) the nature of the relationship between the survivor and the deceased.

4   Delineation and exploration of the cause of death and circumstances surrounding the death.

5   Determination of the bereavement trajectory with differentiation of turning points that can distinguish between vulnerable and resilient survivors.

6   Development, application, and evaluation of intervention strategies that are grounded in empirical bereavement research.

The above recommendations along with other equally pertinent research studies will serve to further validate, modify, and expand this theory of adolescent sibling bereavement. Broadening and modification of the theory will provide for more accurate screening of bereaved individuals at risk and for the development of more effective and developmentally appropriate intervention strategies.

REFERENCES

Balk, D. E. (1981). Sibling death during adolescence: Self-concept and bereavement reactions. (Doctoral dissertation, University of Illinois at Urbana, 1981). *Dissertation Abstracts International, 42*, 386A.

Balk, D. E. (1983a). Adolescents' grief reactions and self-concept perceptions following sibling death: A study of 33 teenagers. *Journal of Youth and Adolescence, 12*(2), 137–159.

Balk, D. E. (1983b). Effects of sibling death on teenagers. *Journal of School Health, 15*, 14–18.

Balk, D. E. (1990). The self-concept of bereaved adolescents: Sibling death and its aftermath. *Journal of Adolescent Research, 5*(1), 112–132.

Balk, D. E. (1991a). Death and adolescent bereavement: Current research and future directions. *Journal of Adolescent Research, 6*(1), 7–28.

Balk, D. E. (1991b). Sibling death, adolescent bereavement and religion. *Death Studies, 15*, 1–20.

Balk, D. E., & Hogan, N. S. (in press). Adolescent sibling bereavement: Religion and spirituality. In D. W. Adams & E. Deveau (Eds.), *Loss, threat to life and bereavement.* Amityville, NY: Baywood.

Bank, S., & Kahn, M. (1982). *The sibling bond.* New York: Basic Books.

Birenbaum, L. K., Robinson, M. A., Phillips, D. S., Stewart, B. J., & McCown, D. E. (1989–1990). The response of children to the dying and death of a sibling. *Omega, 20*(3), 213–228.

Blankemeyer, M. (1994). *Adolescent sibling bereavement: Family factors associated with adjustment to loss.* Unpublished master's thesis, Oklahoma State University, Stillwater.

Bowlby, J. (1969). *Attachment and loss* (Vols. 1–3). New York: Basic Books.

Bowlby, J. (1980). *Attachment and loss: Vol. 3. Loss, sadness, and depression.* New York: Basic Books.

Brent, D. (1983). A death in the family: The pediatrician's role. *Pediatrics, 72*(5), 645–651.

Collins, R. L., Taylor, S. E., & Skokan, L. A. (1990). A better world or a shattered vision? Changes in life perspective following victimization. *Social Cognition, 8*, 263–285.

Davies, B. (1988). The family environment in bereaved families and its relationship to surviving sibling behavior. *Children's Health Care, 17*, 22–31.

Davies, E. B. (1991). Long-term outcomes of adolescent sibling bereavement. *Journal of Adolescent Research, 6*(1), 83–96.

Demi, A., & Gilbert, C. (1987). Relationship of parental grief to sibling grief. *Archives of Psychiatric Nursing, 6*(1), 385–391.

Demi, A., & Miles, M. (1988). Suicide bereaved parents: Emotional distress and physical health problems. *Death Studies, 12*, 297–307.

Dunn, J., & Kendrick, C. (1982). *Siblings: Love, envy and understanding.* Cambridge, MA: Harvard University Press.

Erikson, E. H. (1963). *Childhood and society,* New York: Norton.

Erikson, E. H. (1964). *Identity: Youth and crisis.* New York: Norton.

Fowler, J. W. (1976). Stages in faith: The structural-developmental approach. In T. Hennessy (Ed.), *Values and moral development.* New York: Paulist Press.

Fowler, J. W. (1991). *Stages of faith and religious development: Implications for church, education, and society.* New York: Crossroad.

Frankl, V. F. (1984). *Man's search for meaning: An introduction to logotherapy* (3rd ed.). New York: Simon & Schuster.

Guerriero, A. M. (1983). *Adolescent bereavement: Impact on physical health, self-concept, depression, and death anxiety.* Unpublished master's thesis, York University, Toronto, Canada.

Guerriero, A. M., & Fleming, S. J. (1985). *Adolescent bereavement: A longitudinal study.* Paper presented at the Annual Meeting of the Canadian Psychological Association, Halifax, Nova Scotia.

Hogan, N. S. (1983). Development of the Sibling Inventory of Bereavement. Unpublished raw data.

Hogan, N. S. (1987). An investigation of the adolescent sibling bereavement process and adaptation (Doctoral dissertation, Loyola University of Chicago, 1987). *Dissertation Abstracts, International, 4024A.*

Hogan, N. S. (1990). Hogan Sibling Inventory of Bereavement. In J. Touliatos, B. Perlmutter, & M. Straus, (Eds.), *Handbook of family measurement techniques* (p. 524). Newbury Park, CA: Sage.

Hogan, N. S., & Balk, D. E. (1990). Adolescent reactions to sibling death: Perceptions of mothers, fathers, and teenagers. *Nursing Research, 39,* 103–106.

Hogan, N. S., & DeSantis, L. (1992). Adolescent sibling bereavement: An ongoing attachment. *Qualitative Health Research, 2,* 159–177.

Hogan, N. S., & DeSantis, L. (1994). Things that help and hinder adolescent sibling bereavement. *Western Journal of Nursing Research, 16*(2), 132–153.

Hogan, N. S., & Greenfield, D. B. (1991). Adolescent sibling bereavement: Symptomatology in a large community sample. *Journal of Adolescent Research, 6*(1), 97–112.

Klass, D. (1993). Solace and immortality: Bereaved parents' continuing bond with their children. *Death Studies, 17,* 343–368.

Lamb, M., & Sutton-Smith, B. (1982). *Sibling relationships across the life span.* Hillsdale, NJ: Lawrence Ehrlbaum.

Lehman, D. R., Davis, C. G., Delongis, A., Wortman, C. B., Bluck, S., Mandel, D. R., & Ellard, J. H. (1993). Positive and negative life changes following bereavement and their relations to adjustment. *Journal of Social and Clinical Psychology, 12*(1), 90–112.

Lopata, H. Z. (1973). *Widowhood in an American city.* Cambridge, MA: Schenckman.

Lopata, H. Z. (1975). On widowhood: Grief, work, identity reconstruction. *Journal of Geriatric Psychiatry, 8,* 41–55.

Martinson, I. M., & Compos, R. G. (1991). Adolescent bereavement: Long-term responses to a sibling's death from cancer. *Journal of Pediatric Nursing, 2*(4), 227–235.

Martinson, I. M., Davies, E. B., & McClowry, S. G. (1987). The long-term effects of sibling death on self-concept. *Journal of Pediatric Nursing, 2*(4), 227–235.

McClowry, S. G., Davies, E. B., Kulenkamp, E. J., & Martinson, I. M. (1987). The empty space phenomenon: The process of grief in the bereaved family. *Death Studies, 11,* 361–374.

McCown, D. E., & Pratt, C. (1985). Impact of sibling death on children's behavior. *Death Studies, 9,* 323–335.

Micheal, S., & Lansdown, R. (1986). Adjustment to the death of a sibling. *Archives of Disease in Childhood, 61,* 278–283.

Offer, D. (1969). *The psychological worlds of the teenager.* New York: Basic Books.

Oltjenbruns, K. A. (1991). Positive outcomes of adolescents' experience with grief. *Journal of Adolescent Research, 6*(1), 43–53.

Osterweis, M., Solomon, F., & Green, M. (Eds.). (1984). *Bereavement: Reactions, consequences, and care.* Washington: National Academy Press.

Provence, S., & Solnit, A. (1983). Development-promoting aspects of the sibling experience: Vicarious mastery. In A. J. Solnit, R. S. Eissler, & P. B. Newbaur (Eds.), *The psychiatric study of the child* (pp. 337–351). New Haven, CT: Yale University Press.

Sartre, J. P. (1956). *Being and nothingness: An essay on phenomenological ontology.* New York: Philosophy Library.

Stanner, W. E. H. (1965). The dreaming. In W. A. Lessa & E. Z. Vogt (Eds.), *Reader in comparative religion: An anthropological approach* (3rd ed.) (pp. 269–277). New York: Harper & Row.

Taylor, S. E., Lichtman, R. R., & Wood, J. V. (1984). Attributions, beliefs about control, and adjustment to breast cancer. *Journal of Personality and Social Psychology, 46,* 489–502.

U. S. Bureau of the Census. (1993). *Statistical Abstract of the United States.* (113th ed.) Washington, DC: U.S. Government Printing Office.

U. S. Department of Commerce. (1991). *Statistical Abstract of the United States.* (111th ed.) Washington, DC: U.S. Government Printing Office.

Walker, C. L. (1993). Sibling bereavement and grief responses. *Journal of Pediatric Nursing, 8*(5), 325–334.

Webster's encyclopedic unabridged dictionary of the English language. (1989). New York: Gramercy.

Yalom, I. A., & Lieberman, M. A. (1991). Bereavement and heightened existential awareness. *Psychiatry, 54*, 334–345.

Part Seven

Adoptee Losses

People's experiences with adoption provide new material for looking at the themes running through this book. Although we chose to talk about the dilemmas of adoptees in this book, the examples of birth mothers who surrender their children for adoption can readily be seen as cases of parental bereavement (Silverman, 1981). These women live with only the inner representations of the children they surrendered. They experience the same physical loss as bereaved parents, but often have no socially acceptable way of acknowledging that a loss has taken place. The meaning of conceiving and delivering a baby is often disregarded in the support network, and the meaning of the biological connection between mother and child is minimized. The third member of the adoption triangle, the adoptive parents, are also grieving for the child they could not conceive or carry to term.

Adoption, as it has been codified into Western law, assumes a model of family relationships that reflect modernity. That is, the family, consisting of mother, father, and children, is an autonomous unit with clear parameters and with well-defined, exclusive role relationships. There can be only one mother, so if the role of mother is given to a person to whom the child was not born, birth certificates and other documents are changed to reflect these "facts". The original birth certificate is sealed by the court and is legally inaccessible to the adoptee. The adoption reform movement takes a more post-modern view of these relationships, as reflected in the chapters in this section. However, legitimation of the adoptees' "need to know" about their birth family is interpreted by the opponents of adoption reform as a threat to the family as they know it. The data that are presented by Nickman and Miller-Havens challenge more than the professional view of reality—that is, the need to cut ties with the past—it challenges the folk psychology of a segment of the population who oppose reform. These opponents of reform have politicized these issues with the intent of blocking change in legislation that would allow adoptees to learn about their past and they deny that the birth parent has any part in the adoptees' personal identity.

Both Steven Nickman (Chapter 15) and Susan Miller-Havens (Chapter 16) note the special problems adoptees have in defining their grief to themselves. The difficulty is that their bonds with the birth parents are not socially legitimized. Adoptees are not expected to grieve or feel a connection to their families of origin. As we try to understand the concept of continuing bonds, the nature of the relationship to the missing person becomes important. Nickman argues that even adoptees who were adopted early in their lives have a relationship with their birth parents. In her chapter, Miller-Havens analyzes the birth-origin fantasies of adult adoptees. She looks at how these fantasies function in the adoptee's life.

P. R. S.

S. N.

Chapter 15

Retroactive Loss in Adopted Persons

Steven L. Nickman

In this chapter, it will be argued that it makes sense to speak of adoptees having a relationship with birth parents, even those whom they have never known. The discussion is based on clinical work over a period of 25 years with approximately 250 adoptees (mostly children and adolescents), the adoptive parents in most cases, and 15 birth mothers. We will explore ways to think about adoptees' experiences in relation to the idea of loss and will then give clinical examples of adoptees experiencing loss, along with the interventions that proved necessary in order to help these individuals.

Relationship will be shown partly from the description of some common experiences of adoptees. and partly by drawing parallels with the experience of bereaved individuals, particularly children, for whom constructing an inner representation of the dead parent is an essential process. Once an adoptee is made aware of adoptive status, mental construction of the absent progenitors becomes necessary, and that the internal dialogue between an adoptee and his or her inner representation or construction of the birth parents is as much a relationship as the connection between a bereaved individual and the dead person. The formal characteristics of the connection are similar: In both cases a person has powerful emotions and detailed thoughts about an individual who is not present; this complex of thought and emotion can operate on both a conscious and an unconscious level to influence choices, affect, and behavior (Tessman, 1984).

THE VITAL QUESTIONS

Have Adoptees Experienced a Loss?

Brodzinsky (1990) has compared a child' s experience of adoption, parental death, and divorce on six dimensions. He asks: How permanent is the loss? How common or universal is the experience—that is, how unique or set apart does the person experiencing it feel? How common is public recognition of this type of loss, so that the person experiencing it receives social support? How strong a relationship did the individual have with the absent person? Did the parent bring the situation about voluntarily? And how extensive is the loss of the person seen to be for the individual concerned? Brodzinsky concluded that on a majority of these criteria, adoptees suffer losses that are comparable to or greater than those suffered by individuals who have experienced parental divorce or death.

Nevertheless, to hear adoptees mentioned in the context of loss or bereavement may seem inappropriate to some. Most would concede that, leaving aside the unusual case of an adoptee whose biological parents have actually died, a child who was relinquished or taken from parents in toddlerhood or later might legitimately be seen as bereaved in some sense, but what about those who were placed in the first weeks or months of life with adoptive parents? Do they not have real parents in their adopters? And how important is their connection to the parents they never knew, and who may never have acted toward them in a parental capacity? These questions have been debated at length in the literature of social work, child psychiatry, and psychology since the 1940s, and the debate continues.

By the 1970s a consensus had arisen among professionals that it is normal, rather than neurotic (as used to be asserted) for adoptees to think a great deal about their relinquishing procreators, to wonder about their histories and their personal and physical characteristics as well their motivations in placing the adoptee. It is also generally conceded that a degree of preoccupation with the idea of searching for birth parents is normal, although society discourages actual attempts at search before adulthood. Over time "the search" has come to denote, broadly, a questing state of mind in which the individual actively seeks information about birth parents and personal history, but searching as an activity denotes the pursuit of actual contact. A minority of adoptive parents continues to oppose the search in both broad and narrow senses, even in adoptees well launched on their adult lives, and punitive attitudes toward those who search still exist.

The word loss is appropriate in the case of early-placed adoptees when one broadens the concept to include loss that is recognized retrospectively—that it is an event that is only understood later by the individual who construes it as a loss. The word deprivation might be more accurate but would miss precisely the belief or feeling adoptees have that in some sense they could have had, or almost had, this person in their lives. A parental death or a divorce early in the child's life is no different, when the import of the event is brought home to the child only after some time has passed. "If only I had been born rich," or "If only I had been born with blue eyes" would not be understood by most people as genuine retroactive loss experiences; however, "If I had only been born with the full number of fingers on my left hand," or "If only I had not been placed for adoption, but instead kept by my original parents" express wishes closer to standard human experience than what actually obtains for the child, wishes most people would find understandable. Such wishing on the part of children who have a significant deprivation commonly leads to the development of an active and persistent fantasy life. In Chapter 16 of this volume, Miller-Havens describes ways in which fantasizing contributes to the development of an inner representation of the birth parent.

A rough classification for the losses of adoptees has been proposed (Nickman, 1985). The first is *covert loss:* prolonged or intermittent inner reflection on not having been kept and on having been transferred from one set of caretakers to another, and on not having learned about this until long after the event. ("Long after" could refer to the period around 3 or 4 years, when early disclosure usually begins, or the moment of disclosure could be displaced by the child to age 7 or 8, when cognition becomes more adequate to the situation.) Such reveries are often tinged with depressive feeling and with negative inferences about the self, such as personal unworthiness; children resort to fantasy at such times to explain to themselves the circumstances under which such events might have taken place. These losses are partly relationship ("a relationship that could have been") and partly narcissistic ("there must have been something wrong with me"). If marked, such narcissistic impairment can negatively affect the capacity for future relationships. Covert losses in general are the predominant type found in adoptees placed very early in life, but are present (though not usually predominant) in later-placed adoptees.

Overt loss applies to situations of privation, deprivation, and discontinuity: being transferred from one parent to another during toddlerhood or later, after specific emotional bonds have begun to be laid down and acquired a degree of richness and complexity; experiences of neglect or abuse; experiences of multiple caretaking, leading to the blunting (at times permanent) of a child's capacity to make intimate emotional connections. Overt loss can also be seen to occur when grandparents treat adoptees prejudicially with respect to inheritance, favoring biologically related grandchildren; such situations also share aspects of the next category. Overt losses are the predominant type of loss in later-placed adoptees. They very clearly represent a relationship loss for obvious reasons; additionally, when such losses are marked and repetitive, another kind of relationship loss occurs whereby the individual is deprived of future good relationships by virtue of impairment of the capacity for trust and mutuality, as mentioned above.

Status loss refers to situations in which an individual suffers a narcissistic blow by virtue of being or appearing different from peers—for example, being seen in public with parents who belong to a different racial group, or being singled out in a classroom (ostensibly for educational purposes) to comment on one's country of origin, though one may not remember it. Such losses have their primary effect on an individual's development of healthy narcissism—that is, they may interfere with the formation of positive self-representations and good, resilient self-esteem. While overt and covert losses represent loss of relationship in one way or another, status loss does not.

What/Who Has Been Lost and Was/Is It a Relationship?

As stated above, professionals who work with adoption now largely recognize the legitimacy of seeking information and actualized search as valid expressions of individuals' working out their identities. Do such activities represent relationship in the conventional sense—the sense in which that word is used in this book—or is the kind of knowledge or contact that adoptees desire more inward and personal, related to an individual's pursuit of healthy self-esteem, existential grounding, or both? To frame the question in different terms, do adoptees seek to resume or remake a real relationship that was interrupted, or do they seek the opportunity to redress a wrong, to turn passive to active and, therewith, to claim the right to choose whether to make or not make a relationship that is essentially new, given that they were previously foreclosed from having that relationship? (The first way of putting it would suggest that adoptees are bereft and thus similar to individuals who have lost a person to death; the second way of putting it is different, suggesting not so much loss as a kind of privation *ab initio*.)

Clearly, to pose the question in a dichotomous way is misleading. Adoptees are not a homogeneous group, and individuals are motivated in complex ways. The thoughts of a given adoptee about birth parents are influenced by various circumstances; these include (a) the social and legal structuring of adoption; (b) developmental influences on the adoptee's inner experience of a birth parent; (c) the influence of stressful life events; (d) sustaining fantasy in relation to fantasy about birth parents; and (e) the need for actual knowledge or contact, versus the need for a permitted locus of thought. We will explore these five dimensions using case illustrations, and it will be seen that the question posed above, perhaps best put as "relationship versus enhancement of one's own identity," is not usually answerable in a clear way and that often both ways of seeing the question are valid.

SOCIAL AND LEGAL STRUCTURING OF ADOPTION

Relationship between adoptee and absent birth parent, and whether loss and grief are involved, depend partly on the nature of the laws and transactions governing adoption at a given time and in a given society. Adoption in many traditional societies has provided routine access to birth parents, while adoption from roughly 1920 to 1970 in the United States was hermetically closed. Clearly, adoptees in these two conditions would have had very different experiences of grounding in their biological families and thus, different experiences with respect to loss or privation.

The contemporary movement toward more openness in adoption gives adoptive families more direct and indirect knowledge of birth parents, and at times even early-placed adoptees are acquainted with birth parents. Under such circumstances it can be assumed that wide-ranging, preoccupying fantasy in childhood and adolescence will become less prevalent and that an actual relationship may exist in some adoptions. The following is a naturally evolving open situation:

> Stephen was placed with the Martin family at age 6 months. His mother remained drug-involved and the Martins wanted to adopt him. His maternal grandmother contested custody, but after a clinical intervention she was assured of continuing contact with her grandson and she withdrew her objection to the adoption. Mr. and Mrs. Mar-

tin initially found the grandmother anxious and intrusive but the clinician encouraged them to continue reassuring and welcoming her. Stephen is now 7 and enjoys a warm relationship with his birth-grandmother and her relatives; it is anticipated that this arrangement will alleviate adoption-related confusion and sadness as they may arise in Stephen.

Two adolescent boys will now be described for whom the unavailability of birth parents, or information about them, played a significant role in difficulties. The first boy, age 13, had self-esteem problems and acting-out behavior:

Ari was referred for consultation by his boarding school for repeated stealing. He was the second of three children of his Israeli father and American-born Israeli mother, and the only adopted child. He had been placed with the family in early infancy by an adoption agency in the northeastern United States while the family lived there temporarily; they returned to Israel when Ari was 2 and he had lived there until age 12, when his parents sent him to a specialized boarding school in the same region of the U.S. where they had adopted him. At this time the family returned to the U.S. for another temporary stay, but to a location on the West Coast. Ari's diagnosis was attention deficit disorder with hyperactivity. School officials believed Ari had expulsion as his goal. Developmental information strongly supported the presence of A.D.D. Because Ari's behavior since toddlerhood had been markedly different from that of his siblings, the parents had been puzzled about whether this had any connection with his experience of adoption or their way of handling him; in this sense they were relieved to have a biological explanation. There were further complications with respect to Ari's adoptive status, however: By this time there was a marked emotional component around adoption in the family since Ari's difference was attributed by his siblings to his adoption, and they also capitalized on his not looking like them. Mr. and Mrs. Green had no knowledge of Ari's birth parents but assumed they were not Jewish since he was placed by a Catholic agency. Having Ari at boarding school appealed to them since his situation within the family was difficult; psychotherapy and medication had not helped sufficiently, and the school offered the possibility of a behavior change.

Ari was a handsome boy whose English was fluent though slightly accented. He listed as his three wishes "to be like other people", "to be happier and stronger", and "to not be adopted," then he added a fourth wish: "to be back in Oregon with my family." His self-portrait was well executed and represented a sailor with beret and mustache; he seemed to be representing himself in an idealized way as older, more mobile, and independent. He said he had been "wild like a cougar" in Israel until a doctor had given him medication. He said his siblings taunted him frequently saying "You're not one of us." Of his birth parents he said, "I don't know anything about my first parents. It could be a disaster; I'm not sure I want to know." Nevertheless he said he hoped to find his birth mother when he was 18. He cried when speaking about leaving his family in Oregon to travel cross-country to the school, and he cried again when asked what his good qualities were. "I'm not good for anything. I always had the feeling I was not a good kid when I was living with my parents. I felt like nobody liked me. My parents weren't proud of me. One thing I'm good at is putting myself down—I'm excellent at that for sure." When told that many kids come to feel better about adoption, he said, "Not me, I'll never get over it."

Ari was seen for four interviews and extensive telephone consultations took place with the school counselor and the parents. It was pointed out that Ari's associations in therapy clarified the nature of the stigmatization he felt: partly because of his behavior, and partly because of adopted status. The adopted aspect was further analyzed into the three major areas of loss described above, and Ari could relate parts of his experience to all three; further, he could see that his "A.D.D. behavior" had probably been exacerbated by his adoption-related discomfort. We spoke about theft as a symptom that often has specific meaning for an individual who feels cut off or deprived of something vitally important, and Ari could see that his stealing often occurred when he was feeling intolerably sad, and had the effect of at least partly relieving his sorrow. He expressed satisfaction at the clarifications we arrived at. With the school counselor, we stressed Ari's feelings of isolation and need for a sense of community. With his parents, we emphasized Ari's need for reassurance about family membership and suggested the possible connection between his adoption and the intensity of his hyperactive and impulsive symptoms.

Seen 6 months later, Ari, now 14, said his stealing was much decreased and he was happier. Discussion of adoption-related matters had taken place during a visit to his family, and transfer to a school much closer to the family's place of residence was being discussed. The presence of A.D.D. with hyperactivity clearly influenced Ari's situation in his family and contributed to his low self-esteem and his feeling of alienation from family members who did not understand his behavior; the family's handling of adoption further complicated matters since siblings were allowed to tease him about it, and his exile from the family confirmed his fears that he was not really one of them. One can speculate that if Ari's parents had been given concrete advice about how to minimize adoption-related discomfort, this period of his adolescence might have gone more smoothly and that perhaps placement so far from home might not have been resorted to.

In the next case, identity confusion and self-mutilating behavior occurred.

Scott was 14 when referred, also from a boarding school, where he had been deliberately cutting his arms and abrading his knuckles with sandpaper. He and his older brother had been adopted in infancy by wealthy parents who divorced when Scott was 7. He had been raised in Europe and was bilingual in English and French. He had average intellectual capacity but suffered from dyslexia and related learning disabilities. His mother, who lived in the U.S., was self-absorbed and prone to depression, and his father lived in Europe, where he ran the family business.

"Life's been pretty hard for me," Scott said. "I wonder if I belong anywhere. I'm worried about who my [birth] mother and father were, I went to New York in my last vacation and went to the adoption agency. They wouldn't give me the address." With much feeling he recited the few details the social worker had given him. "I wonder why they gave me up for adoption. I wonder what my mother looks like and sounds like. I was told my mother had brown hair and brown eyes. If I see someone like that I start to wonder. I want to ask if she had a kid and had it adopted. I wonder if my father is mean, or nice, or strict. I lie in my room and listen to music and get this weird dreamy feeling, thinking about going home [to his adoptive mother], seeing my dog and my friends and my girlfriend, then I get mad and start hurting myself." Then he mentioned his best friend at the school, Kevin. "I found out Kevin was adopted, too. He refused to follow the rules. He went to a psychologist and found out he was a battered child. He tried to hang himself once. Right after we found out we both were adopted we figured we might be real brothers, so we cut each other to mix the blood. We think about evil sometimes. If you see it from an adopted kid's view, you're trying to find your parents. Evil is what keeps you from finding them. Once you find your parents and the battle's over, you settle down and live a quiet life. I think my parents are in Canada, or in Germany. . . . ." Asked about his goals, he said, "I don't think about that too much. I want to stay young."

Scott was seen 13 times over a 10-month period. During this time he showed his drawings and a story he was writing; the story had a theme of good and evil and finding out secret knowledge. Three themes that preoccupied him were his learning disabilities, his adoption, and his parents' divorce. He was encouraged to think of himself as the hero of his own life story and to see himself as an individual with specific gifts and abilities that would serve him well in life. It was clear that his use of fantasy served at least two purposes—to connect him with his birth family and to protect him from the anxiety-provoking task of thinking about how to move forward in his life. He was given support for his feelings of sorrow about the parental divorce, for how burdened he felt by his learning disability, and for how worried he was about having a good future; he was also encouraged to view the cutoff from his birth parents as a sad event that was legitimately worthy of being mourned.

Scott was seen again some months after his sessions. His school had written to say that his attitude about school and work had improved, that he was a happier, more active participant in school, and that he had been elected to student council. Scott himself reported, "Things are better. My old friends left and I have new friends. I'm on the wrestling team. I've seen too many bad things. I'm trying to get my life started good now, to get on the right track." He indicated that adoption was no longer as great a preoccupation for him.

"Before, people would ask, 'What religion are you?' or 'What nationality?' and I'd say 'I don't know,' or 'I was raised as a Protestant,' or 'I'm adopted.' Now I figure I don't have to bring adoption into it, I can just tell them about what kind of person I am." As was the case with Ari, Scott demonstrated a connection between his learning disability and his feelings about adoption; in Scott's case, his learning handicap contributed to a feeling of being poorly equipped for life and of not having a good future, and this in turn tipped the balance toward a strong investment in fantasizing about his birth parents in the past and present, and about activities he might engage in to get back into contact with them. (It seems likely that, had more knowledge been available, Scott's sense of isolation might not have been so great.)

It is instructive that Scott construed as evil the forces that kept him from knowledge of his biological parents. To construe this as merely the product of a childhood good–evil mythologizing state of mind would be to miss an important point. While such fantasizing is certainly a developmentally typical activity for late-latency and early-adolescent children, in the case of adoptees it may be resorted to in the absence of specific information that might be much more satisfactory for the individual. While Scott's use of fantasy was adaptive (at least up to the point when he began using it in a self-destructive way), he clearly labeled his lack of genetic information as evil, and this value judgment, stated to his therapist, was in part a statement to the world about its treatment of him.

DEVELOPMENTAL INFLUENCES ON AN ADOPTEE'S INNER EXPERIENCE OF A BIRTH PARENT

As an adoptee matures, birth parents are experienced inwardly in many different ways. The preschool child may have relatively unformed ideas about a man and a woman out there somewhere. The primary school child, beginning around age 7 (Brodzinsky, Schechter, & Brodzinsky, 1986), has begun to understand that relinquishment and adoptive placement go together, and often has a clear perception that something went wrong; the birth parents are now imagined in greater detail. The adolescent boy interested in sports whose adoptive father is a sedentary intellectual may feel the need for a father more in tune with his own wish for athletic instruction and mentoring, and knowing his adoptive status may fantasize about a birth father who is closer to his heart's desire. The young adult entering happily upon marriage may wish altruistically that he or she could reassure an absent birth parent who may be imagined as sad or lonely and wondering whether the adoptee was succeeding in life; there might also be a wish for the birth parent's blessing. Individuals in adolescence or adult life have the capacity to know and care about others in a mature, intersubjective way, and adoptees at this stage may desire not only partial knowledge of a birth parent, but fuller knowledge or direct acquaintance. These differences in individuals' style of constructing the absent birth parent reflect changing developmental capacities in social perception (Kegan, 1982) as well as differences in personality.

Adoptees labor to form an internal working model (in Bowlby's phrase) of their birth parents. During elementary school years, this attempt goes on at the same time the child actively entertains family romance fantasies (Freud, 1908) of an ordinary sort, and the results often have a typical flavor that is illustrated by the following case example.

> Stephanie had been placed with her adoptive parents at 20 days. She was now 6 and entering first grade, but after a week refused to go. She said, "I miss my old teacher, Miss Ashton. I don't like going all day. I miss my mommy." At moments of friction, she would say, "I wish I had stayed with my real mother." Mr. and. Mrs. Davies were puzzled by the connection Stephanie was evidently making between her adoptive placement and her situation at school.

Miss Ashton, the kindergarten teacher, had been young, pretty and gentle. Mrs. Baxter, the new teacher, was somewhat older, kind but businesslike. Stephanie surprised her mother by asking, "Could Mrs. Baxter take me away from you the way you took me away from the young girl who had me in her stomach?"

In the therapist's office she said, "I don't like school at all and I can't help it. I don't want to go. I want to go back to kindergarten, and that is the trouble with me. I really love Miss Ashton." Going to the hand puppets she mused, "I'm going to do a puppet show about how I feel. The teacher takes me away from my mother. I'm gonna put on Adoption if I can."

Putting a mouse puppet on her hand, Stephanie announced theatrically, "My name is Squeaky! I'm gonna have a baby!" Then she remarked aside, "This is the part where they have to adopt. This is hard." She enacted a scene in which a mother dog stole a baby from the mother mouse after a struggle. Showing the baby, she made the dog say, "This is Squeakette. I stole it from the mommy mouse." She invited her parents into the office to observe a repetition of this dramatic action.

Stephanie was seen in short-term therapy. One month later she disclosed a secret that she thought the therapist might laugh at: she had really loved her kindergarten teacher, Miss Ashton, and at times she thought Miss Ashton was her real mother. The therapist said he was not surprised by this and didn't think it was anything to laugh at; he supported her difficulty in separating from Miss Ashton and told Stephanie that when she was in kindergarten, she had been able to imagine she had both of her mothers at the same time. She replied, "Three mothers!", implying that in addition to her adoptive mother she had her beloved teacher, about whom she spun fantasies, and also her unknown birth mother whom she couldn't locate but who was frequently in her thoughts. After a few more sessions the school attendance problem resolved and Stephanie was ready to proceed on her own.

For less fortunate children, the developmental need at times may be for *permission to attach elsewhere,* by means of what might be called definitive disillusionment. This was the case with Michael, age 13, who had been placed with his adoptive family at age 3 after longstanding serious neglect (Mason, 1991). His parents had found him distant and uncooperative almost from the beginning, and this was getting worse. He tormented his sister, did poorly at school, and often wandered off aimlessly on his bicycle for the better part of the day. Individual and family therapy did little to modify a continuing preoccupation with his birth mother, which he expressed openly, and it was felt that he had a painful dilemma involving dual emotional attachments that he perceived as conflicting. In order to diminish his intense involvement with fantasy about his birth mother, his therapist discussed with Michael and Mr. and Mrs. Byrnes the possibility of arranging a meeting between Michael and his birth mother. This was done after painstaking preliminary arrangements and the interview was recorded on videotape (H. Leichtman, personal communication, 1991). The hope was for Michael to experience what his birth mother was actually like, to have some of his early memories validated in conversation with her, to obtain her permission for him to become a committed member of his adoptive family, and to have a better cognitive and emotional understanding of how his placement had come about. The meeting was intensely moving for both participants.

Michael's birth mother emerged clearly as depressed and depleted, but was able to give Michael full permission to live a happy and rewarding life with the Byrnes family. After the meeting, Michael was even more preoccupied for several months and viewed the tape many times, but thereafter he showed much greater acceptance of his adoptive parents and willingness to abide by their rules, while at the same time he seemed more comfortable with himself and his life.

ONGOING LIFE EVENTS: THEIR INFLUENCE ON THE VIVIDNESS OF AN ADOPTEE'S INTEREST IN BIRTH PARENTS AND ON THE INTENSITY OF MOTIVATION TO SEEK KNOWLEDGE OR CONTACT

It is common for adult adoptees to put a search into motion after the death of a beloved person. At such times an individual may feel the need for nurturance to make up for what was lost; the person may also feel the occasion to carry out an activity that has always been of interest but was never compelling enough to claim precedence over daily routines. The possibility also exists that search had been forbidden, explicitly or implicitly, by the deceased. The following case example illustrates at least the first two of these ideas; it also illustrates the fourth point about sustaining fantasy, below, and the fifth point about a permitted locus of thought, and will be discussed under those headings as well.

> Beth S, a 38-year-old unmarried medical secretary, was evaluated because of anxiety that arose principally at times when she was about to see members of her birth family or was thinking about her relationship with them. She later also developed obsessive-compulsive symptoms, eating difficulties and somatic complaints that arose in the same context.
>
> Beth had suddenly become interested in locating her birth mother several years before, after a casual reference by an admiring friend at a health club: "You have nice legs. I'll bet your mother has, too." Beth had grown up as the only child of an Armenian American couple, but was told during grade school that her biological family was Italian. Her mother was warm but a great worrier, and her father gruff, silent, and hardworking. Her parents never encouraged conversation about her adoption nor about her feelings or ideas with respect to her birth parents. The family lived in an apartment in a working-class town near Boston in which much of the adolescent social life was carried out by hanging out on the street. She had a number of friends but, partly through deficient self-esteem and concomitant reluctance to plan, she allowed herself to become sexually involved, got pregnant, and had an abortion. She completed high school as part of a close-knit group of friends. After graduation she became a skilled and successful medical secretary and receptionist.
>
> At times of loneliness within her family, Beth would remember that her birth family was Italian, and when troubled by her mother's anxiety or her father's grumpiness she would fantasize about big family get-togethers on Sunday at which

lasagna and other Italian foods were served in a warm and spontaneous atmosphere. She had several opportunities to marry but remained single for reasons unclear even to herself. As she entered her 30s she began to worry about whether she would ever have children, and regretted her abortion. The immediate context of her search did not seem to include a recent loss by death (though her father, with whom she was not close, had died several years before); rather, the main stimulus seemed to be that she had come to seriously regret a number of life choices and was confronting the possibility that she would never have the loving family life that she had always hoped for.

After meeting her birth mother (whom she found without difficulty) she soon met a number of other birth relatives, and her life took on a new cast: she always took care to dress her best and took along a special present so that she would make a good impression on whichever relative she was about to see. She found that they resembled her physically in an uncanny way, but their behavior was incomprehensible; although they all seemed interested in meeting and knowing Beth, they showed a consistent lack of warmth and an insensitivity to social cues. For example, visiting a half-sister, she was not offered anything to eat or drink although she had brought a gift and dinnertime was approaching. Often birth relatives would telephone to propose introducing her to other members of the family, but after a time she became ambivalent about answering the phone. Ultimately she allowed the contacts to wither, and then experienced a clinical depression with features of anxiety and panic as well as obsessive-compulsive and hypochondriacal symptoms. A vivid expression of her dilemma was her association to the film *Invasion of the Body Snatchers*, in which individuals who appeared human turned out to have a hidden, destructive agenda. Eventually Beth realized that she had had her own agenda in meeting her birth family and had believed unconsciously that they would provide wonderful nurturance to their long-lost relative; the dashing of these hopes had led to a reexperiencing of childhood sadness and feelings of abandonment, and only with difficulty was she able to regain her equilibrium.

It is likely that Beth's vulnerability arose to a large extent from the fact that while growing up she had never been helped to experience in consciousness the sadness or grief about absent birth parents that later manifested itself in her fantasy about a warm, accepting Italian family. During her adolescence it might be said that she did not know she was sad, and instead acted out her sadness and lack of connection by means of an early, unwanted pregnancy. It was only later, after her less than satisfying contacts with her birth family, that she was able to grieve for relationships that never were and, apparently, never were to be.

SUSTAINING FANTASY, FAMILY ROMANCE FANTASY, AND THE FANTASIES OF ADOPTEES

People differ in their use of reverie, make-believe and fantasy, but all children and adolescents use these modalities of thought in the course of development. Tom Sawyer's mock battle with Huck Finn in the woods is a well-known example—the quintessence of play, a shared make-believe, but also a rehearsing of valiant deeds, helping these two preadolescent boys to reassure themselves that they were equal to the challenges the world would present them with. Another use of fantasy that is essentially nonelective is the common *family romance fantasy* as described by Freud (1909) in which a child imagines that one or both parents are really exalted people and the known parents merely substitutes. This is a jack-of-all-trades among the defenses of childhood and serves to shore up the child's self-esteem at critical moments, and to protect parent–child relations at times when a child's disillusionment with parents is prominent.

Sustaining fantasy (A. M. Rizzuto, personal communication,1985; Zelin, 1983) occurs in adult life as well as in childhood and represents an individual's attempt to remain connected to a powerful idea of personal efficacy and success in the face of discouraging circumstances. The "vision quest" of young Plains Indian males is an example. Many myths (Campbell, 1949), children's stories and fairy tales demonstrate the importance of an imaginary mentor (the wise old woman or man; the fairy godmother; in the Star Wars films, the defeated but still powerful Obiwan Kenobi and the dwarflike wizard Yoda). A current example is the orphaned teen-ager in the television series Seaquest DSV, whose protection by an adult officer allows him to live on a submarine and demonstrate his precocious scientific powers. Often a family romance fantasy also has sustaining qualities in childhood. With the contraction and mobility of the nuclear family and the limited access to grandparents, real-life nonparental mentors are in short supply and the importance of sustaining fantasy may be greater now than ever before.

Adoptees engage as often as other children in creating family romance fantasies. The raw material for these, as with nonadopted children, comes mostly from the aspects of the caretaking parents that are not currently disowned by the child. Adoptees commonly have a foreshortened experience with family romance fantasies, however, because no sooner does the child remember adoption than the family romance fantasy (aimed at protecting the child's relationship with his caretakers) takes on other qualities—often a sad reflection that "indeed, I really do have other parents that I don't know." The child may then abandon the original agenda of the fantasy and become preoccupied by the true nature of the relinquishing parents, for their own sake and for the sake of the child's own self-regard (which exists in an injured state because of relinquishment and any other aspects of the adoptive situation that may be troublesome; see Nickman, 1985).

In late adolescence and adult life, adoptees' fantasies about their birth parents, and their potential connection with them, may take on qualities of a sustaining fantasy as the individual gradually crafts a plan—which may be a plan to search and carry out certain transactions, or a plan *not* to search because one does not need or wish to do so. In either case, the maturing adoptee is working on self-definition by taking a position about the piece of self that has to do with the absent others; in either case, the adoptee can salvage self-esteem by turning passive to active and formulating a plan. The fantasy involves self-completion, whether or not it includes a search and a meeting. In the case of Beth, described above, the fantasy of her birth parents as a warm Italian family had sustaining qualities as she grew up with a degree of family conflict. It has already been suggested, however, that Beth's upbringing was lacking in one specific area that was perhaps more important than her parents' personality flaws: their failure to encourage the expression of thoughts and feelings about adoption, and their failure or inability to give Beth any knowledge of her birth family beyond the idea that they were Italian. This points to an important aspect of fantasy in adoptees that professionals have come to respect—namely, the idea that fantasy may be useful at times, especially in early childhood and when it originates in the child rather than the adoptive parents, yet it is always better, from the adoptee's point of view, to have specific information. Miller-Havens (Chapter 16, this volume) describes fantasizing as one type of searching behavior that, along with searching in reality, serves the developmentally essential task of facilitating mourning.

One therefore arrives at a mixed view of sustaining fantasy in adoptees. To the extent that it is a universal phenomenon, it serves the particular needs of adoptees as it does those of people in general; but to the extent that it is required because of a lack of the kind of knowledge that most people have as a birth right, it can be seen as the adoptee's effort to make the most of a deprivation. This point will be discussed further in the next section.

ACTUAL KNOWLEDGE VERSUS A PERMITTED LOCUS OF THOUGHT

As described above, some investigators view adoptees' difficulties as arising partly from their foreclosure from vital information about, or direct contact with, their progenitors. While in full agreement with this position, this author will now suggest that insofar as thought and fantasy serve an adaptive purpose for growing adoptees, that purpose can be defeated by failure of the adoptive parents to recognize its importance.

The point at issue is that any important experience in childhood ideally takes place at the interface between the child and the nurturing parents. The parents assist the child by providing emotional support as well as whatever cognitive framework is necessary for the child to assimilate the experience. The word dialogue symbolizes this process, which is just as essential for a child undergoing sutures in an emergency room as it is for a child coping with the long-term consequences of adoption, chronic illness, parental divorce or death. With or without knowledge of birth parents or contact with them, a young adoptee requires the mediation of the nurturing parents to know what to do with the feelings and thoughts engendered by the fact of adoption. A spatial metaphor may prove useful: once adoption is established as one room in the house of a child's mind, the adoptive parents, who introduced the idea to the child, bear some responsibility for looking into that room from time to time to see who or what may have taken up residence there and what their child's internal guests may be like.

We have used the word locus, meaning place, to refer to the complex set of memories, thoughts, emotions and perceptions relating to birth parents and circumstances of adoption. (In later-placed adoptees, actual memories of the preplacement era form a nucleus for this construct.) What one has been told joins with what one remembers or imagines. The locus and the adoptive parents' awareness of it constitute a unit. A deficiency in parents' awareness of this locus and its importance to the child is potentially causative of problems, as suggested by the following case vignette.

> Kevin, age 14, was one of four adolescent brothers ranging in age from 12 to 19. Kevin and his brother Charlie, age 16, had been adopted in early infancy, while the other two boys had been born to the parents. Mr. Cooper was a construction supervisor, successful at his work, who was warm and participatory with his sons but spoke little. Mrs. Cooper had more education than her husband and was employed part-time as a nurse. Also a warm individual, she was more talkative than her husband. All the boys except Kevin had done well in school and in community activities, sometimes rising to positions of leadership.

Kevin came to clinical attention after numerous episodes of truancy and theft. From the beginning of adolescence he had spoken of himself in negative terms. When asked how he envisioned his birth parents, he first denied thinking about them with any frequency and then said, "She was a slut. He's an asshole; he's probably in jail." No source of these negative judgments could be found in the history of the family's dialogue with Kevin about his adoption. Mr. and Mrs. Cooper had introduced the knowledge of adoption early (at age 3 to 4) and had presented it in a positive light; in dealing with their children they claimed never to have made any discrimination between the adopted and the nonadopted boys, and no reason was found to doubt them. They had promised Kevin and Charlie that they would help them search at age 18 if they wished. Mr. and Mrs. Cooper had not initiated any mention of either boy's birth parents after the boy had reached school age. On the rare occasions when the boys brought the subject up, Mrs. Cooper had tried to respond fully to each boy's expressed thoughts, which had never struck her as unusual or alarming, but she had never gone beyond direct answers to the boys' questions. There had been no shared fantasizing between parents and boys about the parents or their qualities or motivations or attitudes toward the boys, nor had there been any attempt to obtain specific information. Mr. and Mrs. Cooper shared an unspoken belief that for them to bring up adoption to either boy would be intrusive and make the boy feel different from his nonadopted brothers.

Psychiatric and psychological evaluation of Kevin revealed no condition amenable to pharmacotherapy and no specific learning or attentional problems; he emerged from the diagnostic process with the general impressions of "oppositional-defiant disorder" and "conduct disorder," and the only suggested treatment was therapy to enhance Kevin's vision of himself and his future and to increase his behavioral options.

Kevin was repeatedly offered psychotherapy, but his macho stance and rebelliousness precluded his accepting or making use of it. By age 20 he was known to juvenile and adult authorities and was well launched on a career of drug use, dealing, and petty crime, to the anguish of his parents, who wondered how one of their four boys could have done so badly while the others had done so well. This haunting question could be rephrased: Why did Kevin handle his opportunities so differently from his brother Charlie? Insufficiency of the data precludes an adequate answer, but it seems likely that matters of temperament played a part. According to the history provided by the family, Kevin's nature was from the beginning intense and passionate, and he tended to view things in black and white, while his older brother (not biologically related) had a more relaxed attitude in general and toward his adoption in particular. Had more information been available about Kevin's birth parents, it is possible that an anchor in concrete facts would have helped him to see himself independently, rather than as embedded permanently in a mysterious matrix of bad behavior. It seems equally likely that even given a paucity of specific data, Mr. and Mrs. Cooper could still have intervened more effectively with their son if they had had better guidance from the beginning concerning adoptees' needs to have an ongoing dialogue with their parents: a dialogue about reasons for relinquishment and about children's tendency to interpret it in ways that reflect negatively on themselves and their personal worth. It might have helped Kevin if his parents had been able to help him fantasize about his birth parents, neither disparaging nor idealizing them, but rather presenting them as individuals who were sadly unknown to the Cooper family, who were probably sad themselves that they did not know Kevin and the Coopers, and who had various interesting personal qualities that Kevin might think and wonder about. As Kevin matured and was less satisfied by fantasy, Mr. and Mrs. Cooper might have introduced reality into the fantasy system by offering to try to obtain more concrete information.

CONCLUSIONS—THE ARROW OF TIME: CONTRASTS AND PARALLELS WITH BEREAVEMENT

On initial reflection, it might appear that bereavement and adoption have one thing in common—that whatever relationship exists is in the past. Closer inspection reveals that the reverse is true: adoption contains the possibility of earthly reunion, while only heavenly meeting is possible after a death. In adoption, time runs in two directions: back to the moment of biologic unity, and forward to the time of imagined meeting. These two moments—one historical, the other potentially historical—constitute another argument for regarding the adoptee–birth parent nexus as a kind of relationship.

One practical consequence of this relationship aspect is that just as bereaved children engage in constructive activity with regard to a lost relative to preserve the remembered past, adoptees also engage in construction for a variety of reasons: self-esteem, self-definition, existential grounding, empathy for birth parents, preparation for an eventual meeting, and so forth. The component activities of such construction on the part of adoptees are as easily identified as those described for the bereaved (Chapter 6, this volume) and include inquiring, fantasizing, dreaming, planning, and others. Correspondingly, some adoptive parents (though not as many as might be wished) have strategies of their own for assisting their child to form an inner representation of birth parents that is consistent with the child's well-being. They provide information when available; they withhold information as long as they believe such withholding to be beneficial; they encourage children to view birth parents' motivation in a realistic but positive light; they offer to help children search at maturity.

From a formal standpoint, the adoptee families are oriented more toward the future and the bereaved families toward the past, but from the standpoint of parental nurturance there is a sense in which it does not matter. In both cases, what is at issue for the child is to obtain from caretakers a cognitive and emotional map of the world that makes sense and points in positive directions for development. One might liken the parental task, in part, to one of translation or interpretation. The parent and child are confronted by a naked fact that requires understanding by the child in a way that is consistent with the child's best capacities for growth. The parent's task is to foster that understanding, and the language of the process is most often the language of relationship.

REFERENCES

Brodzinsky, D. M., Schechter, D. E., & Brodzinsky, A. B. (1986). Children's knowledge of adoption, developmental changes and implications for adjustment. In R. Ashmore and D. Brodzinsky (Eds.), *Thinking about the family: Views of parents and children* (pp. 205–232). Hillside, NJ: Erlbaum.

Brodzinsky, D. M. (1990). A stress and coping model of adoption adjustment. In D. M. Brodzinsky & M. D. Schechter (Eds.), *The psychology of adoption*. New York: Oxford University Press.

Campbell, J. (1949). *The hero with a thousand faces*. New York: Pantheon.

Freud, S. (1908). Family romances. *Standard edition of the complete psychological works of Sigmund Freud* (Volume 9, pp. 237–241). London: Hogarth Press.

Kegan, R. (1982). *The evolving self: Problem and process in human development*. Cambridge, MA: Harvard University Press.

Mason, E. A. (1991). *Reunion as a therapeutic strategy: A teenage adoptee encounters his birth mother*. (Videotape). University Park, PA: Penn State AudioVisual Services.

Nickman, S. L. (1985). Losses in adoption: The need for dialogue. In A. Solnit, R. Eissler, & P. Neubauer (Eds.), *The psychoanalytic study of the child* (Vol. 40, pp. 365–378). New Haven, CT: Yale University Press.

Tessman, L. H. (1984). The quest for the wanted absent parent in children of the divorced or deceased. In C. Nadelson & D. Polonsky (Eds.), *Marriage and divorce: A contemporary perspective* (pp. 207–224). New York: Guilford Press.

Zelin, M., et al. (1983). The sustaining fantasy questionnaire: Measurement of sustaining fantasies in psychiatric patients. *Journal of Personality Assessment, 47*(4), 427–439.

Chapter 16

Grief and the Birth Origin Fantasies of Adopted Women

Susan Miller-Havens

I thought about my two mothers. I wanted to be the best of both.
—Miller-Havens, 1990

No one escapes loss. When your beloved does not love you anymore or the body of a loved one is lowered into the ground, compelling evidence is provided that the living relationships are gone, although perhaps not over. Historically society has helped its members deal with the inevitable loss of relationships and deaths of loved ones through such means as religious rituals or reminiscing among family and friends. These gatherings are intended to facilitate a natural process of grieving by acknowledging the loss, bearing the pain, and putting the deceased into perspective (Semrad & Chasin, 1966). This book attempts to refute the idea that grief resolution is only complete if the relationship with the object is terminated. It challenges the theory, as do proponents of relational work (Miller, 1976; Sutherland, 1980), that autonomy is the primary psychological goal in life.

In addition, it provides an opportunity to look at other kinds of losses not typically thought of in this context. Adoptees, for instance, have lost their birth parents, but are not necessarily expected to grieve, to experience a connection to their family of origin, nor to develop inner representations.

ADOPTEES AND LOSS

Of the some 6 million adult adoptees in the United States today, a majority were adopted in infancy. It is reasonable to wonder how losses in infancy might affect an adoptee. Are adoptees in fact bereft? After all, adoption is intended to make a contribution to the lives of those most closely involved. The birth mother, without support to raise her child, trusts that another family can and will accept that responsibility. The adopting couple builds a family and the adopted child may acquire a secure situation in which to grow. Until recently, adoption practitioners and adoptive parents were not encouraged to think about an equally important issue that unites the triad—loss; it seemed too negative. (Reitz & Watson, 1992). But the reality is that in most cases the adoptive parents are adopting because they are unable to bear children. This is experienced by them as a profound loss

(Glazer & Cooper, 1988). Birth mothers and birth fathers may have made an informed decision not to parent in order to serve the best interest of the child, while research on relinquishment points to their difficulty in dealing with loss, as manifest in a variety of delayed grief reactions (Deykin, Campbell, & Patti, 1984; Deykin, Campbell, & Ryan, 1988; Silverman, 1981).

Adoptees have lost the mother to whom they were physically bonded in utero and post partum (Bowlby, 1980). Many have also lost at least one foster mother. Recent research indicates that prenatal and postnatal environment contributes to the shaping of the nervous system (Hundert, 1989) Psychological blows, such as early loss, may leave a residue or mark on the nervous system that is later affectually experienced as something missing. Research that connects the physiological to the psychological strengthens Tomkins' (1968) argument that infants do not need cognition or awareness to experience affect; an idea is not necessary in order to have a feeling. The feeling of loss may be salient in the lives of children who have lost a parent early through death or divorce, but the information given to facilitate grieving is decidedly different from what is available to most adoptees. Traditional adoption practice has utilized a sealed record system in an attempt to protect the privacy of the birth mother and to decrease the possibility of social embarrassment for the adopting parents and the child due to infertility and illegitimacy (Burgess, 1977). This closure, however, essentially removes the opportunity to utilize facts indicating whom the adoptee has lost. Children of the closed system usually have been told about their birth parents and the circumstance of their birth, albeit in varying degrees of detail and truth. Although adoptees are often told that their birth parents died or were unable to keep them, few birth parents were or are deceased and fewer still willingly relinquished their babies (Brodzinsky & Schechter, 1990; Deykin, Campbell & Patti, 1984).

The problem for adoptees is that a natural grief process cannot get off the ground. If there is no body to bury, if no one knows if the person is actually dead or has an interest in reviving the early relationship, mourning cannot take its course. Utilizing data from research on the birth origin fantasies of adopted women (Miller-Havens, 1990), the author has argued that adoptees live "suspended" in various conscious or unconscious attempts to deal with early losses. Some adoptees never ask about their birth origins, claim never to fantasize about them, and never actively search for their birth family (Schechter & Bertocci, 1990). The level of grieving and searching activity partly depends on how comfortable the adoptive family is with acknowledging the importance of the loss. Can they talk about the birth mother without becoming threatened or defensive? Do they believe a child adopted in infancy has sustained a loss?

If the birth mother is valued, searching behavior, whether in fantasy or reality, is driven by the need to complete the natural process of grieving (Reitz & Watson, 1992). This activity is similar to that of orphans described by Bowlby (1952), who searched for their missing mothers with their eyes and ears. It is also akin to the families of soldiers missing in action, who still today comb the hillsides of Vietnam for body parts to bury. Grieving does not proceed until the search is over (Bowlby, 1980). In clinical situations it is striking that so many practitioners fail to recognize what the searching behavior of adult adoptees might really mean. By insisting that they get on with grief resolution, some therapists are asking the adoptee to recall what they may know about the circumstances of their relinquishment, to get in touch with the pain and perhaps anger over what might have been, to review the facts they know about their birth family, and then put whatever relationship they had with the birth family into perspective. This is impossible without the help of a completed search.

Some adoptees are encouraged to deny any thoughts of loss or simply feel too loyal and too grateful to their adoptive parents to think about their birth families. But even those who are able to acknowledge their loss struggle over time to create an inner representation of their biological parents, their birth mother in particular. A mental image of the birth parents evolves, depending partly on what adoptees are told about their birth origins. These attempts at gaining an intrapsychic equilibrium are illustrated in my research on adopted women who search for their origins. This group of women, by virtue of their divergent developmental paths, provide an accidental experiment of nature. They have both a biological mother and a nonbiological mother. These women are born of one mother, raised by another. This sets in motion a dual identification with two mothers (Miller-Havens, 1988), as well as the creation of complex inner representations. One way to look at those representations is through birth origin fantasies (Miller-Havens, 1990).

FANTASY FORMATION

Psychology has long recognized fantasy formation as a coping mechanism used against painful affects (Freud, 1917/1957; Sandler & Nagera, 1963). Specific to this study, psychoanalytic theory suggests that prepubertal children create a set of fantasies about other, "better" parents in reaction to the dissolution of the idealization of their parents. Adoption literature reports that adoptees who do not know their birth parents may fantasize about them as early as age 3 (Farber, 1977) and throughout their lives (Rosenweig-Smith, 1988). Unlike nonadoptees, the fantasies are not necessarily about a "better" set of parents (Miller-Havens, 1990). Throughout the adoption literature there is a disharmony among researchers as to the function and meaning of the birth origin fantasies of adoptees. One group claims that the fantasies of birth origin are enmeshed in the classical family romance construct (Clothier, 1943; Glenn, 1985–86; Schechter, 1964; Simon & Senturia, 1966). The other claims that they are contained in a separate system that exists in addition to the family romance (Lawton & Gross, 1964; Miller-Havens, 1990; Stein & Hoopes,1985). There is some evidence that adoptees' fantasies of birth origin may reflect their concerns at a particular developmental stage and that gender difference becomes evident in both the quantity and content of fantasy images (Brodzinksy, 1984; Farber, 1977; Harper, 1984).

To date there are no detailed descriptive studies on the fantasies of female adoptees as separate from male adoptees. While clinicians agree that what children are told about the circumstances of their births will have an impact on the fantasies produced, correlations between the two genders have not been studied extensively.

Those researchers studying women's sense of self and women in relationships (Gilligan, 1982; Miller, 1976, 1988) have not attempted to study a group of women such as those in the sample presented in this chapter. On some level, all adopted women have experienced the loss of their birth mothers, and many have lost at least one foster mother. Female adoptees frequently report relationships with their adoptive mothers that include gratefulness and loyalty. They are thankful to have been adopted rather than remaining an orphan, and often empathize with their adoptive mothers' inability to bear children. For many, it has been hard to come to the decision to search for their birth origins, lest they hurt the relationship with the adoptive mother.

The study presented here has been informed by 25 years of clinical experience and 10 years of research on the psychosocial development of adoptees. The author chose to narrow the focus by using a *non*clinical population consisting of only one gender. Three earlier pilot studies contain narrative and nominal data that are the basis for the measures used in this study. In the largest pilot, 80% of the 281 participants reported having fantasies about their birth origins. Themes and categories quickly emerged in this pilot that reflected two main dimensions or core categories of the fantasies; they have been labeled themes of *disconnection* and *connection*. Disconnection fantasies describe why the individual thinks she was relinquished by her birth mother and connection fantasies refer to physical or psychological features of the birth mother. The fantasies reported in this study shed light on the female adoptee's personal wish to make peace with her archaic sense of self, a self that relates in reality to the adoptive mother and in fantasy to the birth mother. In addition, a much stronger light is shed on themes of connection and disconnection central to all development.

THE DATA

The research was organized around seven questions:

1   Why do adopted women from a nonclinical population search for their birth origins?
2   Do adopted females who search for their origins report having had birth origin fantasies?
3   What are the birth origin fantasies of adopted females?
4   Do the images reveal components that are overlapping or additional to those described in the psychoanalytic literature on birth origin fantasies as defined in the family romance construct?
5   Is there an association between the age at which an individual is adopted and the content of her fantasy?

6   Is there an association between what an adoptee recalls she was told about her birth origins and what she fantasizes?

7   Are there themes in the fantasies of those adopted women who search for their birth origins that are similar to those reported by researchers in women's development?

The coding scheme used for this study is based on the grounded theory of qualitative data as described by Miles and Huberman (1984, pp. 56–65) and Strauss (1987). Checklist responses account for 80% of what the subjects reported fantasizing. In comparison, 89.7% of what the subjects recall being told about why they were relinquished (disconnection) and who their birth mother was (connection) was recorded in the checklists. Statements in the narratives that were not on the checklists were quite readily coded using the coding scheme developed for this study. Intercoder reliability was highest on the main themes ($p = .0001$) and then varied for the coding of more difficult categories such as character traits.

Questionnaires with a cover letter were mailed to 147 female members of The Adoption Connection in Peabody, Massachusetts, and The Adoption Forum in Philadelphia, all of whom had learned about the project through their group newsletters or directors. They were asked to respond in writing using both a narrative and a checklist format. In order to avoid suggesting content to the participants, they were asked to write out fantasies about their birth origins first. Then they were asked to respond to checklists about fantasies that had been derived from participants' responses in the earlier pilots. The same format was used when asking them to record what they had been told about their birth parents.

Fifty-seven percent responded. Their responses have external validity in the nonclinical population of female adoptees who choose to search for their origins. This study is not generalizable to the entire adoptee population.

Of the 84 women who participated in this study, 39% ($n = 32$) had completed their search for their birth origins. Sixty-one percent ($n = 51$) had not completed their search. The age at which the individuals in this sample were adopted varies from birth to 12 years. Sixty-five percent were adopted before 6 months and 35% after 6 months. Forty-five percent were adopted between birth and 2 months. All were adopted in a closed-record adoption system with little or no access to information about their birth origins. Because adoption has largely been an option for middle or upper class Caucasians, there are no participants of color in this study. Eighty percent have had some college education and 67% have jobs that require skill or advanced degrees.

RESULTS

A total of 1,954 responses made by the women who participated were recorded and coded from written narratives and checklists (a questionnaire return rate of 57%). These responses consist of two types: (a) what the adoptee recalls being told about her birth origins, and (b) what she fantasizes about her birth origins. The total fantasy rate reported in the sample was 1,379. The mean number of fantasies was 16.4. The standard deviation from the mean was 8.5. Rates ranged from no fantasies to 36 per subject.

Why Do Adopted Women From a Nonclinical Population Search for Their Birth Origins?

As shown in Table 1, participants reported a variety of reasons for searching, both in their written narratives and in their responses to the checklist provided in the questionnaire.

The evidence in this study supports the hypothesis that a motivation for searching can be a wish for "sameness" (Stein & Hoopes, 1985); however, more detailed descriptions of that wish were revealed. Searching to find someone who looks like the adoptee and to find someone with the same personality predominated the responses. The wish for "sameness," as reported by the subjects in this sample, extends not only to finding someone who physically looks like the adoptee, but someone with the same personality, character, or values. One subject wrote in a narrative about why she searched: "When I was in college, and then

Table 1   Reasons Given to Search for Birth Origins

Reason	Number positive responses indicated in checklists/ Total responding to item/ % of total
To feel connected to my beginnings	77/78/98.7
To know my medical history	78/80/95.0
To let my birth mother know that I am all right	65/74/91.4
To find someone who looked like me	63/74/85.1
To be sure my birth mother was all right	47/63/74.6
To find out why my mother gave me up	52/71/73.2
To find someone with my personality	47/66/71.2
Because of unhappiness in my adoptive situation	17/59/30.5
Other (a)	14/20/70.0

Additional responses in the narratives	
Assorted reasons to search in the narrative (b)	24/27
To give my children knowledge of their heredity	5/5
To solve the puzzle of my life	4/4
To tell her I understand	3/3
To feel at peace with myself	2/2

later on, I just wanted to connect with someone who was like me because I was sure she was just like me."

Empirical evidence from this study contradicts Aumend and Barrett's (1983) theory that adoptees who search are unhappy. Aumend and Barrett argue that adoptees who are interested in searching "report negative feelings toward the adoptive parents and an ignorance of information about birth parents" (p. 37). The present evidence also contradicts findings in other adoption literature where researchers claim that searchers are unhappy or looking for something better (Sobol & Cardiff, 1983; Sorosky, Baran, & Pannor, 1975; Triseliotis, 1973). This research verifies the findings of Geissinger (1984), who found that three quarters of the adults in his study who searched revealed a positive bond with their adoptive parents. Seventy percent of the women in the present study responded that they did not search because they were unhappy. Of those who included unhappiness in reasons for searching, they all cited other motivations as well. The fantasy that their birth parents would be better parents was minimal and the ages at which they were adopted varied.

The reasons to search for birth origins reported by the women in this study confirm the findings often reported in adoption literature (Campbell et al., 1991; Reitz & Watson, 1992; Warner, 1986). The need to obtain a medical history and to find out why the adoptee was relinquished are common responses. However, 98% of the women in the study cited a desire to feel connected to their beginnings as a motivation to search. The magnitude of this finding was not predicted. Although the descriptors "curiosity," "to fill a void," and "to find an identity" (Kowal & Schilling, 1985) are commonly used in adoption literature on search, the women in the pilot study and those in the present study did not describe their interest in searching in those terms. For instance, they used the word "disconnection" rather than void. They did not appear to be writing about the emptiness a void suggests. They describe a disconnection—a severing or a separation. There are missing pieces and unanswered questions. The search is not seen as something that will fill the void, but rather as a way to *reconnect* with someone who has been lost. For instance, a high percentage of the subjects responded that they searched "to let my birth mother know that I am all right" or "to be sure my birth mother is all right".

The subjects quoted here suggest that searching may be a way to reconnect with the birth mother, to be back in relationship with her.

I searched because I miss her. I am totally disconnected. I have always been an outsider. Amazed at families, blood ties, people who look like other people, etc.

I wanted to get to know her and have a relationship with her and her with me.

The main reasons that I searched were to *face* my mother, see what she looked like and that she was alright. I wanted to be *acknowledged* by her and I wanted her to tell me the full story of how I came into the world. I wanted to know that she cared about me.

Do Adopted Females Who Search for Their Origins Report Having Had Birth Origin Fantasies?

The adopted women in this study reported that they had birth origin fantasies. Ninety-six percent reported that those fantasies were about their birth mother, a slightly higher finding than that of Rosenzweig-Smith (1988). The fantasy rate for images about the birth father was considerably lower, about 54%. The fantasy rate for birth mother and birth father as a couple was about 33%. This may reflect the fact that the birth father is often seen as the one who abandons or about whom there is little or no information.

A 31-year-old adoptee writing about her birth father represents in her narrative components frequently found in this sample and others that refer to the birth father's role in the relinquishment.

> He was brought into the fantasy as the one who upon finding out she was pregnant forced her to give me up. She was young and had no money or support of any kind. Only he could have saved her and me but he didn't. He abandoned us both. He broke her heart when he turned away. She went on living but without the man she loved and the child that was born of that love. She never had a one night stand or was raped, although I did wonder that sometimes.

What Are the Birth Origin Fantasies of Adopted Females?

The most frequent fantasy images appear to be those that concern the birth mother's character: her moral, psychological, and social attitudes. For example, these women wrote,

> She was a strong political activist who was courageous and would take great risks to promote social justice.

> She gave me up because she was young, she had no money, because she did not want to try, and because she didn't like children.

Fantasies about the birth mother's physical appearance, why she was unable to keep the adoptee, and what the birth mother has done in her life over time are reported frequently in this study. Fantasies about what the birth mother has done over time is a category that has been eluded to in some studies, but appears with more clarity in the reports of these women.

The fantasies are coded both from statements about what the adoptee thinks the birth mother has done herself over time and her ideas about the birth mother's thoughts regarding the child she relinquished. Sixty-six of the 84 subjects responded to questions in the checklists or wrote in the narratives what they imagined their birth mother did herself or what she thought about the adoptee over the years since relinquishment. Overall, 78% of the group reported a total of 224 fantasy images relating to what the birth mother does or thinks over time. The mean was 2.6 with a range of 0–9 images reported per subject. This is in striking contrast to what the group recalled being *told* about what the birth mother has done since relinquishment. Only one subject reported being told anything and that was simply one statement.

Speculating that fantasy formation for the adopted woman serves to connect her with the birth mother or to be in relationship with her, if only in fantasy, the images about what the birth mother does or thinks about over time are of particular interest to those researchers investigating the paradigm put forth in this book. For example, a 25-year-old woman checked off the following items: She married my birth father, she has lots of children now, she always loved me, she wondered about me, and I thought she would come back for me. A 43-year-old woman wrote,

> I used to think that she was thinking about me all the time and she would give the world to see me and tell me she was sorry she gave me up. I thought she would have a happy life, maybe she had a real good job and was the best mother in the world and that I looked just like her.

The two themes in Table 2 refer to the fantasies about the relinquishment: why the adoptee was disconnected from her birth origins, and what fantasies connect the adoptee to the birth mother. Because categories are not labeled as positive or negative, these themes provide a more neutral way of organizing categories of fantasies while providing a new framework for examining the way

Table 2   Main Themes of Disconnection and Connection

	Number positive responses out of 84 questionnaires	% of total responding
Fantasies of disconnection		
Why the adoptee was relinquished		
Birth mother was unable to keep the child	69	82.1
She was forced to relinquish	60	71.4
The child was unwanted	44	53.0
The birth mother died	17	20.0
Fantasies of connection		
Who the birth mother was		
Her character—moral psychological, social	72	85.7
Physical appearance	70	83.3
What she has done or thought over time	66	78.0
Her talents—arts, athletics, etc.	50	59.0
Other relatives she has or adoptee has	48	57.1

adopted women who search for their birth origins conceive this part of their adoptive experience.

Do the Images Reveal Components That Are Overlapping or Additional to Those Described in the Psychoanalytic Literature on Birth Origin Fantasies as Defined in the Family Romance Construct?

This research supports the contention that birth origin fantasies are not produced using the same configuration as Freud's concept of the family romance construct, that for the adoptee, fantasies are different from those of the nonadoptee (Lawton & Gross, 1964; Stein & Hoopes, 1985). The images in the Freudian paradigm are of another set of parents who are better than the child's parents. The fantasized parents are often imagined to be kings, queens, or superstars. For the female adoptees in this study, the fantasies of the birth mother are three times as numerous as those about the birth father, the birth parents are imagined as a couple by half of the subjects, and as better parents than the adoptive parents by only one quarter of the subjects. The idea that the birth parents are from royalty or famous is cited by few of the respondents (see Table 3).

Table 3   Components of the Family Romance Construct

Type of fantasy— Who the fantasy is about	Number of positive responses	
	Total responding to item	Percentage
The birth mother alone	78/84	96.3
The birth father alone	43/80	34.0
The birth mother and birth father as a couple	27/82	53.0
Type of fantasy— **Content of the fantasy**		
The birth mother would be a better mother than the adoptive mother	23/78	29.8
The birth parents would be better parents than the adoptive parents	14/77	18.0
The birth father would be a better father than the adoptive father	8/77	10.5
The birth mother was famous	5/5	5.0
The birth mother was a movie star	3/3	3.0
The birth mother was a queen	3/3	3.0
The birth mother was a singer	2/2	2.0

Is There an Association Between the Age a Female Child Is Adopted and Her Fantasy Content?

The total fantasy rate reported in the sample was 1,379. The standard deviation from the mean was 8.5. Rates ranged from no fantasies to 36 per subject.

There was no association or correlation found between the ages of the women in this sample that were adopted and the their total production of fantasy images. However, looking at specific time periods revealed some significant findings. Those individuals in the present study who were adopted at under 2 weeks of age had fewer fantasies of either disconnection or connection than was expected given the mean fantasy rate. How can this be accounted for?

Infant researchers such as Tomkins (1968), Sander (1969), deCasper & Carstens (1981), Stern (1983), and Demos (1984) argue that theories that rely on instinct and cognition to define early child development overlook the preverbal capabilities of infants. Particularly relevant to this discussion is the theory that infants do not need cognition to experience affect, that an idea is not necessary to have a feeling (Tomkins, 1968). Infants organize themselves around affective states and their inner experience becomes relevant to what happens to the self (Sander, 1969). Contemporary infant research supports empirically and deepens theoretically Sullivan's (1935) and Bowlby's (1969, 1972, 1980) argument that without the cognitive abilities to process a representation of the mother, her loss in infancy is experienced as an affect: It becomes a residue of something missing or disconnected. It could be argued that the women in the present study who were adopted between birth and 2 weeks had or have no mental representation of the loss of the birth mother. They cannot think about it. Like retrospective loss, they are only left with the feeling that something has been lost (Balint, 1952). Perhaps that feeling becomes the most salient thing in their affective experience. Adoption studies, narratives in popular books on the adoptive experience, and clinical case presentations often report that persons adopted as infants, who have known about the fact of their adoption from an early age, describe memories of feeling anywhere from a vague to nagging sense of loss over time (Brodzinsky & Schecter, 1990; Lifton, 1979; Maxtone-Graham, 1983). Adoptees who were not told that they were adopted until they were adults report in retrospect that they felt something was missing but they had no idea what (Stack, 1994).

Freudian theory emphasizes the importance of grieving for the mental health of all individuals. The process of grieving requires expressing the yearnings for and the anger with the lost one. Without the opportunity to mourn, Freud (1917/1957) described people who fell into melancholic states, those disorders that present-day psychiatry terms depressive reactions. Bowlby (1961), observing grief reactions in young children, theorized that unsuccessful grieving at any age increases fantasy production because the affect is repressed.

The finding in the present study that women adopted under 2 weeks of age reported less fantasy than was expected should not be confused, however, with the aspect of Bowlby's theory that claims that successful grief resolution decreases fantasy formation. Bowlby is assuming that the aggrieved child has a mental representation of his mother (1969). Such a representation is part of Bowlby's working model. This is assumed to be in place at the time "attachment is clear for all to see" (about 6 months). However, an image is developing from birth and Bowlby claims it can be conceptualized using Piaget's (1971) description of infant cognitive development. At 2 weeks of age or younger, the adoptee does not have a representation of the lost mother. Without the mental model of the birth mother, how can fantasy images of her be created and how can she be mourned? For example, two women adopted at birth who had fewer fantasies than expected wrote,

> I didn't fantasize until I was 17, when I found my adoption papers with my name and her name. It was then that I realized that she existed, that she was a real person.

> I had no fantasies. I really can't tell you why I am doing a search, I just felt I had to do it because something is missing. Maybe it has something to do with the loss of my adoptive parents who I loved very much.

Neither of the women in these examples had a foster mother, and therefore most likely had only one experience of loss in infancy, that of their birth mother. In the first example finding the names, the birth mother's and her own, gives the subject a mental model to elaborate. In the second example, the second loss in adulthood triggers the memory of the early loss when there was no mental model.

The women adopted at 6 months or under in the present sample produced fewer fantasies of disconnection than was predicted. They also produced fewer fantasies than those adopted after 6 months. This finding may only reflect the fact that 65% of the subjects were adopted under 6 months and that fantasies of disconnection were consistently dominated by those of connection, 2 to 1. It may also be that, according to Bowlby (1952), fantasy formation increases when the child is unable to complete the grieving process. Fantasy is part of keeping the image and hope for reunion alive. In the case of adult adoptees there is reason to believe that the same mental mechanisms used by children who are separated from their birth mothers operate in adoptees over a lifetime.

In the following examples, the adoptees adopted at 6 months may have possessed the cognitive ability to have the representation of the mother, but because she is not dead or because they think about her as lost, they cannot express the yearning and anger necessary for grieving to proceed.

> I saw myself as an "Oliver Twist". I romanticized that I was this poor orphan child who came from the gentry. I envisioned my birth mother as this beautiful, young woman who had to give me up. She was forced by circumstances to give me up for adoption and she was heartbroken. Her lover left her to go in the service.

> I wanted to believe she was a warm, caring person so I wouldn't hold it against her for giving me up for adoption. But, I always have had mixed emotions about how I

feel about her. In other words, if she was such a good, warm, caring person, why didn't she try to or keep me? . . . By believing good traits about her it is easier for me to give her an out for giving me up. I can honestly say I never felt any hostile or negative feelings towards her.

One way to conceptualize these findings is to look at the way in which the content of these fantasies could reflect affect, cognition, and the attempt to grieve. The examples of the two women adopted under 2 weeks mark a starting place. Perhaps some residual affect was there for both subjects, but it was not until, as seen in a previous example, the adoptee saw her adoption papers that she realized there actually was a birth mother. As shown, maybe the loss of her beloved adoptive parents touched off a little residual affect and set the subject to thinking about her birth mother.

The subjects adopted at 6 months may possess both the residual affect of the loss and the cognitive abilities to have made some sort of representation of the birth mother (Bowlby, 1969; Tomkins, 1968). It is important to emphasize that any subject adopted at 3 months or older most likely had a foster mother whom she then eventually lost. The loss of the foster mother is a second early loss; this time a loss that includes a proto-model, a full mental model of the foster mother. This additional loss might affectually remind the neurological system (Hundert, 1989) or it may inform the developing cognitive apparatus of the original loss of the birth mother.

Continuing with the theories of Freud and Bowlby that grieving does not resolve loss without the expression of positive and negative feeling for the lost one, the following examples reflect the subjects' struggles, in fantasy, to place in perspective the birth mothers whom they have never known, but apparently have some feelings about:

It was always just she had to . . . for whatever reasons she couldn't keep me. There were lots of cruel fantasies when I was younger that I was worthless, that she hated me.

Sometimes I thought she was the most beautiful loving person alive. Other times I thought she was a prostitute and/or a drug addict.

In spite of my internal anger at her giving me up, I suppose it was too threatening for me to think of her as a "loser in the crowd," so to speak. Perhaps I built her up in my mind as someone famous and beautiful to compensate for how I really saw her deep inside. I wanted her to be what I felt I couldn't be because of the "missing pieces." Not knowing the story of my conception and birth forced me to want to fantasize about my birth mother. I was looking for my connection with my beginning!

The older an individual when he/she is adopted, the more developed will be the representations of either the birth mother or, more likely, the foster mother. Clothier first emphasized the "archaic sense of loss" in her 1943 paper. However, until very recently the loss of the birth mother and/or the loss of the foster mother were not considered losses necessary to grieve, adoption was not considered a separation from the birth mother, and searching was not considered an important step to take along the road to the resolution of a loss either through reunion or grieving (Andersen, 1989).

Is There an Association Between What an Adoptee Recalls She Was Told About Her Birth Origins and What She Fantasizes?

This study shows some empirical evidence to support the hypothesis that what a female adoptee is told about her birth origins will have some association with what she then fantasizes (Table 4).

Most adoptive parents are instructed to tell their adopted child something about her birth origins (Brodzinksy, 1984). The most common story told is that the birth mother was unable to keep the child because she was too young or too poor. Because she loved the child so much, she decided to give her to a couple who could take better care of her. The story changes sometimes as the child grows older, perhaps with nonidentifying information made available by the adoption agency that reveals ethnic background, physical appearance, education, or occupation (Nickman, 1985). There is a range of stories told from the selfless,

Table 4   What Was Told and What Was Fantasized

	Told fantasy (%)	Told no fantasy (%)	Not told fantasy (%)	Not told no fantasy (%)	Chi sq.	P
Appearance of birth mother	38	0	45	17	10.338	.001**
Birth mother died	5	2	16	77	8.629	.003**
Child was unwanted by birth mother	16	5	37	43	4.959	.026*
Birth mother's talents	15	4	44	37	3.872	.049*
Birth mother's character traits	26	1	60	13	2.555	.110
Birth mother forced to relinquish	25	6	46	23	1.610	.205
Relatives of birth mother	26	14	31	29	1.334	.248
Birth mother unable to keep	55	10	27	47	.954	.329

* p < .05
** p < .02

good birth mother story described above to the truncated story that the birth mother simply died, to a harsher story that portrays the birth mother as someone who did not want her baby.

What is interesting in the present study is that first of all, telling the subject something about the birth mother produced more fantasy formation rather than less. For example, a 44-year-old social worker recalls,

> Based partly on what I was told (that she was short, plump, blue-eyed, and 40 when I was born, and a teacher) I pictured her as Margaret Mead; intellectual, practical not glamorous, fairly serious, in a study with lots of books, sad but wise, purposeful, competent.

The frequencies that reflect this increase in fantasy as a result of what was told were seen in the following collapsed categories: The adoptee was told that the birth mother was unable to keep the child, that she was an individual forced to relinquish her child, or that she was an individual with particular character traits. Secondly, four sets of obtained frequencies that were significantly different from those that were expected, showed that telling the subject something about the birth mother produced less fantasy formation rather than more. These frequencies contain collapsed variables that refer to being told something about the appearance of the birth mother, that the birth mother was dead, that the adoptee had been unwanted by the birth mother, or what the birth mother's talents were. In the first set, it appears that the subjects were so consumed with what their birth mother looked like that those who were told nothing about her appearance fantasized as frequently as did those who were told something. In the second set, adoptees who were told that their birth mother died were less likely to fantasize that she was dead than those who were not told she died ($r = .32, p = .003$). For example, a 35-year-old college graduate wrote about it this way:

> I never really had any fantasies about why I was placed for adoption because I was told that my parents were killed in a car accident and although I was never thoroughly convinced that this was true, I never had the desire to question it or challenge it.

One way to interpret this finding is that being told that the birth parents died closes the case for some. For those who weren't told that they died, the fantasy may protect them from having to think about the relinquishment. This line of reasoning follows Gould's (1973) theory that fantasy serves to shield an individual from painful affect. In the case of the adoptee, the affect to avoid is that of loss (Andersen, 1989; Bowlby, 1969; Clothier, 1943).

The third unexpected frequency concerns the adoptees who are told that they were unwanted. Only 15% of those who had a fantasy of being unwanted had been told that they were unwanted. Like being told that the birth mother is dead, it is a hard fact to process. Either there is very little fantasy produced or as in the following narrative, the adoptee tries to explain to her self why she was unwanted.

> I always felt I was the child of either a very sick person who could not take care of me for health reasons or that my real mom had me out of wedlock and was ashamed of me or was not able to keep me for this reason, but would someday try to get me back!

Half the sample fantasized that they had been unwanted even though they had not been told that. One young woman recalled being told only that her birth mother was an unmarried teenager who liked school and was bright. She wrote the following about being unwanted: "Sometimes I wonder if she just didn't want me if she didn't want to be tied down."

Again, this closure by telling the adoptee that she was unwanted may shut down another affectively painful piece of information, the fantasies of being unwanted. The frequency of the fantasies that contain an image of being unwanted confirm the findings of Triseliotis (1973) and Brinich (1980), who report the fear of having been unwanted as central to some adoptees' self-perceptions. In the absence of facts, these fantasies represent one way an adoptee can explain the reason for relinquishment.

In the fourth set of frequencies that were significant, very few subjects were told about their birth mother's talents (3% of the sample) but almost two thirds fantasized about their mother's artistic, musical, or athletic abilities. Perhaps, like appearance, these fantasies bring the birth mother more into focus as a person.

> She could sing and write lovely poems and stories. She played the piano. I love the piano. Many of the things about my fantasy carried over into my real life. I grew up to be more like my fantasy of my birth mother than like my real-life adoptive mother.

Exploring these findings further, it was found that it can be statistically predicted that an adoptee who is told that her birth mother is dead will fantasize less about her being dead ($r = .32, p = .003$) and that those who are told very little about her talents will fantasize more about her talents ($r = .21, p = .0498$).

Let us return to the main themes around which the data in this study are organized: disconnection and connection. What the adoptee recalls being told about the reason that she was relinquished (the theme of disconnection) is positively correlated with what she fantasizes about that separation ($r = .30, p = .0054$). What the adoptee recalls being told about who her birth mother was or what she was like (the theme of connection) is more highly correlated with what she then fantasizes ($r = .59, p = .0001$). The two themes of connection and disconnection are positively correlated between what was told and what was fantasized ($r = .31, p = .004$). Investigating this further, however, yields the finding that there is no linear relationship between the two. This confirms the earlier findings that there may be some associations between what is told and what is fantasized, but knowing what a subject has been told will not necessarily predict what she will fantasize.

Are There Themes in the Fantasies of Those Adopted Women Who Search for Their Birth Origins That Are Similar to Those Reported by Researchers in Women's Development?

There is evidence in this research to support the findings in previous pilot studies that point to the wish to be in relationship with the birth mother, whether through fantasy or by searching for her. The beginning of a self in relation is viewed by Chodorow (1970) and Miller (1976) as the early infant relationship with the mother. The affiliative nature of women is reflected in their efforts at continuity and connection in future meaningful relationships.

For the purpose of this discussion, it is argued that: Adopted women who search have acknowledged the fact that they have been disconnected from their birth mother. Given what is known now about the strength of mother–daughter ties, of being in relationship as essential to women's' sense of self and mental health (Stiver & Miller, 1989), and the ethic of care (Gilligan, 1982), the acknowledgement of disconnection from the birth mother may not be easy. It is particularly difficult for those who either have little affect tolerance (Sashin, 1989) or suffer from overwhelming loyalty to the adoptive parents who took them in (Kirk, 1964).

The images reported in this study reveal the attempt to explain why there was a disconnection, why a mother would relinquish her child. The attempts to cognitively and emotionally come to terms with the severing of the in utero and neonatal bond is seen repeatedly in the present study. The data support theory from the object relations school, the interpersonal theory on women's development, and infant research that the preverbal relationship with the biological mother may prove to be rich, valid, and long-lasting. This study not only gives evidence for the attempt through fantasy to explain the loss of the birth mother, but also illustrates the function denial has as a coping mechanism. For example, fantasies ranged from total denial of the disconnection to complete realization. Here the powerful defense of denial is seen so vividly in the narratives below, as these women struggle to avoid the acknowledgment of disconnection from the birth mother. Stories are relayed that provide comfort to the adoptee:

> I had no fantasies. As a child I had a great imagination and did fantasize, but never about my birth mother. The main reason for this, I believe, is that being adopted was so very painful to me that I preferred not to think about it at all.

> My fantasies have always been romantic ones. The birth mother always has her heart torn away from her when I am taken from her. That has always been a great comfort

to me. The comfort has come from always believing that she loved and wanted me. She would have kept me.

I could not understand how a mother could give up a child for adoption so I internalized that something must be wrong with me.

Since I was not adopted until I was 10 months old, I used to think that maybe my birth mom kept me sort of on the lam, living in different parts of the country trying to figure out a way to earn a living. . . . The reason I was in the home for so long was that she was away on business. The courts decided. This took some of the responsibility off my birth mother since I fantasized that she was not directly responsible for my relinquishment.

How anyone who was pretty and very loving could have given me away was a mystery to me.

Researchers investigating women's development have noted that women will go to great ends to maintain relationships even if the situations are fraught with complications (Miller, 1976, 1988). The women in this study do not view their wish to be in relationship with their birth mother as a wish for a better mother. The two relationships are very different. Each relationship carries its own meaning and there is concern for both relationships, that the adoptive mother not be hurt and that the birth mother be found to be alive and well. The subjects quoted below express this common concern:

I was encouraged by my adoptive parents to search if I wanted to. I was told by my adoptive mother that she would do it with me. I always knew that I was free to do it but somewhere in my own mind I was afraid that it would hurt her if I did. I loved my parents so much I would never hurt them like that.

I asked my mom for pieces of the puzzle less and less frequently. I felt that I was hurting her to ask and I was a "good" daughter.

The empirical evidence in this research indicates that the fantasy images relating to the wish to be connected to the birth mother outweigh those describing fantasized reasons for disconnection, 2 to 1. These findings support theories of Chodorow (1970), Miller (1988), and Gilligan (1982) while bringing statistically significant findings to an area of human development that is often difficult to defend through narratives or clinical work alone. The fantasy images reported in this research bring alive the quality of the attempts by the subjects to be in relationship with their birth mothers, to be connected to them again if only in fantasy. These attempts are reflected in the following example.

She was very much life to me. I fantasized that she looked like me. She was very musical, passionate, intelligent, educated, religious, and a victim. She is very sad as I am very sad I fantasize she is me; she is my soul mate. She is the me that I have lost. She is the presence beneath this huge sense of loss that I have always lived with. She is home, a place of beginning and return, the wholeness that I have never been able to acquire. She is my mother, a connection, a belonging that I have never had. She is the child in me, my spirit. I hope that she has come to terms with this loss and pray that she is happy. But I think that we are both very sad. I want to find her, hold her, touch her more than anything else.

The wish for connection and to be in relationship with the lost birth mother is supported by not only the fact that the ratio of fantasies of connection outnumbered those of disconnection in this study, but that individual categories of connection reached statistical significance. The fantasies of appearance, talents, and character can all be seen as ways in which the adoptee connects herself to her beginnings, no matter what she is or is not told. In the first example below, the subject was told nothing about her relinquishment or her birth mother. She reports having had 30 fantasies about her, well over the mean of 16. The second example represents an attempt to bring a mental representation of the birth mother's appearance to mind.

> I had a vivid picture in my mind. I assumed she was young and looked like me. [In terms of appearance, talents and character the following are examples from this subject's checklist responses: She was beautiful, short, thin, artistic, athletic, sensitive, warm, has the same values as mine, she's just like me, and she wanted the best for me.]

> I used to dream of her but I never could really see or feel in my head what she looked like. . . . I knew it was her but it was like a camera that wouldn't focus.

A surprising number of adoptees indicated that they fantasized that they had a twin (25 out of the 53 who answered the question). This finding needs further investigation, but it might represent the ultimate description of being just like someone; the connection then is a merging of two people. In this case, it could be seen as a displacement of the image of the birth mother onto an image of a twin.

One of the most compelling categories is the one that describes the fantasies of a pretend relationship with the birth mother, where the adoptee imagines what the birth mother is doing over time and what she thinks about the adoptee. In this way, fantasy images serve to keep the adoptee in relationship with the birth mother. These sets of images may soften the reality of the separation. Of the 66 women who responded to these questions or wrote about the subject in their narratives, over three quarters reported relevant fantasy images. Examples below bring these statistics to life:

> All during my search I just knew deep down that she loved me and she never stopped thinking about me.

> She gives good advice, exactly how she feels, not holding anything back. She is truthful and honest. In her heart she cannot forget about a baby girl she gave birth to

22 years ago. [This subject also checked off in the checklists; She always loved me and She always wondered about me.]

I sometimes thought that she had married perhaps someone locally, more for convenience than for love, perhaps did or did not have any children and never told her husband about me even though she has thought about me often and especially on 1 November every year. Since she probably didn't have much money, she would not have had enough to pay anyone or any group to search for me without telling her husband. Frequently I would think that perhaps she was dead.

In terms of the new paradigm presented in this book, the present research adds data in support of the idea that individuals, adopted or not, are drawn toward a resolution of loss that incorporates the inner representation of a loved one into their everyday life rather than terminating or amputating the relationship. Those adoptees who are unencumbered by denial, like the families of MIAs, search for evidence to learn if the lost one is indeed gone. Only then can mourning proceed. The content in the birth origin fantasies presented in this study contributes to the idea that part of grief resolution is keeping the lost one alive. Adoptees' representations of their birth mothers, often based on very little information, may illuminate a basic human desire to remain connected or in relationship to our origins of birth as well as to our loved ones.

REFERENCES

Andersen, R. (1988). Why adoptees search: Motives and more. *Child Welfare League of America, 67*(1), 15–19.

Andersen, R. (1989). The nature of adoptee search: Adventure, cure, or growth? *Child Welfare League of America, 68*(6), 623–631.

Aumend, S., & Barrett, M. (1983). Searching and non-searching adoptees. *Adoption and Fostering, 101*, 23–31.

Balint, M. (1952). *Primary love and psychoanalytic technique.* London: Hogarth Press.

Bowlby, J. (1952). Maternal care and mental health: A report prepared on behalf of the World Health Organization as a contribution to the United Nations Programme for the Welfare of Homeless Children. (Monograph Series 2, 2nd ed.). Geneva: World Health Organization.

Bowlby, J. (1961). Children's mourning and its implications for psychiatry. *American Journal of Psychiatry, 118*, 481–498.

Bowlby, J. (1969). *Attachment and Loss* (Vol. 1). New York: Basic Books.

Bowlby, J. (1972). *Attachment and Loss* (Vol. 2). New York: Basic Books.

Bowlby, J. (1980). *Attachment and Loss* (Vol. 3). New York: Basic Books.

Brinich, P. (1980). Some potential effects of adoption on self and object representations. *Psychoanalytic Study of the Child, 35*, 107–133.

Brodzinsky, D. (1984). New perspectives on adoption revelation. *Early Child Development and Care, 18*, 105–118.

Brodzinsky, D., & Schechter, M. (Eds.). (1990). *The psychology of adoption.* New York: Oxford University Press.

Burgess, L. (1977). *The art of adoption.* Washington, DC: Acropolis.

Campbell, L., Silverman, P., & Patti, P (1991). Reunions between adoptees and birthparents. *Social Work, 36*(4), 329–335.

Chodorow, N. (1970). *The reproduction of mothering: Psychoanalysis and the sociology of gender.* Berkeley: University of California Press.

Clothier, F. (1943). The psychology of the adopted child. *Mental Hygiene, 27,* 222–230.

DeCasper, A. J., & Carstens, A. A. (1981). Contingencies of stimulation: Effects on learning and emotion in neonates. *Infant Behavior and Development, 4,* 19–35.

Demos, V. (1984). Empathy and affect: Reflections on infant experience. In J. Lichtenberg, M. Bornstein, & D. Silver (Eds.), *Empathy II* (pp. 9–34). Hillsdale, NJ: The Analytic Press.

Deykin, E., Campbell, L., & Patti, T. (1984). The postadoption experience of surrendering mothers. *American Journal of Orthopsychiatry, 54,* 271–280.

Deykin, E., Campbell, L., & Ryan, T. (1988). Fathers of adopted children: A study of the impact of child surrender on birth fathers. *American Journal of Orthopsychiatry, 58,* 240–248.

Farber, S. (1977). Sex differences in the expression of adoption ideas from birth through latency. *American Journal of Orthopsychiatry, 47,* 639–650.

Freud, S. (1957). Family romances. In J. Strachey (Ed. and Trans.), *The standard edition of the complete psychological works of Sigmund Freud* (Vol. 9, pp. 237–241). London: Hogarth Press. (Original work published 1908)

Freud, S. (1957). Mourning and melancholia. In J. Strachey (Ed.), *The standard edition of the complete psychological works of Sigmund Freud* (Vol. 14, pp. 243–258). London: Hogarth Press. (Original work published 1917)

Geissinger, S. (1984). Adoptive parents' attitudes towards open birth records. *Family Relations, 33*(4), 579–585.

Gilligan, C. (1982). *In a different voice.* Cambridge, MA: Harvard University Press.

Glazer, E., & Cooper, S. (1988). *Without child.* Lexington, MA: Lexington Books.

Glenn, J. (1985–86). The adopted child's self and object representations. *The International Journal of Psychoanalytic Psychotherapy, 11,* 309–313.

Gould, R. (1973). *Child studies through fantasy.* New York: Quadrangle Books.

Harper,. J. (1984). Who am I ? A crisis of identity for the adopted adolescent. *Mental Health in Australia, 1*(13), 16–18.

Hodges, J. (1984). Two crucial questions: Adopted children in psychoanalytic treatment. *Journal of Child Psychotherapy, 10,* 47–55.

Hundert, E. (1989). *Philosophy, psychiatry and neuroscience: Three approaches to the mind.* London: Oxford University Press.

Kirk, D. (1981). *Adoptive kinship.* Toronto: Butterworths.

Kirk, H. D. (1964). *Shared fate.* New York: Free Press.

Kowal, K. A., & Schilling, K. M. (1985). Adoption through the eyes of adult adoptees. *American Journal of Orthopsychiatry, 55*(3), 354–362.

Lawton, J., & Gross, S. (1964). Review of psychiatric literature on adopted children, *Archives of General Psychiatry, 11,* 636–643.

Lifton, B.J. (1979). *Lost and found: The adoption experience.* New York: Dial Press.

Maxtone-Graham, K. (1983). *An adopted woman.* New York: Remi Books.

Miles, M., & Huberman, A. (1984). *Qualitative data analysis.* Beverly Hills, CA: Sage.

Miller, J. B. (1976). *Towards a new psychology of women.* Boston: Beacon Press.

Miller, J. B. (1988). Connections, disconnections, & violations. *Work in Progress.* Working paper series, #33. Wellesley, MA: The Stone Center.

Miller-Havens, S. (1988). *The early psychosexual development of adopted women: A literature review.* Unpublished qualifying paper, Harvard University, Cambridge, MA.

Miller-Havens, S. (1990). *The birth origin fantasies of adopted women who search.* Unpublished doctoral dissertation, Harvard University, Cambridge, MA.

Nickman, S. (1985). Loss in adoption: The importance of dialogue. *Psychoanalytic Study of the Child, 40,* 365–398.

Piaget, J. (1971). The affective unconscious and the cognitive unconscious. In *The child and reality* (pp. 31–48). London: Penguin Books.

Reitz, M., & Watson, K.(1992), *Adoption and the family system*. New York: Guilford Press.

Rosenzweig-Smith, J. (1988). Factors associated with successful reunions of adult adoptees and biological parents. *Journal of Policy, Practice and Program Child Welfare League of America*, *67*(5), 411–422.

Sander, L. (1969). The longitudinal course of early mother—child interaction: Cross-case comparison in a sample of mother child pairs. In B.M. Foss (Ed.), *Determinants of infant behavior* (Vol. 4, pp. 189–227). New York: John Wiley & Sons.

Sandler, I., & Nagera, H. (1963). Aspects of the metapsychology of fantasy. *Psychoanalytic study of the child* (Vol. 18). New York: International Press.

Sashin, J. (1989). Duke Ellington: The creative process and the ability to experience and tolerate affect. In V. D. Volkan & E. W. Johnston (Eds.), *Muse and melancholia,* Charlottesville: University of Virginia Press.

Schechter, M. (1960). Observations on adopted children. *Archives of General Psychiatry, 3*, 109–118.

Schechter, M. (1964). Emotional problems in the adoptee. *Archives of General Psychiatry, 10*, 37–46.

Schechter, M., & Bertocci, D. (1990). The meaning of the search. In D. Brodzinsky & M. Schechter (Eds.), *The Psychology of Adoption* (pp. 69–90). New York: Oxford University Press.

Semrad, E., & Chasin, R. (1966). Interviewing the depressed patient. *Journal of the American Psychiatric Association, 17*(10), 91–94.

Silverman, P. R. (1981). *Helping women cope with grief.* Beverly Hills, CA: Sage.

Simon, M., & Senturia, A. (1966). Adoption and psychiatric illness. *American Journal of Psychiatry, 122,* 858–868.

Sobol, M., & Cardiff, J. (1983). A sociopsychological investigation of adult adoptees' search for their birth parents. *Family Relations, 32*(4), 477–483.

Sorosky, A., Baran, A., & Pannor, R. (1975). Identity conflicts in adoptees. *The American Journal of Orthopsychiatry, 45*, 18–27.

Sorosky, A., Baran, A., & Pannor, R. (1978). *The adoption triangle.* Los Angeles: Anchor Press.

Stack, J. (1994). *Well kept secrets: Adoptees who were never told.* Unpublished paper presented at American Adoption Congress conference, New Orleans.

Stein, L., & Hoopes, J. (1985). *Identity formation in the adopted adolescent.* New York: The Child Welfare League of America.

Stern, D. (1983). The early development of schemas of self, other, and "self with other." In J. Lichtenberg & S. Kaplan (Eds.), *Reflections on self psychology.* Hillsdale, NJ: The Analytic Press.

Stiver, I., & Miller, J. B. (1989). From depression to sadness in women's psychotherapy. *Work in Progress.* Working paper series, #36. Wellesley, MA: The Stone Center.

Strauss, A. (1987). *Quantitative analysis for social scientists.* Cambridge, Cambridge University Press.

Sullivan, H. S. (1935). *The interpersonal theory of psychiatry.* New York: W. W. Norton.

Sutherland, J. D. (1980). The British object relations theorists: Balint, Winnicott, Fairbairn, Guntrip. *Journal of the American Psychoanalytic Association, 28*, 829–860.

Tomkins, S. (1968). Affects—Primary motives of man. *Humanitas III, 3*, 321–345.

Triseliotis, J. (1973). *In search of origins.* Boston: Beacon Press.

Warner, L. (1986). Adopted women's search for the biological mother. *Dissertation abstracts international.* 46, 3610B.

Wieder, H. (1978). The family romance fantasies of adopted children. *The Psychoanalytic Study of the Child, 197,* 185–199.

Part Eight

Meanings and Implications

The next three chapters deal with findings from research and clinical practice without reference to the type of loss. The first two explore the way continuing bonds function in the individual's ongoing life. The people studied are university students, a popular group with researchers because they are so readily available. Both studies point the direction for more research with a broader range of people. The third chapter is a report of a clinical intervention.

In Chapter 17, Samuel Marwit and Dennis Klass ask about attachment in terms of the ongoing role the dead person plays in the survivor's life. Marwit and Klass let their subjects choose the deceased person. This is different from most research, which predetermines what relationship will be asked about, usually the person's deceased parent, child, sibling, etc. The first discovery of the research was that people did not have any problems understanding the question. When asked to name a person who had died, and then to write about the role that person plays in their life now, everyone could do it. Thus, the folk psychology includes interaction with the inner representation of the dead, even though the official psychology does not. The second discovery was that a much wider range of people were named than expected. Peers, friends/acquaintances, grandparents, and neighbors were important to them, not just the expected immediate relationships. Marwit and Klass found categories by which they could describe the different roles that the inner representations of the deceased play. To some extent, the roles were different depending on who died. For example, those respondents who lost a friend were more likely to see their connection as helping with value clarification.

In Chapter 18, David Balk uses a standardized measure to assess the degree of attachment his subjects maintained. He observes that with time these respondents seemed to display less attachment than those who were relatively new mourners. He is measuring the amount of attachment people experienced. He finds that those with a good deal of attachment were more likely to display greater distress and sorrow. We cannot ignore these findings, since they challenge one of the assumptions of this book: that ongoing attachments usually play positive roles in the survivor's life. Balk's findings point to the need for more research. It may be premature to quantify this phenomenon before we clarify and reach some consensus about what is being measured. In addition, if we talk of only the presence or absence of a phenomenon, then we may miss the subtleties in the way that survivor integrates the bond or how the bond changes over time.

Normand and her colleagues, as well as other contributors to this book, found that with time the attachment changes and takes on a different form and function. Balk also considers Ainsworth's research on patterns of attachments (i.e., secure and insecure) and extends those patterns to assessing the prior relationship between the deceased and the surviving mourners, and by implication to the present relationship between the living and the dead. We might ask whether this is the same phenomenon and the same use of the word attachment that we have been describing here.

Lora Heims Tessman's chapter (19) is an extended description of a psychotherapeutic intervention. Because of his Nazi past, an adult daughter does not feel that she can associate herself with the father she once loved. The problem of the parent whose behavior is not acceptable, either to the child or the society in which the child lives, is one that is not attended to in other chapters of this book. It is an interesting question, for abusive and neglectful parents are mourned, as are children and siblings with whom the survivors have very ambivalent bonds. Tessman's chapter provides us with a sensitive clinical narrative of her patient's struggles with the ambivalence in the bond with her father and with the resolution she finally achieved. She needed to learn to distinguish between the social meaning of what her father represented from his role in her life as a caring parent. Only when she could hold a more realistic image of her father as a man and as a father could she acknowledge what was lost. When she was able to define her father for herself, the image of the deceased began to evolve from where it had been frozen in psychic time. As she reconstructed the bond with her father, significant bonds in the present, such as with her husband, changed. Tessman provides a guide, using one therapeutic strategy, to work with a client through difficult grief. In the end this is what this book is about—helping people deal with their losses and the meaning of these losses in their lives.

P. R. S.
S. N.
D. K.

Chapter 17

Grief and the Role of the Inner Representation of the Deceased

Samuel J. Marwit and Dennis Klass

Predominant 20th-century Western theories of grief stress that successful resolution of grief occurs when the griever withdraws emotional ties to the deceased. The idea that successful grief resolution involves the withdrawal of bonds with the deceased so as to release emotional energy for future "healthy" attachments undergirds much of the contemporary grief counseling literature. Worden (1991), for example, posits four tasks of mourning and refers to the final task as "to emotionally relocate the deceased and move on with life" (p. 17). Conceptualizing grief therapy as helping the griever toward the eventual withdrawal of emotional ties to the deceased is supported by others as well (Dietrich & Shabad, 1989; Raphael & Nunn, 1988; Sanders, 1989).

There is, however, an emerging, though still minority, alternative view of successful grief resolution. M. Stroebe, Gergen, Gergen, and W. Stroebe (1992, 1993) have challenged the prevailing orientation as being specific to this culture at this historical period. They claim that the modern psychological theory of grief is a rejection of the equally valid earlier romanticist notions that valued "bonding with" the deceased. They further claim that contemporary psychological theory is unsupported by cross-cultural studies. They note that some other cultures value attachments to, and guidance provided by, recently deceased as well as long-deceased ancestors (e.g., Yamamoto, Okonoji, Iwasaki, & Yoshimura, 1969). M. Stroebe et al. (1992) present a case for the healthy presence of the deceased in the ongoing lives of survivors and claim that at different times and different places, the cultural zeitgeist values continued attachments, even when healthy resolution of grief has been achieved. In similar fashion, Klass (1988) has shown that the definition of healthy and unhealthy resolution of grief is more grounded in the various theoretical models of grief than in research on the lives of survivors.

The conceptualization of healthy resolution that incorporates rather than rejects the deceased is supported by existing models of grief that, at present, seem to pose a minority position. Mogenson (1992) talks of the "images of the dead which animate bereavement." He says, "Though medical psychology defines

The authors wish to express their appreciation to Michael Trusty for his help with statistical analyses.

This chapter is adapted from *Omega—Journal of Death and Dying*, Vol. 30, No. 4, pp. 283–298 (1994/1995). Copyright © 1994/1995 by Baywood Publishing Company. Adapted by permission.

mourning as the process by means of which the living detach themselves from the dead, the fantasies to which the bereaved are subject . . . belie this definition" (p. xi). M. Stroebe et al. (1992) cite evidence from their earlier studies, and from those of Rosenblatt (1983) and Rosenblatt and Meyer (1986), that "images" of the deceased serve a positive function guiding the bereaved as role models and in decision-making. Likewise, Vaillant (1985) states, "Contrary to folklore and psychiatric myth, separation from and loss of those we love do not cause psychopathology. Rather, failure to internalize those whom we have loved causes psychopathology" (p. 59). Similarly, Rubin (1985) states, "The greater the comfort and fluidity with which one can relate to the representations of the deceased, the more one can refer to 'resolution' of the loss" (p. 232).

The literature on the role(s) played by the inner representation of the deceased provides a theoretical framework for thinking about the place of the deceased in the ongoing lives of the living. Fairbairn (1952) defines the inner representation as (a) those aspects of the self that are identified with the deceased, (b) characteristics or thematic memories of the deceased, and (c) emotional states connected with those characterizations and memories. Phenomena that indicate interaction with the inner representation of a deceased person are a sense of presence, hallucinations in any of the senses, belief in the person's continuing active influence on thoughts or events, or a conscious incorporation of the characteristics or virtues of the dead into the self.

The active and healthy role of the inner representation is supported in the bereavement literature across the life span. Buchsbaum (1987) views a firm preservation of the deceased parent in the mind of surviving children and adolescents as vital to their ongoing development. Similarly, Silverman and Worden (1992) state, "Prior analysis of data from the Child Bereavement Study suggests that children do not detach from the deceased but rather find a way of carrying an inner representation of the deceased with them. This representation is dynamic and may change with time" (p. 329). Viederman (1989), writing about the death of parents, sees inner representations as important components that shape the survivor's world. Analogous conclusions are drawn by Klass (1988) and Klass and Marwit (1988) with parental bereavement and by Moss and Moss (1984) and Silverman (1986) with spousal bereavement.

The present research is an attempt to (a) investigate the existence of inner representations of deceased in the lives of the living, (b) define the nature of such representations, if they exist, (c) consider their relationship to the resolution of grief, and (d) look for variables that might predict membership in representational categories. Because there is no similar empirical research to date, this investigation is exploratory in nature.

INVESTIGATION METHODS

Participants

Ninety-one research participants were recruited from a variety of university classes. This allowed for neutralizing any ascertainment bias that might result from exclusively recruiting participants from classes whose content is that of death and dying. Seventy-one participants were retained in the final sample. Eliminated were four respondents who addressed the death of a pet instead of a person, three who addressed divorce rather than death, two who addressed the death of public figures unknown to them, one who addressed an "eventual" death, and 10 who supplied unintelligible or grossly inadequate responses (providing information to fewer than 15 of 18 categories).

The final sample consisted of 26 males aged 18 to 42 ($M = 25.19$; $SD = 7.29$) and 45 females aged 19 to 54 ($M = 26.53$; $SD = 8.40$). All participants were Caucasian. Among the 26 male participants, 6 described the death of a grandfather, 4 the death of a grandmother, 6 the death of a peer, and 6 the death of an older friend (often described as a mentor). Only one each described the death of a father, aunt, uncle, or spouse. Among the 45 female participants, 10 described the death of a grandfather, 10 the death of a grandmother, 11 the death of a friend, 4 the death of an older friend, 4 the death of a father, 2 the death of an uncle, and 1 each the death of a mother, brother, sister, and aunt. The chi-square for participant gender by relationship to deceased was nonsignificant. Gender differences within category were also nonsignificant and so were collapsed to provide relationship categories of parent, grandparent, aunt/uncle, peer, and older friend.

Testing Procedure

Participants were tested in three groups of approximately 30 per group. They were asked to identify themselves by age and gender and then to identify an important person in their lives who had died, as well as the timing and circumstances of that death. They were then asked to address the following questions: immediate reactions when learning about the death, reactions 6 months later, how the death changed their lives, the role the deceased played in their lives when alive, the role the deceased currently plays in their lives (if any), and a subjective estimate of the degree of resolution of their grief. Each question was presented orally with sufficient time allotted for a written response before proceeding to the next question. A minimum of 15 minutes was allowed for each of the two most relevant inquiries; that is, the role the deceased played and the role the deceased now plays in the lives of the research participants. It was not unusual to receive several pages of written comments on each of these.

Rating Procedure

The two authors and an advanced psychology graduate student independently read each of the 71 responses. Each then made ratings regarding the participant's stated perception of the closeness, conflictedness, and degree of idealization (negative, balanced, overidealized) of the relationship with the target person while that person was alive. Similar ratings were made of the degree of idealization, amount of longing still present, and degree of emotionality remaining now that the target person is dead. Lastly, ratings were made of the suddenness and appropriateness of the death, with "appropriate" being defined as deaths that are expected either because they are age appropriate or appropriate to physiological circumstances (similar to Weissman, 1972). Since this study was exploratory in nature, questions frequently asked in bereavement research were included here as independent variables.

Table 1 lists subjectively rated variables and the percent agreement and Kappa coefficients as determined by the independent rating of the two authors. It will be noted that the percent agreements are uniformly high, allowing differences to be resolved by using the third rater's rating in those few cases where disagreement remained.

To determine what roles, if any, are played by the deceased in the ongoing lives of the research participants, 20 randomly selected written responses were first read by the two authors and one graduate student. Four categories repeatedly emerged. These were labeled:

1 *Role model*, operationally defined as a global identification with the deceased. Examples:

P42: "Mother is my role model. I still draw upon her wisdom and learn vicariously many things, and make decisions the way she would."
P10: "My grandmother reminds me that I can be just as independent and strong as she was."
P48: "I remember him as the ideal dad; someone I would like to imitate as a parent."

Table 1 Interrater Reliability of Subjectively Evaluated Dimensions

Dimension	*N*	Percent Agreement	Kappa
Close	71	83%	.66
Sudden	57	96%	.93
Approp.	60	93%	.87
Quality	70	94%	.70
Att. alive	71	89%	.67
Att. dead	71	87%	.47
Role	70	77%	.68
Longing	71	93%	.67
Emotional	68	100%	1.00

Note: Close = close to deceased while alive (yes, no), Sudden = suddenness of death (yes, no), Approp. = appropriateness of death (appropriate, not appropriate), Quality = quality of relationship (conflicted, nonconflicted), Att. alive and Att. dead = attribute while alive and after death (negative, idealized, balanced), Role = inner representation (situation specific guidance, role model, values clarification, remembrance formation), Longing = longing present (yes, no), Emotional = emotionally charged record (yes, no).

2   *Situation specific guidance*, defined as situations where the primary function of the deceased is to help the living deal with a specific situation. Examples:

> P8: "My grandma, to me, is a strong memory of strength and livelihood. Especially now, when I am about to finish school and things are hard with grades and work. I remember when I first started college, how she told me that things would get better and that I should take advantage of my opportunity. To this day, when things get bad and I think about what she said and her personality somehow seems to give me an extra push to go on and keep trying."
>
> P45: "I always think about her when I'm trying to make a decision on some big event in my life. I think 'What would she do?' She is always in my thoughts and I try to build my life the way I think she would have liked for me to be.")

3   *Values clarification*, defined as adopting or rejecting a moral position identified with that of the deceased. Examples:

> P11: "Thinking about him [mentally handicapped brother] makes me more appreciative that I am alive. It has made me and my family more caring towards all underpriveledged people."
>
> P3: "Rick is sort of a motivation for me to continue being sensitive and patient with people, along with knowing that sometimes times can get tough, but situations can also turn around with time. Rick makes me want to understand people, and I find myself taking a lot of time out to listen to other people's problems."

4   *Remembrance formation*, defined as "memory" of the deceased without the deceased performing any active function. Examples:

> P56: "She [great aunt] still means a lot to me in positive ways. Sometimes when I'm having a bad day, I think about the way she laughed so hard, and it automatically brings a smile to my face. When I think of her, I get a warm feeling inside."
>
> P17: "He is part of my history. Every time I hear the band 'Rush' on the radio, I think about him because it was his favorite band."
>
> P65: "Now my dad is someone we enjoy reminiscing about. He is still missed by the entire family. We wonder what he would be like 12 years older and what he would be doing."

In this intitial sampling, the four representational functions were approximately equally represented (5, 4, 5, 6, respectively). It should be noted that raters had no preconceived notions about what categories, if any, would derive from these data. In other words, these four categories were not imposed upon the data, but instead emerged from it.

Next, using these four categories, 15 additional subject responses were rated by the same three raters, but this time independently. Two-out-of-three agreement was reached on 14 cases, with unanimous agreement being obtained in 8 cases. In five cases of nonunanimity, one author indicated that he could have rated the response in one of two ways. Incorporating the alternative rating increased agreement to 12 out of the 15.

Lastly, all 71 cases were rated independently by all three raters. Two-out-of-three agreement was reached in 68 cases (96%). The remaining three cases were easily resolved by discussion. The resulting frequencies for each category are as follows: 11 cases of situation specific guidance, 18 cases of role model, 13 cases of values clarification, and 29 cases of remembrance formation.

The methodology used to arrive at these four categories—namely, allowing the categories to emerge from the data—has been used in other research (Glaser & Strauss, 1967). It is interesting to note that the resulting categories coincide with less systematically derived concepts in the existing literature (M. Stroebe et al., 1992; Wortman & Silver, 1987; see Discussion).

STUDY RESULTS

Participant Gender and Relationship to Deceased

Chi-squares were run for variables relevant to participant gender and for participant's relationship to the deceased. With regard to participant gender, a significant chi square was obtained with the dimension of closeness, $\chi^2(1, N = 71) = 6.84, p < .01$. In this instance, 67% of female participants but only 33% of male participants reported having been close to the deceased. For all remaining variables, male and female participants showed remarkable similarity. For quality of relationship, 88% of males' and females' responses were rated as nonconflicted. As to whether there was longing still present, 92% of males' and 82% of females' responses were rated as no longing present. For rating the reports as emotionally charged or not, more than 90% of both males and females presented nonemotionally charged accounts. In rating attitude toward deceased when alive and after death (negative, balanced, idealized), more than 80% of males and females reported balanced attitudes.

With relationship of deceased to participant, significant chi-squares were obtained with appropriateness of death, $\chi^2(4, N = 57) = 34.35, p < .0001$, suddenness of death, $\chi^2(4, N = 55) = 18.40, p = .001$, and quality of relationship, $\chi^2(4, N = 68) = 24.32, p < .0001$. For this sample, appropriate deaths were reported, as expected, for 95% of grandparents, 75% of aunts/uncles, 6% of peers, and 44% of older friends. Only 25% of parental deaths were rated as appropriate, although the total number of appropriateness ratings of parental deaths is small ($n = 4$) and so may not be a representative sample. These figures correspond, as expected, with suddenness of death. Sudden deaths are less often appropriate. Consequently, 67% of parental deaths and 75% of peer deaths were reported as sudden, while only 14% of grandparental deaths and 0% of aunt/uncle deaths were sudden. Older friends deaths were about evenly divided on suddenness. Lastly, with regard to quality of relationship, less than 10% of relationships with aunts/uncles, grandparents, peers, and older friends were rated as conflicted, whereas 67% of relationships with parents were seen as conflicted. However, caution must be exercised in interpreting this latter since only six parental deaths could be rated for conflictedness. Still it is interesting to note that five of these six parental deaths are fathers, and four of those are reported as conflicted.

Table 2 presents the distribution of inner representational roles for each relationship to deceased. Treating this table as a chi-square results in a significant finding, χ^2 (12, $N = 68$) $= 23.36$, $p < .05$, although a large percentage of cells have expectancy counts of less than 5 and so this finding must be approached with caution. Regardless, it is interesting to note that remembrance formation, which is the least active role, is the most frequent role in this small samples of parental deaths. Also of specific interest is that values clarification is the predominant role played by deceased peers but the least apparent role played by older deceased relatives and friends. Seventy-five percent of the values clarification reports were attributed to deceased peers. None were attributed to parents. Values clarification, or at least values synchrony, appears to be clearly generational for this cohort.

A stepwise discriminant function analysis was performed using nine variables as predictors of membership in the four inner representational role groups. The nine variables were participant's age and gender, deceased's age and gender, participant's age at time of death, suddenness of death, closeness and appropriateness of relationship, and degree of resolution as reported by subject. As a result of unusually large amounts of missing data for deceased's age at time of death ($n = 29$), this variable was eliminated from the analysis.

Table 2 Relationship to Deceased and Inner Representational Role

Relationship		SSG	RM	VC	RF
Parent	Frequency	1	1	0	4
	Percent	1.47	1.47	0.00	5.88
	Row %	16.67	16.67	0.00	66.67
	Column %	10.00	5.88	0.00	13.79
Aunt/uncle	Frequency	0	2	0	3
	Percent	0.00	2.94	0.00	4.41
	Row %	0.00	40.00	0.00	60.00
	Column %	0.00	11.76	0.00	10.34
Grandparent	Frequency	5	10	2	13
	Percent	7.35	14.71	2.94	19.12
	Row %	6.67	33.33	6.67	43.33
	Column %	50.00	58.82	16.67	44.83
Peer	Frequency	2	1	9	5
	Percent	2.94	1.47	13.24	7.35
	Row %	11.76	5.88	52.94	29.41
	Column %	20.00	5.88	75.00	17.24
Older friend	Frequency	2	3	1	4
	Percent	2.94	4.41	1.47	5.88
	Row %	20.00	30.00	10.00	40.00
	Column %	20.00	17.65	8.33	13.79

Note: SSG = situation specific guidance, RM = role model, VC = values clarification, RF = remembrance formation.

The discriminant function analysis using the remaining eight variables showed closeness and suddenness to be predictive of membership in groups (Wilks' Lambda = .69, $F(6, 94) = 3.27, p < .01$). These two variables accounted for 84% of the between group variability. Means relevant to this finding are presented in Table 3. As can be seen, the discriminant function separates group 3, clarification of values, from the other three groups. Closeness appears to have a greater association with clarification of values, whereas suddenness of death is a stronger contributor to situation specific guidance, role model and remembrance formation.

Resolution

It was decided to do an additional stepwise regression using degree of resolution as the dependent measure, especially since there were so many potentially related variables. This was not the primary purpose of this investigation, but was a compelling question throughout. Degree of grief resolution was determined by participant's self report on a 10-point Likert-type scale ranging from "totally unresolved" to "fully resolved." Deceased's age was eliminated as an independent variable due to its low frequency. This left participant's age and gender, deceased's gender, participant's age at time of death, time since death, appropriateness and suddenness of death, and closeness to deceased as independent variables. Results showed participant's age at time of death to be the only variable to reach significance ($F[1, 56] = 5.93, p = .01$). This relationship is supported by a significant inverse correlation ($r [68] = -.34, p = .01$); that is, the greater the participant's age at the time of death, the lower is the reported degree of resolu-

Table 3   Closeness of Relationship and Suddenness of Death for Inner Representational Categories

	Variable	
Category	Closeness	Suddenness
Situation specific guidance ($N = 9$)		
Mean	1.22	1.55
SD	.44	.53
Role model ($N = 14$)		
Mean	1.29	1.71
SD	.47	.47
Values clarification ($N = 12$)		
Mean	1.83	1.67
SD	.39	.39
Remembrance formation ($N = 22$)		
Mean	1.50	1.77
SD	.51	.43

tion. Interestingly, time since death was not significant. Therefore, it appears that participant's age at time of death, regardless of elapsed time, is the primary predictor variable. Participant age at time of death ranged from 7 to 39 with a mean of 19.71 and a *SD* of 6.11. While there was a slight skew toward the younger end of the distribution with half of the participants (*n* = 33) being between 16 and 22 at the time of death, there was sufficient representation at both extremes to make this finding interesting (*n* = 12, ages 7–15; *n* = 16, ages 23–39).

INTENT OF INVESTIGATION: A DISCUSSION

The primary intent of the current investigation was to determine whether or not the deceased play an active role in the ongoing lives of survivors and, if so, whether the nature of these roles can be delineated. It was originally expected that inquiring about the current role of the deceased would be viewed as highly esoteric and very difficult to address. As it turned out, no participant had trouble with the concept and many wrote two or three pages. The idea of an active inner representation of a valued deceased individual seems to be a concept readily and naturally available to many people.

The current data provide empirical support for the existence of active inner representational figures that function as role models or behavioral guides to the living and that operate even in the presence of reportedly high degrees of grief resolution. Four categories reliably emerged: role model, situation specific guidance, values clarification, and remembrance formation. In doing so, these data provide support for the positions recently espoused by M. Stroebe et al. (1992), Rubin (1985), Vaillant (1985), and others who claim that positive grief work involves "remembering, not forgetting; it is a process of internalizing, not extruding. Attachment, if properly treated, provides us strength forever" (Valliant, 1985, p. 63).

The four categories identified are noticeably similar to the descriptions of constructive roles mentioned elsewhere. For example, M. Stroebe et al. (1992) mention Rosenblatt and Meyer's (1986) "discussion of internal dialogues with a deceased person (which) serve the positive function of helping the bereaved clarify thoughts, deal with unfinished and emergent relationships, and prepare for the future" (p. 1210). Gergen's (1987) work on "social ghosts" that "provide models for action, offer attitudinal perspectives, and lend esteem and emotional support to those who engage with them" (p. 1210). W. Stroebe and Stroebe (1989) add their own findings that "results indicate that the deceased continued to have strong psychological influences over the way the widowed organized and planned their lives" (p. 209).

The validity of the labels arrived at are further supported by their concurrence with concepts summarized by Wortman and Silver (1987):

> Continued attachment between the grieving person and the lost object may take many forms, such as through continued affective involvement with the loss (Parkes, 1972;

Rubin, 1981) [parallels *values clarification*]; through turning to the deceased for help with decision making (Zisook & Shuchter, 1986) [parallels *situation specific guidance*]; through various types of legacies, in which the wishes or commitments of the deceased are carried out by family members (Goin, Burgoyne, & Goin, 1979) [parallels *role model*]; through hallucinations or dreams (cf. Rees, 1971); or merely through a continued sense of presence of the lost object (Bors, 1951; Zisook, DeVaul, & Glick, 1982; Zisook & Schuchter, 1986) [parallels *remembrance formation*]. (p. 209)

The current data are further interesting because of their failure to confirm some of the anticipated predictors of membership in these categories. For example, it is interesting that degree of resolution or age of participant at time of death bear no relationship to the existence or quality of the inner representational role. One might think that the less active function of remembrance would correspond to higher degrees of resolution while the more active roles would correspond to lower degrees of grief resolution. Indeed, Horowitz, Wilner, Marmor, and Krupnick (1980) and Marris (1974) build theories on that supposition. However, this was not the case.

The finding most noteworthy with regard to inner representational categories was that closeness of the relationship and suddenness of death accounted for most of the between group variance. The impact of closeness is understandable in that the closer one feels to the deceased, the greater the prospect for retaining aspects of that person. Suddenness of death is a little more difficult to understand. However, it is interesting that the one category where closeness appears to be a stronger predictor variable than suddenness is that of values clarification. This may bear some relationship to the finding that values clarification is the role predominantly played by deceased peers. Values clarification may be a function of the nature of the sudden deaths experienced by peers. Sudden deaths of peers tended to be suicides and therefore, it may be the dramatic nature of these deaths that clarified values relating to living. Examples:

P27: "John's death probably affects me more than it did when it happened. If I think about the tragedy, a wasted life, promises unfulfilled, etc., his death carries a strong message. Life is momentary and precious. Make the most of each day or moment in the best possible manner. Live in today."

P 67: "He is a constant reminder of how extreme people can be and to what extremes they may go to get a point across, or let someone know they exist and feel also. He made me more aware of other people and what they may be feeling inside."

Relationships to the deceased were uniformly reported as nonconflicted, non-emotionally charged, and with very little longing still present. This may be a function of the relatively high degree of resolution of grief reported by both men and women. Over half of the sample (57%) reported resolution in the 8–10 range on a scale where 10 was "complete resolution." There were no significant differences between mean grief resolution scores for inner representational categories.

While the specific purpose of the present investigation was to explore the inner representational roles played by the deceased in the ongoing lives of the living and not to focus on grief resolution, there was a secondary interest in treating resolution as a dependent variable. Stepwise regression showed participant age at time of death to be the single predictor variable, unrelated to elapsed time, and correlational analysis showed these to be inversely related. This seems to indicate that younger people are either less invested in death to begin with, experience less intense grief as a function of their age, or have greater recuperative powers. It may also, however, be a function of the nature of the relationship to the deceased. It is interesting that 50% of participants in the first quartile for age at time of death described grandparent deaths as did 47% in the second quartile, whereas only 31% and 38% are the respective figures for the third and fourth quartiles. Grandparent deaths are the most expected and predictable and therefore, possibly the easiest to resolve. It may be that the sample sizes were simply not large enough to allow this trend to reach significance.

One limitation of the current research design is that it requested participants to "choose a *significant* death in their lives" but failed to inquire about other deaths experienced. Therefore, it cannot be determined whether targets (deceased) selected are the participant's only encounter with death or represent one experience from a number of death encounters. Future research needs to control for this. However, it is interesting that the deaths reported are predominantly grandparent deaths, followed by peer and older friend deaths, followed by parent and aunt/uncle deaths, followed, lastly, by an insignificant number of sibling ($n = 2$) and spousal ($n = 1$) deaths. This is probably a function of the age and circumstances of the participant population.

The number of reported peer and, especially, older friend deaths was not expected. It was anticipated that, for this age group, grandparent followed by parent deaths would have accounted for the vast majority of cases. It may be that participants experienced more parent deaths than they chose to report and that they reported peer and older friend deaths because these are less anticipated and therefore more dramatic, noteworthy, and personally involving. It may also be true, however, that friends play a more central role in peoples' lives than previously understood. This role may be as strong, if not stronger at times, than that of relatives. Support for this is found in the social support literature as it relates to loss, specifically situations of bereavement and divorce. Regardless, it is interesting that 14% of participants described the death of older friends (mentors) and that this was more true for male (23%) than for female (9%) participants. This is a category of grief rarely dealt with in the literature, and possibly one that requires more attention.

Given recent literature (e.g., M. Stroebe, 1992; M. Stroebe et al., 1992) questioning the rigidity of contemporary Western viewpoints of grief resolution and given the results of the present investigation, it appears reasonable to think of active inner representations of the deceased as playing important functions in the postgrief lives of survivors. It is reasonable to think of grief therapy as valuing, validating, and even encouraging the activity of these roles. Before encouraging these steps, however, it may be necessary to empirically examine the nature and function of inner representations for different populations and different death circumstances. As M. Stroebe (1992) notes, grief work must account for cultural styles and individual differences with regard to personality, coping styles and situational variables. Exploratory work in some of these areas has already been done and it is anticipated that, given the recent challenges to prevailing theory, much more will occur in the near future.

REFERENCES

Bors, E. (1951). Phantom limbs of patients with spinal cord injuries. *Archives of Neurology and Psychiatry, 66*, 610–631.

Bowlby, J. (1971). *Attachment and loss: Vol. 1. Attachment.* Hammondsworth, England: Pelican Books.

Buchsbaum, B. C. (1987). Remembering a parent who has died: A developmental perspective. *The Annual of Psychoanalysis, 15*, 99–112.

Dietrich, D. R., & Shabad, P. C. (1989). *The problem of loss and mourning: Psychoanalytic perspectives.* Madison, CT: International Universities Press.

Fairbairn, W. D. (1952). *An object relations theory of the personality.* New York: Basic Books.

Gergen, M. M. (1987, August). *Social ghosts: Opening inquiry on imaginal relationships.* Paper presented at the 95th Annual Convention of the American Psychological Association, New York.

Glaser, B. G., & Strauss, A. L. (1967). *The discovery of grounded theory: Strategies for qualitative research.* Chicago: Aldine.

Goin, M. K., Burgoyne, R. W., & Goin, J. M. (1979). Timeless attachment to a dead relative. *American Journal of Psychiatry, 136*, 988–989.

Horowitz, M., Wilner, N., Marmor, C., & Krupnick, J. (1980). Pathological grief and the activation of latent self-images. *American Journal of Psychiatry, 137*(10), 1157–1162.

Klass, D. (1988). *Parental grief: Solace and resolution.* New York: Springer.

Klass, D., & Marwit, S. J. (1988). Toward a model of parental grief. *Omega: Journal of Death and Dying, 19*(1), 31–50.

Kurdek, L. (1988). Social support of divorced single mothers and their children. *Journal of Divorce, 11*, 167–188.

Marris, P. (1974). *Loss and change.* London: Routledge & Kegan Paul.

Mogenson, G. (1992). *Greeting the angels: An imaginal view of the mourning process.* Amityville, NY: Baywood.

Moss, M. S., & Moss, S. Z. (1984). Some aspects of the elderly widow(er)'s persistent tie with the deceased spouse. *Omega: Journal of Death and Dying, 15*(3), 195–205.

Parkes, C. M. (1972). Components to the reaction to loss of a limb, spouse or home. *Journal of Psychosomatic Research, 16*, 343–349.

Raphael, B., & Nunn, K. (1988). Counseling the bereaved. *Journal of Social Issues, 44*, 191–206.

Rees, W. D. (1971). The hallucinations of widowhood. *British Medical Journal, 4*, 37–41.

Rosenblatt, P. (1983). *Bitter, bitter tears: Nineteenth century diarists and twentieth century grief theories.* Minneapolis: University of Minnesota Press.

Rosenblatt, P., & Meyer, M. (1986). Imagined interactions and the family. *Family Relations, 35*, 319–324.

Rubin, S. (1981). A two-track model of bereavement: Theory and application in research. *American Journal of Orthopsychiatry, 51*(1), 101–109.

Rubin, S. (1985). The resolution of bereavement: A clinical focus of the relationship of the deceased. *Psychotherapy, 22*(2), 231–235.

Sanders, C. (1989). *Grief: The mourning after*. New York: Wiley.

Silverman, P. R. (1986). *Widow-to-widow*. New York: Springer.

Silverman, P. R., & Worden, W. J. (1992). Children's understanding of funeral ritual. *Omega: Journal of Death and Dying*, 25, 319–331.

Stroebe, M. (1992). Coping with bereavement: A review of the grief work hypothesis. *Omega: Journal of Death and Dying*, 26, 19–42.

Stroebe, W., & Stroebe, M. (1989). Determinants of adjustment to bereavement in young widows and widowers. In M. Stroebe, W. Stroebe, & R. O. Hansson (Eds.), *Handbook of bereavement* (pp. 208–226). New York: Cambridge University Press.

Stroebe, M., Gergen, M. M., Gergen, K. J., & Stroebe, W. (1992). Broken hearts or broken bonds: Love and death in historical perspective. *American Psychologist*, 47, 1205–1212.

Stroebe, M., Gergen, M. M., Gerger, K. J., & Stroebe, W. (1993). Hearts and bonds: Resisting classification and closure. *American Psychologist*, 48, 991–992.

Stylianos, S. K., & Vachon, M. L. S. (1993). The role of social support in bereavement. In M. Stroebe, W. Stroebe, & R. O. Hansson (Eds.), *Handbook of Bereavement: Theory, Research, and Intervention* (pp. 397–410). New York: Cambridge University Press.

Vaillant, G. E. (1985). Loss as a metaphor for attachment. *American Journal of Psychoanalysis*, 45(1), 59–67.

Viederman, M. (1989). Personality change through life experience. III: Two creative types of response to loss. In D. R. Dietrich and P. C. Shabad (Eds.), *The problem of loss and mourning: Psychoanalytic perspectives* (pp. 187–212). Madison, CT: International Universities Press.

Weissman, A. (1972). *On dying and denying: A psychiatric study of terminality*. New York: Behavioral Publications.

Worden, W. J. (1991). *Grief counseling and grief therapy: A handbook for the mental health practitioner* (2nd ed.). New York: Springer.

Wortman, C. B., & Silver, R. C. (1987). Coping with irrevocable loss. In G. R. VandenBos and B. K. Bryant (Eds.), *Cataclysms, crises, and catastrophes: Psychology in action* (pp. 189–235). Washington, DC: American Psychological Association.

Yamamoto, J., Okonoji, K., Iwasaki, T., & Yoshimura, S. (1969). Mourning in Japan. *American Journal of Psychiatry*, 126, 74–182.

Zisook, S., DeVaul, R. A., & Glick, M. A. (1982). Measuring symptoms of grief and bereavement. *American Journal of Psychiatry*, 139, 1590–1593.

Zisook, S., & Shuchter, S. R. (1986). Time course of spousal bereavement. *General Hospital Psychiatry*, 7, 95–100.

Chapter 18

Attachment and the Reactions of Bereaved College Students: A Longitudinal Study

David E. Balk

The majority of bereavement research in the past several decades presents grief as a natural consequence of forming attachments and losing them (Jacobs, 1993). Loss through death would be the principal example of ruptured attachments producing grief. Freud (1917/1957) maintained that bereavement resolution involved gradually detaching libido investment from the inner representation of the deceased. Bowlby (1969, 1973, 1980) revolutionized thinking on bereavement with his assertion that resolution of grief involved letting go of attachment to the one who died and forming new attachments in the social world.

According to the attachment theory of bereavement resolution, ongoing attachment following a death is unhealthy, if not pathological. In particular, grief resolution is considered most problematic when death disrupts relationships marked by insecure attachment (Bowlby, 1980; Parkes, 1991; Parkes & Weiss, 1983; Weiss, 1993). Some of the signs of insecure attachment are ambivalence and dependency. Shanfield and his colleagues (Shanfield, Benjamin, & Swain, 1984; Shanfield & Swain, 1984; Shanfield, Swain, & Benjamin, 1986–87) used signs of insecure attachment to explain why parents of adult children killed in traffic accidents had significantly more distress than parents whose adult children had died from cancer. Scharlach (1991) explained adult children's greater problems in grief resolution following the death of their parents were significantly influenced by insecure filial attachments.

NEW THINKING ABOUT ATTACHMENT AND GRIEF

The attachment view of bereavement resolution has been revisited. Stroebe and her associates (M. Stroebe, Gergen, Gergen, & Stroebe, 1993a) have argued that forgoing attachments to the deceased is a contemporary phenomenon, and that

The Prevention Research Branch of the National Institute of Mental Health provided the great bulk of the funds to conduct this study (MH 45044). The William T. Grant Foundation and the Graduate College at Kansas State University also funded the project.

former generations suffered "broken hearts" rather than "broken bonds." This view was quickly challenged (Peskin, 1993) as a misreading and misrepresentation of Bowlby. In their reply, Stroebe et al. (1993b) reasserted their understanding of Bowlby and depicted Peskin's position as idiosyncratic.

In-depth, qualitative research with bereaved parents led Klass (1987–88) to ask serious questions about the accepted views of attachment and bereavement. He reported that bereaved parents in self-help and support groups commonly mentioned ongoing attachments to their dead children (1992–93, 1993). Hogan and DeSantis (1992) discovered that bereaved adolescents typically maintained ongoing attachments to their dead siblings. Silverman, Nickman, and Worden (1992) noted that bereaved children made conscious efforts to sustain connections to their dead parents and incorporated those attachments into their ongoing social environment. Tyson-Rawson (1993), who studied 20 college women whose fathers had died, reported that 14 of her 20 research participants mentioned "an ongoing attachment to the deceased, indicating a continuing bond with the significant other who died" (p. 166). Ten of these 14 students felt comforted with this ongoing attachment, felt it as a real presence in their lives, but were loath to report experiences of their father's presence lest people consider them crazy. These 10 women "were also more likely to report that they viewed themselves as having reached some resolution of their grief" (p. 171).

In addition to these empirical studies, bereaved individuals have emphasized in therapy conversations that they do not accept that bereavement resolution requires relinquishing emotional investments in their dead loved ones. As one widow said, "If that is what experts think grief resolution is all about, then I want nothing to do with their ideas."

Shuchter and Zisook (1993) recognized that ongoing attachments to the deceased represented for some persons a sign of healthy adaptation. However, these same authors noted that ongoing attachment denoted an enduring aspect of grief "for a significant proportion of otherwise normal bereaved individuals" (p. 25).

AN IDEA FOR A STUDY ON BEREAVEMENT AND ATTACHMENT

Bereavement resolution during the late adolescent college years is not a developmental task expected of most undergraduates. Furthermore, the college campus does not present a benevolent niche within which to resolve grief. Indeed, few environments in the human ecology provide such niches. As an instance, are there many situations in which expressions of grief do not prompt discomfort among observers? Are there many situations in which expressions of ongoing attachment to the deceased would be considered healthy?

This chapter presents an investigation of the role that the level of ongoing attachment plays in the trajectory of responses reported by bereaved college students. Among the questions investigated are:

- Do bereaved college students report ongoing attachment to the deceased?
- Is greater attachment to the deceased marked by more acute and enduring bereavement responses than found in bereaved individuals with less attachment?
- Do bereavement responses over time differ according to the bereaved college student's level of attachment?

RESEARCH METHOD

The analysis presented here was part of a larger project aimed at investigating the efficacy of social support as a secondary preventive intervention on college students' bereavement. This overall project included 180 students—110 bereaved and 70 not bereaved. The bereaved students were randomly placed in control and treatment groups. The students completed multiple data instruments on several occasions; among these instruments, to be described in greater detail later, were the Beck Depression Inventory (BDI), the Impact of Event Scale (IES), the SCL-90R, and the Texas Inventory of Grief (TIG). Analyses of the social support intervention were reported elsewhere (Balk, 1993b; Balk & Hogan, in press; Balk, Tyson-Rawson, & Colletti-Wetzel, 1993).

Over a span of three data gathering sessions, the project retained 78% ($n = 141$) of the participants: 46 bereaved support group members, 34 bereaved control group members, and 61 nonbereaved control group members. The data-gathering sessions were about 6 weeks apart. The attrition of more bereaved control group members than any other participants prompted some reflections on issues of ethics and bereavement research (Balk, 1993a, 1995b; Balk & Cook, 1995).

Data analyses of the efficacy of the support group intervention have been restricted to the 141 participants who remained in the project. In brief, MANOVA indicated significant group differences existed, and repeated-measures MANOVA identified significant group $\times$ time effects and significant group effects. Because of the significant group $\times$ time effects, the social support intervention was demonstrated as having an effect on some responses over time.

Sample

The sample for this investigation included the 80 bereaved college students (15 males, 65 females, with an average age of 24.4) who remained in the NIMH project for three data-gathering sessions. The analysis focused on the influence that attachment to the deceased had on bereavement responses.

Instruments

Multiple data instruments were used on multiple occasions. Among these instruments were four established, standardized inventories, plus a bereavement inventory in its early stages of use. We discuss below each instrument in turn and provide Cronbach alpha coefficients identifying the high internal consistency of the instruments across the three data-gathering sessions of this study.

Beck Depression Inventory (BDI)   The BDI is a 21-item, self-report inventory with several decades of use. The BDI has excellent psychometric properties and has been used successfully with college students (Beck & Steer, 1984; Beck, Steer, & Garbin, 1988; Bumberry, Oliver, & McClure, 1978; Byrne, Baron, & Campbell, 1993; Hammen, 1980; Reynolds & Gould, 1981).

The instrument measures cognitive, behavioral, somatic, and emotional aspects of depression. Each item provides four statements scaled from 0 to 3, and respondents are to choose which statement best represents them over the past 7 days. Total BDI scores can range from 0 to 63, and higher scores are indicative of more severe depression. College students typically produce lower mean scores on the BDI than do persons in clinical treatment (Kendell, Hollon, Beck, Hammen, & Ingram, 1987). One approach interprets BDI responses in terms of cutoff scores: 0–10 indicates normal ups and downs, 11–16 indicates mild mood disturbance, 17–20 indicates borderline clinical depression, 21–30 indicates moderate depression, 31–40 indicates severe depression, and over 40 indicates extreme depression (Burns, 1981).

Shanfield and Swain (1984) used the BDI in their study of parental bereavement over death of adult children in traffic accidents. Some other bereavement studies that featured the BDI include the University of Southern California longitudinal investigation of spousal bereavement (Gallagher-Thompson, Futterman, Farberow, Thompson, & Peterson, 1993), the Tubingen Longitudinal Study of Bereavement (W. Stroebe, Stroebe, & Domittner, 1988), and Robinson and Fleming's (1989, 1992) analyses of depression in bereaved and in clinically disturbed individuals.

Texas Inventory of Grief (TIG)   The TIG is a self-report inventory available since the middle 1970s. The instrument has good psychometric properties (Faschingbauer, DeVaul, & Zisook, 1977; Miller, Dworkin, Ward, & Barone, 1990; Zisook, DeVaul, & Click, 1982). An 8-item scale measures grief at the time of the death (Past Behavior), and a 13-item scale measures present reactions to the death (Present Behavior). An example of an item measuring Past Behavior would be, "I was angry that the person who died left me." An example of an item measuring Present Behavior would be, "I still cry when I think of the person who died." Each TIG item is answered on a 5-point scale ranging from "Completely True" to "Completely False." Responses are coded so that higher scores are indicative of more acute feelings of grief.

In addition to gathering typical demographic information, the TIG has an item measuring the respondent's relationship to the person who died. This relationship item, a gross measure of attachment, has choices ranging from "Closer than any relationship I've ever had before or since" to "Not very close at all."

SCL-90R   The SCL-90R is a 90-item, self-report inventory measuring nine dimensions of distress. These dimensions are Somatic Distress, Obsessive–Compulsive Behavior, Interpersonal Difficulties, Depression, Anxiety, Hostility,

Phobic Reactions, Paranoia, and Psychotic Distress. In use since the 1970s, the SCL-90R has several studies testifying to its psychometric properties (Clark & Friedman, 1983; Derogatis & Cleary, 1977; Derogatis, Rickels, & Rock, 1976; Johnson, Ellison, & Heikkinen, 1989; Pauker, 1985; Payne, 1985). Horowitz, Krupnick, Kaltruder, Leong, and Marmer (1981) and Shanfield and his associates (Shanfield et al., 1984; Shanfield & Swain, 1984; Shanfield et al., 1986–87) used the SCL-90R in their studies of adult bereavement. Gallagher-Thompson and her associates (1993) used a brief version of the SCL-90R in their study of spousal bereavement.

SCL-90R responses are scaled from 0 to 3, with higher scores indicative of greater distress. Raw scores on each SCL-90R dimension can be transformed to standardized scores with a mean of 50 and a standard deviation of 15. Such transformations were performed for this study.

Examples of symptoms within each SCL-90R dimension are:

- Somatization—Headaches, a lump in the throat, pains in heart or chest.
- Obsessive–Compulsive—Problems getting things done, problems concentrating, having to recheck work.
- Interpersonal Distress—Critical of others, feeling misunderstood, self-conscious.
- Depression—Crying easily, feeling worthless, lonely, hopeless.
- Anxiety—Nervous, fearful, restless.
- Hostility—Annoyed, outbursts of temper, arguing often.
- Phobic Anxiety—Feeling nervous when alone, fearful of going out of the house, avoiding places or activities that are frightening.
- Paranoia—Blaming others, distrusting others, feeling watched by others, having ideas and beliefs not shared by others.
- Psychoticism—Feeling lonely when with others, thinking something is wrong with one's mind, bothered by thoughts about sex, not feeling close to someone else.

Impact of Event Scale (IES) The IES is a 15-item, self-report inventory available since the late 1970s (Horowitz, Wilner, & Alvarez, 1979). Each item is scaled from 0 to 3.

The IES measures both intrusive and avoidant responses to traumatic stress: 8 items measure intrusive behavior and 7 items measure avoidant. An example of intrusive behavior would be thinking about something even when you don't want to. IES intrusive scale scores can range from 0 to 24, and higher scores indicate more unprompted (perhaps unwanted) thoughts and feelings about the traumatic life event. An example of avoidant behavior would be avoiding reminders of an unpleasant event. IES avoidant scale scores can range from 0 to 21, and higher scores indicate greater efforts at avoiding thinking or feeling about the traumatic life event.

The IES has commonly been used in a variety of studies investigating responses to life crises, and frequently has been used in conjunction with the TIG, the BDI, and the SCL-90R (Arata, Saunders, & Kilpatrick, 1991; Cella, Perry, Poag, Amand, & Goodwin, 1988; Rynearson & McCreery, 1993; Sloan, 1988). Zilberg, Weiss, and Horowitz (1982) reported cross-validation evidence for the use of the IES in studies of reactions to stress.

Grant Foundation Bereavement Inventory (GFBI)   The GFBI, developed by members of the Research Consortium on Adolescent Bereavement, is still exploratory. The GFBI assesses several aspects of bereavement, such as coping, feelings of disloyalty, emotions, influence of religion, identification with the deceased, and recovery. Nearly all items are scaled from 1 to 5 ("Never" to "Almost all the time") or 1 to 4 ("Not at all" to "Very much"). Room is left in several cases for open-ended probes. Respondents are asked to answer in terms of their reactions during the past month.

The following is an Attachment Scale that was constructed from 29 GFBI items. Each item is answered on a 1 to 5 scale. More attachment is indicated by higher scores.

How often during the past month have you . . .

1   Talked about him/her with other people.
2   Remembered things you did together, places where you and he/she had been.
3   Played his/her favorite songs or records.
4   Made a special effort to look at pictures, videotapes, or home movies of him/her.
5   Had everyday places remind you of him/her.
6   Made a special effort to visit places that remind you of him/her.
7   Thought of things you'll never get a chance to do with him/her.
8   Thought of things that he/she never had a chance to do with his/her life.
9   Worn or carried with you something that belonged to him/her.
10   Stored things that are reminders in a special place.
11   Gone to this special place to look at any of the items.
12   Asked questions to find out more about his/her life.
13   Thought about him/her when awake.
14   Pictured him/her in your mind.
15   Tried to recall how his/her voice sounded.
16   How often have your thoughts of him/her been comforting?
17   How often have your thoughts of him/her been distressing?
18   Thought about how he/she died.
19   Thought about other things going on that same day.
20   Thought about the last time you saw him/her.
21   Thought about the good times you shared together.
22   Thought about ways you wish you had behaved.
23   Done something to keep from thinking about him/her.
24   Done something to avoid having a conversation about him/her.
25   Avoided going to places that might remind you of him/her.

26   Avoided doing something that reminds you of him/her.
27   Done something to keep from thinking about him/her.
28   Missed him/her during the past month.
29   How often will you miss him/her in the coming months and years?

The internal consistency of the several scales used in this study remained very high. In most cases, the alpha coefficients were in the .80s or .90s. Table 1 provides the coefficients for each scale across the three data-gathering sessions.

In addition to very high internal consistency scores on the Attachment Scale, Pearson product–moment correlation coefficients were calculated on the Attachment Scale and the relationship item from the TIG. There was a significant positive association between the scale and the TIG item at each data session:

- *rho* = .654, *p* = .000 for the first data session,
- *rho* = .445, *p* = .000 for the second data session, and
- *rho* = .377, *p* = .000 for the third data session.

Having established the internal consistency of the Attachment Scale and the association of the Attachment Scale with a single variable that measures closeness of relationship to the person who died, the Attachment Scale scores for the three data sessions was transformed into one overall score. This transformation amounted to adding each person's three scores and dividing by three. The scores, which ranged from 31.04 to 115.74, were reviewed and collapsed into three categories: Little Attachment, Some Attachment, and Much Attachment. There were 15 persons with Little Attachment, 49 with Some Attachment, and 16 with Much Attachment.

Table 1   Cronbach Alpha Coefficients Depicting the Internal Consistency of All Scales Used in the Study

Scale	Time 1	Time 2	Time 3
BDI	.89	.91	.91
IES Avoidance	.83	.88	.83
IES Intrusion	.89	.88	.90
TIG Past	.91	.91	.88
TIG Present	.93	.92	.93
SCL Somatic	.86	.86	.88
SCL Obsessive	.88	.89	.88
SCL Interpersonal	.90	.91	.91
SCL Depression	.91	.92	.92
SCL Anxiety	.90	.89	.91
SCL Hostility	.87	.88	.87
SCL Phobia	.80	.82	.77
SCL Paranoia	.85	.81	.82
SCL Psychotic	.80	.85	.81
Attachment	.94	.93	.94

Grouping students according to level of attachment did not lead to gender differences, age differences, or differences in membership in the social support or control groups. There were no differences regarding religious affiliation: 54.4% reported they were Protestant, 26.6% Catholic, and 7.6% Other (Muslim, Jewish, Buddhist); 11.4% said they were not members of any religious group. Over the course of the project, time since the death (an average of 2 years upon entering the study) did not prove a significant influence on responses of the attachment groups. However, at entrance to the study, there were group differences in terms of attachment and time since the death, F (2, 78) = 3.15, $p < .05$. When they entered the study, the students with much attachment had on average been bereaved less than 1 year, those with some attachment had been bereaved for 2.1 years, and those with little attachment had been bereaved for 3.1 years.

A plurality of the deaths (47.5%) had been to immediate family members. Twenty-five percent had been to other relatives, frequently grandparents, and 27.5 % to friends, including boyfriends and girlfriends. The majority of deaths (58.8%) had been caused by illnesses, 26.3% by accidents, and 14.9% by other causes (murder, suicide, unknown). Nearly all of the deaths due to illness happened to immediate family members or other relatives (40 of 47), and the majority of deaths due to accidents happened to friends (12 out of 20). The 12 deaths from "other causes" were evenly divided between immediate family members, other relatives, and friends.

Analysis of Data

MANOVA, univariate F-tests of group differences, repeated measures MANOVA, and discriminant function analysis were used to test whether grouping respondents by level of attachment to the person who died produced significantly different group results. In short, grouping the bereaved college students according to Little Attachment, Some Attachment, and Much Attachment provided the independent variable. Responses to the BDI, TIG, IES, and SCL-90R scales formed the dependent variables.

RESEARCH FINDINGS

Repeated-measures MANOVA revealed that support group members and bereaved control group members did not differ in terms of Attachment Scale scores, F (1, 78) = 2.95, $p = .090$. The support group and control group members also did not differ in their responses to the relationship variable from the TIG, F (1, 77) = 0.33, $p = .565$.

The Wilks' procedure for assessing multivariate tests of significance indicated overall significant effects differentiating responses of the students grouped according to Little Attachment, Some Attachment, and Much Attachment, F = 2.42, $p = .003$. Univariate F-tests identified significant differences in 40 out of 42 scaled responses. These univariate F-test results are provided in Table 2.

Table 2   Univariate F-tests With Respondents Grouped by Attachment Level

Scale	Time	Attachment Level			F ratio*	p value
		Little	Some	Much		
BDI	1	7.94	12.33	15.00	3.53	.036
BDI	2	5.50	9.50	14.11	7.82	.001
BDI	3	6.78	8.18	14.33	7.74	.001
Avoidance	1	14.74	16.80	21.01	8.22	.001
Avoidance	2	12.18	14.58	19.45	11.67	.000
Avoidance	3	11.79	14.59	20.00	33.55	.000
Intrusion	1	16.95	22.25	29.41	19.15	.000
Intrusion	2	12.64	18.24	24.45	22.27	.000
Intrusion	3	12.05	18.10	25.35	27.97	.000
Past Grief	1	16.92	23.06	29.07	11.17	.000
Past Grief	2	18.54	22.56	29.00	7.83	.001
Past Grief	3	18.20	21.56	29.33	13.53	.000
Present Grief	1	32.63	45.57	51.20	14.45	.000
Present Grief	2	30.54	41.35	51.31	17.38	.000
Present Grief	3	28.39	40.82	48.92	24.53	.000
Hostility	1	55.11	62.02	66.55	6.32	.003
Hostility	2	53.47	59.78	65.00	5.69	.006
Hostility	3	48.47	59.90	63.60	9.48	.000
Somatic	1	55.11	62.02	66.55	3.62	.033
Somatic	2	50.26	55.54	60.40	6.84	.002
Somatic	3	48.89	53.98	58.55	2.85	.066
Obsessive	1	57.47	65.17	69.70	9.19	.000
Obsessive	2	55.42	61.41	65.55	9.58	.000
Obsessive	3	50.79	60.07	64.45	7.76	.001
Interpersonal	1	57.95	66.85	68.10	6.08	.004
Interpersonal	2	54.54	60.28	64.53	3.09	.053
Interpersonal	3	51.21	61.10	65.30	9.48	.000
Depression	1	58.00	65.39	67.60	7.71	.001
Depression	2	55.32	61.56	65.15	7.52	.001
Depression	3	51.58	60.34	64.50	12.87	.000
Anxiety	1	55.53	60.90	67.20	6.53	.003
Anxiety	2	50.58	58.24	62.75	11.43	.000
Anxiety	3	48.21	57.61	62.40	10.13	.000
Phobia	1	51.95	60.66	62.25	5.04	.010
Phobia	2	50.42	58.46	56.20	5.03	.010
Phobia	3	48.63	54.80	57.35	4.95	.010
Paranoia	1	53.63	58.90	62.50	3.95	.025
Paranoia	2	50.39	55.63	60.73	3.98	.024
Paranoia	3	47.84	54.98	61.10	12.68	.000
Psychosis	1	58.63	65.44	67.50	5.13	.009
Psychosis	2	55.37	59.73	64.25	5.28	.008
Psychosis	3	51.89	58.85	65.45	10.50	.000

*DF (2, 57)

Discriminant function analysis clearly differentiated group membership for the bereaved college students grouped according to Little Attachment, Some Attachment, and No Attachment (χ^2 = 140.41, 40 *df*, *p* = .000). The small Wilks' lambda of .052 indicated the power of Attachment Scale grouping as a discriminating function was great. The large canonical correlation of .93 indicated a very strong relationship between the discriminant function coefficients and the group centroids. Group centroids clearly separated the three groups. A continuum can be used to represent these group differences; the scores are the group centroids.

Responses to the multiple scales proved powerful predictors of group membership categorized by Little Attachment (−3.99), Some Attachment (−0.28), and Much Attachment (4.06). Chance alone would predict that in this study one could make correct group classification in 33% of the cases; the discriminant function procedure correctly classified group membership in 94.03% of the cases. These classification results are presented in Table 3.

Of the 42 scaled responses, 19 emerged as significant predictors of group membership. The mean scores of each attachment group to these 19 scaled responses are provided in Table 4. The standardized canonical discriminant function coefficients are also listed.

DISCUSSION

Three main questions guided this study. The first question to be answered was whether bereaved college students report ongoing attachment to the deceased. The evidence suggests a majority do remain attached, with up to 20% having considerable or much attachment to the person who died. However, attachment levels of students upon their entrance to the study correlated significantly with time since the death. It is plausible that over time the majority of bereaved students will become less attached to the person who died. Such a finding would be consistent with the received view of attachment theory (Bowlby, 1980). That a minority remained much attached would be in agreement with Shuchter and Zisook's (1993) assertion that ongoing attachment was present "for a significant proportion of otherwise normal bereaved individuals" (p. 25).

The second question was whether greater attachment to the deceased was marked by more acute and enduring bereavement responses than found in be-

Table 3   Classification of Group Membership From Responses to BDI, TIG, SCL-90R, and IES Scales

		Predicted Group Membership		
Actual Group	# of Cases*	1	2	3
1. Little Attachment	15	13	0	2
2. Some Attachment	36	0	35	1
3. Much Attachment	16	0	1	15
Total	67	13	36	18
Percent of grouped cases correctly classified = 94.03%				

*13 cases had at least one missing discriminating variable and were thus removed from the analysis.

Table 4 Mean Scores and Standardized Canonical Discriminant Function Coefficients: Significant Predictors of Group Membership

| | | Attachment Level | | | |
Scale	Time	Little	Some	Much	Discr Coeff*
BDI	1	8.85	11.84	16.87	−1.344
BDI	2	5.62	8.03	14.27	−0.662
Avoidance	3	8.69	14.00	19.00	1.051
Intrusion	1	16.08	21.00	27.56	0.447
Intrusion	2	11.32	17.76	20.87	0.476
Past Grief	3	18.20	21.56	29.33	0.692
Present Grief	3	28.39	40.82	48.97	−0.166
Somatic	1	54.15	60.28	63.20	0.667
Somatic	3	49.85	53.47	59.13	−1.090
Obsessive	1	56.46	63.97	70.93	1.403
Obsessive	3	50.08	58.41	64.73	−1.436
Depression	1	57.69	65.13	68.20	1.237
Anxiety	1	54.23	60.00	68.60	−0.890
Anxiety	2	46.31	56.66	63.93	0.846
Anxiety	3	45.38	56.19	63.87	0.553
Phobic	2	48.62	57.44	56.13	0.724
Paranoia	3	46.85	52.84	3.47	0.785
Psychotic	1	57.31	65.34	68.60	0.718
Psychotic	2	51.46	58.59	63.73	−1.163

*Group Centroids: Little Attachment = −3.99, Some Attachment = −0.28, Much Attachment = 4.06.

reaved individuals with less attachment. The overall MANOVA results give a resounding "Yes" to this question.

The third question was whether bereavement responses over time differed according to the bereaved college students' level of attachment. In all but one case, it was always the group with much attachment whose responses signified greater distress. For instance, students with much attachment had significantly higher depression scores on all administrations of the BDI. They had significantly higher avoidance and intrusion scores as measured by the IES. Their past and present grief responses as measured by the TIG were more acute. Their symptoms of distress as measured by the SCL-90R were significantly higher than the responses of the other two attachment groups. Given all this evidence obtained over multiple data-gathering sessions, it is clear that greater bonds to the person who died involved more acute distress and enduring grief than experienced by students with little or some attachment.

Limitations of This Study

Various patterns of attachment behavior have been identified in the research literature. The overall patterns are secure attachment and two types of insecure attachment: anxious and resistant attachment plus anxious and avoidant attachment (Ainsworth, 1979, 1988; Bowlby, 1979). Descriptions of each pattern are:

• Secure attachment—A person has close emotional bonds and can be independent of the person with whom these bonds have formed.

• Anxious and resistant attachment—A person forms ambivalent emotional bonds, is wary of strangers, and resists contact after a separation from the person with whom bonds have been formed.

• Anxious and avoidant attachment—A person cares little if separated from the person with whom bonds have been established and tends basically to disregard this person.

Secure attachment is as important for adolescent as for infant development. Early and middle adolescents' secure attachment to parents is positively associated with secure peer relations. Late-adolescent college students who have secure attachments to parents are also likely to have secure attachments with peers. Insecure peer attachments are much more likely for adolescents who have anxious bonds with their parents (Cooper & Ayers-Lopez, 1985; Hazen & Shaver, 1987; Hill & Holmbeck, 1986; Kobak & Sceery, 1988). Some depression during adolescence has been linked to insecure parent-adolescent relationships (Burbach, Kashani, & Rosenberg, 1989; Kobak, Sudler, & Gamble, 1991)

Inability to determine whether attachment patterns were secure or insecure is a limitation of this study. Further investigations must analyze type of attachment as well as extent of attachment. One hypothesis building on Bowlby's (1979, 1980) work is that students with secure attachment will resolve grief differently than students with insecure attachment. Another hypothesis is that healthy grief resolution will be found in students with a secure, ongoing attachment.

Profiles of Grief Identified in This Study

What can we deduce beyond concluding that greater attachment produces more acute grief and more intense distress? We can use the information from the discriminant function analysis to produce a psychologically meaningful profile (Tatsuoka, 1970) of students grouped by their attachment level.

Profile of a Bereaved Student with Little Attachment   Students with little attachment to the deceased had noticeably low depression scores, were hardly ever bothered by intrusive thoughts and feelings about the death, and did not try to avoid reminders of the death. They were not troubled much at the time of the death, nor did they currently have acute grief reactions. All of their responses regarding symptoms of distress were like the responses of a normal, nonclinical population. That is, they looked like other persons their age who were not emotionally troubled.

Profile of a Bereaved Student with Some Attachment   These students' BDI scores were not much different from the scores of their less-attached bereaved peers. The students with some attachment engaged in avoidant behavior about the death, and they were bothered by intrusive thoughts and feelings. Their grief at the time of the death was more acute than the students with less attachment, but not nearly as acute as the students with much attachment. The same pattern recurred in their present grief reactions. Their symptoms of distress indicated somatic complaints, anxiety, and obsessive–compulsive behavior nearly one *SD* above the norm of peers who are not in clinical treatment. Their symptoms of psychotic distress and depression as measured by the SCL-90R were a full *SD* above the norm.

Profile of a Bereaved Student with Much Attachment These students were clearly the most distressed and hurting of all the groups. Their BDI scores were indicative of mild mood swings. They often tried to avoid reminders of the death but were overcome by intrusive thoughts and feelings. Their grief at the time of the death was very acute, as was their current grief. Nearly all of their SCL-90R symptoms of distress exceeded a full *SD* above the norm of a nonclinical population. Their distress was particularly manifested in obsessive–compulsive behavior, depression, anxiety, paranoia, and psychotic symptoms.

CONCLUDING REFLECTIONS

The results of this study run counter to the thesis of this book that continuing attachment marks grief resolution. Maybe it does in some persons, but it surely does not in all. Perhaps an issue centers on what determines resolution of grief and on how to measure resolution of grief. The ongoing symptoms of distress in the participants of this study are not signs of grief resolution, but of ongoing grief work.

The findings in this study indicate that greater levels of continuing attachment are accompanied by greater distress and sorrow. It hardly seems plausible that in the first few years of their grief, individuals with more attachment would feel less distress than persons who were less invested in relationships severed by death. Conversely, it seems likely that persons with less attachment to those who died would be buffered from distress symptoms. When M. Stroebe et al. (1993a) said bonds were not broken, they emphasized hearts were.

We are still left without a clear notion of the trajectory of grief resolution based on level of attachment. It is possible that a 5- or 10-year longitudinal study will indicate that grief resolution occurs with no dampening of attachment in the lives of persons with strong bonds when the death occurred.

A longer-term longitudinal study could show a decrease in attachment by students who were at present much attached to the persons who died. The significant association between time since the death and level of attachment cannot be dismissed. However, only by bringing in research participants with the same general span of time since the death could this issue be studied rigorously. It may be that persons who now feel little or no attachment have felt that way since the death, and have not become detached from the deceased over time. The students currently with the most attachment may relinquish their emotional bonds and become at the same time less aggrieved and less distressed.

At the same time, however, we cannot predict with certainty such a lessening of attachment will occur. What may occur is an enduring attachment, but with a moderation of grief and distress. It is not impossible that these persons will remain bonded to their dead friends or family members and will find their pain lessens.

Grief may become a lifelong companion for students who maintain some or much attachment to the persons they loved in life. Silver and Wortman (1980) over a decade ago accented that outsiders seldom appreciate the intensity and the duration of grief reactions. Again, we are reminded that M. Stroebe and her colleagues (1993a) write about broken hearts.

We must also remember that Wortman and Silver (1989) assailed some myths prevalent in the received views about death and bereavement. One of these myths is that an absence of grief is always a sign of troubled or complicated mourning. Perhaps level of attachment is a covariate influence on feelings of grief. Little or no attachment would correspond with little or no grief, and that conclusion is surely consonant with the attachment theory of bereavement and with the findings in this study.

We should consider the developmental and ecological niche within which college students live out their bereavement. For students suffering from acute and enduring grief, there are risks to completing the normal developmental tasks one expects of late adolescents. Among these tasks are forging intimate relations outside one's family of origin, gaining autonomy and independence from one's parents, and forming a sense of occupational identity (Balk, 1995a). For late adolescents the college environment typically has salutary effects on these developmental tasks (Pascarella & Terenzini, 1991). However, rather than a source of nourishment and growth, the campus can become a place of loneliness, isolation, nonproductivity, and dread for students dealing with grief. Would the obstructions to development be all the greater for persons whose ongoing attachment was also accompanied by enduring, severe grief reactions?

This last question raises some important concerns about vulnerability during bereavement in college, and I want to address the issue of risk that emerges from the data in this study. There is little doubt that unresolved grief can be psychologically and physically injurious (Osterweis, Solomon, & Green, 1984). Should we conclude that bereaved students with an enduring attachment to those who died are at risk of debilitating consequences should appropriate interventions not be available? This author suspects such a conclusion is on target.

But such a conclusion leads to issues about helpful interventions. Findings that link attachment level to enduring, acute grief champion the design, delivery, and evaluation of secondary prevention efforts to assist at-risk students. The NIMH-sponsored social support intervention that led to these findings was successful in providing stress reduction in some critical areas. Other programs are needed to extend those efforts.

REFERENCES

Ainsworth, M. D. S. (1979). Infant-mother attachment. *American Psychologist, 34*, 932–937.

Ainsworth, M. D. S. (1988, August). *Attachments beyond infancy.* An invited address presented at the Annual Convention of the American Psychological Association, Atlanta, Georgia.

Arata, C. M., Saunders, B. E., & Kilpatrick, D. G. (1991). Concurrent validity of a crime-related post-traumatic stress disorder scale for women within the Symptom Checklist 90 Revised. *Violence and Victims, 6*, 191–199.

Balk, D. E. (1993a, April). *Bereavement research using control groups: Ethical obligations and questions.* Paper presented at the Annual Conference of the Association for Death Education and Counseling, Memphis, Tennessee.

Balk, D. E. (1993b, August). *Trajectory of grief among bereaved college students: Longitudinal results of a preventive intervention.* Paper presented at the Annual Convention of the American Psychological Association, Toronto, Canada.

Balk, D. E. (1995a). *Adolescent development: Early through late adolescence.* Pacific Grove, CA: Brooks/Cole.

Balk, D. E. (1995b). Bereavement research using control groups: Ethical obligations and questions. *Death Studies, 19*(2), 123–138.

Balk, D. E., & Cook, A. S. (Eds.). (1995). Ethics and bereavement research. *Death Studies, 19*(2), 61–88.

Balk, D. E., & Hogan, N. S. (1995). Religion, spirituality, and bereaved adolescents. In D. Adams & E. Deveau (Eds.), *Beyond the innocence of childhood: Helping children and adolescents cope with threats to their lives, dying, death and bereavement: Vol. 3. Helping children and adolescents cope with death, bereavement, and other losses.* Amityville, NY: Baywood.

Balk, D. E., Tyson-Rawson, K., & Colletti-Wetzel, J. (1993). Social support as an intervention with bereaved college students. *Death Studies, 17*, 427–450.

Beck, A. T., & Steer, R. A. (1984). Internal consistencies of the original and revised Beck Depression Inventory. *Journal of Clinical Psychology, 46*, 1365–1367.

Beck, A. T., Steer, R. A., & Garbin, M. G. (1988). Psychometric properties of the Beck Depression Inventory: Twenty-five years of evaluation. *Clinical Psychology Review, 8*, 77–100.

Bowlby, J. (1969). *Attachment and loss: Vol. 1. Attachment.* New York: Basic Books.

Bowlby, J. (1973). *Attachment and loss: Vol. 2. Separation: Anxiety and anger.* New York: Basic Books.

Bowlby, J. (1979). *Secure attachment.* New York: Basic Books.

Bowlby, J. (1980). *Attachment and loss: Vol. 3. Loss: Sadness and depression.* New York: Basic Books.

Bumberry, W., Oliver, J. M., & McClure, J. N. (1978). Validation of the Beck Depression Inventory in a university population using psychiatric estimate as the criterion. *Journal of Consulting and Clinical Psychology, 46*, 150–155.

Burbach, D. J, Kashani, J. H., & Rosenberg, T. K. (1989). Parental bonding and depressive disorders in adolescents. *Journal of Child Psychology and Psychiatry and Allied Disciplines, 30*, 417–429.

Burns, D. D. (1981). *Feeling good: The new mood therapy.* New York: New American Library.

Byrne, B. M., Baron, P., & Campbell, T. L. (1993). Measuring adolescent depression: Factorial validity and invariance of the Beck Depression Inventory across gender. *Journal of Research on Adolescence, 3*, 127–143.

Cella, D. F., Perry, S. W., Poag, M. E., Amand, R., & Goodwin, C. (1988). Depression and stress responses in parents of burned children. *Journal of Pediatric Psychology, 13*, 87–99.

Clark, A., & Friedman, M. J. (1983). Factor structure and discriminant validity of the SCL-90 in a veteran psychiatric population. *Journal of Personality Assessment, 47*, 396–404.

Cooper, C. R., & Ayers-Lopez, S. (1985). Family and peer systems in early adolescence: New models of the role of relationships in development. *Journal of Early Adolescence, 5*, 9–22.

Derogatis, L. R., & Cleary, P. A. (1977). Confirmation of the dimensional structure of the SCL-90: A study in construct validation. *Journal of Clinical Psychology, 33*, 981–989.

Derogatis, L. R., Rickels, K., & Rock, A. F. (1976). The SCL-90 and the MMPI: A step in the validation of a new self-report scale. *Journal of Psychiatry, 128*, 280–289.

Faschingbauer, T. R., DeVaul, R. A., & Zisook, S. (1977). Development of the Texas Inventory of Grief. *American Journal of Psychiatry, 134*, 696–698.

Freud, S. (1957). Mourning and melancholia. In J. Strachey (Ed. and Trans.), *The standard edition of the complete psychological works of Sigmund Freud*, (Vol. 14, pp. 243–258). London: Hogarth Press. (Originally published 1917)

Gallagher-Thompson, D., Futterman, A., Farberow, N., Thompson, L. W., & Peterson, J. (1993). The impact of spousal bereavement on older widows and widowers. In M. Stroebe, W. Stroebe, & R. O. Hansson (Eds.), *Handbook of bereavement: Theory, research, and intervention* (pp. 227–239). New York: Cambridge University Press.

Hammen, C. L. (1980). Depression in college students: Beyond the BDI. *Journal of Consulting and Clinical Psychology, 48*, 126–128.

Hazen, C., & Shaver, P. (1987). Romantic love conceptualized as an attachment process. *Journal of Personality and Social Psychology, 51*, 511–524.

Hill, J. P., & Holmbeck, G. N. (1986). Attachment and autonomy during adolescence. *Annals of Child Development, 3*, 145–189.

Hogan, N., & DeSantis, L. (1992). Adolescent sibling bereavement: An ongoing attachment. *Qualitative Health Research, 2*, 159–177.

Horowitz, M. J., Krupnick, J., Kaltruder, N., Leong, A., & Marmer, C. (1981). Initial psychological responses to parental death. *Archives of General Psychiatry, 38*, 85–92.

Horowitz, M. J., Wilner, N., & Alvarez, W. (1979). Impact of Event Scale: A measure of subjective stress. *Psychosomatic Medicine, 41*, 209–218.

Jacobs, S. (1993). *Pathologic grief: Maladaptation to loss*. Washington, DC: American Psychiatric Press.

Johnson, R. W., Ellison, R. A., & Heikkinen, C. A. (1989). Psychological symptoms of counseling center clients. *Journal of Counseling Psychology, 36*, 110–114.

Kendell, P. C., Hollon, S. D., Beck, A. T., Hammen, C. L., & Ingram, R. E. (1987). Issues and recommendations regarding use of the Beck Depression Inventory. *Cognitive Therapy and Research, 11*, 289–299.

Klass, D. (1987–88). John Bowlby's model of grief and the problem of identification. *Omega, 18*, 13–32.

Klass, D. (1992–93). The inner representation of the dead child and the worldviews of bereaved parents. *Omega, 26*, 255–272.

Klass, D. (1993). Solace and immortality: Bereaved parents continuing bond with their children. *Death Studies, 17*, 4, 343–368.

Kobak R. R., & Sceery, A. (1988). Attachment in late adolescence: Working models, affect regulation, and representations of self and others. *Child Development, 59*, 135–146.

Kobak, R. R., Sudler, N., & Gamble, W. (1991). Attachment and depressive symptoms during adolescence: A developmental pathways analysis. *Development and Psychopathology, 3*, 461–474.

Miller, F., Dworkin, J., Ward, M., & Barone, D. (1990). A preliminary study of unresolved grief in families of seriously mentally ill patients. *Hospital and Community Psychiatry, 41*, 1321–1325.

Osterweis, M., Solomon, F., & Green, M. (1984). *Bereavement: Reactions, consequences, and care*. Washington, DC: National Academy Press.

Pascarella, E. T., & Terenzini, P. T. (1991). *How college effects students: Findings and insights from twenty years of research.* San Francisco: Jossey-Bass.

Parkes, C. M. (1991). Attachment, bonding, and psychiatric problems after bereavement in adult life. In C. M. Parkes, J. Stevenson-Hinde, & P. Marris (Eds.), *Attachment across the life cycle* (pp. 268–292). London: Routledge.

Parkes, C. M., & Weiss, R. (1983). *Recovery from bereavement.* New York: Basic Books.

Pauker, J. D. (1985). Review of SCL-90R. In J. V. Mitchell, Jr. (Ed.), *The ninth mental measurements yearbook* (Vol 2, pp. 1325–1326). Lincoln, NE: The Buros Institute of Mental Measurements.

Payne, R. W. (1985). Review of SCL-90R. In J. V. Mitchell, Jr. (Ed.), *The ninth mental measurements yearbook* (Vol 2, pp. 1326–1329). Lincoln, NE: The Buros Institute of Mental Measurements.

Peskin, H. (1993). Neither broken hearts nor broken bonds. *American Psychologist, 48,* 990–991.

Reynolds, W. M., & Gould, J. W. (1981). A psychometric investigation of the standard and short form Beck Depression Inventory. *Journal of Consulting and Clinical Psychology, 49,* 306–307.

Robinson, P. J., & Fleming, S. J. (1989). Differentiating grief and depression. *Hospice Journal, 5,* 77–88.

Robinson, P. J., & Fleming, S. J. (1992). Depressotypic cognitive patterns in major depression and conjugal bereavement. *Omega, 25,* 291–305.

Rynearson, E. K., & McCreery, J. M. (1993). Bereavement after homicide: A synergism of trauma and loss. *American Journal of Psychiatry, 150,* 258–261.

Scharlach, A. W. (1991). Factors associated with filial grief following the death of an elderly parent. *American Journal of Orthopsychiatry, 61,* 307–313.

Shanfield, S. B., Benjamin, G. A. H., & Swain, B. J. (1984). Parents' reactions to the death of an adult child from cancer. *American Journal of Psychiatry, 141,* 1092–1094.

Shanfield, S. B., & Swain, B. J. (1984). Death of adult children in traffic accidents. *Journal of Nervous and Mental Disease, 172,* 533–538.

Shanfield, S. B., Swain, B. J., & Benjamin, G. A. H. (1986–87). Parents' responses to the death of adult children from accidents and cancer: A comparison. *Omega, 17,* 289–297.

Shuchter, S. R., & Zisook, S. (1993). The course of normal grief. In M. Stroebe, W. Stroebe, & R. O. Hansson (Eds.), *Handbook of bereavement: Theory, research, and intervention* (pp. 23–43). New York: Cambridge University Press.

Silver, R. L., & Wortman, C. B. (1980). Coping with undesirable life events. In J. Garber & M. E. P. Seligman (Eds.), *Human helplessness: Theory and applications* (pp. 279–340). New York: Academic Press.

Silverman, P. R., Nickman, S., & Worden, J. W. (1992). Detachment revisited: The child's reconstruction of a dead parent. *American Journal of Orthopsychiatry, 62,* 494–503.

Sloan, P. (1988). Post-traumatic stress in survivors of an airplane crash-landing: A clinical and exploratory research intervention. *Journal of Traumatic Stress, 1,* 211–219.

Stroebe, M., Gergen, M. M., Gergen, K. J., & Stroebe, W. (1993a). Broken hearts or broken bonds: Love and death in historical perspective. *American Psychologist, 47,* 1205–1212.

Stroebe, M., Gergen, M. M., Gergen, K. J., & Stroebe, W. (1993b). Hearts and bonds: Resisting classification and closure. *American Psychologist, 48,* 991–992.

Stroebe, W., Stroebe, M., & Domittner, G. (1988). Individual and situational differences in recovery from bereavement: A risk group identified. *Journal of Social Issues, 44,* 143–158.

Tatsuoka, M. (1970). *Discriminant analysis: The study of group differences.* Champaign, IL: Institute for Personality and Ability Testing.

Tyson-Rawson, K. (1993). *College women and bereavement: Late adolescence and father death.* Unpublished doctoral dissertation, Kansas State University, Manhattan, Kansas.

Weiss, R. (1993). Loss and recovery. In M. Stroebe, W. Stroebe, & R. O. Hansson (Eds.), *Handbook of bereavement: Theory, research, and intervention* (pp. 271–284). New York: Cambridge University Press.

Wortman, C. B., & Silver, R. C. (1989). The myths of coping with loss. *Journal of Consulting and Clinical Psychology, 57,* 349–357.

Zilberg, N. J., Weiss, D. S., & Horowitz, M. J. (1982). Impact of Event Scale: A cross-validation study and some empirical evidence supporting a conceptual model of stress response syndrome. *Journal of Consulting and Clinical Psychology, 50*, 407–413.

Zisook, S., DeVaul, R. A., & Click, M. A. (1982). Measuring symptoms of grief and bereavement. *American Journal of Psychiatry, 139*, 1590–1593.

Chapter 19

Dilemmas in Identification for the Post-Nazi Generation: "My Good Father Was a Bad Man?"

Lora Heims Tessman

Memories are the only paradise from which you cannot be evicted.
—Victor Hugo, quoted by Inge's father, a Nazi official

Access to memory is valued by Inge's father. It is startling that Inge invoked this quotation in her therapy, as it came from a man who was subject to the Nazi mandate of silence, of memory aborted. But it had not lost its impact on the daughter 30 years hence. Was she somehow heedful of Santayana's wisdom that those who cannot remember the past are condemned to repeat it? In this chapter I will try to explore what value, as well as what risks, access to dreaded memory may have. For traumatized individuals, when denial of a dreaded past is replaced by remembrance, intolerable dilemmas in identification may emerge. Such dilemmas are profound for the post-Nazi generation of Germans, and perhaps especially for the children of Nazis. The narrative of Inge highlights such a dilemma, compounded by bereavement. It raises the question: Under what conditions can memories also be a secret ally in acknowledging and facing these dilemmas? I suggest that highly positive features in identification with a parent, prior to loss and disillusionment, may foster the individual's capacity to tolerate access even to those memories in which the dreaded identifications are rooted. Although, understandably, both individuals and whole cultures may intend to block out memories connected to a sense of "evil", extruded memories frequently continue to exert pressure for enactments—for example, self-destructive behavior. Paradoxically, memories feared because of their overwhelming negative force may also contain hidden potential for resilience.

In my earlier writings about children of parting parents (Tessman, 1978), I stressed the dynamic interplay between identification, the quest for the wanted absent parent, and mourning. Identifications do not replace the quest for the wanted absent parent as an external presence, a quest that emerges at many levels and in many guises (Tessman, 1984). In adolescence one struggles with an internally altered image of the parents (in the direction of some disillusionment) to whom the relationship becomes altered but eventually not lost. However, a reality-based disillusionment (such as having a Nazi father) may interfere traumatically with the ability to risk partial internal decathexis. Under the threat of actual loss of a central identification figure, dealing with the disillusionment becomes too threatening (Tessman, 1978). Adolescents forced to acknowledge substantial "badness" in the formerly admired parent are prone to severe depressions, at times with suicidal ideation. In past work I have noted that these adolescent depressions were of the introjective type, in which harsh self-judgments replicated identification with a devalued object. The devalued attributes of the absent parent often evolved from the adolescent's internalization of a loss of value in the eyes of the remaining parent and social network, and were then compounded by the child's own anger about the loss. It was noted that frequently the bond of devaluation could not be resolved in the usual course of therapeutic alleviation of depressive self-criticism, but involved a reexamination of the discontinuity in transmitted values. In Inge's case, a distillation of her individual experience of her father as distinct from the social meanings of his behavior seemed prerequisite to her needed tolerance for her own ambivalence.

The inner quest for a sense of contact with a dead person may need to remain unconscious for several reasons: it conflicts with what the individual knows is rational; it draws the person toward wanting to experience deadness (in suicidal ideation); it jeopardizes the security of other needed relationships by being experienced as disloyal to them; or it may arouse more pain and longing than the individual can cope with at the time. However, if the form of quest can be recognized in a safe context and becomes focused instead on memories, mourning, and associated alterations in the image of the wanted person in accordance with renewed emotional development, the person has begun to acknowledge what was lost, and ironically regains those aspects of the self and the lost other that had been frozen in inner psychic time.

When Inge first sat in the office revealing that her father was a Nazi, I thought, "Can I treat a Nazi's child without unconscious reproach, revulsion that would interfere? Will I try?" I knew that she had been suicidal. She pictured a man intensely loved and irreparably lost. I thought, "Must the self be lost too?" Her tale was of wrestling with the pain of love gone awry, somewhere between the ordinary triangles of childhood and extraordinary, unspeakable reasons for blame, and forgiveness withheld. Her own integrity needed commitment to truth. It was soon learned that her father was always willing to help people, to talk and to listen to them, perhaps a good sign for the talking and listening needed to establish a treatment relationship. Inge continued in psychotherapy for several years in the early 1970s and was seen again in 1990 when the reunification of Germany was about to take place.

Once she understood the implications of Nazi ideology during her adolescence, Inge abhorred the shared beliefs that had been part of the loving interchanges between her father and herself in childhood. She considered suicide to lay at rest her identification with him, her sense that she had his ideology within her. She had not been able to mourn him, but felt drawn to enact his death. Eventually in her therapy, memory fueled her unfinished involvement with him at an affective level, thus allowing her the sense of emotional contact with him she seemed to need to separate her ego ideal from his, and revive its disrupted development. This chapter comprises excerpts from the initial year of her treatment.

EXCERPTS FROM INTERVIEWS

Therapist: *What brings you . . . ?*

Inge: *If I were clear what is making my life so miserable, I wouldn't be here. Currently I don't see the point of going on with life. I don't feel good about myself and my life is so awful. I don't even believe in a good afterlife. I grew up in Germany, during World War II. Then I managed to get away to America . . . and quickly ended up getting married. It's a terrible marriage. Hans is also German—he escaped, too. My question is, if I should have a divorce?*

T: *Important question. What troubles you most of all?*

I: *I don't feel I have a capacity to love people and I feel very unlovable.*

T: *Can you tell me about that?*

I: *Basically, I feel guilty for not having been able to love my mother . . . or brother. She is a very cold woman who I never could please. Mother was given to unreasonable punishments and nothing I did every seemed to please. I just couldn't get along with her. My father was a high Nazi official—but I loved him very much. After the war he was arrested by the Russians along with other important Nazis and we never saw him again. We had news that he died in prison.*

T: *And you then . . .?*

I: *I grew up feeling guilty because I know I would have been a Nazi, too, if he had lived. I hadn't realized everything that would involve. Feeling superior and agreeing to extermination of Jews. That had never been spoken about. When I found out after he was gone that he must have believed those things, I felt horrified and betrayed because I had always believed what he taught me.*

T: *It sounds like you had two images of him . . . and they didn't fit together.*

I: *Yes, during the war everyone admired him. He was kind to everyone and kinder to me than my mother. All kinds of people turned to him for help and he never let them down.*

T: *So whatever else it turned out he thought, you had the experience of some good in him and between you and him.*

As she was devastated by the negative components of her identification with him, it seemed important to prepare her to face the negative feelings by establishing that these feelings did not constitute the whole of her reality sense. Inge had said that what troubled her most was the feeling of being unloving and unlovable. I wanted to clarify between us, before she plunged further into her sense of guilt and desolation, that a loving relationship had once existed for her (and hence could exist again) even if it were now lost.

Next Session

Inge: *At home my parents hardly ever talked to each other. Mother was also an active Nazi in the volunteers. After my father was arrested, we first didn't dare flee because we thought it might be harder for him to find us. But when whole families were getting arrested we fled to my mother's family. Mother's sister's husband got interested in me. I fell in love with my uncle and we made a lot of kinky oral sex. The whole family knew perfectly well, but nobody stopped it. But I felt it was wrong, I felt it was incest and thought I might go insane. And at 16 I went off on my own.*

She had now brought up another area of guilt, this time around "falling in love" and sex. We might note that she considered this incest, although the uncle was not her blood relative. This hints at displacement from her sexual love for Father, by whom she had felt "betrayed", and whom they left behind in fleeing.

Next Session

Inge: *Maybe if I felt things were under my control more, I could straighten out.*
Therapist: *During the war, what happened to you and your family wasn't under your control at all. You must have been horrified at being so helpless. But when you were a child, from what you said, your father seemed to be a person in control and you admired that . . . and then that image came crashing down, too. You've had to manage, and have managed an impossible lot.*
I: *I do have an excellent job. I've gotten promoted several times so I administer a department now. I finished college in night school, when Hans had no job and wouldn't look for one. Somebody in the family had to have a stable job.*
T: *So you've kept things under control in that way, but within you now?*
I: *I wish I was dead, but I'm not happy at that prospect either. All week I was aware of the feeling of worth I did not have. I grew up very unreligious. My father agreed, said it was pure hypocrisy. But after all the disaster and my father was lost, I began to feel a need for religion. With each religion, I found an obstacle because I couldn't believe all of it: I felt I would be dishonest joining a church. I was struggling about free will versus determinism. I kept asking If there is so much misery, how could a good God create it?*
T: *That was much like what troubled you about your father . . . if he were in control like he seemed to be, how could your good father let such disasters happen . . . and turn out to believe something different than he showed you.?*
I: *When I started thinking about it, I made an appointment with a psychiatrist. He thought I was O.K., that I didn't need anything. But he was wrong, actually I had a complete feeling of desolation, was suicidal. I*

had a kitchen knife in my purse to kill myself. This whole business of failure of faith is out of normal logical reality. My framework of reality can't be put in any conventional one . . . but it includes two sides of a question; perhaps it means living with both.

T: *There are many kinds of reality . . . and being able to live with both sides of a question—or feeling—may be very important.*

I: *You asked about being a victim. For many years after we were first married, if we had an argument, Hans would hit me, push me against the wall and I was full of bruises, but never questioned it. I would try to appease him or blame myself, thinking I'm so unattractive. He constantly called me stupid and still does. Last week, I realized I was angry about it.*

T: *With reason! So a question is why have you put up with it for so long?*

I: *My whole adolescence undermined my confidence. I believed in the whole Nazi ideology When I found out what it really involved, it shook me up very badly. I couldn't trust my judgment about anything anymore.*

T: *When you found out more about what your father had believed? Tell me what beliefs you shared.*

I: *That we were indeed superior, that I had to be that way. That the war, the suffering were justified in the cause of the Nation. Where he died in prison . . . later we heard my father was given a lot of credit for lifting morale there. He had a lot of charisma, he was a leader type, had been a hero. I am ashamed to say my feelings for him were wiped out . . . I couldn't forgive him for having been a believer and for staying where we were . . . we could have left earlier, we knew we were likely to get occupied. During the occupation, he still talked of "going down with the flag flying." It was awful. I didn't get raped but my mother almost did. When they arrested him in the middle of the night he went elegantly dressed and dignified still. He said, "I would like to say good-bye first," and then he went.*

T: *I don't believe your feelings about him have been wiped out. I think they have been in limbo . . . because they've needed to be.*

Next Session

She told of the pressures of one week that most people would have considered harrowing. I was struck by the fact that she did not complain.

Therapist: *What are you trying to make up for, to have to be such a superwoman all the time?*

Inge: *I guess it's an attempt to be like the God I look for . . . the best I can come up with is the evil and incompleteness in the world that I . . . this striving in me to be more perfect. Not only does it not make sense, but it is a sin to be, to try to be without sin . . . just to justify yourself. It is really arrogant. Because of my inability to believe anything I was totally alienated from everything . . . society. I couldn't be part of anything and always felt like an outsider. Now that I'm coming here I feel supported and protected by society. My big quarrel has been, "Who*

let all this misery happen?" . . . It's the huge discrepancies I can't re-
member that I bitterly resent.
T: *Discrepancies in you, too?*
I: *Yes, because I totally feel anger at being betrayed and deserted. I re-*
member my mother and others were very angry at me because I didn't
show any feeling of loss or grief about my father. I couldn't cry. I felt
nothing . . . only betrayed because I believed whatever he told me, and
he told me that we had to go on no matter what.
T: *You felt betrayed but I think in some ways you tried not to betray him.*
You tried staying true to the idea that you have to be the strong one, no
matter what. That way you wanted to stay in touch with him and the
ideas you'd shared.
I: *My first suicidal attempt—it seems to me now that that's what it*
was . . . was when my mother sent me to the store for some milk. There
was an air raid warning and everyone took cover. I didn't, but just stood
there watching the planes, thinking, "Gee, I wish I were there in that
airplane." It shot at me, right close by. I remember being aware I could
have been dead. "There is blood on me." . . . That was me shooting at
me . . . like an attempt by myself to commit suicide . . . a part of me I
have known about, that would come at me sometime.
T: *I'm glad it missed you.*
I: *Thanks.*

The image of "me shooting at me" seems the epitome of simultaneous identification with victim and with aggressor.

Next Session

Inge brought in a small picture on a brooch of herself with her father. I felt sad
and used my sadness as a clue that the bittersweet memories characteristic of
mourning were about to emerge. After she revisited the meanings of her father,
she could then reconsider the meanings in her relationships to other men: husband Hans and Uncle Klaus.

Therapist: *There you are together!*
Inge : *I feel there are a lot of good things and bad things to work on*
now. I wonder if I'm not casting Hans in the role of the bully because he
is really not as strong as I would like him to be. Sometimes I feel Hans
would prefer if I was a man. He liked me during the period when I drove
a bus, learned to fly an airplane, while he wouldn't look for a job. I must
have been afraid that if I married someone as strong as my father I
would be . . . my own strength would be reinforced and I would end up
like my father. I always wanted to end up like my father when I was a
child, but never after he was arrested. My mother thought as a female I
was a total flop . . . I didn't have boyfriends from age 11 to 15 . . . I ma-
tured late, with my first period at 14 and that made me look like a freak
in her eyes. This week, I've been able to think more about my father. He

was very absorbed in his work, and his meetings, seldom at home in the evening. But when he was there he was easy to talk to, we went on a lot of walks and we always admired the same things. He had a telescope. We used to go out and look into the sky and he would explain stars and how marvelous everything in the distance was.

T: *So your looking up at the sky, wishing you were in the airplane . . . like you mentioned last week . . . didn't come out of nowhere . . . it was connected to the kind of image you had had with your father . . . when things were harmonious between you.*

I: *That hadn't occurred to me, but yes, we looked at the sky a lot. And vacations were happy, we sat and loafed and picked flowers. I never saw my father angry because my parents didn't quarrel in front of me.*

T: *You said they didn't talk to each other either . . . but you and he?*

I: *We talked . . . he liked to talk, and would listen, too. My father used to give a lot of parties. People would drop in for supper and much of the time somebody would be living with us, friends or relatives in trouble. My father was always willing to help. There would be grand parties for New Year's Eve and he would make up a box full of sayings, supposed to be prophetic for the year to come.*

T: *Like what, can you remember one?*

I: *Like I think the last New Years' Eve together one was about: "Memories are the only paradise from which you cannot be evicted."—a quote from Victor Hugo.*

T: *"Memories are the only paradise from which you cannot be evicted"!! [Silence]*

I: *He made me aware of the importance of things, made everything more alive. [Tears fill her eyes for the first time.] I see him as an equal now and he would respond and know how I felt. [Inge now put her head into her hands and wept. I was deeply moved at her grief, her having retrieved words about memory as the Paradise from which she had been evicted.]*

I: *Now I see myself in an embrace with him. [She wraps her own arms around her shoulders.] We are both saying, "It's all right." I am very much like him, not only thinking in terms of genetic influence but through his guidance and passing on of his values.*

T: *You feel yourself forgiving him and each other. . . . I think you feel he would have liked you again.*

I: *Yes, and I think he would have been proud of me, too. There is an awareness I have from him of the capacity for evil. I have to, I want to accept that as a part of myself, too.*

T: *What you talk of as "evil" is tied up with your anger. Anger isn't evil in itself; anger usually has grown out of fear. You had reason for terror in your abandonment. The question is what one does with it.*

I: *I have always been afraid of it; but it is probably a great gift because it has made me feel more related to a collective humanism . . . so that I can participate in the achievement of that humanity* *as well as in the evil. That's important to me. I mean if you feel tied into the awareness of evil, you have a right to be tied into the achievements as well.*

T: *You've always done your part in that . . . and then some. But what exactly is the evil you talk about, not in the Nazi party, but in you?*

I: *What I don't want is his participation in the idea of superiority and his enjoyment of power. I can't see how he wasn't aware of what was going on; it must have been part of the organization, But he never talked of eliminating anyone, just didn't discuss it. He said those who were superior in I.Q. and willpower and moral sense had a moral obligation to preserve that potential to the fullest—a gift given to a collective-type entity . . . conceivably a genetic accident. He should have told me more.*

T: *Yes, he should have. You are arguing with your father now, talking again.*

Next Session

"I wish the suffering in my marriage would end—that the marriage would end—but divorce is like death and destruction, and it is like an existential statement that I am now against death," Inge began. She reported realizing that week that she had been making an intense effort for years to keep "the evil in me" at bay. It occurred to her that "I do not really need to be afraid of my subconscious because maybe I'm not that bad."

Therapist: *What comes to your mind?*

Inge: *After the war, I had not gone back to school. Instead I worked for a year with refugee children. I remember being on duty by myself with 30 kids and 12 sick with whooping cough. I was exhausted. There was some Lysol next to the cough medicine and I was so exhausted I started to give the wrong thing . . . the kid spit it out and was all right. Why couldn't I have just said "I'm too darn tired," and let someone else do it? Somehow, that was like when I stood in front of the airplane. I'm beginning to know what my problem is . . . in many situations I can't tell what is good and what not.*

In describing the near accident with the child, she was moving closer to her potential role in contributing to death. It was connected with the image of herself as strong enough to do anything, an image that combined her identification with the father of her childhood with a necessary defense against the helplessness she experienced when death and disaster had actually surrounded her. The possibility of her own death wishes toward a child (her brother) was still far from consciousness and would not emerge for another year.

Next Session

Inge discussed the sexual interlude with Uncle Klaus, after her father's arrest:

Inge: *His advances I first took as simple shows of affection. My real anger is at my mother about that. She was totally dependent on our relatives to keep us, and wasn't willing to risk any trouble. It was like she sold me in order to be allowed to stay. I don't think she is capable of sympathy. When my younger brother tried to commit suicide and was sent to a sanitarium a few years ago, she just wrote me that it was proof of how "weak" he is.*

Inge was dealing with the lack of sympathy between herself and her mother. Like Hans, her mother could not tolerate weakness. Inge expected criticism rather than protection from her mother. She expected me to be critical too.

Next Session

Inge: *Last time, after I told you the incident about the Lysol, I thought you might be so appalled by me that you wouldn't want to see my anymore; that you would see me as a potential murderess.*
Therapist: *No, I wasn't appalled by you. But I think you have been. There you were surrounded by death . . . at a time you felt deeply deserted and angry . . . feeling as though you might have a part in the killing. But you haven't destroyed anyone and there's no way you could have stopped the war deaths. You weren't that powerful and guilty as you felt. But you have been in conflict, distraught about that, and we will want to understand how the thought of death and having evil in you got connected.*
I: *You know the trouble with my marriage now is that I'm not acting like a robot; I'm beginning to feel free to be me. And I don't know if Hans can take that or not. Making peace with my father here was terribly powerful for me. I realized . . . that forgiveness to my father is also forgiveness to myself. I had been wishing I was dead, but couldn't face that because the idea of life after death . . . in my mind before that would be a picture of a kind of hell . . . I know you know I don't believe that literally . . . but still, and it had the idea of meeting my father in it.*

With my mother it is different. My guilt is not that I hate her, but that I just don't care. I would think about "what if there is a disaster and one died," and I would have rather had father and me be left. Toward the end of the war we were all unreasonable. Near the time when I almost got killed by the bomb, there were also great periods of joy. We didn't know what would happen next, so there was no real reason not to pick all the daisies there were . . . I picked them and made garlands for me and many of our friends . . . we got used to the sound of gunshots at night. Sometimes people were returning from prison camp, musicians would be at the window celebrating . . . at that time I didn't yet feel betrayed by my father or Germany . . . I didn't realize what we had done to Jews 'till a year later.

Next Session

In this session Inge recalled her childhod fantasy that she first belonged to a man rather than to her mother. Parting from him and his care was symbolized by a wrenching wound, like hand torn from limb.

> **Inge:** *I think I had a real attachment to my maid, who left when my brother was born. Then I was punished for things I didn't know what it was. Mother would put me in the cellar with the coal and the potatoes, in the dark. Once I broke one of the slats.*
> **Therapist:** *What were your thoughts about your mother then?*
> **I:** *For a long time, I even thought I wasn't my mother's child! I remember a story she once told at the dinner table. She told about watching a merry-go-round one day and there was an accident—and the man had his hand torn off—and that's what brought me!*
> **T:** *Is there more?*
> **I:** *I interpreted that he couldn't take care of me and handed me to my mother and that's how she got me. For the longest time I thought I was a foster child.*
> **T:** *So you felt you had really been the man's before your mother took you. Maybe we can find out more about what that meant to you. I would guess it involved a remarkable effort on your part to explain to yourself why you and your mother didn't feel closer like you wished for. You tried hard not to blame anybody, so you decided for a while that the distance between you was because it wasn't your real mother. You must have wanted to preserve an image of her you needed to love, to split her up like that.*

Next Session

> **Inge:** *Last week, I left here feeling enormously elated. I had an image of my own subconscious that I can trust myself and not fear so much. If what you said came out of my mind, the strength in me to explain the trouble between myself and Mother like that . . . I must have a strong will to live! I visualized the man with the bleeding stump crying out and holding me cradled and saying will someone take care of my baby? [Her own arms form a cradling position as she talks.]*
> **Therapist:** *That kind of cradling, embracing, is what you pictured between yourself and your father when you were forgiving each other.*
> **I:** *The time before my father died, I guess I still felt secure. I expected I would finish high school and probably study physics or philosophy. I would get married and have 12 children and the servants would help take care of the house. My father wouldn't have interfered with what I wanted. The months before they took my father . . . I was busy dreaming up a storm about boyfriends that I didn't have yet. And then I went through a state of shock . . . months of shock when I didn't look at the future at all . . . the past and the future were a black wall and there was*

only the terrible present. I didn't want to think of my father because by then he had betrayed me. First he was a hero and then he was a criminal and so I was a criminal too.
T: *You didn't want to think of him, but in your mind you shared his fate.*
I: *People would say, "Here comes that Nazi's brat." When the invasion came, the enemy soldiers had us do all kinds of ugly work; they said, "Let them clean up the mess, they did the damage." My mother was too weak, so she sent me as the substitute . . . all the other women were adults. One day . . . we were shoveling bodies . . . the ground was hardened blood . . . we didn't know if there was another layer of bodies underneath or not . . . maggots were all over crawling up my legs. Everyone else vomited and couldn't go on, but I was still digging. One of the soldiers finally felt sorry for me and brought me a can of liverwurst and I took it home to my relatives.*

Next Session

Inge: *That last session was hard, but I think it was valuable. I think through the week I was able to carry a thread and define one area of tension in me. We talked about it here. The question of what values I discarded and what I kept.*

She discussed her new awareness of the enormous resentment she felt whenever she needed to maintain the role of the strong and invulnerable one, while others abandoned their tasks or leaned on her. Another woman at work was goofing off while "I am responsible and get blamed. For the first time I took the attitude, 'It's tough beans if she has to work late, too, and miss going to a party, it's not fair for her to go around bitching while I do all the work.'"

We related this to the last session in which she had described her endurance in substituting for her mother by continuing to bury the bodies, while others vomited and gave up.

Next Session

She brought in an erotic dream of a doctor she liked.

Inge: *We were sitting together and he was slowly and in a loving way starting to undress me. This probing and dragging things up and laying things bare may be doing me some good. In the dream, he got slightly undressed, too.*

Consciously, she had felt betrayed by this doctor, because she had assumed that she believed the unpleasant things her husband had told him about her and expected him to feel critical of her. (The dream is also a reference to the transference.) When she realized the discrepancy between the dream and her expectation, I pointed out her habits of criticizing herself in ways that left her expecting criticisms from others. Still, in the dream his approach was loving . . . was something changing?

Inge: *That would fit with . . . well, lately I feel I don't have to defend and justify myself all the time. One thing I'm really pleased about . . . to tell you an idea that is a risk because it is entirely irrational. Why can I tell you so serenely? If it comes to my integrity about my ideas . . . I would go to a mental hospital before giving them up.*

Therapist: *You won't have to . . .*

I: *I feel I'm not really as threatened as I thought I was . . . like I have finally gotten to the innermost part of my being of which I was afraid . . . and it is light . . . like a combination of my feeling and my being . . . what I want to be and what I am. There has always been a tension of being capable and powerful . . . and then of being evil. There has been a continued effort on my part not to have the evil use of power. You have said it is just anger about not having my needs met. I see the tension now not because I am evil but because I choose to give up . . . if I choose to give up wanting greatness, I can let go now because it is not actual evil I have committed, but only thought about. What I am getting to is that I can rely on the good . . . that that is almost as reliable as my breathing . . . I don't know if it would be true under all circumstances. One good thing after we talked about that last session: I rethought my relationship with Klaus: I overrated my guilt. He had enormous charisma and power over me. Maybe he was a necessary affirmation of my femininity. The relationship ended when I really pressured him to have real sex with me. He gave a romantic speech of how it would ruin my life and was embarrassed. After that it was intolerable to keep going. With real sex he would have had to acknowledge I was a woman. He put me on a train . . . I cried and cried for 2 weeks and then realized it was over. I felt cheapened, not good enough. My preoccupation with it is really a kind of arrogance, as though we were equal. Under the circumstances I was really much more vulnerable, and might as well not pretend otherwise.*

T: *So you were in a state of being stirred up by him, and then were rebuffed. You describe him as jolting you into feeling not equal, not good enough, a difference in generations he suddenly acted on, backtracking on being lovers, so that you felt cheapened, not great at all. And probably shades of a flop as a woman that started for you vis-a-vis mother. . . . Meanwhile, what you said about choosing to give up greatness is interesting, too . . . it's been such a tie to your father. Do you think you might be afraid that if you want to give some of that up, you would be getting rid of your father at the same time?*

Next Session

Inge: *I think I am finally making some progress. What you said last time made me think, "How much of my parents is in me; and how much I'm afraid I would kill them off if I threw some of those notions of power out." It feels like that is a gate I'm afraid to open right now, but like I have it now anytime to tell myself, "Do I want to look at that?" and feel reasonably happy about it. My feelings about my* *mother when I was little . . . I was mainly afraid I would hurt her and that I had. People would say, "Don't get Mutti upset." She suffered from migraines, so it would be "You'll bring on one of Mutti's headaches." She would say, "When you are naughty, I can't love you." It would be things like break a dish, stain a dress, or not being nice to grandma. I think I was already afraid of being accused of things I didn't do to an extraordinary degree.*

Next Session

Inge: *I'm feeling somewhat low . . . started thinking about my parents with an unexpected result: it took the form of feeling sorry for myself and my present situation.*
Therapist: *That's not so surprising; perhaps it's time for letting yourself care about yourself.*
I: *That brings up how I feel about pain generally . . . I would say I haven't felt I have wanted to discard it. But I realized that much of what bothered me at 15 has still been going on in my present life with Hans. I have had the assumption that I have to continue it, endure it, no matter what. But I'm beginning to question that. There is no doubt about it, my satisfaction has been in being the Rock of Gibraltar and having people lean on me. There is still a fantastic wish of salvaging the whole thing. Last week I left here partly angry at you and partly elated.*
T: *You let yourself get angry at me! Congratulations! Can you tell me more about being mad at me?*
I: *[laughs] You raised the question of when Hans hurts me, whether I somehow welcome it as a punishment, and then feel more justified . . . or something like that. First, that hurt my feelings and I was angry with you. Then I realized that what there is, is that if suddenly I was very happy I would have to pay for it with a big disaster.*
T: *That was a sequence in your life that you didn't bring about. Happiness and then disaster. You know, we've questioned that you're not that powerful after all, and don't need to be. Maybe my questioning that power makes you angry, too.*

Next Session

Inge: *I was proud of myself last week—I actually started an argument with Hans and didn't even short-circuit it like usually. I stuck it out. Even if I've messed things up in the past, my mother messed things up for me and I can see now it didn't destroy me. Do you remember the fantasy of the genie in the bottle I had . . . that I was afraid to let it out, that I thought it might kill me?*
Therapist: *Yes, the genie seemed to be something within yourself you were afraid to let out.*
I: *I realized that the genie was about my being power-hungry, to arrange and have everything my way, so that I won't have to suffer. It would be not to depend on anybody who is unreliable and who will let*

me down. It has a lot of anger in it at my father for having trusted him to be in the picture . . . instead of in prison, leaving us unprotected about any of the horrible things they did to us, like the nights of freezing in cattle cars.
T: *Once you thought him powerful enough.*
I: *I think of my father as a powerful man and think of myself as powerful and I am proud that I am like my father; but maybe really good parents are not those like my father. His power failed him and I'm afraid my power will fail me. I'm not as powerful as I want to be . . . and now I realize that has its benefits.*

Next Session

Inge: *Last week, you asked me about the moment I first remember feeling unprotected—and I have been thinking of the duality in me. What I was afraid of was not only power . . . but what happened when I felt unprotected by my father . . . the first moment must really have been my attempt to revenge myself on my father.*
Therapist: *And how did you do that?*
I: *With Klaus . . . no one protected me. He was always putting my father down . . . he said he would never have gotten caught and dragged to prison while his family was deserted. Of course all that time Klaus was fiddling around with me and ignored his family. I identified very much with my father, but I never defended my father to Klaus. I betrayed him like that.*
T: *So that added to your guilt, and somewhere in you, you defined yourself as a betrayer, too. Just before your father was taken, when you were 13 and 14 already, how were things between you then?*
I: *This is how close I was to my father and yet wasn't: The night that Dresden went up in flames . . . I was on duty putting out incendiary bombs. It meant being up on the roof with my father and I thought it was neat. That night Dad and I were standing on the factory roof. He said:"I think tonight this city is going to be destroyed . . . it is too dangerous . . . I want you to go downstairs." I was terribly, terribly hurt.*
T: *A different message than his usual "we are companions" . . . though, you know, he was protecting you, cared about what would happen to you.*
I: *I felt like he didn't love me like before. I remember thinking, "I'll show my father somebody loves me," and I was really ready for Klaus then. But then I also thought, "My father is a criminal so I am a criminal, so I will be as bad as I can." I ended up admiring Klaus enormously and felt I was being disloyal to my father. My father knew Klaus and didn't approve of him as a person. Klaus had a sparkling personality, spoke five languages, played the piano, and read poetry. My father was much more spiritual. Klaus was practical—work and pleasure. My father was work and duty oriented. Both were serene in what they represented—and having the wonderful illusion they were always right. My*

father would have suffered about the way Klaus lived. Both were quite oblivious to the damage they might leave in their wake.
T: *Yes, you in their wake! In relationship to Klaus you ended up feeling "put in your place": fiddled with, but not loved—oral sex but not real sex—nor acknowledged as a woman. Of course, real sex would have brought other worries; you said you were afraid of going insane. What do you think went on in you about that?*
I: *Funny, I let myself cry for him and not for my father.*
T: *You didn't care as much; it wasn't as overwhelming a loss.*
I: *I guess I was lucky to have known two splendid men. After that, the run-of-the-mill guy doesn't look so good. Maybe I can't have the splendid feeling participating in building the country that my ancestors did. But the guilt I have is well balanced by the fact that I am able to enjoy beautiful and good things.*

Next Session

Inge: *I have been feeling miserable, thinking of my parents and Klaus and how I've adapted my whole identity toward them. I feel sorry for me. I am beginning to worry whether I am an alcoholic—I now have three beers and a scotch after Hans goes to bed at 8. Maybe I'm just more able to show when I'm feeling bad.*
Therapist: *You have had a great deal to cause you sadness in your life. But you still have choices now.*
I: *I tried so hard not to be sad after my father was taken. I think in order not to be bitter. I don't want to be a drag for everyone. Maybe I was even the Rock of Gibraltar for my father. Then there is the admission of the fact that I'm not as powerful as I want. There's a tremendous relief that I wasn't able to do something about what happened to me and my father. Maybe some of the feelings of fear, punishment and false accusation were unnecessary, but I have always been ready for that. I always felt that if Hans tells lies about me, he will be believed and not I.*
T: *Who is believed in public must be an issue for you in all kinds of ways. With Klaus you had a real experience and a lot of feeling about it. But it was secret and you felt guilty. You knew it existed, but there was no validation in reality, no one wanted to believe it or have it said. And in front of others, he acted as though it wasn't happening. And in Germany everyone acted as though what was happening wasn't happening.*

Next Session

Inge: *When I was naughty, my mother and father talked of needing to break my will.*
Therapist: *Both of them?*
I: *No, it is not both of them! I always knew my father admired someone with a strong will. He told me one of the things he liked about me was having a strong will. That that was necessary to survive and live a meaningful life. But it was mother's and father's expressed policy that*

any disagreements have to be concealed. It was his great striving for harmony.

T: *Klaus concealed his disagreements with his wife, but excluded you when his wife was there. Not quite harmony. Your father and you shared an admiration for willpower, but he talked of "breaking your will" when he was with your mother? [Her pain at being suddenly ignored by Klaus when they were with others had been discussed further last session.]*

I: *I remember once, a kid who lived on the block and I went for an adventure walk without telling. My father was upset with me, and I felt very betrayed. I thought he would like that. I felt, "You are acting like my mother, how could you do that to me?" Father had treated me as a kid, with respect. Mother expected me to act only like a girl.*

Later Sessions

During the next months, Inge brought up a number of new perspectives on her mother:

> **Inge:** *I think during my early childhood she was a very lonely and scared and unhappy woman—and to some extent Dad treated her with the same unresponsiveness that Hans treats me. I am sort of seeing her from the outside in now; it hadn't occurred to me to think from her point of view.*

She became aware of the many restrictions on her mother's role of German hausfrau, and the degree to which she felt devalued as a person herself. She began to see how Mother's inhibitions limited the expression of warmth toward her little daughter. Inge had sorely missed this and assumed it was caused by her own naughtiness. She recovered some memories of a warm-hearted grandmother with whom she felt more free to be herself and accepted.

At about this time, a minor skirmish in which her adolescent son was involved brought a police car to her home late at night. After the police left, Inge made an emergency call to me; something she resorted to only in extreme crisis. The following session:

> **Therapist:** *Did the police visit strike terror into you?*
> **Inge:** *Yes, I had the image of when they came to arrest my father. I've had a terror of anyone in uniform. I used to not be able to buy a postage stamp because they have uniforms in the post office.*

We now talked at some length about recognizing the terrifying realities of her past life and the remaining vulnerability associated with any reminder of those realities (such as the police). We needed to differentiate those from the conflicts in her childhood and the complicated feelings about her father that had given rise to so much guilt and sadness in her. The effects of her wish for power, and her anger after being disillusioned about Father, had to be separated from the guilt she felt about what happened in Germany, so that she could choose to let herself have some happiness without being followed by the disaster that she had said earlier she expected. She talked of her past fears of being put away in a mental institution, seeing it now as her way of joining her father (in prison). We linked her first suicidal impulse (to stand up to the airplane to be shot at, instead of seeking shelter) to a mixed act of love and self-punishment. She knew her father admired her willpower in standing up to adversity; she and father had stood on duty together on the roof the night of the bombings. He had talked of going down with flags flying, but had sent her downstairs for safety. She felt not only hurt, but also as though she had failed him. The next time, she would not go down to the shelter and fail him again, even if it cost her her life. An additional, powerful meaning (which she explored during the second year of therapy) was this: Being sent away by father in "mid-flame," during a state of intense excitement, was like being sent away by Klaus during a state of high sexual arousal. Both rebuffs were a rude reminder of the generation gap, a comedown from the sense of equality that had been stimulated, but eventually a relief in limiting the power of her Oedipal desires.

One day she stated,

> Only lately have I been able to see my father as one man, with both good and evil. But there is no continuity in his good and evil. So much time has passed and so much else has colored things. I've kept thinking how much I am like him. I don't know how much this is a fallacy—how much I have reconstructed him to be like me, and finally then thinking we are alike . . . to keep feeling close to him. But wanting to be dead was part of that. I've come to the painful conclusion that I'm kidding myself with all my fancy talk of moral responsibility for Hans. I no longer think it is my moral responsibility to stay together no matter what, resenting it all the time. But I don't know if I would be capable to uproot myself from my past again. The first time that happened—when my father was taken and I was cut off from my past and everything I believed—it was as though I and everyone around me had died. What has been of value to me lately . . . is that I can trust my integrity . . . that it would stand by me . . . I think that what I am finally achieving is peace with the memory of my father.

Inge concluded her first year of treatment with a sense of arguable difference (rather than silence) as well as connection to the memory of her father. This helped to sustain her during continued therapy in subsequent years, omitted here (see Tessman, 1990) when transference deepened and intensified around the issues of the mutual harshness in the mother–daughter relationship. Startling herself with a further insight, she portrayed her mother, herself a survivor of harsh mothering, as having conveyed that Inge was "unworthy to live, just like Jews and homosexuals," at those times when Inge had longed for emotional intimacy rather than self-containment as a child. Inge became aware that the most intimate aspects of the affective ambiance between parent and child are enmeshed with the content of the prevalent cultural values and transmitted by child-rearing practices to future generations. Eventually some compassion for her mother's plight and for her own residual longings fueled a courageous journey to face her mother in her homeland, to replace silence with "humongous arguments" with which she tried to make their relationships more alive and real. A continuing interplay between her efforts to make change in her inner and outer worlds continued over the next two decades, but beyond the scope of this chapter.

REFERENCES

Tessman, L. H. (1978). *Children of parting parents*. New York: Jason Aronson.

Tessman, L. H. (1982). A note on the father's contribution to the daughter's ways of loving and working. In S. Cath, A. Gurwitt, & J. M. Ross (Eds.), *Father and child: Developmental and clinical perspectives* (pp. 219–238). Boston: Little, Brown.

Tessman, L. H. (1984). The quest for the wanted absent parent in children of the divorced or deceased. In C. Nadelson & D. Polonsky (Eds.), *Marriage and divorce: A contemporary perspective* (pp. 207–224). New York: Guilford Press.

Tessman, L. H. (1990). Dilemmas in identification for the post-Nazi generation: My good father was a bad man? Paper presented at meetings of the American Psychoanalytic Association, Miami.

Part Nine

Conclusion

Chapter 20

Concluding Thoughts

Phyllis R. Silverman and Steven L. Nickman

To write a "conclusion" for this book seemed inappropriate to us. We framed this book as part of a conversation, in order to leave things open and in recognition of the need for a continuing dialogue. We have tried to expand our understanding of the bereavement process, which we see as a dynamic part of human life that has no real end. We think, however, we have learned some things from editing this book and we would like to bring these thoughts together here.

DEFINING THE CONTINUING BOND

The central theme of this book is that survivors hold the deceased in loving memory for long periods, often forever, and that maintaining an inner representation of the deceased is normal rather than abnormal. It also is more central to survivors' experience than commonly has been recognized. We suggest that these relationships can be described as interactive, even though the other person is physically absent. We see, too, that other relationships characterized by physical absence (i.e., birth parents who surrender children for adoption, or a parent with whom there is little contact after a divorce) can have a similar influence on the lives of the individuals involved.

We can describe the survivor's experience in terms of interfaces—with the survivor's inner representation of the deceased, and with the living community that surrounds the survivor. Each of these influence the other. The relationship with the inner representation influences how survivors behave in the community of the living people. The living, whether they are immediate family, cultural group, or larger society, can influence the individual's desire and ability to remain involved with the deceased.

When we describe the dynamics of the construction of the inner representation of the dead or absent person, it should be clear that we do not have a common definition of what is meant by an inner representation or an interactive relationship. Marwit and Klass describe an inner representation of the deceased in four ways that the deceased may influence the behavior or inner status of the survivors. These are similar to what Normand and her colleagues call a living legacy. Several authors describe how the role the deceased plays in the mourner's life changes over time. Balk developed an Attachment Scale, which primarily describes activities that keep memories of the deceased alive—that is, thinking or talking about him or her. Hogan and DeSantis describe the continuing connection in terms of an ongoing conversation that the bereaved sibling has with the deceased: expressing their regret about what happened, asking why it happened, bringing them up to date and asking for their help. There are many dimensions to continuing-bond phenomena, some of which focus on the inner conversation where the deceased is assigned an active role, and others in which the deceased is passive. Activity or passivity of the deceased or absent person does not seem related to the age or other demographic characteristics of the survivors.

Many mourners feel visited by the deceased, as if the deceased lives on another plane and initiates the interaction. To some extent this relates to the mourner's belief system, yet in part, the belief system is irrelevant. Clearly some of the elements of a continuing bond with an absent other are perhaps different from the elements of attachment to a living person. With absent persons we rely more on dreams, memories, conversations about them, and cherished objects that remind us of them. Memories, dreams, internal conversations, and cherished objects, however, are part of the bond with the living, as well.

Attachment, as used by Bowlby, refers to the bond that develops between parent and infant. It involves giving and receiving care. The concept evolved from the observation that infants are predisposed to relational experiences that are essential for their growth and development. The term has come to be used to refer to many different kinds of relationships as if attachment were a static phenomenon. Attachment between adults may have different components than does the attachment between an infant and a parent. We should, however, ask whether the use of the term *attachment* is appropriate when we talk about a continuing bond to the deceased. Attachment, as defined in Webster's dictionary, means affectionate regard or devotion. Devotion and affection do not end with a death. Caring about someone seems to emanate from the bond that exists between the deceased and his or her surviving loved ones. But, there are differences. We cannot ignore that we are talking about connections that, in part, depend on the memory and the ability of the survivor to maintain an inner dialogue. This ability, as Buchsbaum points out, changes with stages of development.

As we try to understand the nature of the bond with an absent person, we also need to understand the relationship that existed prior to the loss. How much, we can ask, are these bonds like other bonds that have been studied in detail? How are these bonds related to other bonds in a person's life? Can we use Ainsworth's characterizations of secure and insecure attachment to define the nature of the prior relationship? Does it apply to how we characterize the continuing bond? Inge, as described by Tessman, had to better understand her relationship with her father and the meaning of that relationship before she could find a way to remember him. As she reworked the attachment to her father, other attachments in her life changed. This is equally true for the adopted children Nickman describes.

The book has begun to flesh out this concept and to define some of its parameters, but much work remains.

THE PARADOX OF LETTING GO AND REMAINING INVOLVED

We cannot ignore a central fact about death: it is forever. The silence from the grave can be deafening. We are talking about relationships with the dead or with people whom the adoptees never knew. The term *paradox* seems to be the best way to describe what we are dealing with: an irreconcilable tension. The chapters by Moss and Moss and by Lopata both deal with this paradox. We hope that by talking about the value of bonds to the deceased, it does not seem we are advocating living in the past. The gratification that was available when the deceased lived is no longer available in the same way. Yet, as mourners move on with their lives to find new roles, new directions, and new sources of gratification, they experience the past as very much a part of who they are. The deceased are both present and not present at the same time. It is possible to be bereft and not bereft simultaneously, to have a sense of continuity and yet to know that nothing will ever be the same. The reality is that there is an inner system that continues to be centered on the person who is no longer physically present. This inner reality may encourage the mourner to carry on. Klass and Conant point to parents and widows who feel that the deceased are encouraging them to live and to enjoy life, to move on, but this does not involve severing their tie or their obligation to the deceased.

The bond may shift so that it is not as central to the lives of the bereaved. The bond can take on a new form with time. But the connection is still there. In time, people may feel less guidance from the dead. At the same time, people may need help from their social support networks to keep their bonds alive. The social support networks may also help survivors let the deceased rest and be a part of the past. What has traditionally been called the mourning period may simply be the period in which the survivor is learning to live within this paradox.

Rituals, such as those described in the chapter on Japan, facilitate and legitimate this process. Rituals give language and form to the paradox, and are prescriptive in terms of how to deal with it and live with it. As we develop a new model of grief, we may find differences in people's tolerance for living with a paradox. In Western society we seek consistency and logic. It may be that the new model of grief will be a part of a less linear Western world view. Since we live in a world in which death is inevitable, perhaps we must consider that what mourners need is to learn to live with contradiction and the inexplicable. Even if different subcultures would develop rituals and beliefs that would maintain rigid boundaries, clinicians and researchers need to give up the hope of understanding grief in the context of a neat, orderly package that follows a single set of rules.

LEGITIMATION OF OLD GRIEF

A continuing attachment to the deceased has consistently been the defining symptom of people diagnosed with what was called at one point "pathological grief," and is now often called "complicated mourning." When people talk about the deceased or behave in deference to a desire of the deceased for more than a few months after the death has occurred, they are very likely to be labeled with a diagnosis indicating problem behavior. Diagnosis is a judgmental statement that implies some behaviors, thoughts, or feelings are good (usually called "healthy") and others are not good ("unhealthy" or "pathological"). A diagnosis of pathological grief or complicated mourning has been one of the society's ways of enforcing the view that bonds must be severed. Clearly such a diagnosis cannot be made using the understanding of grief that emerges in this book.

Just as our understanding of grief rules out much of what has been called pathology in grief, the concept of grief being finished becomes irrelevant. The survivors may reach a point where grief no longer dictates their behavior but is instead in their control. Occasional tears are no longer upsetting, remembering brings comfort, and sadness is not something to avoid.

There is at present no language for describing the diminution of grief, or that accounts for the ongoing activity that appears to be similar to acute mourning behavior. The editors had many discussions about the concept of *resolution*. It seemed the word had been intended by those who have used it to mean the end of grief—that is, grief is resolved and therefore over. However, *resolve* is a word with complex meanings. It implies "resolute" with the implication of courageous intention. In the new technology it means "clarity," as in high-resolution television. It means decision, as in a resolution passed by Congress. In the end, we agreed with Rubin that resolution may be an appropriate word if it reflects the dynamic ongoing process we have been trying to capture. Rubin's definition reads:

> Resolution is the process that supplements and continues on beyond adaptation and/or coping with loss. The connections to the representations of the deceased and to the memories of the relationship to the deceased continue on across the life cycle.

So we seek a language for describing how these representations change as people mature and develop over the life cycle. Here the work of several adult developmental theorists can be brought into the conversation. Rubin refers to the work of Blatt et al. as a model for conceptualizing adult development. Silverman and Nickman have used Kegan's work to characterize developmentally the conceptualization of the role of the "other"—in this case, the "absent other" in the mourner's life. As children grow to adulthood and beyond, their understanding of who died will evolve and change, having different meaning for them at each stage of the life cycle. So the nature of the connection changes, and the part it plays changes in the child-becoming-adult's life. Adoption provides a good example of this process. As children mature, they revisit what it means to be adopted; as their capacity to understand evolves, the chosen child story has long since passed its usefulness.

The bereavement process comprises many pieces. When we talk about accommodation or adaptation, we refer to the way people reorganize their lives and their sense of self in a way that enables them to live in the present. This also involves learning to deal with the extreme sadness and pain associated with loss. An ongoing construction of a deceased person is propelled by the sense of the deceased that is embedded in the mourner from the relationship before the death. The construction of the new relationship uses some different elements. All of this takes place over time at speeds determined by individual circumstances and history. There is no fixed formula, no one way of arriving at a resolution.

PROBLEM BEHAVIOR

There are people for whom the pain remains high, and in whom there seems to be little transformation of the bond with a deceased or absent individual. There are people whose sense of the deceased does not change, who look to the past as the only time when life was worthwhile. Some of these people cling to their relationship with the deceased. That might lead us to wonder if they were trying to reconstruct the past rather than develop a new perspective and relationship with it. It is not clear whether these patterns relate to behaviors that are not associated with the death, with ambivalences or conflicts that preceded death, or with difficulties in the present that defy solution.

We need not rush to invent new categories of "pathology." We have seen in this book that often the pathologies defined by the old model of grief were not based on research or clinical experience, but were based on the cultural values from which that model of grief emerged. As we help the new model take shape, we need not repeat the mistakes of the past. The heart of this book has been descriptions of people suffering many kinds of losses as they make their way toward resolution. If there is such a thing as pathology in bereavement, it needs to be carefully described, not simply proscribed. Rubin provides us with an example of how idealizing the past and not allowing for any comfort in the present causes problems for a sibling who finds his own solutions outside the family. Tessman reports on how the inability to mourn and to find some way of affirming a patient's connection to her father causes the woman problems in her subsequent relationships with men.

Many of the contributors to this book support the idea that constructing an affirming image of the lost person is helpful. To be helpful the image has to be part of the present, and not lock the mourner into a rigid relationship with either the deceased or with the people in the present. We need to be cautious that we do not impose the concept of an ongoing attachment as a rigid requirement. We should not impose any requirements for what healthy grief looks like. We need to allow individuals room to make their own meaning and their own peace.

IMPLICATIONS FOR THERAPEUTIC
INTERVENTION

A detailed discussion of helping techniques for the bereaved is beyond the scope of this book. We can draw some conclusions, however, from the various contributions that would bear on how to be helpful for individuals who have lost someone dear to them. These ideas apply whether the intervention takes place immediately after the death or whether it occurs many years afterward. They may even apply to helping a person with a loss that has not even been mentioned as a pressing problem.

The first level of help is in the natural support systems—families and communities. People need concrete assistance; they need support over time, and they need people who can listen and recognize their ongoing needs for friendship, care, and concern. They need people who can share the bond with the deceased, and make that bond part of their ongoing relationship with the survivor. No individual or family should have to deal with a death and their subsequent grief alone. It is an obligation of everyone in the community to be informed and available at such times.

As our culture develops new rituals of helping to match the new model of grief, we may find that mutual-help or self-help organizations such as Compassionate Friends, Widow to Widow Programs, THEOS, Parents Without Partners, or the American Adoption Congress have pioneered the way. These groups have formed in part because their members' experience was not legitimated in the larger society. As part of their shared resolutions, they have developed the folk psychology and "folk remedy" to match their lived experiences. They find comfort, acceptance, and legitimation of their feelings. In the context of these organizations, the survivors are helped to express their feelings, to see that there is a future, and to find role models in people who have successfully managed their grief and continue to thrive. In this context they learn the "tricks of the trade," using Irving Goffman's term. Adoptees learn that it is acceptable to search for their birth parents and learn the practical details of how to conduct the search. Bereaved parents learn how to include the child in the holidays, and how to tell people how many children they "have." In these groups, people may move from the role of recipient to that of helper. Helping others is one of the ways to find new meaning for the pain they have experienced, and a way to express the meaning of the transformed bonds with their loved ones. Together they find new ways to remember and to include the deceased in the community and family life. In a group meeting, an elderly widow, whose husband had saved every tie he ever owned, shared that she made quilted pillows from the ties for each of her grandchildren. She then told them the story attached to each tie. In this way they were given an opportunity to know their grandfather. In his chapter, Klass describes the balloons sent up at a Compassionate Friends gathering. Parents of children killed by drunk drivers honor their children and give meaning to their deaths by lobbying for legislation that will protect the public from similar catastrophes.

Professionals who offer individual or family therapy for grief or lead support groups are more likely to be guided by the model of grief used by scholars and researchers. Normative approaches based on a prescribed period of mourning, with the idea that one should have "moved on" after that length of time, are a Procrustean bed for therapy. Professionals can focus on support, educating people about the range of appropriate behaviors, how to use their inner strength, and how to use community resources to facilitate coping. A significant part of professional intervention can be focused on facilitating the survivor's construction of a bond with the person who has died.

In closing, we see the importance of this book in providing researchers and clinicians with a new perspective on grief—to shift their focus from the end of the living bond to the place of the inner representation of the dead or absent person in the inner world of the survivor, and on the place of the inner representation in the survivor's social world. In addition, we think that it is important to bring death into the conversation about living. We can no longer see it as an isolated phenomenon, insulated from the way we think about life and living. We are not sure what form a new model of the resolution of grief will take, nor can we describe the rituals and social interactions that will express the new model. We are sure, however, that any new model that emerges will understand the centrality of the connection in the human family to others, both living and dead. We look forward to the conversations among the bereaved, researchers, and clinicians in which the new model will take shape.

Index